Warrantless Searches

A Guide for Police-Citizen Contacts, Cell Phones, and Exclusions

Mike R. Galli

POLICE PUBLISHING
A division of POLICE TECHNICAL
Terre Haute, Indiana

POLICE PUBLISHING books may be purchased for educational or sales promotional use. For information please write:

POLICE PUBLISHING
661 Poplar Street
Terre Haute, IN 47807

Parts of this manual were edited and reviewed by the California District Attorneys Association.

Designed by POLICE PUBLISHING
Manufactured in the United States of America

The Library of Congress Cataloging –in-Publication Data
Galli, Mike R.
Warrantless Searches: A Guide for Police-Citizen Contacts, Cell Phones, and Exclusions

ISBN 978-1-63180-007-8 Paperback
Library of Congress Control Number: 2014958606

This book is dedicated to the men and woman in law enforcement, who put their lives on the line each day for justice and make society a safer place for all. Included in the "law enforcement" category are prosecutors. They are not exposed to the same dangers as police officers, but they strive to uphold their efforts in the courtroom.

Table of Contents

Forward

There are several books written on search and seizure law, but their primary audience is lawyers. This book is by no means intended to be an authoritative analysis of the Fourth Amendment. Many such multi-volume works already exist that accomplish that task. This book is different. I have been a prosecutor for over 30 years and have taught search and seizure law and search warrant drafting to hundreds of law enforcement officers. All of the cases discussed in this book have been personally read by me and synthesized down to the key points. For important cases, the facts and the court's rationale of the case have been provided.

I know that the first rule of search and seizure for any officer is safety. No officer sets out to violate anyone's rights. My goal is to provide law enforcement officers and district attorneys a simple guide to the first portion of the Fourth Amendment, which states that "The right of the people to be secure in their persons, houses, papers, and effects, against unreasonable searches and seizures, shall not be violated." I also hope officers who take the time to educate themselves on search and seizure law will never lose a case because of a bad, warrantless search.

While I am a California lawyer, and a large number of the citations relate to California appellate cases, many of the legal precedents discussed refer to United States Supreme Court cases. Individual states have always had the power to grant greater rights to individuals under their own State constitutions than those granted by the U.S. Supreme Court under the United States Constitution. However, on June 8, 1982, the People of California passed a voter initiative known as Proposition 8 or the "Victims Bill of Rights." It added article I, §28(d) to the California Constitution, which fundamentally changed California's rules of criminal procedure and restricted the State court's ability to base criminal procedure decisions on "independent state grounds." Evidence obtained in what was formerly an illegal search and seizure under California law, is now admissible in a California criminal proceeding, unless federal constitutional standards, as established by the U.S. Supreme Court, mandate exclusion of the evidence. Therefore, U.S. Supreme Court decisions regarding the admissibility of evidence in criminal cases have even greater weight in California cases and are discussed in greater detail in the pages that follow.

For those in law enforcement, and those who plan to enter the field, remember that it is a noble calling. Remain safe and have a long, happy and productive career.

Thank you,
Mike R. Galli

Acknowledgements

I want to thank Police Technical and Thomas Manson, its CEO, for recognizing the value of this work and deciding to market and publish it. I also wish to thank Brianne Hofmann for her editing skills and valuable assistance in completing this work. Last, but not least, I wish to thank the California District Attorneys Association (CDAA), which published the Search Warrant Law & Practice Manual, 3rd Edition and provided me with the knowledge and skills necessary to organize this work.

1.0 – Basic Constitutional Provisions

The United States and California governments derive their powers from the People. The United States and California Constitutions enumerate those powers and the People's limitations imposed on the use of those powers. Therefore, any analysis of search and seizure law must begin with those documents.

The Fourth Amendment to the United States Constitution initially placed limits only on searches and seizures federal officials conducted by federal officials. In 1961, in **Mapp v. Ohio** (1961) 367 U.S. 643, the United States Supreme Court ruled for the first time that the Fourth Amendment is applicable to the States through the Fourteenth Amendment to the United States Constitution.

The Fourth Amendment only protects a citizen from governmental action; it does not protect a citizen from private party actions that law enforcement officers do not instigate or direct, even if those actions are illegal.

In **Burdeau v. McDowell** (1921) 256 U.S. 465 the U.S. Supreme Court rejected the defendant's attempt to suppress private books, papers and memoranda taken from his private office by a third party and then turned over to Joseph Burdeau, a Special Assistant to the United States Attorney General. Mr. Burdeau intended to use those documents before a federal grand jury as evidence proving the defendant committed mail fraud. In rejecting the defendant's claim, the Supreme Court ruled:

> The papers having come into possession of the government without a violation of petitioner's rights by governmental authority, we see no reason why the fact that individuals, unconnected with the government, may have wrongfully taken them, should prevent them from being held for use in prosecuting an offense where the documents are of an incriminatory character." (**Id**. at 476.)

1.1 – United States Constitution

During its first meetings, the United States Congress began work on enacting a Bill of Rights. Their efforts resulted in the creation of the first 10 amendments to the United States Constitution, which the States quickly ratified. The desire for a Bill of Rights arose out of the former colonists' general objections to the manner in which Great Britain governed them before the Revolutionary War and the desire to place limits on the powers of the new United States Government.

The Fourth Amendment specifically grew out of the colonist's objection to writs of assistance and general warrants that allowed the authorized enforcing agents to rummage through one's house and possessions searching when, where and whomsoever they desired for smuggled goods. The British used general warrants and writs of assistance to enforce British trade laws in the colonies in the 1760s. The differences between the two, as well as the problems associated with both, were best described by the U.S. Supreme Court in **Steagald v. United States** (1981) 451 U.S. 204.

> The **general warrant specified only an offense** – typically seditious libel – and left to the discretion of the executing officials the decision as to which persons should be arrested and which places should be searched. Similarly, the **writs of assistance** used in the Colonies **noted only the object of the search** – any uncustomed goods – and thus left customs officials completely free to search any place where they believed such goods might be. The central objectionable feature of both warrants was that they provided no judicial check on the determination of the executing officials that the evidence available justified an intrusion into any particular home. (**Id**. at 220 [**Emphasis** added].)

Because of the language in the Fourth Amendment, as well as its historical origins, federal and state courts will always invalidate any warrant that resembles a general rummaging warrant.

1.1.1 – Fourth Amendment

The Fourth Amendment states that "[t]he right of the people to be secure in their persons, houses, papers, and effects, against unreasonable searches and seizures, shall not be violated, and no Warrants shall issue, but upon probable cause, supported by Oath or affirmation, and particularly describing the place to be searched, and the persons or things to be seized."

Searches performed without a search warrant are per se unreasonable, except for well-defined exceptions.

While the Fourth Amendment refers to warrants, it does not distinguish between arrest warrants and search warrants. However, the two protect very different interests. As the U.S. Supreme Court explained in **Steagald vs. United States**, **supra**, there is an important difference between the interests protected by an arrest warrant and the interests protected by a search warrant. The Court said:

> While an arrest warrant and a search warrant both serve to subject the probable cause determination of the police to judicial review, the interests protected by the two warrants differ. An arrest warrant is issued by a magistrate upon a showing that probable cause exists to believe that the subject of the warrant has committed an offense and thus the warrant primarily serves to protect an individual from an unreasonable seizure. **A search warrant, in contrast, is issued upon a showing of probable cause to believe that the legitimate object of a search is located in a particular place,** and therefore safeguards an individual's interest in privacy of his home and possessions against the unjustified intrusion of the police. [**Emphasis** added.] **Id**. at 212-213.

1.1.2 – Search Warrant Advantages

Officers should use search warrants for the following reasons:

- The courts give deference to searches conducted with search warrants
- An officer can make a warrantless arrest if serving a search warrant in a residence

- An officer never has to be concerned about a person withdrawing their consent to search
- Search warrants are a very useful way to protect a confidential informant's identity
- An officer has qualified immunity from a civil lawsuit while lawfully serving a search warrant. (See **Malley v. Briggs** (1986) 475 U.S. 335[1].)

1.2 – California Constitution

In California, Article I, 13 of the California Constitution places limits on searches and seizures by California law enforcement officers and mirrors the language of the Fourth Amendment.

1.2.1 – Article I, Section 13

This provision reads as follows: "The right of the people to be secure in their persons, houses, papers, and effects, against unreasonable seizures and searches may not be violated; and a warrant may not issue except on probable cause, supported by oath or affirmation, particularly describing the place to be searched and the persons and things to be seized."

It is apparent that the wording is almost identical to that found in the Fourth Amendment to the United States Constitution.

The individual states have always had the power to interpret their own State constitutions more broadly than the U.S. Supreme Court has interpreted the United States Constitution. When a state court, specifically a state's Supreme Court does so, the court's action is justified under the doctrine of "independent state grounds". The U.S. Supreme Court explained this rule best in **Arkansas v. Sullivan** (2001) 532 U.S. 769, while quoting from its own decision in **Oregon v. Hass** (1975) 420 U.S. 714:

> "[A] State is free *as a matter of its own law* to impose greater restrictions on police activity than those this Court holds to be necessary upon federal

[1] In **Malley v. Briggs**, the U.S. Supreme Court confronted the issue of the degree of immunity accorded a police officer in a federal civil rights lawsuit (42 U.S.C. 1983) damages action when the suit alleged that the officer caused the plaintiff to be unconstitutionally arrested by presenting a magistrate with a complaint and supporting affidavit that failed to establish probable cause. In a 7-2 decision, the Court ruled that an officer "will not be immune if, on an objective basis, it is obvious that no reasonably competent officer would have concluded that a warrant should issue; but if officers of reasonable competence could disagree on this issue, immunity should be recognized." (**Malley**, **supra**, at 341.) While the Court refused to set a standard of absolute immunity, it did afford an officer qualified immunity, as long as the officer's actions were objectively reasonable. As it relates to search warrants, the Court noted the following: "Although the case before us only concerns a damages action for an officer's part in obtaining an allegedly unconstitutional arrest warrant, the distinction between a search warrant and an arrest warrant would not make a difference in the degree of immunity accorded the officer who applied for the warrant." (**Id**. at 344, fn. 6). The Court also stated that "[o]nly where the warrant application is so lacking in indicia of probable cause as to render official belief in its existence unreasonable, **Leon**, **supra**, *at 923* [**United States v. Leon** (1984) 468 U.S. 897], will the shield of immunity be lost." (**Malley**, **supra**, at 344-345.)

> constitutional standards, . . . [a State] . . . may not impose such greater restrictions as a matter of *federal constitutional law* when this Court specifically refrains from imposing them. **Oregon v. Hass**, at 719." (**Arkansas v. Sullivan**, **supra**, 532 U.S. at 772 [*Italics* in original].)

Up until June 8, 1982, California courts were free to interpret the California constitution as granting greater rights to their citizens in the area of criminal procedure than were granted by the United States Constitution. However, on that date, the People of California passed a voter initiative known as Proposition 8 or the "Victims Bill of Rights". It added Article I, 28(d) [2] to the California Constitution, which fundamentally changed California's rules of criminal procedure and restricted a California State court's ability to base criminal procedure decisions on "independent state grounds."

1.2.2 – Article I, Section 28(f)(2)

This Constitutional amendment reads as follows:

> Right to Truth-in-Evidence. Except as provided by statute hereafter enacted by a two-thirds vote of the membership in each house of the Legislature, relevant evidence shall not be excluded in any criminal proceeding including pretrial and post-conviction motions and hearings, or in any trial or hearing of a juvenile for a criminal offense, whether heard in juvenile or adult court. Nothing in this section shall affect any existing statutory rule of evidence relating to privilege or hearsay, or Evidence Code Sections 352, 782 or 1103. Nothing in this section shall affect any existing statutory or constitutional right of the press.

The California Supreme Court upheld the constitutionality of this amendment in the case of **In re Lance W.** (1985) 37 Cal.3d 873.

The result of the amendment is that California is now bound to follow federal rules on search and seizure law. Evidence obtained in what was formerly an illegal search and seizure under California law, is now admissible in a California criminal proceeding, unless federal constitutional standards, as established by the U.S. Supreme Court, mandate exclusion of the evidence. Although California's State exclusionary rule will no longer apply to the suppression of evidence in criminal proceedings, California police officers might still be subject to civil liability for a violation of a person's rights under the California Constitution.

---

[2] On November 4, 2008, the California electorate passed initiative measure Proposition 9, known as "Marcy's Law". That proposition added several victims' rights to the California Constitution. It also renumbered Article I, §28(d) to Article I, §28(f)(2).

2.0 – Basic Search and Seizu re Law

2.1 – Standing To Challenge a Search or Seizure

The legal concept of standing addresses the issue of whether a person has a legitimate expectation of privacy in the property searched and whether it is one society is prepared to recognize. Although the concept is simple, its application to a given fact pattern may be difficult.

There are a number of situations where a defendant's lack of standing to challenge a search, will result in the denial of the defendant's motion to suppress the seized evidence. These situations include the abandoning of property, co-conspirators' actions, disclaimers of ownership, mere presence at a crime scene, storing things in or at other people's property and trash containers left at the curbside for collection. Situations involving guests, babysitters and home visitors, passengers in cars, possessory offenses and tenant's rights are not easily subject to such a blanket rule.

2.1.1 – Standing Defined

The California Supreme Court has stated that the term "standing" should be avoided when analyzing Fourth Amendment claims to avoid confusion with the U.S. Supreme Court abandonment of that terminology since **Rakas v. Illinois** (1978) 439 U.S. 128. Instead, the focus should be on the nature of the inquiry stated below. (See **People v. Ayala** (2000) 23 Cal.4th 225, at 254, footnote 3.)

The **Ayala** case involved a triple murder robbery and an attempted murder in an automobile body shop office in San Diego. The police conducted a warrantless search of the office and seized beer cans, vodka containers and orange juice containers that were left behind by the defendant, his brother and another co-conspirator. The defendant's fingerprints were lifted from beer cans found in the office. The Court found the defendant lacked standing in the abandoned property and ultimately affirmed the convictions and death sentence.

The question to ask in every case involving a standing issue is

> Did the challenged search or seizure violate the Fourth Amendment rights of a criminal defendant who seeks to exclude the evidence obtained during it? (See **Rakas v. Illinois** (1978) 439 U.S. 128, 140.) That inquiry in turn requires a determination of whether the disputed search and seizure has infringed an interest of the defendant which the Fourth Amendment was designed to protect. (**Id**. at 140.)

Phrased another way, the question to ask is does the person who claims the protection of the Fourth Amendment have a legitimate expectation of privacy in the invaded place and is it an expectation that society is prepared to recognize as being reasonable?

2.1.2 – Burden of Proof

The burden of proof in establishing a legitimate expectation of privacy in the area searched rests with the defendant. Because Fourth Amendment rights are personal, a defendant must show a personal, reasonable and legitimate expectation of privacy in the property searched or seized. A defendant's assertion of a third party's right to object to a police search is no longer sufficient to establish standing.

2.1.3 – Categories and rules

2.1.3.1 – Abandoned property

The Court of Appeal ruled in the case of **In re Baraka H.** (1992) 6 Cal.App.4th 1039 that a minor had no standing to object to the search of a brown paper bag containing marijuana that was hidden in some nearby weeds, because the minor lacked a reasonable expectation of privacy in the bag or its contents.

FACTS (In re Baraka H. (1992) 6 Cal.App.4th 1039)

The police watched the defendant waive down three cars at an intersection in a 10-minute period. After conversing with each of the occupants, the minor went over to a brown paper bag that was concealed in a grassy area, a short distance away. The minor then returned to the vehicles and exchanged something small for money with the occupants of the cars. Following the minor's arrest, the paper bag was searched and found to contain eight small, Ziploc baggies of marijuana.

In **People v. Shaw** (2002) 97 Cal.App.4th 833, the Court of Appeal reached a similar result when it ruled that Mr. Shaw had no legitimate expectation of privacy in the hole where he stored his cocaine base, which was located in the backyard of an apartment complex. The hole was located in a yard area that was a common area accessible to all occupants of the building and therefore no reasonable expectation of privacy existed. Unlike a private residence, Mr. Shaw was not in exclusive control of the area in which he hid the narcotics.

FACTS (People v. Shaw (2002) 97 Cal.App.4th 833)

Lorenzo Shaw lived at a fourplex at 4779 Auburn Drive, San Diego, which was known to the police as the "number one address in mid city" for rock cocaine offenses. (**Id**. at 836.) Between the evening of November 8 and November 9, 2002, Officers Lynn and Newquist, with the permission of the property owner, were standing behind a fence at a residence on Wrightman, which was directly behind the fourplex. The officers saw several people go to apartment #3 and leave a short time later. The officers also saw Mr. Shaw go into the backyard of the complex on two occasions, reach down to the ground near the fence and then return to the apartment. Officer Newquist subsequently entered the backyard of the complex, lifted a 4"x4" piece of wood from the ground and found a bag containing several pieces of rock cocaine in the hole in the ground. At trial, Mr. Shaw was convicted of possessing cocaine base for sale and sentenced to state prison.

2.1.3.2 – Bank Records

The U.S. Supreme Court ruled in a 7-2 opinion in **United States v. Miller** (1976) 425 U.S. 435, which is a case involving an illegal distillery operation, a warehouse fire and the failure to pay taxes on 175 gallons of whiskey, that a depositor has no standing to object to a financial institution turning over the depositor's checks, deposit slips, financial statements and monthly statements to the government.

The Court stated that it

> has held repeatedly that the Fourth Amendment does not prohibit the obtaining of information revealed to a third party and conveyed by him to Government authorities, even if the information is revealed on the assumption that it will be used only for a limited purpose and the confidence placed in the third party will not be betrayed. (**Id**. at 443.)

In **People v. Slaton** (1990) 222 Cal.App.3d 1041, the defendant was convicted of 11 counts of grand theft and two counts of attempted grand theft arising from the defrauding of homeowners and lending institutions by a refinancing scheme. He was sentenced to six years and eight months in prison. The Court held that the defendant had no standing, under the Fourth Amendment, to object to the warrantless seizure of the documents he submitted to various institutional lenders to obtain refinance loans. The documents obtained consisted of loan applications, real estate purchase and sale contracts, escrow instructions, preliminary title reports, lists of properties owned, and rental agreements.

The appellate court noted that

> A potential borrower must assume the risk that the information he offers a lender, in support of a loan application, will be conveyed by the lender to the government. This is especially true where, as here, the borrower sought to defraud the lender. A defendant cannot claim a reasonable expectation of privacy in documents he offers to defraud his victim. Thus, the government's seizure of the lenders' loan files here, although warrantless, was proper. (**Id**. at 1047.)

2.1.2.4.5 – Co-conspirators

The U.S. Supreme Court ruled in **United States v. Padilla** (1993) 508 U.S. 77 that belonging to a conspiracy or being married to someone whose property is searched does not establish standing.

2.1.3.4 – Criminals and Stolen Property

Generally, a defendant lacks standing to object to the search of a stolen item.

The defendant in **People v. Satz** (1998) 61 Cal.App.4th 322 was found to lack standing because she rented the motel room with a stolen credit card, and had thereby defrauded an innkeeper. Since she was a trespasser, she lacked a possessory or property interest in the room. The Court of Appeal also held that the defendant voluntarily consented to the search of the room and her purse.

FACTS (People v. Satz (1998) 61 Cal.App.4th 322)

> Julie Gavina Satz rented room 301 at the Ventura Pierpoint Inn with an American Express credit card and without luggage. The next day, Cynthia McMahan, the hotel manager, became suspicious of the way the defendant rented the room. The manager contacted American Express who advised her that Julie Gavina Satz was not authorized to use the credit card. The manager then called the police and asked for assistance in evicting the defendant from the room.
>
> When the police officer arrived, the manager and police officer went to the motel room. The manager knocked on the door several times announcing herself as the manager. When there was no response after several attempts to arouse the defendant in the room, the manager unlocked the door with a passkey and again announced herself as management.
>
> Ms. McMahan announced that the defendant was not authorized to use the credit card in question and asked her how she was paying for the room. The defendant said she had no money. It was noted that two other people were in the room but not checked in as guests.
>
> The officer, who remained outside the doorway, asked if she could "check out the room." The defendant consented and said, "That would be fine. I didn't do anything wrong." The officer then asked the defendant if she "could look through her things." The defendant said, "Sure, you can check anything." The officer searched the defendant's purse and seized 0.41 grams of methamphetamine.

In **People v. Shepherd** (1994) 23 Cal.App.4th 825, the court ruled that a woman lacked an expectation of privacy in her purse, which was left in a stolen car.

The Court of Appeal in **People v. Melnyk** (1992) 4 Cal.App.4th 1532 held that an auto thief has no standing to object to a search of the stolen car.

In **People v. Danielson** (1992) 3 Cal.4th 691, the defendant was found to lack standing to object to the search of a stolen duffel bag taken from the murder victim two years earlier.

In **People v. Solario** (1977) 19 Cal.3d 760, the Court of Appeal ruled that a burglar cannot invoke the homeowner's Fourth Amendment rights.

2.1.3.5 – Ownership Disclaimers

A number of cases hold that a disclaimer of ownership generally bars one from later challenging a search or seizure. See **Alderman v. United States** (1969) 394 U.S. 165; **People v. Stanislawski** (1986) 180 Cal.App.3d 748; **People v. DaSilva** (1989) 207 Cal.App.3d 43; **People v. Mendoza** (1986) 176 Cal.App.3d 1127 and **People v. Allen** (1993) 17 Cal.App.4th 1214.

In **People v. Dees** (1990) 221 Cal.App.3d 588, the Court of Appeal ruled that the District Attorney (DA) is estopped from raising standing if the DA uses the admission of ownership to connect the defendant to the seized contraband.

FACTS (People v. Dees (1990) 221 Cal.App.3d 588)

In the afternoon of January 19, 1988, Contra Costa County Deputy Sheriff Frederick Gray was dispatched to 2460 Fordham in San Pablo, regarding a disturbance. When the deputy arrived, he spoke with Phillip Newman, who resided at that location.

Mr. Newman told the Deputy that Mr. Dees was his friend and was in Mr. Newman's backyard removing property. As Deputy Gray walked around the corner to look in the backyard, he saw a brown colored Cadillac parked on Rollingwood Drive. The Cadillac had expired registration, the keys were in the ignition and the driver's window was rolled down. The defendant was approximately 150 feet east of the car and was walking down the road towards Deputy Gray when the Deputy noticed him. Mr. Dees appeared slightly agitated.

Deputy Gray gestured toward the Cadillac and asked Mr. Dees if it belonged to him; Mr. Dees said, "Yes." While Deputy Gray was conversing with the defendant about Mr. Newman's complaint, Sergeant Ford arrived.

After observing Mr. Dees for about two minutes, Sergeant Ford advised Deputy Gray that Mr. Dees was under the influence of drugs and told Deputy Gray to search the Cadillac. Deputy Gray found a canvas bag on the floorboard of the Cadillac. He could feel the distinct outline of a set of scales. As he touched them, Mr. Dees said, "Oh, yeah, they're scales there but they're not mine."

When Deputy Gray opened the bag, he found several plastic bags containing a white powder, 10 syringes and some colored pills.

At the motion to suppress, the parties argued over standing. The Court held that "The out of Court admission does not give the Defendant standing and I don't think there was any other sufficient proof of standing." (**Id**. at 592.) The defendant was held to answer on the drug charges.

RATIONALE

- The only evidence at the preliminary hearing tying Mr. Dees to the Cadillac was his admission.
- In order to hold Mr. Dees to answer, the Court had to accept his admission of ownership to be true.
- The People failed to introduce registration, a bill of sale or other indicia of ownership of the car.
- The People in essence argued that the car and its contents belonged to Mr. Dees because he said so.

2.1.3.6 – Guests, Babysitters, and Visitors

In **Minnesota v. Olson** (1990) 495 U.S. 91, the U.S. Supreme Court ruled that overnight guests have a reasonable expectation of privacy in the residence and may have standing to object to a search.

The U.S. Supreme Court ruled in **Minnesota v. Carter** (1998) 525 U.S. 83, that Mr. Carter and Mr. Johns, who were packaging cocaine while visiting another person's apartment, lacked standing to challenge the apartment search for the following reasons:

- The purely commercial nature of the transaction involved
- Their relatively short period of time on the premises, as opposed to being overnight social guests
- The lack of any previous connection to the premises by Mr. Carter and Mr. Johns.

FACTS (Minnesota v. Carter (1998) 525 U.S. 83)

Thomas Carter and Melvin Johns were inside the apartment of Kimberly Thompson, where the three of them were bagging cocaine. While they were inside, Officer James Thielen went to the apartment to investigate an informant's tip regarding cocaine activity. The informant had told Officer Thielen that the informant had walked by the ground floor window of the apartment and saw people putting white powder into bags.

Officer Thielen looked through a gap in the closed blinds of the window and watched the bagging operation for several minutes. Officer Thielen notified headquarters so that a search warrant affidavit could be prepared and then returned to the building.

Mr. Carter and Mr. Johns left the building in a Cadillac and were stopped by the police. When the police opened the car door to let Mr. Johns out, they observed a black zippered pouch and a loaded handgun, on the car's floorboard. The suspects were arrested and a car search the next day yielded several pagers, a scale and 47 grams of cocaine in plastic sandwich bags.

Upon returning to the apartment, Ms. Thompson was arrested and a search conducted. The apartment search yielded cocaine residue on the kitchen table along with plastic baggies similar to those found in the Cadillac. The police later learned that Mr. Carter and Mr. Johns lived in Chicago, had never been to the apartment before, and were only in the apartment for about 2 ½ hours before being arrested. Mr. Carter and Mr. Johns gave Ms. Thompson an eighth ounce of cocaine in exchange for use of the apartment.

The Court of Appeal ruled in **People v. Dimitrov** (1995) 33 Cal.App.4th 18, that Russian Paul lacked standing to contest the search based on his testimony that he had no possessory interest in the premises or expectation of privacy in them. He specifically testified that he had did not live in apartment 301, had no key to the apartment, had no clothes or possessions in the apartment, and had no "expectation of privacy" in the apartment because "People were always coming and going."

FACTS (People v. Dimitrov (1995) 33 Cal.App.4th 18)

The police had received information that "Russian Paul" was selling cocaine from apartment 301 with the assistance of a woman named "Olga." The police did a control buy out of the apartment, with an informant buying cocaine from "Russian Paul." The police then obtained a search warrant for the apartment.

When the police attempted to serve the search warrant, the front door was barricaded and they could not make entry without the use of a battering ram. While they were attempting entry, the police saw Olga toss two large bags to "Russian Paul," who was standing by the balcony. "Russian Paul" threw the bags to the ground, three stories below. The bags were later retrieved and found to contain contraband.

In **People v. Cowan** (1994) 31 Cal.App.4th 795, the Court of Appeal ruled that Cowan had no standing to contest the apartment search for the following reasons:

- No evidence that he had authority to be in the apartment alone
- No evidence that Mr. Cowan could enter the apartment without permission
- No evidence that Mr. Cowan could store anything in the apartment
- No evidence that Mr. Cowan could invite anyone over without the owner's permission
- No evidence that Mr. Cowan could visit without advance notice.

FACTS (People v. Cowan (1994) 31 Cal.App.4th 795)

Police went to a residence to investigate a report of drug use. Hoyt Henry opened the door and allowed the officers to enter. Mr. Cowan and a female were also inside the residence. Mr. Cowan was seated on a couch and attempted to conceal something between a gap in the couch. Mr. Henry was arrested for stimulant influence.

The officers retrieved the container from the couch and found it to contain methamphetamine. Mr. Cowan testified that he was a friend of the person who owned the apartment and had a "standing" invitation to visit.

In **People v. Scott** (1993) 17 Cal.App.4th 405, the Court of Appeal ruled that an overnight guest has no standing to object to a search under furniture in the host's living room and in **People v. Hamilton** (1985) 168 Cal.App.3d 1058, the Court of Appeal ruled that an overnight guest has no standing to object to the search of another's bedroom.

People v. Moreno (1992) 2 Cal.App.4th 577 held that babysitters have standing to complain about searches that occur in their presence, but **People v. Koury** (1989) 214 Cal.App.3d 676 held that daytime visitors have no standing to object to searches of the premises, even in their presence.

2.1.3.7 – Passengers and Non-Owner Drivers of Cars

In **Brendlin v. California** (2007) 551 U.S. 249, the U.S. Supreme Court finally addressed the issues of whether or not a passenger is detained by virtue of a car stop and if so, whether the passenger has standing to object to the lawfulness of the stop. A unanimous Supreme Court held that a passenger, just like the driver, is seized within the meaning of the Fourth Amendment when an officer makes a traffic stop. Accordingly, a passenger has standing to object to the lawfulness of the stop based on that detention.

People v. Carvajal (1988) 202 Cal.App.3d 487 and **People v. Leonard** (1987) 197 Cal.App.3d 235 hold that a driver who is not the owner of a car, but has the owner's permission to use the car, has standing to object to a search.

2.1.3.8 – Possessory Offenses

In **United States v. Salvucci** (1980) 448 U.S. 83, the U.S. Supreme Court ruled that being charged with a possessory offense does not automatically confer standing. In reaching that decision, the Court expressly overruled its earlier decision in **Jones v. United States** (1960) 362 U.S. 257, which held that it did confer automatic standing.

FACTS (United States v. Salvucci (1980) 448 U.S. 83)

John Salvucci and Joseph Zackular were charged with 12 counts of unlawful possession of stolen mail. Massachusetts police seized the 12 checks during the service of a search warrant on an apartment rented by Mr. Zackular's mother.

The District Court held that the search warrant affidavit was deficient because the affiant relied on double hearsay and failed to specify the dates on which the information in the affidavit had been obtained.

> The District Court and the Court of Appeals incorrectly ruled that since the defendants were charged with possessory offense, under the **Jones** rule, they had automatic standing to challenge the search.

It has been held that even ownership of contraband alone does not automatically confer standing. In **People v. Nelson** (1985) 166 Cal.App.3d 1209, the Court of Appeal ruled that the defendant lacked standing to object to the search of the trunk of a car he was driving that belonged to his mother, and for which he had lost the keys.

In **People v. Ooley** (1985) 169 Cal.App.3d 197, the appellate court ruled that the defendant had no standing to object to the police's entry of an apartment to arrest him on an outstanding warrant where he was merely a guest. At the suppression hearing, the defendant failed to put on any evidence to contradict the record that apartment 108 was occupied by "Jerry Philips and his family."

The Court of Appeal ruled in **People v. Root** (1985) 172 Cal.App.3d 774 that the defendant lacked standing to object to the stop of a vehicle he was neither driving nor riding in at the time of the stop, and in which he had placed a bag of cocaine. The Court found no expectation of privacy based on the following factors:

- The defendant placed the bag in another's car
- The defendant then walked away from the car
- The 3rd party then drove away in the car.

2.1.3.9 – Presence at Crime Scenes

In **Rakas v. Illinois** (1978) 439 U.S. 128, the U.S. Supreme Court refused to adopt a standard that "any criminal defendant at whom a search was 'directed' would have standing to contest the legality of that search; i.e., 'a target theory.' " (**Id**. at 132.) Mere presence at a crime scene does not confer standing. In order to contest the legality of the search, the aggrieved party must show that they had a reasonable expectation of privacy in the area invaded and that it is an expectation that society is prepared to recognize as reasonable.

FACTS (Rakas v. Illinois (1978) 439 U.S. 128)

> A police officer, who was on routine patrol, received a radio call advising him of the robbery of a clothing store in Bourbonnais, Illinois, and provided him with a description of the getaway car. The officer spotted a car that he thought matched the description and, after the arrival of additional units, stopped the car.
>
> Officers ordered Frank L. Rakas and two female passengers out of the car. Two officers then searched the interior of the car and found a box of rifle shells in the locked glove compartment of the car and a sawed off rifle under the front passenger seat.

Before trial, the parties moved to suppress the evidence. The women conceded that while they did not own the car, Mr. Rakas did, and that they were merely passengers. The women also did not claim ownership of the rifle or shells.

2.1.3.10 – Storing Things in or at Other People's Property

In **Rawlings v. Kentucky** (1980) 448 U.S. 98, the U.S. Supreme Court ruled that Mr. Rawlings lacked a legitimate expectation of privacy in Ms. Cox's purse and therefore could not challenge the lawfulness of that search. The Court based that decision on the following factors:

- When Mr. Rawlings dumped thousands of dollars of drugs into Ms. Cox's purse, he had only known her for a few days
- Mr. Rawlings never sought or received access to Ms. Cox's purse before this incident
- Mr. Rawlings had no right to exclude others from Ms. Cox's purse.

FACTS (Rawlings v. Kentucky (1980) 448 U.S. 98)

On October 18, 1976, six police officers, armed with an arrest warrant for Lawrence Marquess for drug distribution charges went to Mr. Marquess' house in Bowling Green, Kentucky. When the police arrived, Mr. Marquess' roommate, four other visitors, and David Rawlings were at the residence.

While searching through the house for Mr. Marquess, the police smelled marijuana smoke and saw marijuana seeds on the mantel in one of the bedrooms. Four officers remained at the residence, while two other officers went to obtain a search warrant.

The officers detained the occupants and told them they could only leave if they consented to a body search. Two of the visitors consented to a search and were allowed to leave after the search found nothing. Mr. Rawlings was seated on a couch to the left of Vanessa Cox, with her handbag located between them.

Forty-five minutes later, the two officers returned with a search warrant for the house. Officer Eddie Railey read the warrant to the assembled group, along with their *Miranda* rights. After the warrant was read, Officer Don Bivens approached Ms. Cox and ordered her to empty her purse on the coffee table in front of the couch. When Ms. Cox emptied her purse, a jar containing 1,800 tablets of LSD as well as a number of smaller vials containing additional drugs fell out.

Ms. Cox turned to Mr. Rawlings and told him to take what was his. Mr. Rawlings immediately claimed ownership of the contraband. The officers searched Mr. Rawlings' person and found $4,500 in cash located in his shirt pocket, and a sheathed knife located at his side.

In **United States v. Payner** (1980) 447 U.S. 727, the U.S. Supreme Court ruled that the defendant lacked standing to object to an unlawful search of a bank vice-president's briefcase, which ultimately led to information establishing that the defendant had a foreign bank account that he failed to claim on his 1972 IRS Return.

in **United States v. Miller** (1976) 425 U.S. 435, the U.S. Supreme Court ruled that a depositor has no expectation of privacy, and therefore no "protectable Fourth Amendment interest" in copies of checks and deposit slips retained by the depositor's bank.

In **People v. McPeters** (1992) 2 Cal.4th 1148, the California Supreme Court ruled that a defendant lacked any reasonable expectation of privacy in a murder weapon he gave to his cousin for safekeeping. The Court observed that while the defendant still had a property interest in the weapon, he had abandoned his expectation of privacy by turning it over to his cousin.

FACTS (People v. McPeters (1992) 2 Cal.4th 1148)

The defendant shot and killed a woman. The night before the killing, he stayed as a guest at the house of his cousin, Sabrina. After the killing, he gave the gun to Sabrina, and asked her to hold it for him. She placed the weapon under her pillow in her bedroom. The police later confiscated the weapon from her.

In **People v. Ybarra** (1991) 233 Cal.App.3d 1353, the Court of Appeal ruled that the defendant had standing to object to the search of a locked toolbox he left in a friend's motel room for the following reasons:

- The defendant had placed the locked tool box in his friend's motel room with the friend's permission
- The defendant had a key to the motel room
- The defendant had taken normal precautions to keep the contents of the box private and therefore reasonably expected it would remain free from governmental intrusion
- The defendant testified that when he left the room, no one was inside and he secured the door before leaving.

FACTS (People v. Ybarra (1991) 233 Cal.App.3d 1353)

Kern County Deputy Sheriff Joslin obtained a search warrant for Mr. Ybarra, his car, and a motel room at 1030 Wible Road. On August 24, 1989, the deputy observed Mr. Ybarra driving his car and stopped him. A search of the suspect's person yielded a pipe containing marijuana, a pager and $484 in cash. A search of the car resulted in the seizure of a soft drink can containing eight bags of methamphetamine, a small bag of marijuana and a small bag of psilocybin mushrooms.

The deputy then went to 3620 Wible Road, which was not listed in the warrant, and continued the search. The motel manager unlocked the motel room door and let the deputy inside. The deputy seized a locked, red toolbox and a triple beam balance scale inside the room. Inside the toolbox was less than three ounces of marijuana, packaged in three bags.

In **People v. Stanley** (1999) 72 Cal.App.4th 1547, the Court of Appeal ruled that a search warrant was not required to install and monitor the surveillance meter on the utility pole standing in Mr. Stanley's backyard.

FACTS (People v. Stanley (1999) 72 Cal.App.4th 1547)

About two months before Jack Mace Stanley and David Singerman were arrested, Deputy Sheriff Lori Erickson received information from a citizen informant. The CI told Deputy Erickson that Mr. Singerman said he was illegally growing marijuana inside a residence in Ventura County. The CI also provided the deputy with an accurate description of Mr. Singerman and identified the make, model, and license number on the truck Mr. Singerman drove.

Deputy Erickson and another deputy followed Mr. Singerman from his home in North Hollywood to a house in Ventura Mr. Stanley owned. The deputies watched the house for several weeks and made the following observations:

- Overgrown trees and shrubs surrounded the house, yet there was no lawn, swimming pool or Jacuzzi
- The drapes and blinds on the front windows were always drawn
- Very little activity occurred at the house other than Mr. Stanley and Mr. Singerman coming and going
- Mr. Stanley did not place any household trash receptacles at the curbside for pick-up for three weeks.

The preceding factors led Deputy Erickson to conclude that the house was not being used as a residence. Without a search warrant, the house was scanned with a thermal imagining device, which showed significantly more heat escaping from the roof, roof vents, and eaves of the house than from similar residences in the neighborhood.

Four days after the thermal scan, the deputies chatted with the electric company and learned that the billing records showed normal power use for the house. Believing that the suspects were illegally diverting electricity into the house, the deputies asked the electric company to install a surveillance meter on the utility pole on Mr. Stanley's property. The electric company gained access to the pole in Mr. Stanley's yard by leaning a ladder against it from a neighbor's yard.

The surveillance meter showed that electricity was being diverted into Mr. Stanley's house. The electric company's records showed normal household usage of about 11 KWH per day, whereas the surveillance meter showed 411 KWH per day being delivered.

Deputy Erickson obtained a search warrant for the residence after rendering an opinion in the affidavit that the electricity usage was consistent with the use of 30, 1000-watt grow lights. Growing marijuana plants were seized from the residence.

RATIONALE

The court ruled that the defendants possessed no reasonable expectation of privacy in devices used by the electric company to deliver electricity to the house. The poles, wires, transformers, and meters were owned by the utility and these devices are in plain view.

The technology used to show the diversion of electricity did not peer inside Mr. Stanley's house or otherwise penetrate the inner sanctum of the home.

> The technology employed does not tell those monitoring it what electrical devices are inside the house or what activities the power supports. The meter does not discriminate between electricity used to fire pottery and power used to grow orchids, tomatoes or marijuana. It only tells officers how much electricity is being delivered by the utility and, by comparison to billing records, whether it is being diverted or stolen. (**Id**. at 1554.)

The Court of Appeal also found that sufficient probable cause existed for the issuance of the search warrant based on the information provided by a citizen informant, the police officers' observations and the hidden surveillance utility meter.

2.1.3.11 – Tenants

In **People v. Thompson** (1996) 43 Cal.App.4th 1265, the Court of Appeal ruled that the defendant, who had an outstanding restraining order against him, had standing to object to the search of the room because the restraining order did not divest the defendant of his legitimate expectation of privacy in his rented room. Until he was formally evicted, the defendant still had certain lawful possessory rights under the terms of his rental agreement.

FACTS (People v. Thompson (1996) 43 Cal.App.4th 1265)

The defendant lied about having been convicted of a crime when he applied for work at various group homes. The detective had gone to the rooming house where the defendant lived and spoke to his landlord. The landlord had obtained a restraining order against the defendant, preventing the defendant from coming within 100 yards of the landlord or boarding house. The defendant had not been evicted from the residence at that time.

The landlord told the detective that the defendant was violating the restraining order so the detective arrested the defendant inside his bedroom at the boarding house. The detective conducted a 90-minute search of the room for evidence.

The Court of Appeal ruled in **People v. Thomas** (1995) 38 Cal.App.4th 1331, that the defendant lacked a reasonable expectation of privacy in his wooden pallet and heavy cardboard box residence, which was located on a public sidewalk, erected without a permit or permission and violated a Los Angeles Municipal Code ordinance (41.18) that made his actions illegal. The Court also rejected Mr. Thomas' contention that the box was a "container" and therefore entitled to Fourth Amendment protection. The Court ruled that it was not a container because it was not closed on all sides and because it was not an open or closed repository for personal effects.

FACTS (People v. Thomas (1995) 38 Cal.App.4th 1331)

Los Angeles Police Officers Moeller and Long responded to a burglary call at Lucy's Fashions, which is a manufacturer of denim clothing, in the early morning hours of July 17, 1994. A witness reported that a man had thrown boxes and bags of clothing from a second floor window to two other men on the street below, who then ran off with the items. A search of the store showed a forced entry with boxes and clear plastic bags of denim clothing stacked near a window.

Earlier that morning the officers observed a group of men at a nearby corner (4th and Towne Streets) looking at some denim clothing. The officers therefore returned to that location where they found several homeless people. Some were wrapped in blankets, some covered by boxes and others in makeshift shelters.

The officers approached a box where they saw the gathering earlier that morning. Officer Moeller "banged" on the box, said "police" a couple of times, waited about 10 seconds and then lifted a corner of the box and looked inside. Both officers saw a clear plastic bag of denim clothing similar to the bags used at Lucy's and saw Mr. Thomas and a woman asleep in the box.

The officers requested the two to step out, which they did. Mr. Thomas volunteered that he had the clothing because a friend "ripped it off." The clothing did come from Lucy's Fashions and the defendant was arrested for a felony violation of California Penal Code 496.

At Mr. Thomas' suppression hearing he took the stand and testified that he had been living on the public sidewalk at 4th and Towne Streets since February 1993 (July 1994 crime date) in a four-sided, 4'x12' "residence" made from wooden pallets and heavy cardboard propped up against the exterior wall of a building. The structure partially blocked the sidewalk and lacked utilities or locks. Mr. Thomas had no permit for the structure and paid no rent or taxes for the use of the property. Around Christmas in December 1993, a City of Los Angeles street maintenance crew had hauled away his box and others in the area, but he rebuilt it and continued to sleep in the box until his arrest on July 17, 1994.

In **People v. Llamas** (1991) 235 Cal.App. 3d 441, the Court of Appeal ruled that the defendant lacked standing to object to the car stop and arrest of the co-defendant. However, the defendant could challenge the voluntariness of the co-defendant's consent to search their common motel room. Despite this ruling, the Court found Mr. Torregroza's consent to be valid and based on an independent act of his free will.

FACTS (People v. Llamas (1991) 235 Cal.App. 3d 441)

On March 4, 1990, San Jose Police Department (SJPD) Officer Hector Gutierrez stopped a car being driven by Eric Torregroza within seconds of its leaving a motel parking lot. Mr. Torregroza told the officer that he and his girlfriend (a passenger) had just checked out of a room at the motel and were on their way to buy beer.

The officer discovered Mr. Torregroza was driving with a suspended California driver's license (CDL) and appeared to be under the influence of alcohol and stimulants. The officer then arrested him.

Mr. Torregroza gave the officer permission to move his car to a nearby parking lot so it would be off the street. The girlfriend had left by that time.

Officer Gutierrez found a motel key in the front seat and asked Mr. Torregroza for permission to check his motel room for contraband. Mr. Torregroza said, "Go ahead," thus giving consent.

Upon returning to the motel room, the officer entered the room with the key and found the defendant (Llamas) and a companion sitting on the bed. Narcotic paraphernalia and narcotics were in plain view on a counter in the room. Both the defendant and the companion were under the influence of stimulants and arrested.

The Court of Appeal ruled in **People v. Hernandez et al**. (1988) 199 Cal.App.3d 1182, that the resident of one bedroom (Paz), who has never been given permission to enter a second occupant's bedroom (Rodriguez), has no legitimate expectation of privacy or standing to object to contraband officers seized in violation of the Fourth Amendment in the second occupant's bedroom.

FACTS (People v. Hernandez et al. (1988) 199 Cal.App.3d 1182)

Based on external information and police surveillance, a Sacramento police officer suspected the residents at 149 Cathcart Street were involved in narcotics activity and were using their cars to facilitate that activity. On June 25, 1986, officers stopped a car in which Mr. Rodriguez and Mr. Paz were riding. Both were found to be illegal aliens and taken to the police station for booking and then to jail.

Detective Backer spoke with Mr. Rodriguez at the jail shortly after the arrest. Mr. Rodriguez admitted that he was an illegal alien, that he lived at 149 Cathcart Street and gave Detective Backer permission to search the residence.

Detective Backer brought Officer Schiele into the room and asked for permission to search for heroin. Mr. Rodriguez indicated he was in control of the house and again gave consent saying, "Yes, let's go."

The officers took Mr. Rodriguez back to the house. Enroute, Mr. Rodriguez told Detective Backer that other people lived in the house and that Mr. Rodriguez and his wife occupied one bedroom and Mr. Paz another.

Inside the northeast bedroom, Officer Bettenhausen found and seized two guns. The officer also saw a piano bench in the room that he intended to use as a platform for packaging the seized evidence and for writing notes. When he went to pick it up, the lid opened and he discovered a scale, a dinner plate, and individually packaged pieces of tar heroin.

After the discovery of the contraband in the piano bench, Mr. Rodriguez claimed that Mr. Paz used the bedroom. Detective Backer called the police station, and Officer Garcia obtained Mr. Paz's permission to search the room.

Mr. Paz testified at the Penal Code 1538.5 hearing that he lived in the house for three days, neither paid rent nor shared in the household expenses, received no mail at the house, that the northeast bedroom was not his, that he had never been inside the northeast bedroom and had no permission to go into the room.

Mr. Rodriguez and Mr. Paz were convicted of offenses involving the sale of heroin.

2.1.3.12 – Trash Containers

In **California v. Greenwood** (1988) 486 U.S. 35, the U.S. Supreme Court ruled that a person has no expectation of privacy in trash left at the curbside for pick-up.

2.2 – Three Types of Police-Citizen Contacts

There are three types of police-citizen contacts: consensual encounters, detentions and arrests. Each contact involves a different level of restraint on a citizen's freedom of movement. A consensual encounter involves no restraint at all on an individual's liberty. A detention is more restrictive and involves a short restraint on personal liberty while an officer investigates a potential criminal violation. An arrest is the most restrictive of all and is the highest restriction on one's personal liberty.

The table below graphically illustrates the distinctions between the three types of police-citizen contacts discussed in the previous paragraph:

CATEGORY	DEFINITON	TEST	STANDARD
Consensual	Interaction **w\no restraint** of an individual's liberty.	Would a reasonable person feel free to leave?	None.
Detention	Interaction of **limited scope, purpose, and duration.**	Would a reasonable person feel free to leave?	**Reasonable suspicion** criminal activity is afoot and suspect detained is connected with it.
Arrest	Seizure **not limited in scope, purpose or duration.**	None.	**Probable Cause** to believe a crime has been committed and the person arrested committed that crime.

2.2.1 – Consensual Encounters

A consensual encounter is an interaction between an officer and a citizen and involves no restraint of an individual's liberty. Officers can initiate consensual contacts by merely approaching someone or by simply saying, "Hello."

Officers can act on hunches when they make consensual contacts, provided there is no detention. The test for determining if the contact is a consensual encounter or a detention hinges on whether a reasonable person would feel free to leave or otherwise terminate the encounter. If the answer to that question is "Yes," then the encounter is a consensual encounter. However, if the answer is "No," then a court will construe the encounter to be a detention, requiring compliance with all the rules necessary for a lawful detention. (See **United States v. Mendenhall** (1980) 446 U.S. 544.)

2.2.1.1 – Identification Requests

In **INS v. Delgado** (1984) 466 U.S. 210, the United States Supreme Court ruled that questions about one's identity or a request for identification (ID) by the police do not constitute a Fourth Amendment violation, unless the circumstances of the encounter are so intimidating that a reasonable person would believe that they were not free to leave without answering the questions.

In a 5 to 4 decision in **Florida v. Bostick** (1991) 501 U.S. 429, the U.S. Supreme Court ruled that no detention occurred because the defendant's person was not seized during his initial contact with police on a bus. In that case, the police boarded a bus and asked the defendant for ID. The ID matched. They then asked the defendant for, and received consent to search his luggage, which resulted in the seizure of cocaine.

The defendant's freedom of movement was not restricted by the police, but by the bus. Therefore, that independent fact makes the "free to leave test" inapplicable. Instead, the correct test to apply is to ask if "a reasonable person would feel free to decline the officer's request or otherwise terminate the encounter." If the answer is "Yes," then no detention occurred. If the answer is "No," then the defendant was detained.

In **People v. Lopez** (1989) 212 Cal.App.3d 289, the Court of Appeal refused to suppress the seized evidence and held that asking a man who is sitting on the hood of a car for ID did not constitute a detention. The court found that the brief questioning in this case, which did not relate to criminal activity, did not constitute a detention.

FACTS (People v. Lopez (1989) 212 Cal.App.3d 289**)**

An officer saw Mr. Lopez sitting on the hood of a car and asked him if the car belonged to him. Mr. Lopez said "No" and the officer asked Mr. Lopez why he was there. Mr. Lopez said that he was waiting for his friends who were playing pool. The officer asked Mr. Lopez where his pool stick was and did not receive an answer. The officer then asked for ID and Mr. Lopez handed the officer his wallet. Upon opening the wallet, the officer found cocaine.

In **People v. Clark** (1989) 212 Cal.App.3d 1233, the Court of Appeal refused to suppress the evidence and ruled that asking for a person's name did not constitute a detention and that inspection of a watch was okay because the officer had a reasonable suspicion that it was stolen.

FACTS (People v. Clark (1989) 212 Cal.App.3d 1233**)**

An officer saw Mr. Clark slumped on a park bench and approached to see if Mr. Clark was okay. When Mr. Clark awoke, the officer asked him his name. Mr. Clark not only gave the officer his name, but voluntarily provided paperwork from his pocket. As Mr. Clark did so, the officer illuminated the area and noted numerous watches and other jewelry in the pocket. The officer removed the watch and asked Mr. Clark where he got the items. Mr. Clark said he bought them and then fled, but the officer quickly apprehended him.

In **People v. Bouser** (1994) 26 Cal.App.4th 1280, the Court of Appeal ruled that an officer's initial contact with an individual by asking, "Hey, how you doing? You mind if we talk?" constituted a consensual encounter. The officer did not transform that consensual encounter into a detention merely because the officer conducted a warrant's check.

FACTS (People v. Bouser (1994) 26 Cal.App.4th 1280**)**

The officer saw Mr. Bouser in an alley known for drug dealing, standing near a dumpster and looking for something. Upon seeing the officer, Mr. Bouser appeared nervous and began walking in the opposite direction.

The officer stopped his patrol car behind Mr. Bouser and said, "Hey, how you doing? You mind if we talk?" Mr. Bouser stopped in response to the officer's inquiry. The officer asked Mr. Bouser his name, date of birth and about his prior arrest record. The officer also asked what Mr. Bouser was doing in the alley. Mr. Bouser said he was visiting a nearby friend but could not provide an address.

The officer did a warrant check and filled out a field interview (FI) card, while engaging the suspect in "small talk." The warrant check revealed an outstanding traffic warrant and the officer arrested Mr. Bouser. During a booking search, the officer found tar heroin in Mr. Bouser's pants pocket.

RATIONALE

The Court of Appeal found the contact in this case to be consensual for the following reasons:

- The officer did not order the suspect to do anything
- The officer did not order the suspect to hand him anything (driver's license, wallet, etc.)
- The officer did not draw a weapon, use threatening gestures or activate any of the emergency equipment on the police car.

In **People v. Terrell** (1999) 69 Cal.App.4th 1246, the Court of Appeal upheld the trial court's denial of the defendant's motion to suppress evidence. The Court of Appeal ruled that the suspect's initial encounter with the police was consensual, including the defendant's handing over of his California driver's license (CDL) to the police officer.

FACTS (People v. Terrell (1999) 69 Cal.App.4th 1246)

On October 28, 1997, at about 3:30 p.m., Los Angeles Police Department (LAPD) Officer Trevino, along with his partner Officer Day, saw the defendant and two other men seated on a park bench in the area of 51st Street and Avalon in Los Angeles County. One of the other two men appeared to be under the influence of a controlled substance.

Officer Trevino had a brief conversation with the defendant and then asked if he had any ID. The defendant produced a CDL. After running a warrant check, which took about three minutes, Officer Trevino arrested the defendant for an outstanding warrant. A search of the defendant's fanny pack resulted in the seizure of a syringe that contained .22 milliliters of heroin.

The defendant testified at the suppression motion and claimed that he was standing in the background behind the park bench when the officer summoned him and four other individuals over to the police car. The defendant denied ownership of the fanny pack and claimed that he only learned about it at the police station. He also denied possession of the heroin and syringe.

After a court trial, the court convicted the defendant of possession of heroin and a syringe and sentenced him to 16 months in prison.

RATIONALE

The defendant's encounter with Officer Trevino was a consensual encounter for the following reasons:

- At no time did the defendant ask Officer Trevino for his driver's license back
- The entire encounter lasted about three minutes
- At no time during the consensual encounter did either police officer, by words or conduct, indicate that the defendant was not free to leave
- Based on the totality of the circumstances, no reasonable inference could be drawn that the encounter was a detention.

2.2.1.2 – Officer Focused Scrutiny

In **Michigan v. Chesternut** (1988) 486 U.S. 567, a unanimous U.S. Supreme Court ruled that a person, who panicked and discarded packets of codeine pills in front of the officers driving beside him was not detained prior to discarding the contraband.

FACTS (Michigan v. Chesternut (1988) 486 U.S. 567)

Four Detroit police officers were riding in a marked police car in the early afternoon of December 19, 1984. While engaged in routine patrol activities, they saw the defendant standing alone on a street corner. The officers saw a car pull to the curb, a man exit the car, approaching Michael Mose Chesternut on foot. When the defendant saw the police car, he began to run. The officers, while still in the patrol car, followed to see where Mr. Chestnut was headed.

Upon catching up to Mr. Chesternut, the police cruiser drove along side of him for a short distance. As they did, they saw Mr. Chesternut reach into his right side pocket, pull out a number of packets, and discard them. Officer Peltier exited the patrol car and retrieved the abandoned packets. Based on his experience as a paramedic, he believed the pills contained codeine. The defendant, who ran only a few paces away, stopped on his own. Officer Peltier arrested Mr. Chesternut for possession of the codeine tablets and took him to the police station for processing.

At the police station, a search of the hatband on Mr. Chesternut's hat yielded another packet of pills, a heroin packet and a hypodermic needle. The defendant was charged with possession of heroin, codeine and valium, in violation of Michigan state law.

At the preliminary hearing, the magistrate granted Mr. Chesternut's motion to dismiss the evidence and found that the police "chase" constituted an unlawful seizure of the defendant's person. The Michigan trial court upheld that decision, as did the Michigan Court of Appeals. The Court of Appeals ruled that the "investigatory pursuit" constituted an unjustified seizure and that any "investigatory pursuit" constitutes a seizure under **Terry v. Ohio**, (1968) 392 U.S. 1. The U.S. Supreme Court granted a writ of certiorari to address the constitutional question and reversed the lower court's decision to suppress the seized evidence.

RATIONALE

"[A]ny assessment as to whether police conduct amounts to a seizure implicating the Fourth Amendment must take into account 'all of the circumstances surrounding the incident' in each individual case. *INS v. Delgado* 466 U.S. 210, 215, 104 S.Ct. 1758, 1762, 80 L.Ed.2d 247 (1984) quoting *United States v. Mendenhall* 446 U.S. 544, 554, 100 S.Ct. 1870, 1877, 64 L.Ed.2d 497 (1980) (opinion of Stewart, J.)." **Michigan v. Chesternut, supra**, at 572.

The police conduct "would not have communicated to the reasonable person an attempt to capture or otherwise intrude upon respondent's freedom of movement. The record does not reflect that the police activated a siren or flashers; or that they commanded respondent to halt, or displayed any weapons; or that they operated the car in an aggressive manner to block respondent's course or otherwise control the direction or speed of his movement. Tr. of Oral Arg. 2, 11, 20. While the very presence of a police car driving parallel to a running pedestrian could be somewhat intimidating, this kind of police presence does not, standing alone, constitute a seizure." (**Id**. at 575.)

In **People v. Gonzales** (1985) 164 Cal.App.3d 1194, the Court of Appeal ruled that questioning the driver of a parked car in a high burglary area at night did not constitute a detention. However, once the radio check established that the defendant was in possession of a stolen car, the officer could lawfully detain the defendant.

FACTS (People v. Gonzales (1985) 164 Cal.App.3d 1194)

At 12:30 a.m., an officer noticed a car parked in a residential area, with two occupants in the car. The officer was aware of drug and burglary problems in the area so he stopped his car and approached the driver's side of the car.

The officer asked the driver for a CDL and learned that the driver had none, nor did he possess any other ID. The officer asked the driver his name, but the driver could not pronounce or spell his name. This raised the officer's suspicion so he ran a radio check and learned that the car was stolen.

In **People v. Franklin** (1987) 192 Cal.App.3d 935, the Court of Appeal refused to suppress the evidence seized from Mr. Franklin and noted that "direct scrutiny" does not always constitute a detention.

FACTS (People v. Franklin (1987) 192 Cal.App.3d 935)

An officer noticed Mr. Franklin walking down the street wearing a full-length coat at midnight on a warm night. The officer shone his spotlight on Mr. Franklin and noticed that the man was carrying a cloth like object, which he appeared to try to conceal from the officer's view.

The officer pulled his car in behind Mr. Franklin and radioed that he was making a stop. As the officer made contact with Mr. Franklin, he noted that Mr. Franklin appeared jittery and had his hands in his pockets.

The officer asked Mr. Franklin to remove his hands from his pockets. When he did, the officer noticed the defendant's bloodstained hands. This was due to a murder that Mr. Franklin had just committed. The officer searched Mr. Franklin's person and found a vial of white powder in his pocket.

The Court of Appeal in **People v. Perez** (1989) 211 Cal.App.3d 1492, refused to suppress PCP evidence and held that an officer's mere spotlighting of a parked car did not constitute a detention. A detention only occurred when the officer recognized the smell of marijuana emanating from the vehicle.

FACTS (People v. Perez (1989) 211 Cal.App.3d 1492)

An officer saw a car parked in a motel parking lot that was known for drug use. The occupants slouched down in the front seat, so the officer spotlighted the interior of the car, approached it and asked the driver to roll down his window. When the driver did, the officer smelled marijuana. He then searched the car and found PCP.

In **People v. Ross** (1990) 217 Cal.App.3d 879, the Court of Appeal ruled that the officer did not transform his initial consensual encounter with Ms. Ross into a detention when he asked her to take her hands out of her pockets.

FACTS (People v. Ross (1990) 217 Cal.App.3d 879)

Vallejo Police Officer Ketchum was patrolling the 800 block of Grant Street on the evening of September 30, 1988. Officer Ketchum was aware of a letter the landlord of an apartment complex on that block sent to his tenants advising them that visitor loitering was prohibited. "No Trespassing" signs were also posted on the exterior of the buildings.

Officer Ketchum's nightly routine was to patrol the area, contact people who were unknown to him as tenants of the complex, find out if they were visitors and, if they were not, tell them to move along.

Officer Ketchum saw a group of four to six people standing in front of the complex. He recognized two as residents. Except for Elan Ross, the others in the group walked away when he approached. Officer Ketchum asked Ms. Ross to come over and talk to him, which she did. She also identified herself in response to Officer Ketchum's question and said she lived in one of the apartments.

Officer Ketchum asked her if she had any ID and noticed that she had both hands in her coat pockets. Because she was some distance away from him, he asked her to walk over to him so he would not have to yell. As Ms. Ross walked toward the officer, she kept her hands in her pockets.

After he spoke to her for two or three minutes about the trespassing signs, he asked her to remove her hands from her pockets. He did that out of concern for his safety or the possibility that she could be hiding something. Officer Ketchum said that it is his standard practice when talking to persons with their hands in their pockets to ask them if they would mind taking them out of their pockets. As Ms. Ross removed her right hand from her pocket, she clenched her fist and threw two cellophane wrapped, white chunky rocks of cocaine behind her. Officer Ketchum retrieved them and arrested her for possession for sale of cocaine.

Following her arrest, the officer pat searched her and found her to be in possession of $168 in cash. After waiving her Miranda rights, the defendant admitted to selling cocaine for about 1 ½ hours before the officer arrived and that the money came from those sales. Following the denial of her suppression motion, she plead guilty to violating California Health and Safety Code 21350(a) (Possession of Cocaine) and received a 90-day jail sentence.

RATIONALE

Officer Ketchum's initial questions regarding the defendant's name and residence constituted a consensual encounter. His request to see her ID to verify the information provided did not transform the nature of the encounter into a detention.

Asking the defendant to remove her hands from her pocket also did not constitute a show of authority, which would have transformed the consensual encounter into a detention. Even if the nature of the contact became a detention, Officer Ketchum acted reasonably by asking Ms. Ross to remove her hands from her pocket based on his safety concerns.

The defendant's action in tossing the cocaine behind her was a voluntary act and was unrelated to Officer Ketchum's conduct.

In **People v. Bennett** (1998) 68 Cal.App.4th 396, the Court of Appeal ruled that no detention occurred when an officer approached a known parolee on the street and asked to speak with him. The fact the officer observed the parolee talking to a prostitute, who had just offered sex to an undercover officer in exchange for money prior to the contact, did not somehow convert the encounter into a detention.

FACTS (People v. Bennett (1998) 68 Cal.App.4th 396)

Santa Ana Police Officers were conducting a prostitution sweep when they saw Michael Edward Bennett talking to a prostitute who had just offered sex to an undercover officer for $40. Officer Gonzales asked the defendant, "Can I talk to you a moment?" and the defendant said "Yes."

During the contact, the officer remembered the defendant from a previous contact and asked if he was still on parole, to which the defendant replied, "Yes." Officer Gonzales next asked the defendant if he would be willing to sit in his patrol car while he "ran him for warrants." The defendant once again said, "Yes."

The officer described the defendant as being "very cooperative" and the conversation tone as "calm." No physical force was required, threatened, or used. The officer used no handcuffs or other restraints. While the defendant remained in the patrol car, Officer Gonzales ran a computer check that revealed the following facts about the defendant:

- He failed to stay in touch with his parole officer
- His wife reported him missing and, because of a death in his family, there was a concern that he might be a danger to himself.

The officer drove the defendant away from the area to avoid interfering with the undercover prostitution operation, while he attempted to verify the computer information. Within 30 minutes, the officers had contacted Rochester Jackson, the defendant's parole officer. Mr. Jackson directed the police to arrest the defendant for violating his parole. Officers then arrested the defendant, placed him in a holding cell and searched his person. The officers found cocaine base in the defendant's shoe.

ADDITIONAL POINTS

The defendant appears to be a three striker, although the appellate court did not discuss sentencing. The appellate court disapproved of the trial court's decision to give the defendant a second full-blown Penal Code 1538.5 suppression hearing because of the trial judge's belief that the earlier one was not adequate.

2.2.2 – Detentions

A detention is a seizure strictly limited in duration, scope and purpose. (See **Wilson v. Sup. Court** (1983) 34 Cal.3d 777, 784.) An officer is required to have a reasonable suspicion, based on articulated facts that criminal activity is afoot before the officer can detain someone.

The U.S. Supreme Court stated in **United States v. Mendenhall** (1980) 446 U.S. 544 that "[a] person has been seized within the meaning of the Fourth Amendment only if, in view of all of the circumstances surrounding the incident, a reasonable person would have believed that he [or she] was not free to leave." (**Id**. at 554.) If a reasonable person would feel free to leave, then the encounter is a consensual encounter. If a reasonable person would not feel free to leave, then the contact is a detention.

FACTS (**United States v. Mendenhall** (1980) 446 U.S. 544)

Ms. Mendenhall, 22 years old, arrived at the Detroit Metropolitan Airport on a commercial flight from Los Angeles early in the morning on February 10, 1976. She had not graduated from high school and was a black woman. Two Caucasian DEA agents saw her exhibit conduct that they believed appeared to be characteristic of persons smuggling narcotics. The conduct Ms. Mendenhall exhibited, which fit the so-called "drug courier profile" consisted of the following: 1) Ms. Mendenhall was arriving on a flight from Los Angeles, a city believed by the agents to be the place of origin for much of the heroin brought into Detroit; 2) Ms. Mendenhall was the last person to leave the plane, "appeared to be very nervous," and "completely scanned the whole area where [the agents] were standing"; 3) after leaving the plane, Ms. Mendenhall proceeded past the baggage area without claiming any luggage; and 4) Ms. Mendenhall changed airlines for her flight out of Detroit.

The officers approached her as she was walking through the concourse, identified themselves as federal agents, and asked to see her ID and airline ticket. Ms. Mendenhall produced her driver's license, which was in her true name of Sylvia Mendenhall, and her ticket, which was issued in the name of "Annette Ford." The agents questioned her briefly regarding the discrepancy between the two documents and Ms. Mendenhall said she "just felt like using that name." The agents asked how long she'd been in California and she said she had only been in California for two days.

Agent Anderson then specifically identified himself as a federal narcotic's agent and noticed that Ms. Mendenhall "became quite shaken, extremely nervous, and had a hard time speaking." After first returning the ticket and driver's license to her, Agent Anderson asked Ms. Mendenhall if she would accompany them to the airport DEA office for further questioning. She agreed to do so. The office, which was located one flight of stairs up and about 50 feet from where Ms. Mendenhall had first been approached, consisted of a reception area adjoined by three other rooms. At the office, the agent asked her if she would allow a search of her person and purse and told her that she had the right to decline the search if she so desired. Ms. Mendenhall said, "Go ahead," and handed her purse to the agent. The purse contained a receipt for an airline ticket that had been issued to "F. Bush" three days earlier for a flight from Pittsburgh through Chicago, to Los Angeles. Agent Anderson asked if this was the ticket that Ms. Mendenhall had used for her flight to California, and she said it was.

A female police officer, who had arrived to conduct the person search of Ms. Mendenhall, asked the agents if Ms. Mendenhall had consented to be searched. The agents said that she had, and Ms. Mendenhall followed the policewoman into a private room. The policewoman asked Ms. Mendenhall if she consented to the search, and she said she did. The policewoman explained to Ms. Mendenhall that she would have to remove her clothing. Ms. Mendenhall said she had a plane to catch and was assured that if she was not carrying narcotics there would be no problem. Ms. Mendenhall began to undress without any further comments and removed from her undergarments two packages, one of which appeared to contain heroin, and handed them to the policewoman. Ms. Mendenhall was then arrested for possession of heroin.

The District Court denied her motion to suppress evidence and concluded that the agents' conduct in initially approaching her and asking to see her ticket and ID was a permissible investigative stop, based on facts justifying a suspicion of criminal activity. The District Court also concluded that Ms. Mendenhall had accompanied the agents to the DEA office voluntarily and voluntarily consented to the search of her person in the office. After trial, Ms. Mendenhall was convicted, but the Court of Appeals reversed her conviction and found that she was unlawfully detained and therefore had not validly consented to the search. The Supreme Court reversed that holding in a 5-4 decision.

In a 7 to 2 decision in **California v. Hodari D.** (1991) 499 U.S. 621, the U.S. Supreme Court ruled that cocaine discarded by a juvenile fleeing from the police did not amount to the fruit of an illegal seizure, where the officer had not touched the person at the time the cocaine was discarded.

The Supreme Court specifically ruled that a seizure of a person requires either the application of physical force upon the person or a submission to the officer's assertion of authority. Since an officer had not touched the minor at the time he discarded the cocaine, there was no application of force. The Court also held that even if the foot pursuit constituted a show of authority by the police, the minor did not stop in response to that show of authority and that no seizure occurred until after the police tackled the minor, which occurred after the minor discarded the cocaine.

The California Supreme Court ruled in the case of **In re Tony C.** (1978) 21 Cal.3d 888, 893, that a detention is justified where the circumstances known or apparent to the officer include specific and articulable facts causing him to suspect that:

1. Some activity relating to crime has taken place or is occurring or about to occur, and
2. The person the officer intends to stop or detain is involved in that criminal activity.

The Court also stated that the facts justifying the detention must be such that any reasonable officer in a like position, drawing when appropriate on his training and experience, would suspect the same criminal activity and the same involvement by the person in question.

This reasonable officer standard is significant because California law previously required that an officer also subjectively entertain a belief that the person was involved in criminal activity, but that is not required under United States Constitutional principles. Pursuant to **In re Lance W.** (1985) 37 Cal.3d 873 and the passage of Proposition 8, federal law governs this area and therefore a subjective belief is no longer required under California law. This position is specifically recognized and articulated in **People v. Lloyd** (1992) 4 Cal.App.4th 724, at 733, fn. #3.

In **People v. Garry** (2007) 156 Cal.App.4th 1100, the Court of Appeal overruled the trial court and found, in a case of first impression, that the officer illegally detained the defendant by shining his white spotlight on him and then rushing toward him, while asking the defendant about his legal status. The Court of Appeal also found that the trial court placed undue emphasis on the fact the officer did not issue any verbal commands to the defendant and thereby failed to consider the officer's combined, intimidating actions.

FACTS (People v. Garry (2007) 156 Cal.App.4th 1100)

Officer Crutcher testified at the suppression hearing that on May 3, 2005, at approximately 11:23 p.m., he was in an area of Vallejo known as "The Crest." This area is a high-crime, high-drug area where drugs are often sold and where officers have been assaulted. Officer Cruther saw Mr. Garry standing for between five to eight seconds, next to a car parked on the corner of Janice and McGrue streets. While Officer Crutcher had never made any arrests at that corner, he testified to making over 40 drug-related arrests in the last seven years and to making "several" arrests on Janice Street, about 100 to 150 yards from where Mr. Garry was standing, including one, six months earlier.

Officer Crutcher activated the white spotlight on his patrol car and illuminated Mr. Garry. He was about 35 feet away and noticed that Mr. Garry looked nervous. The officer briskly walked toward Mr. Garry, who looked nervous and shocked as he retreated a few steps. The officer estimated that he traveled the 35 feet between two and one-half and three seconds. Mr. Garry said, "I live right there" and pointed to a house on his right. The officer said, "Okay, I just want to confirm that" and asked Mr. Garry if he was on probation or parole. Mr. Garry said he was on parole, so the officer decided to detain him and find out why he was there.

The officer testified that after arriving at Mr. Garry's location, and learning he was on parole, Mr. Garry "kind of paused" and the officer reached out and grabbed him, but Mr. Garry started to "violently" pull away. The officer put Mr. Garry in an arm-shoulder lock, put him on the ground and handcuffed him. A search incident to the arrest yielded a brown paper bag in Mr. Garry's right front jacket pocket. Inside were two sandwich bags containing 13 individually wrapped pieces of rock cocaine. Mr. Garry was charged with possession for sale of cocaine base and two prison priors.

The trial court denied Mr. Garry's motion to suppress evidence and found Officer Crutcher's testimony "credible" and the initial encounter was consensual. As the trial court explained, "[Crutcher] didn't yell anything at Mr. Garry. He didn't yell 'Stay where you are. You're under arrest,' or anything like that. He simply approached him, and as he was approaching him, started to speak to Mr. Garry. And one of the things he asked was, 'Are you on probation or parole?' And Mr. Garry was responding to that question and told him that he was on parole. Once Mr. Garry told him he was on parole, I find that the officer had a legal basis to detain Mr. Garry for the purpose of conducting a parole search, which is exactly what he did." (**Id**. at 1105.)

A jury convicted Mr. Garry of the charged crimes and he was placed on three years of probation and ordered to be placed in a Delancey Street residential treatment program, or a "Category 1" treatment program determined by the probation department. The appeal followed.

RATIONALE

In finding a detention, the Court of Appeal observed that "Crutcher's testimony makes clear that his actions, taken as a whole, would be very intimidating to any reasonable person. Crutcher testified that after only five to eight seconds of observing defendant from his marked police vehicle, Crutcher bathed defendant in light, exited his police vehicle, and, armed and in uniform, 'briskly' walked 35 feet in 'two and one-half to three seconds' directly to him while questioning him about his legal status. Furthermore, Crutcher immediately questioned defendant about his probation and parole status, disregarding defendant's indication that he was merely standing outside his home. In other words, rather than engage in a conversation, Crutcher immediately and pointedly inquired about defendant's legal status as he quickly approached. We think only one conclusion is possible from this undisputed evidence: that Crutcher's actions constituted a show of authority so intimidating as to communicate to any reasonable person that he or she was 'not free to decline [his] requests or otherwise terminate the encounter.'" (In re Manuel G. [(1997) 16 Cal.4th 805] at p.821)" (**Id**. at 1111-1112.)

"We find a detention occurred despite the fact that Crutcher did not make any verbal commands. 'It is not the nature of the question or request made by the authorities, but rather the manner or mode in which it is put to the citizen that guides us in deciding whether compliance was voluntary or not.' (*Franklin [1987) 192 Cal.App.3d 935 at p. 941*]) No matter how politely Crutcher may have stated his probation\parole question, any reasonable person who found himself in defendant's circumstances, suddenly illuminated by a police spotlight with a uniformed, armed officer rushing directly at him asking about his legal status, would believe themselves to be 'under compulsion of a direct command by the officer.' (*People v. McKelvy [(1972) 23 Cal.App.3d 1027] at p. 1034 . . .*) Crutcher's actions set an unmistakable 'tone,' albeit largely through non-verbal means, 'indicating that compliance with the officer's request might be compelled.' (*In re Manuel G. supra, 16 Cal.4th at p. 821 . . .*)" (**Id**. at 1112.)

In **People v. Strasburg** (2007) 148 Cal.App.4th 1052, the Court of Appeal held that the Compassionate Use Act of 1996 (H&S 21362.5) did not provide one with a shield against reasonable investigations and searches for marijuana. It only provided a limited defense against prosecution.

FACTS (**People v. Strasburg** (2007) 148 Cal.App.4th 1052)

On October 25, 2005, at approximately 1:40 p.m., Napa County Deputy Sheriff Aaron Mosley was on patrol in Calistoga. While in the area of the Petrified Forest Road and Foothill Boulevard, he saw Mr. Strasburg and another person sitting in a car in the parking lot of a Mobil gas station. The deputy drove his patrol car into the parking lot and parked to the left and rear of Mr. Strasburg's car, but did not block the car from leaving. He also did not activate any emergency equipment on his patrol car. The deputy approached the driver's side of the car. Mr. Strasburg opened the driver's door, which caused the deputy to smell immediately the odor of marijuana coming from the car. Mr. Strasburg immediately told the deputy that he had "a medical marijuana card," but the deputy did not ask to see it. In fact, he never saw a medical marijuana card because he never asked to see one.

The deputy asked Mr. Strasburg if he had marijuana on his person or in the car. Mr. Strasburg said he did and retrieved a Ziploc bag, which he gave to the deputy, and claimed it contained about three quarters of an ounce of marijuana. At that point, the deputy asked Mr. Strasburg to get out of the car. The deputy saw another bag of marijuana in the car in plain sight, which Mr. Strasburg also gave to the deputy. The second bag contained approximately 2.2 g of marijuana. Once Mr. Strasburg got out of his car, Mr. Strasburg again told the deputy that he had a medical marijuana card and asked the deputy to look at it. The deputy refused saying, "We don't buy that here in Napa County." The deputy was aware of the medical marijuana law and knew that someone with a doctor's recommendation could legally possess marijuana. The deputy said, "We don't buy that" because he was under the mistaken impression that medical marijuana cards weren't recognized Napa County. In fact, they were.

Before placing Mr. Strasburg in the back of his patrol car, the deputy asked Mr. Strasburg if there was more marijuana in the car and was told there was more than an ounce. The deputy searched the rest of the car and found 23 ounces of marijuana (approximately 1.4 pounds) and a scale. The scale was not a mini pocket scale but a full powered scale that could easily weigh 23 ounces at one time.

RATIONALE

In rejecting Mr. Strasburg's contention that once he produced a doctor's prescription for marijuana, the deputy had no basis to detain him, frisk him or to even search his car, the court noted that the status of a qualified patient does not confer immunity from arrest. The Compassionate Use Act also does not impair reasonable police investigations and searches.

> "An officer with probable cause to search is not prevented from doing so by someone presenting a medical marijuana card or a marijuana prescription. Given the probable cause here, the officer is entitled to continue to search and investigate and determine whether the subject of the investigation is in fact possessing the marijuana for personal medical needs..." **Id**. at 1060.

"Defendants argument that his prescription showed a lack of probable cause is inaccurate. Because cause was created by the odor and presence of

> marijuana in a parked car occupied by two persons...[the deputy] did not have to stop searching in the face of the marijuana prescription and the circumstances of how the smoking occurred. Otherwise every qualified patient would be free to violate the intent of the medical marijuana program expressed in section 11362.5 and deal marijuana from his car with complete freedom from any reasonable search." **Id**. at 1060.

A similar result was reached in **People v. Waxler** (2014) 224 Cal.App.4th 712, where both the trial court and Court of Appeal found that the odor of burnt marijuana coming from a car, coupled with the observation of a marijuana pipe inside the car, created probable cause for a search of the car for more marijuana. The Court of Appeal specifically ruled that "a law enforcement officer may search a vehicle pursuant to the automobile exception to the warrant requirement where the officer smells burnt marijuana and sees burnt marijuana in the defendant's car. The automobile exception is not limited to situations where the officer smells or sees more than 28.5 grams of marijuana in the vehicle (11357, subd.(b)); the observation of any amount of marijuana—which is currently illegal to possess except as authorized by the CUA [Compassionate Use of Marijuana Act]—establishes probable cause to search pursuant to the automobile exception."

FACTS (People v. Waxler (2014) 224 Cal.App.4th 712)

In February 2012, Del Norte County Deputy Sheriff Richard Griffin learned that someone was illegally dumping trash in a parking lot behind a Crescent City Safeway. The deputy drove to the Safeway and stopped next to Michael Waxler's truck. The deputy smelled the odor of burnt marijuana and saw a marijuana pipe that appeared to contain for marijuana in the bowl. The pipe was on the bench seat and next to Mr. Waxler. The deputy searched the truck and found a methamphetamine pipe and a small bindle containing methamphetamine with a street value of about $50.

Deputy Griffins partner detained Mr. Wexler and obtained Miranda I's statement from him. Mr. Waxler told several different stories during his interview. At some point during a conversation, Mr. Waxler told Deputy Griffin that he "had a 215 card" and showed it to him. Deputy Griffin learned about this card after he began searching the truck.

Mr. Waxler was charged with possession and transportation of methamphetamine. He brought a motion to suppress in the trial court arguing that since the amount of un-smoked marijuana was "miniscule" (approximately 0.3 grams) and possession of less than one ounce of marijuana is an infraction, the amount of marijuana observed could not support his arrest. The People argued that the Compassionate Use Act did not protect one from a valid search or arrest.

In denying Mr. Waxler's motion, the trial court ruled that in the absence of an affirmative defense being asserted at the beginning of the officer's investigation, the officer had the right to proceed as he did. The trial court also erroneously noted that once the 215 card was brought to the officer's attention, the officer would have no further justification to search.

2.2.2.1 – Factors Justifying Detentions

Court cases have held that detentions may be justified if they occur in a high crime area, as documented by police bulletins and a large number of prior arrests. Other factors that may justify a detention are those based on an officer's expertise regarding recognized crime profiles, unprovoked flight by a suspect, visible weapons, traffic violations, truancy checks and the similarity of a suspect or vehicle to a crime perpetrator. Under certain circumstances, detentions based on informant information are also permissible.

2.2.2.2 – Hunches

In the context of detentions, officers may not act on mere hunches. In **Delaware v. Prouse** (1979) 440 U.S. 648, the U.S. Supreme Court stated:

> Except in those situations in which there is at least articulable and reasonable suspicion that a motorist is unlicensed or that an automobile is not registered, or that either the vehicle or an occupant is otherwise subject to seizure for violation of law, stopping an automobile and detaining the driver in order to check his driver's license and the registration of the automobile are unreasonable under the Fourth Amendment. (**Id.** at 663.)

The Delaware Supreme Court based its decision on both the Delaware and United States Constitutions, but none of the courts that heard the facts of this case found the search valid.

FACTS (Delaware v. Prouse (1979) 440 U.S. 648)

> At 7:20 p.m. on November 30, 1976, a New Castle County police officer was on a patrol in his police car when he stopped a car occupied by four persons. The patrol officer later identified William Prouse III as a passenger in the backseat of the car. As the officer approached, he smelled burning marijuana and later seized marijuana that was in plain view on the car's floorboard.
>
> The officer testified at a suppression hearing that he neither observed traffic or equipment violations before stopping the car and that he made the stop only to check the driver's license and registration. The officer was not acting according to any standard procedures or guidelines. Because he was in the area and was not responding to any calls he decided to pull the car over and do a spot check for driver's license and registration.

In **Brown v. Texas** (1979) 443 U.S. 47, a unanimous U.S. Supreme Court held that a Texas statute that made it a crime to fail to identify one's self to a police officer on demand violated the Fourth Amendment and was therefore unconstitutional.

In this case, the Court found that the police clearly had no lawful reason to detain Mr. Brown, even though they wanted to identify him.

FACTS (<u>Brown v. Texas</u> (1979) 443 U.S. 47)

At 12:45 p.m., on December 9, 1977, El Paso Police Officers Venegas and Sotelo were on patrol in their police car. The officers saw Zackary Brown and another man walking in opposite directions and away from each other in an alley in a high drug area. Although the men were a few feet apart, the police officers believed the two were about to meet but for the patrol car's arrival.

Officer Venegas got out of the police car when it entered the alley and asked Mr. Brown to identify himself and explain his reason for being in the alley. The police never detained or questioned the other man. Officer Venegas said he stopped Mr. Brown for the following reasons:

- The situation "looked suspicious and we had never seen the suspect in that area before."
- The area has a high incidence of drug activity.

Officer Venegas also said that he did not suspect that Mr. Brown had engaged in any specific misconduct or have any reason to believe he was armed. Mr. Brown refused to identify himself and angrily asserted that the police had no right to stop him. Officer Venegas then told Mr. Brown that he was in a "high drug problem area". Officer Sotelo then "frisked" Mr. Brown, but found nothing.

When Mr. Brown continued to refuse to identify himself, he was arrested for violating Texas Penal Code Title 8, 38.02(a)[Failure to Identify as Witness]. The section reads as follows:

> "[a] person commits an offense if he intentionally refuses to report or gives a false report of his name and residence address to a peace officer, who has lawfully stopped him and requested the information."

Following his arrest, the police again searched Mr. Brown and again found nothing. Enroute to the jail, Mr. Brown identified himself, but the police still held him in custody. During the booking process, the police searched Mr. Brown a third time and once again found nothing.

Mr. Brown was convicted in the El Paso Municipal Court and fined $20, plus court costs. He appealed to the County Court. At his de novo trial in the El Paso County Court, he challenged the constitutionality of the Texas law under the First, Fourth and Fifth Amendments to the United States Constitution. After waiving a jury trial, the court convicted him and imposed a $45 fine, plus court costs.

Under Texas law, if the penalty is under $100, no further appellate review can occur. Mr. Brown therefore appealed directly to the U.S. Supreme Court, which granted a hearing.

RATIONALE

There was no reason to detain Mr. Brown. The police lacked any reasonable suspicion that Mr. Brown was engaged in criminal conduct.

The Court also noted the following:

- There was nothing unusual about people being in the alley where Mr. Brown was detained
- Mere presence in a neighborhood frequented by drug users, without more, is not a basis to conclude that Mr. Brown was engaged in criminal conduct
- Mr. Brown's actions were no different from the activity of other pedestrians in the neighborhood.

In a 5 to 4 decision in **Hiibel v. Nevada** (2004) 542 U.S. 177, the U.S. Supreme Court held that in the context of an investigative detention (see **Terry v. Ohio**, **infra**,), a State (*not the Fourth Amendment*) can require a suspect to disclose his name to the police. The U.S. Supreme Court noted that questions concerning a person's identity are a routine part of many **Terry v. Ohio** investigative stops and that "[a]nswering a request to disclose a name is likely to be so insignificant in the scheme of things as to be incriminating only in unusual circumstances." **Hiibel**, **supra**, 159 L.Ed.2d 292, at 306.

The Court observed that Mr. Hiibel apparently refused to identify himself because he thought it was none of the deputy's business and stated that "[w]hile we recognize petitioner's strong belief that he should not have to disclose his identity, the Fifth Amendment does not override the Nevada Legislature's judgment to the contrary absent a reasonable belief that the disclosure would tend to incriminate him." (**Id**. at 306.)

The case holding appears to be unique to those states like Nevada that have "stop and identify" statutes that require a person detained under suspicious circumstances by an officer to identify him or herself verbally. There is no requirement in the Nevada statute that a suspect produce a driver's license or any other document. California has no such law and this case does not grant a California peace officer the authority to demand ID from a person detained pursuant to a **Terry v. Ohio** investigative stop.

FACTS (Hiibel v. Nevada (2004) 542 U.S. 177)

The Humboldt County Sheriff's Department in Nevada received a call in the afternoon reporting an assault. The caller claimed to see a man assault a woman in a red and silver GMC truck on Grass Valley Road. Deputy Sheriff Dove was dispatched to investigate the call.

Upon arrival, the deputy found the truck parked on the side of the road and saw Larry Dudley Hiibel standing by the truck and a young woman sitting inside the truck. The deputy saw skid marks in the gravel behind the truck, which caused him to believe the truck came to an abrupt stop.

Deputy approached Mr. Hiibel, explained why he was there and asked to see any identification in the possession of Mr. Hiibel. Mr. Hiibel appeared intoxicated and refused to provide any identification despite Deputy Dove's 11 repeated requests over several minutes. Despite Deputy Dove's warning to Mr. Hiibel that he would be arrested if he continued to resist, he still refused to give his name. Mr. Hiibel taunted the deputy by putting his hands behind his back and told Deputy Dove to arrest him and take him to jail, which the deputy ultimately did.

Mr. Hiibel was charged with violating Nevada Revised Statute (NRS) 299.280 by "willfully resist[ing], delay[ing], or obstruct[ing] a public officer in discharging or attempting to discharge any legal duty of his office." **Hiibel, supra**, 159 L.Ed.2d 292, at 300. NRS 271.123 requires that any person who is lawfully detained shall identify themselves. Mr. Hiilbel was tried and convicted in the Justice Court of Union Township and fined $250. He appealed to Nevada's Sixth Judicial District Court, which affirmed his conviction. In a divided opinion, the Nevada Supreme Court affirmed the conviction. The U.S. Supreme Court granted certiorari and upheld the conviction.

In **People v. Durazo** (2004) 124 Cal.App.4th 728, the Court of Appeal ruled that officers acted on a mere hunch, without the objectively reasonable suspicion necessary to detain Mr. Durazo, when they stopped his car on a public roadway.

FACTS (People v. Durazo (2004) 124 Cal.App.4th 728)

At about 1 a.m. on September 5, 2003, California State University at Channel Islands (CSUCI) Police Sergeant Cowgill responded to a call from James Ash and went to Mr. Ash's campus apartment on Cathedral Cove in Camarillo. Mr. Ash told the Sergeant that he had received several phone calls that day from individuals who claimed to be from Oxnard. Mr. Ash said the callers were Mexican gang members, but gave no facts to support that conclusion. Mr. Ash said that the callers told him they were coming to his apartment at 6 a.m. the next morning and that he did not know why they were threatening him. When pressed for more details, he provided none, became non-responsive and refused to answer questions.

Sergeant Cowgill arranged for the university police to patrol the area the next morning and had a note placed in the department's briefing book so that other officers would become aware of the report.

Nothing happened on September 5, 2003. On September 9, 2003, Officer Shawn Bartlett reviewed the briefing book entry and decided to patrol the area because the threat had not yet occurred. At about 7 a.m., Officer Bartlett saw a car turn left onto a street at the intersection of Cathedral Cove and Anacapa. Officer Bartlett noted two Hispanic males in the car. He also noted that both looked in the direction of the three-story building where Mr. Ash lived and found the activity suspicious because both occupants turned their upper bodies in their seats to look at the building. Mr. Ash lived in a building containing 10 or 20 units and housed 40 to 50 residents. Other buildings, which housed about 700 students, surrounded Mr. Ash's building.

The car did not stop at the building, but continued driving at the posted speed limit. Officer Bartlett followed the car for about three miles and did not observe any vehicle code violations. During this time, he ran the license plate and discovered that the car was registered to a woman who lived in Oxnard. Finding it strange that the driver appeared to drive very cautiously, he initiated a car stop. Officer Bartlett felt the stop was justified for the following reasons:

- The occupants were Hispanic
- Both had looked in the direction of Mr. Ash's building
- The driver was very careful to observe all traffic laws as the officer followed him.

After he activated his emergency lights, but before the car stopped, Officer Bartlett observed the passenger move around in his seat and appear to manipulate an unknown object. Officer Bartlett now had a "gut feeling" that the passenger was hiding contraband. Upon stopping the car, Officer Bartlett discovered that the passenger was subject to search and seizure. A search under the passenger seat yielded a semiautomatic pistol, a 30-round magazine and a pair of gloves. Mr. Durazo was on parole and the officer arrested him.

Mr. Durazo's motion to suppress the evidence was denied and he plead guilty to being a felon in possession of a gun. He received a six-year state prison sentence.

In **People v. Hernandez** (2008) 45 Cal.4th 295, the California Supreme Court correctly found that an officer's stop of a car for false registration amounted to acting on a hunch and was therefore illegal.

FACTS (People v. Hernandez (2008) 45 Cal.4th 295)

Sacramento County Sheriff's Deputy Anthony Paonessa saw Mr. Hernandez driving a pickup truck with no license plates, but displaying a temporary operating permit in the rear window. Nothing about Mr. Hernandez's permit appeared wrong and the Deputy observed no other vehicle code violations. Nevertheless, Deputy Paonessa decided to make a traffic stop because, in his experience, permits are "very often" forged or have been issued for a different car, or the car itself was stolen. After making the car stop, the Deputy contacted Mr. Hernandez and told him that he was stopped because he had no license plates. Mr. Hernandez pointed out that he had a temporary permit in the rear window of the car. The Deputy asked for Mr. Hernandez driver's license, registration, and proof of insurance. According to the Deputy, Mr. Hernandez "appeared nervous. His speech was very rapid and abrupt, and his hands were shaking very badly." **Id.** at 298. In response to a question from the Deputy, Mr. Hernandez said he was on probation, but would not identify the offense. After repeatedly refusing to get out of the truck, Deputy Paonessa pepper sprayed Mr. Hernandez. Because Mr. Hernandez continued to resist, Deputy Paonessa and his partner pulled Mr. Hernandez from the truck and handcuffed him.

Mr. Hernandez was charged with violations of California Penal Code 69 (obstructing an officer in the performance of his duties), 148(a)(1) (resisting arrest), California Health & Safety Code 11550(a) (under the influence of methamphetamine) and California Vehicle Code 23152(a) (driving under the influence of drugs). Following the denial of his motion to suppress evidence, the jury convicted Mr. Hernandez of all charges and he appealed.

The Court of Appeal reversed the judgment and remanded the case to the lower court. The California Supreme Court affirmed the Court of Appeal judgment.

RATIONALE

The California Supreme Court quoted from the United States Supreme Court's decision in **Delaware v. Prouse** (1979) 440 U.S. 648, where the United States Supreme Court observed that "[E]xcept in those situations in which there is at least articulable and reasonable suspicion that a motorist is unlicensed or that an automobile is not registered, or that either the vehicle or an occupant is otherwise subject to seizure for violation of law, stopping an automobile and detaining the driver in order to check his driver's license and the registration of the automobile are unreasonable under the Fourth Amendment...[P]ersons in automobiles on public roadways may not for that reason alone have their travel and privacy interfered with at the unbridled discretion of police officers." **Prouse**, **supra**, at 663.

The California Supreme Court stated that "[t]he failure here is that, although Deputy Paonessa knew that some people driving with a temporary permit may be violating the law, he could point to no articulable facts supporting a reasonable suspicion that Mr. Hernandez, in particular, may have been acting illegally. **Hernandez**, **supra**, 45 Cal.4th at 299.

By way of contrast, in the companion case of **In re Raymond C.** (2008) 45 Cal.4th 303, which was decided the same day, the California Supreme Court unanimously upheld the trial court's finding that the stop of the minor's car was reasonable under the circumstances.

FACTS (In re Raymond C.. (2008) 45 Cal.4th 303).

At approximately 1 a.m. on October 24, 2004, Officer Timothy Kandler saw the minor driving an Acura without license plates or temporary operating permit in the rear window. From the officer's vantage point, he was unable to see if there was a temporary permit affixed to the front window. The officer stopped the Acura for the perceived license plate violation. The officer asked the minor for his driver's license, registration, and proof of insurance. The minor provided the driver's license and proof of insurance and said that the temporary permit was displayed in the front window of the car.

In the course of the officer's discussion with the minor, he observed signs and symptoms consistent with alcohol intoxication. The minor failed some field sobriety tests and was arrested for driving under the influence of alcohol.

At a motion to suppress evidence, the minor's father testified that he bought the 2005 Acura on October 2, 2004, and did not receive license plates for the car until early December. The father testified that the two-week-old car was "shiny and new" when the minor was arrested and that there was a temporary permit in the front window.

The trial court denied the motion to suppress evidence and found that the minor drove a vehicle while under the influence of alcohol and with a blood alcohol level of 0.08% or more. The trial court found the minor to be a ward of the court and placed him on probation with conditions, including a 10-day work program. The court of appeal later affirmed that finding and ruled that "[T]he absence of a rear plate or, from the officer's vantage point, a temporary tag substituting for the plate, justified the stop." **Id.** at 306. The California Supreme Court upheld the Court of Appeal decision.

RATIONALE

The California Supreme Court agreed with the Court of Appeal finding that the facts of the case justified the officer's reasonable suspicion that the car was being driven in violation of the vehicle license requirements. The Supreme Court said the question was whether Officer Kandler was allowed to stop the car and continue his investigation. The minor argued that the officer should have driven around the car to see all the windows before stopping it.

In rejecting the minor's argument, the Court noted that "[s]uch maneuvering would require driving alongside the Acura on both sides and driving ahead of it while scanning the windshield in the officer's rear view mirror. Even assuming the officer could have engaged in these potentially dangerous maneuvers, he was not required to do so. 'The reasonableness of [an] officer's decision to stop a suspect does not turn on the availability of less intrusive investigatory techniques.' (*United States v. Sokolow* (1989) 490 U.S. 1, 11, 109 S.Ct. 1581, 104 L.Ed.2d 1.) Nor is an officer required to eliminate all innocent explanations that might account for the facts supporting a particularized suspicion. (*People v. Glaser* (1995) 11 Cal.4th 354, 373, 45 Cal.Rptr.2d 425, 902 P.2d 729.) The course Kandler followed was reasonable as well as safer for him, Raymond, and other motorists. Moreover, if Kandler had passed Raymond in order to check his windshield for a temporary permit, he would have lost control of the situation. Raymond could have turned into a side street and driven away before the officer could turn around and follow. If the car had been stolen, allowing the driver to fall in behind the officer would place the officer in danger of attack by a felon seeking to avoid arrest. The course taken by Kandler was entirely reasonable under the circumstances." **Id.** at 308.

The Court of Appeal refused to uphold the pat search of a minor in the case of **In re H.H.** 174 Cal.App.4th 653, where the officer's stated justification for the pat search was the minor's statement that he did not give consent to be searched.

FACTS (In re H.H. (2009) 174 Cal.App.4th 653)

Albany Police Officer Ted Allen was on patrol late one evening when he saw H.H. riding a bicycle with defective lighting. Due to the vehicle code violation, he stopped the minor, asked him to step from the bike and to remove a backpack that the minor was wearing. H.H. removed the backpack and said, "I'm not on probation." The minor then said that he did not give his consent for a search of his person.

Officer Allen thought both of these comments were strange and that the minor might have a weapon on his person. Based on this hunch, and in the absence of articulable facts that the minor was armed and dangerous, Officer Allen pat-searched H.H. and found a loaded revolver in H.H.'s jacket.

H.H. was charged with a variety of weapons charges. However, after the trial court denied his motion to suppress the evidence based on its conclusion that "the officer's specific articulated reasons for conducting the pat-down search under the circumstances were reasonable [.]" (**Id**. at 657), H.H. admitted to a misdemeanor violation of possession of a deadly weapon. The trial court than placed H.H. on probation and placed him with his father.

RATIONALE

A refusal to consent to a search cannot itself form the basis for reasonable suspicion: "it should go without saying that consideration of such a refusal would violate the Fourth Amendment." [Citations.] If refusal of consent were a basis for reasonable suspicion, nothing would be left of Fourth Amendment protections. A motorist who consented to a search could be searched; and a motorist who refused consent could be searched, as well. (**Id**. at 658. [Citations].)

> The minor's refusal to consent did not – as the People suggest – necessarily indicate the minor "had something illegal to hide." The minor simply informed the police officer that he would not consent to the search of his backpack or his person. (**Id**. at 660).

The Court of Appeal did acknowledge that

> "[t]he judiciary should not lightly second-guess a police officer's decision to perform a pat-down search for officer safety. The lives and safety of police officers weigh heavily in the balance of competing Fourth Amendment considerations." (**Dickey**, **supra**, 21 Cal.App.4th at p. 957) Here, however, there simply were no specific and articulable facts at the suppression hearing that the minor was armed and dangerous. (**Id**. at 660)

In **People v. Lujano** (2014) 229 Cal.App.4th 175, the Court of Appeal ruled that the police acted on a hunch when they conducted a warrantless intrusion into a private home and detained the resident. The Court found that the warrantless detention of Mr. Lujano inside his residence lacked probable cause, and therefore violated the Fourth Amendment.

FACTS (People v. Lujano (2014) 229 Cal.App.4th 175)

> In the evening of December 19, 2010, a Riverside liquor store was robbed by two men wearing black colored sweatshirts, gloves, and masks. One of the robbers brandished a handgun. The robbery was captured on the store's multiple surveillance cameras. The man who brandished a firearm appeared to be about six feet tall and weigh about 300 pounds, while the second robber was shorter (five feet eight inches or five feet nine inches tall) and thinner. Based on the surveillance video, the officers identified the gun used in the robbery, but never recovered, as a .38 caliber or .357 hammerless revolver. During the robbery, the two victims--later identified as the store manager and a friend who happened to be at the store--were both sprayed in the face with pepper spray. Neither victim was able to identify either robber.
>
> In the afternoon of December 28, 2010, two Riverside police officers were on patrol when they observed a man in the driveway in front of a house stripping copper wire from an air conditioning unit that might have come from the residence. The officers approached the man and spoke with him. The man was later identified as "Albert Vargas," who told the officers that he was visiting a friend named "Rick." Mr. Vargas did not know Rick's last name, but he was later identified as Ricardo Lujano, the defendant in this case. Mr. Vargas also admitted that he was on probation "for narcotics," and that he was stripping copper wire from the air conditioner because it no longer worked.
>
> The officers noticed that a side door that led from the driveway into the house was ajar, but not wide enough for someone to walk through it. Officer

Bryan Galbreath approached the door, leaned inside, identified himself as a police officer, and commanded anyone in the house to come to the door. Mr. Lujano responded to the officer's commands and came out from the bedroom area of the house and into the officer's view. Mr. Lujano followed Officer Galbreath's instructions, turned around and walked backwards out of the door, and onto a concrete step. While Officer Galbreath did not handcuff Mr. Lujano at that time, he did take physical control of him and required Mr. Lujano to keep his hands clasped behind his back. Officer Galbreath asked Mr. Lujano for consent to search his person, which Mr. Lujano gave. During the search, Officer Galbreath located a plastic bag of methamphetamine in Mr. Lujano's pants pocket, at which point he arrested him.

Mr. Lujano then consented to a search of his residence, as did the owner of the home, which turned out to be Mr. Vargas's mother, who was summoned to the residence by the police. During a search of the residence, the officers found a nine-millimeter semi automatic handgun, as well as a speed loader for a .38 caliber revolver. The officers also recovered a pair of shoes, three pairs of work gloves, two black hooded sweatshirts--one sized 2XL and the other sized 3XL--two cans of pepper spray, one of which was empty and one of which was full. All of the items, with the exception of the smaller of the two sweatshirts, were found in Mr. Lujano's bedroom.

Officer Jeffrey Adcox, was involved in the earch of Mr. Lujano's residence and had also participated in the investigation of the robbery and reviewed the surveillance video. Officer Adcox noted that Mr. Lujano appeared to be about the same height and weight as the larger armed robber in the video. Based on a further review of the crime video, he opined that the shoes recovered in the search matched those worn by one of the robbery suspects, as did the gloves, pepper spray bottle and black hooded sweatshirt. At the suggestion of Officer Adcox, Officer Park also reviewed the surveillance video and came to the same conclusion as Officer Adcox. Officer Park also noted the similarity in height, build, and facial hair between Mr. Lujano and the larger of the two robbers.

Mr. Lujano's motion to suppress the evidence seized was denied and he pled guilty to possession of controlled substances, receiving stolen property, and being a felon in possession of a firearm. Mr. Lujano went to trial on the robbery charge. A jury found him guilty of that charge and also found the enhancement for personally using a firearm during the commission of the robbery to be true. The trial court sentenced Mr. Lujano to 14 years four months in prison. Mr. Lujano promptly appealed.

RATIONALE

The Court of Appeal found that the motion to suppress the evidence should have been granted, but in so ruling, the court held that only the robbery and firearm enhancement convictions needed to be reversed because Mr. Lujano waived his right to appeal on the remaining charges as part of his plea bargain, and also failed to obtain a certificate of probable cause.

The court found that an individual stripping copper wire from an air conditioner in front of a residence does not necessarily show that one is engaged in criminal activity. However, in light of an officer's training and expertise, it is not unreasonable inference for an officer to believe that such a person might be engaged in criminal activity. The appellate court found that the record was devoid of any evidence that Mr. Vargas had entered the house and that when officer Galbreath first contacted Mr. Lujano, he was unaware of any specific, articulable facts particular to Mr. Lujano suggesting that he might be involved in criminal activity. The court also found that the officer's observations outside the house prior to making contact with Mr. Lujano failed to yield any facts that would lead the officer to conclude that a burglar was inside the residence. The appellate court went on to observe that there was nothing in the record establishing that Officer Galbreath was aware of any facts at that time that were particular to the defendant, which would be sufficient to persuade someone that Mr. Lujano had committed a crime.

As the court said,

> There is nothing in the record establishing that Officer Galbreath, at the time he detained defendant, was aware of facts particular to defendant sufficient to "persuade someone of 'reasonable caution'" that defendant had "committed a crime"--nothing to support the belief defendant even was trespassing, let alone committing burglary.

(**Id**. at 187.)

Finally, the court observed:

> In short, we do not doubt that the responding officers had a good faith suspicion defendant was engaged in criminal activity. That suspicion, however, was not supported by objective facts rising to the level of probable cause, as required to justify the warrantless detention of the resident inside a dwelling. As such, defendant's detention was in violation of his Fourth Amendment rights.

(**Id**. at 188.)

2.2.2.3 – Detentions and Drug Courier Profiles

Based on their expertise, officers may detain persons who meet a recognized drug courier profile. (See **United States v. Mendenhall** (1980) 446 U.S. 544 and **United States v. Sokolow** (1989) 490 U.S. 1.)

In **People v. Daugherty** (1996) 50 Cal.App.4th 275, the Court of Appeal found the initial encounter to be consensual and ruled that at the point when the officer told Ms. Daugherty that he only spoke to people who he believed were carrying drugs through the airport, the officer had a sufficient reasonable suspicion to justify a detention.

FACTS <u>People v. Daugherty</u> (1996) 50 Cal.App.4th 275)

Narcotics officers were working the Burbank Airport when they saw Ms. Daugherty arrive with several bags. They watched her for a while and believed she might be transporting narcotics.

Officer Gillespie approached, identified himself and asked to speak to Ms. Daugherty for a moment. Officer Gillespie advised Ms. Daugherty that she was not under arrest, was free to leave at any time, and did not have to speak with him. He told her he wanted to ask her a few questions if she did not mind. He then asked for ID and Ms. Daugherty verbally identified herself as "Linda Washington" and said she had no written ID.

In response to the officer's request, Ms. Daugherty handed him her ticket, which was a one-way ticket to Detroit. Officer Gillespie returned the ticket to Ms. Daugherty and advised her that he and his partner worked narcotics and only interviewed people they suspected were transporting drugs through the airport. When asked by Officer Gillespie if she was carrying any drugs, Ms. Daugherty said "No."

Officer Gillespie asked for consent to search Ms. Daugherty's luggage, but she refused. After the refusal, Officer Gillespie advised Ms. Daugherty that he believed she was carrying drugs and would be detained in an office until a police dog could be summoned to sniff the luggage. Thirty minutes later, a dog arrived and alerted to the three kilograms of cocaine in Ms. Daugherty's luggage.

2.2.2.4 – Informant Information

In **<u>Draper v. United States</u>** (1959) 358 U.S. 307, the U.S. Supreme Court ruled in a 6 to 1 decision, with only Justice Douglas dissenting, that a federal narcotics agent had probable cause and reasonable grounds to arrest and search Mr. Draper based on information provided to him by a confidential reliable informant (CRI). Justice Whittaker, writing for the majority of the court, observed that when the agent "saw a man having the exact physical attributes and wearing the precise clothing and carrying the tan zipper bag that Hereford [the CRI] had described, alight from one of the very trains from the very place stated by Hereford and start to walk at a 'fast' pace toward the station exit, Marsh [the agent] had personally verified every facet of the information given him by Hereford except whether petitioner had accomplished his mission and had the three ounces of heroin on his person or in his bag. And surely, with every other bit of Hereford's information being thus personally verified, Marsh had 'reasonable grounds' to believe that the remaining unverified bit of Hereford's information – that Draper would have the heroin with him – was likewise true." (**<u>Id</u>**. at 313.)

FACTS (<u>Draper v. United States</u> (1959) 358 U.S. 307)

Federal Narcotic Agent Marsh, with 29 years of experience, was stationed in Denver, Colorado. He had worked with a CRI named Hereford, who had worked as a "special employee" for the Bureau of Narcotics at Denver for about six months. From time to time, the CRI gave information to Agent Marsh that always proved accurate and reliable. The CRI received small sums of money as compensation for the information provided.

On September 3, 1956, the CRI told Agent Marsh that James Alonzo Draper recently began living at a particular address in Denver and "was peddling narcotics to several addicts" in Denver.

On September 7, 1956, the CRI told Agent Marsh "that Draper had gone to Chicago the day before [September 6] by train [and] that he was going to bring back three ounces of heroin [and] that he would return to Denver either on the morning of the 8th of September or the morning of the 9th of September also by train.' Hereford also gave Marsh a detailed physical description of Draper and of the clothing he was wearing, and said that he would be carrying "a tan zipper bag," and that he habitually 'walked real fast.' "(**<u>Id</u>**. at 309.) The CRI described Mr. Draper to Agent Marsh as ". . . a Negro of light brown complexion, 27 years of age, 5 feet 8 inches tall, weighed about 160 pounds, and that he was wearing a light colored raincoat, brown slacks and black shoes." (**<u>Id</u>**. at 309, FN 2.)

On September 8, 1956, Agent Marsh and a Denver police officer went to the Denver Union Station and watched incoming trains from Chicago, but saw no one matching Mr. Draper's description. On September 9, 1956, he repeated the process and this time saw Mr. Draper, who matched the exact physical and clothing description provided by the CRI alight from an incoming Chicago train and start walking fast toward the exit. Mr. Draper was carrying a tan zipper bag in his right hand and had his left hand trust into his raincoat pocket. Agent Marsh and the Denver police officer caught up to Mr. Draper and arrested him. A search incident to arrest revealed two envelopes containing heroin that were held in his left hand inside the raincoat pocket and a syringe in the tan zipper bag. Agent Marsh seized a total of 865 grams (30.5 ounces) of heroin from Mr. Draper. The CRI died four days after Mr. Draper's arrest and was not available to testify for the government at the suppression motion.

Mr. Draper's motion to suppress the seized evidence was denied by the District Court and a jury convicted him of knowingly concealing and transporting narcotics. The Court of Appeals affirmed the conviction, as did the U.S. Supreme Court, which granted certiorari to address the alleged Fourth Amendment violation.

The U.S. Supreme Court, in a 6 to 3 decision in **Alabama v. White** (1990) 496 U.S. 325, upheld a car stop based on the totality of circumstances in what it classified as a "close case" based on information from an anonymous informant that was partially corroborated by the police.

FACTS (Alabama v. White (1990) 496 U.S. 325)

On April 22, 1987, at about 3 p.m., Montgomery Police Department Corporal Davis received a telephone call from an anonymous caller. The caller said that Vanessa White would be leaving 235-C Lynwood Terrace Apartments at a particular time in a brown Plymouth station wagon with a broken right taillight lens. She would go to Dobey's Motel, which is about four miles away, and would be in possession of an ounce of cocaine inside a brown attaché case.

Corporal Davis and his partner, Corporal Reynolds, went to the Lynwood Terrace Apartments and saw a Plymouth matching the description parked in the parking lot in front of building 235. The corporals saw Ms. White leave building 235 and watched her enter the station wagon. However, she was not carrying anything when she entered the car. The corporals followed the car as it took the most direct route to Dobey's Motel and requested a marked patrol unit stop the car when it reached the Mobile Highway, which is the roadway where the Dobey's Motel is located.

Officers made a car stop at 4:18 p.m., just short of Dobey's Motel. The officer made this car stop approximately 68 minutes after the corporal received the anonymous caller's information. Corporal Davis contacted Ms. White, asked her to get out of the car and then explained that she was stopped because she was suspected of carrying cocaine. Ms. White gave the Corporal consent to search the car. The officers found a locked, brown attaché case in the car and Ms. White provided Corporal Davis with the combination to the lock. Inside the brief case, officers found marijuana and arrested her. Ms. White also had three mgs of cocaine in her purse.

Following the denial of her motion to suppress evidence, Ms. White plead guilty to possession of marijuana and cocaine and reserved her right to appeal the denial of the suppression motion. The Alabama Court of Criminal Appeals reversed the trial court and suppressed the evidence. The Alabama Supreme Court declined to hear the case. The U.S. Supreme Court granted a writ of certiorari because of differing views in federal and state courts as to whether an anonymous tip could provide reasonable suspicious for a stop and ultimately upheld the lawfulness of the stop and search.

RATIONALE

The U.S. Supreme Court found the tip in this case similar to the one in **Illinois v. Gates** (1983) 462 U.S. 313, where the tip in this case "provide[d] virtually nothing from which one might conclude that [the caller] is either honest or his information reliable; likewise, the [tip] gives absolutely no indication of the basis for the [caller's] predictions regarding [Vanessa White's] criminal activities." (**Id**. at 329.)

"Reasonable suspicion is a less demanding standard than probable cause not only in the sense that reasonable suspicion can be established with information that is different in quantity or content than that required to establish probable cause, but also in the sense that reasonable suspicion can arise from information that is less reliable than that required to show probable cause. *Adams v. Williams, supra* [(1972) 407 U.S. 143], demonstrates as much. We there assumed that the unverified tip from the known informant might not have been reliable enough to establish probable cause, but nevertheless found it sufficiently reliable to justify a *Terry* [**Terry v. Ohio** (1968) 392 U.S. 1] stop. Reasonable suspicion, like probable cause, is dependent upon both the content of information possessed by police and its degree of reliability. Both factors-quantity and quality-are considered in the 'totality of the circumstances-the whole picture,' *United States v. Cortez, 449 U.S. 411, 417, 101 S.Ct. 690, 695, 66 L.3d. 2d 621 (1981)*, that must be taken into account when evaluating whether there is reasonable suspicion. (**Id**. at 330.)

"Contrary to the court below, we conclude that when the officers stopped respondent, the anonymous tip had been sufficiently corroborated to furnish reasonable suspicion that respondent was engaged in criminal activity and that the investigative stop therefore did not violate the Fourth Amendment." (**Id**. at 331.)

"As for the caller's prediction of respondent's destination, it is true that the officers stopped her just short of Dobey's Motel and did not know whether she would have pulled in or continued past it. But given that the 4-mile route driven by respondent was the most direct route possible to Dobey's Motel, . . . but nevertheless involved several turns, . . . we think respondent's destination was significantly corroborated." (**Id**. at 331.)

"We think it also important that, as in *Gates* 'the anonymous [tip] contained a range of details relating not just to easily obtained facts and conditions existing at the time of the tip, but to future actions of third parties ordinarily not easily predicted.' . . . The fact that the officers found a car precisely matching the caller's description in front of the 235 building is an example of the former. Anyone could have 'predicted' that fact because it was a condition presumably existing at the time of the call. What was important was the caller's ability to predict respondent's *future behavior,* because it demonstrated inside information-a special familiarity with respondent's affairs. The general public would have had no way of knowing that respondent would shortly leave the building, get in the described car, and drive the most direct route to Dobey's Motel. Because only a small number of people are generally privy to an individual's itinerary, it is reasonable for police to believe that a person with access to such information is likely to also have access to reliable information about that individual's illegal activities. . . . When significant aspects of the caller's predictions were verified, there was reason to believe not only that the caller was honest but also that he was well informed, at least well enough to justify the stop." (**Id.** at 332. [*Italics* in original].)

Unlike the holding in **Alabama v. White**, **supra**, the U.S. Supreme Court ruled in **Florida v. J.L.** (2000) 529 U.S. 266, that an anonymous report that a young black male was standing at a particular bus stop, wearing a plaid shirt and carrying a gun, without more, was insufficient to justify a **Terry v. Ohio**, **infra**, stop.

FACTS (Florida v. J.L. (2000) 529 U.S. 266)

On October 13, 1995, an anonymous caller reported to the Miami-Dade Police that a young black male was standing at a particular bus stop, wearing a plaid shirt and carrying a gun. There was no audio recording of the anonymous tip and the police knew nothing about the informant.

Two officers were dispatched to the location sometime after the call was received and arrived within six minutes of the dispatch. They saw three black males "just hanging out [there]." J.L. was wearing a plaid shirt. J.L. was also 10 days shy of his 16th birthday at the time of this incident.

Aside from the tip, the officers had no basis to suspect any illegal conduct and did not see a firearm. J.L. also did not make any threatening or otherwise unusual movements towards the police officers. One of the officers approached J.L. and told him to put his hands up on the bus stop, frisked him, and seized a gun from J.L.'s jacket pocket.

The trial court granted the defendant's motion to suppress, but the intermediate appellate court reversed. The Florida Supreme Court reversed the appellate court and held that the tip provided no predictions of future conduct and did not contain any other qualifying indicia of reliability. Two justices dissented and argued for the creation of a "firearm exception" to the **Terry v. Ohio**, **infra**, rule.

RATIONALE

The Supreme Court noted, "All the police had to go on in this case was the bare report of an unknown, unaccountable informant who neither explained how he knew about the gun nor supplied any basis for believing he had information about J.L." **Florida v. J.L.**, **supra**, at 271.

The Supreme Court noted that an anonymous tip alone would seldom demonstrate the informant's basis of knowledge or veracity. In this case, the caller provided no predictive information and therefore failed to provide the police with any means to test the informant's knowledge or credibility. The fact that J.L. turned out to have a gun is not sufficient to establish that the officers had a reasonable basis for suspecting J.L. of engaging in criminal conduct prior to the frisk.

The Supreme Court also refused to adopt the government's proposal that because firearms are dangerous, the Court should modify its standard **Terry v. Ohio**, **infra**, analysis to create a "firearm exception." The Court noted, "[s]uch an exception would enable any person seeking to harass another to set in motion an intrusive, embarrassing police search of the targeted person simply by placing an anonymous call falsely reporting the target's unlawful carriage of a gun." **Florida v. J.L.**, **supra**, at 272.

In **People v. Coulombe** (2001) 86 Cal.App.4th 52, the Court of Appeal considered the holding in **Florida v. J.L.**, **supra** but ruled that officers were justified in detaining and pat searching the defendant in a public place after being told by two separate citizen informants that the defendant was in possession of a firearm at a crowded, civic New Year's celebration, which the officers were patrolling.

FACTS (People v. Coulombe (2001) 86 Cal.App.4th 52)

On New Year's Even 1999, at about 11 p.m., two separate citizens, approximately 5 to 10 seconds apart, approached two uniformed Santa Rosa Sergeants at the "1st Night" celebration in downtown Santa Rosa. Both citizens pointed to the nearby Cantina restaurant, which was approximately 75 feet away, and told the Sergeants that a man wearing a white cap had a gun. Neither citizen provided any identifying information about themselves.

Three police officers immediately went to the restaurant and saw the defendant, who was wearing a white cap, seated in a wheelchair. He was the only person in the area who matched the citizen informants' description. The police pat searched the defendant and found a "small snub-nosed stainless steel revolver" in the defendant's right side pocket.

The district attorney charged the defendant with felony violations of California Penal Code 22021(a)(1) (Felon with a gun), PC 22025(a)(2) (Possession of a concealed firearm) and 22316(b)(1) (Possession of ammunition by a felon). The trial court granted the defendant's motion to suppress the evidence, but the appellate court reversed.

RATIONALE

"Any reasonable person would conclude, given two independent reports by citizens that an individual matching defendant's description, in defendant's location, at that particular point in time, was carrying a firearm in a crowd of New Year's Eve revelers, constituted 'specific and articulable' facts giving rise to a reasonable suspicion that defendant was engaged in criminal activity and was armed." (**Id.** at 57.)

The Court of Appeal found the case distinguishable from **Florida v. J.L., supra**, based on the following factors:

- The Santa Rosa Officers received two independent tips from citizen informants within the span of 5 to 10 seconds of each other
- The tips were not made anonymously over the telephone, but were provided during face-to-face contact with the officers who could observe the informants' credibility and where the informants ran the risk of losing their anonymity
- The circumstances under which the defendant allegedly possessed a gun occurred in a throng of thousands of New Year's celebrants as opposed to a bus stop with only two other persons present.

In **People v. Ramirez** (1996) 41 Cal.App.4th 1608, which was decided four years before the decision in **Florida v. J.L., supra**, a California Court of Appeal panel ruled that the police sufficiently corroborated anonymous information to justify the temporary detention of the defendant and his associates.

FACTS (People v. Ramirez (1996) 41 Cal.App.4th 1608)

Police received an anonymous report that stated three Hispanic male adults (HMA) were in a two door blue Buick, with license plate number 1MBK445. The reporting party said the three HMAs were dealing drugs from their vehicle on the east side of Golden Hill Park in San Diego.

Within five minutes of the report, the police arrived in the area. The officers saw three HMAs talking inside a car that matched the description. The officers ordered all three HMAs out of the car and pat searched them for weapons. One officer obtained Mr. Ramirez's consent to search a jacket he had worn and found drugs inside the jacket.

RATIONALE

The Court of Appeal found the information sufficiently corroborated for the following reasons:

- The officers confirmed the physical description of the suspects, vehicle and location
- The location was known as a high narcotics trafficking area
- The men were conversing inside the car, which the Court found to be an activity consistent with the anonymous informant's statement that the men were dealing drugs
- Some exigency existed in view of the report of a "crime in progress."

2.2.2.5 – Identification Requests

California Courts have held that if a detention is valid and officer may request ID from the detained suspect.

In **People v. Loudermilk** (1987) 195 Cal.App.3d 996, the Court of Appeal ruled that an officer lawfully detained the defendant and that there is no constitutional proscription against asking a detained person for ID. Based on that lawful detention, the court found that the police lawfully seized a wallet from the defendant's person during a weapons pat search and that the wallet constituted evidence showing a violation of California Penal Code 248.9 (False Information to a Peace Officer).

The Court of Appeal upheld the wallet search on the independent grounds of a search incident to arrest. The arrest was justified based on the fact that the defendant's description substantially matched that of an attempted murder suspect, that the defendant was alone and hitchhiking in the middle of the highway at a late hour.

FACTS (People v. Loudermilk (1987) 195 Cal.App.3d 996)

Benjamin Bill was sleeping in a tree grove near a highway ramp when he was awakened around 3 a.m. by what sounded like three firecrackers. Mr. Bill had been shot below the right earlobe and the bullet exited at the base of the right side of his chin.

The officers obtained a description from Joey Lightfoot of the man who fired the shots. The suspect was running east along Dry Creek Road toward Healdsburg. Mr. Lightfoot described the suspect as a White male adult, approximately 5 feet 8 inches tall, with an average build, wearing a long-sleeve shirt and dark pants and carrying a .22 caliber pistol.

At approximately 4:30 a.m., Deputy Sheriffs Geaslin and Haran heard the broadcast and were searching an area north of Healdsburg on Highway 101 when they spotted the defendant, who matched the description of the shooter. Deputy Geaslin asked the defendant for ID, but the defendant claimed to have none. During a weapons pat search, Deputy Geaslin felt a wallet in the defendant's right rear pocket. The deputy retrieved the wallet from the pocket, opened it and began searching for ID. Deputy Geaslin handed two pieces of paper with several names on them to Deputy Haran. He also gave Deputy Haran some pieces of ID from the wallet, which Deputy Haran took to the car and used to run an ID check.

The defendant then began crying and said, "I shot him. Something went wrong in my head. I thought he was going to shoot me, so I shot him." He also said, "Come on, I'll show you where the gun is by the old boxcar." The defendant was "really excited" and "stressed out." After the deputies handcuffed him, they placed the defendant in a police car and took him to several spots where he said the gun was located. However, the gun could not be located.

At the police station, Detective Giovannoni read the defendant his Miranda rights. Although he initially invoked his right to remain silent, the defendant later reinitiated contact and led Detective Giovannoni to the gun.

In **People v. Long** (1987) 189 Cal.App.3d 77, the Court of Appeal ruled that it was permissible for officers to ask a bar patron to step outside when he was found in the company of an underage woman. Once outside, the police could lawfully ask the defendant for ID.

FACTS (People v. Long (1987) 189 Cal.App.3d 77)

San Jose Police Department (SJPD) Officer Brian Blackford and his Field Training Officer Dennis Luca saw the defendant inside a bar and in the company of a 19-year-old woman. Upon seeing this, they asked the defendant to step outside, which he did. The officers asked for ID and the defendant retrieved his wallet and began fumbling inside looking for ID. Officer Luca asked for and received permission to look in the wallet for ID but instead found methamphetamine.

The defendant appeared under the influence of methamphetamine, but due to a statutory drafting error by the California Legislature, it was legal to be under the influence of a controlled substance at that time. Therefore, this case does not fall within the category of a search incident to a lawful arrest.

2.2.2.6 – Suspect or Vehicle Similarity to Crime Perpetrator

The U.S. Supreme Court unanimously ruled in **United States v. Hensley** (1985) 469 U.S. 221 that if the police have a reasonable suspicion, grounded in specific and articulable facts that a person was involved in or is wanted in connection with a completed felony, they may make an investigative stop even absent probable cause to arrest.

Furthermore, if the police make an investigative stop in objective reliance on a "wanted flyer" or bulletin issued by another police agency, any evidence uncovered during the stop is admissible as long as the police who issued the flyer or bulletin possessed a reasonable suspicion justifying that stop and if the stop that in fact occurred was not significantly more intrusive than would have been permitted the issuing department.

This was the first case where the Supreme Court dealt with a situation where the police stopped someone after a completed crime. Previous cases involving investigative stops related to crimes that were either about to be committed or were being committed at the moment of the stop.

FACTS (United States v. Hensley (1985) 469 U.S. 221)

On December 4, 1981, two armed men robbed a tavern in the Cincinnati suburb of St. Bernard, Ohio. Six days later, St. Bernard Police Officer Davis, interviewed an informant who told him that Thomas Hensley had driven the getaway car during the robbery. After obtaining a written statement from the informant, Officer Davis issued a "wanted flyer" to other police departments in the Cincinnati metropolitan area.

The flyer contained the following information regarding Mr. Hensley:

- He was wanted for investigation of aggravated robbery
- It described both Mr. Hensley and the date and location of the alleged robbery
- It asked other departments to pick up and hold Mr. Hensley for the St. Bernard Police should he be located
- It warned other departments to use caution and to consider Mr. Hensley armed and dangerous.

The Covington Police Department received the teletype of the wanted flyer on December 10, 1981. Covington is a Kentucky suburb of Cincinnati and is about five miles from St. Bernard. The flyer was read aloud at each shift change between December 10 and 16. Some of the Covington officers knew Mr. Hensley and, after December 10, periodically looked for him at places in town he was known to frequent.

On December 16th, Covington Officer Eiger saw a white Cadillac convertible stopped in the middle of Covington Street. He saw Mr. Hensley in the driver's seat and asked him to move along. As Mr. Hensley drove away, Officer Eiger asked the dispatcher if Mr. Hensley had an arrest warrant outstanding. The police never confirmed the existence of an arrest warrant prior to the subsequent stop and arrest of Mr. Hensley.

Covington Officer Cope reported that he had sighted the Cadillac and it was approaching him on Holman Street. The officer activated his emergency equipment and Mr. Hensley pulled to the curb. Officer Cope approached the Cadillac with his weapon held in the air and ordered Mr. Hensley and a passenger to get out of the car. A few moments later, Officer Rassache arrived and recognized the passenger as Albert Green, who he knew to be a convicted felon. When Officer Rassache stepped up to the open passenger door and saw the butt of a revolver sticking out from under the passenger seat, he arrested Mr. Green.

A search of the passenger compartment, following Mr. Green's arrest, resulted in the seizure of a second handgun that was wrapped in a jacket in the middle of the front seat. The police later found a third handgun in a bag in the back seat.

A federal grand jury in the Eastern District of Kentucky ultimately indicted Mr. Hensley for being a felon in possession of a firearm. The District Court denied his motion to suppress the evidence. Following a court trial, the court convicted Mr. Hensley and sentenced him to two years in federal prison.

On appeal, the 6th Circuit Court of Appeal reversed the conviction and held that the stop and subsequent seizure of the weapons were illegal for the following reasons:

- The crime was not ongoing or imminent, but instead had already been completed
- The wanted flyer was insufficient to create a reasonable suspicion that Mr. Hensley had engaged in criminal conduct.

RATIONALE

"The justification for the stop did not evaporate when the armed robbery was completed. Mr. Hensley was reasonably suspected of involvement in a felony and was at large from the time the suspicion arose until the stop by the Covington Police. A brief stop and detention at the earliest opportunity after the suspicion arose is fully consistent with the principles of the Fourth Amendment." (**Id**., at 615-616.)

In **People v. Monroe** (1993) 12 Cal.App.4th 1174, the Court of Appeal ruled that the police lawfully stopped a car that William Monroe was riding in as a passenger to investigate whether or not he was a murder fugitive (he wasn't), based on the following factors:

- He matched the description of the suspect in several respects, especially from the profile view that the officer was able to observe
- He was in a neighborhood frequented by the wanted suspect
- He was in a rental car from Ohio, which is the state where the suspect was reported to have recently been
- He turned away from the officers when they pulled up alongside of him at a stop light and remained in that position until the light changed.

During that lawful car stop, officers found Mr. Monroe to be in possession of an open container of alcohol. He was arrested pursuant to California Vehicle Code 40302(a) when he could not produce any satisfactory ID. Incident to that arrest, officers searched his person resulting in the seizure of cocaine.

2.2.2.7 – Truancy Checks

There are two statutes in the California Education Code that deal directly with the arrests of truants and the transportation of truants. Each of these statutes is an important element in the analysis of the lawfulness of arresting truants.

California Education Code 48264 is entitled "Arrest of Truants" and states that "[t]he attendance supervisor or his or her designee, a peace officer, a school administrator or his or her designee, or a probation officer may arrest or assume temporary custody, during school hours, of any minor subject to compulsory full-time education or to compulsory continuation education found away from his or her home and who is absent from school without valid excuse within the county, city, or city and county, or school district."

California Education Code 48265 is entitled "Delivery of Truant" and states that "[a]ny person arresting or assuming temporary custody of a minor pursuant to section 48264 shall forthwith deliver the minor either to the parent, guardian, or other person having control, or charge of the minor, or to the school from which the minor is absent, or to a nonsecure youth service or community center designated by the school or district for counseling prior to returning such minor to his home or school, or to a school counselor or pupil services and attendance officer located at a police station for the purpose of obtaining immediate counseling from the counselor or officer prior to returning or being returned to his home or school, . . ."

The California Supreme Court ruled in the case of **In re James D.** (1987) 43 Cal.3d 903, that youthful appearance alone was not enough to detain a minor for suspicion of truancy. However, in that case, the officer had the additional factors of the minor carrying a book bag, observations made during school hours and the fact the minor was crossing a bridge that was at least three miles away from the nearest school, which justified the detention.

2.2.2.8 – Unprovoked Flight

In a 5 to 4 decision in **Illinois v. Wardlow** (2000) 528 U.S. 119, the U.S. Supreme Court ruled that Mr. Wardlow's unprovoked flight, coupled with the high crime area, justified a **Terry v. Ohio**, **infra**, type of stop based on the totality of circumstances.

FACTS (Illinois v. Wardlow (2000) 528 U.S. 119)

On Sept. 9, 1995, Sam Wardlow was standing on a Chicago street at about noon. Officers Nolan and Harvey were driving in the last Chicago police car in a caravan of four that were converging on an area of high drug activity. The officers were driving together because they expected to find a crowd of people in the area, including lookouts and customers. However, Officer Nolan could not recall if the cars were marked or unmarked units.

As the caravan approached the area of 4035 West Van Buren, Officer Nolan saw Mr. Wardlow standing next to a building carrying a white colored, opaque bag under his arm. Mr. Wardlow looked in the officer's direction, and then fled on foot. Mr. Wardlow ran through a gangway and an alley, but officers eventually cornered him on the street.

Officer Nolan exited the police car and performed a protective weapons pat-down search on Mr. Wardlow. He did this because of his experience that it was common for there to be weapons near narcotics transactions.

During the frisk, Officer Nolan squeezed the bag and felt a heavy, hard object, similar in shape to a handgun. The officer opened the bag and recovered a .38 caliber handgun with five live rounds of ammunition. Mr. Wardlow was arrested and prosecuted.

The Illinois trial court denied Mr. Wardlow's motion to suppress the evidence. The Illinois Appellate Court reversed the trial court and held that the gun should have been suppressed because Officer Nolan did not have a reasonable suspicion of criminal activity sufficient to justify and investigative stop pursuant to **Terry, infra**. The Illinois Supreme Court agreed with the appellate Court. The U.S. Supreme Court granted certiorari and reversed the Illinois Supreme Court.

RATIONALE

Chief Justice Rehnquist wrote the majority opinion for the Supreme Court and stated that an individual's presence in an area of expected criminal activity, standing alone, is not enough to support a reasonable, particularized suspicion that the person is committing a crime.

In the present case, "it was not merely [the defendant's] presence in an area of heavy narcotics trafficking that aroused the officers' suspicion but his unprovoked flight upon noticing the police." (**Id**. at 124.)

"Headlong flight – wherever it occurs – is the consummate act of evasion. It is not necessarily indicative of wrongdoing, but it is certainly suggestive of such." (**Id**. at 124.)

". . . the determination of reasonable suspicion must be based on commonsense judgments and inferences about human behavior." (**Id**. at 125.) "Unprovoked flight is simply not a mere refusal to cooperate. Flight, by its very nature, is not 'going about one's business'; in fact, it is just the opposite." (**Id**. at 125.)

In his dissenting opinion, Justice Stevens stated that inferences that can be drawn from a person's flight depend on a number of different circumstances and factors such as:

- The time of day
- The number of people in the area
- The character of the neighborhood
- Whether the officer was wearing a uniform or in plain clothes
- Whether the officer was driving a marked or unmarked police car
- Whether the person ran after the police car passed
- What the runner was wearing (jogging clothes or a business suit)
- The direction and speed of the flight
- Whether the person's behavior was otherwise unusual.

The California Supreme Court unanimously reached a similar conclusion regarding flight in **People v. Souza** (1994) 9 Cal.4th 224, which was decided six years before **Wardlow, supra**, when it ruled that flight can be a key fact in determining whether an officer has a reasonable suspicion to justify a detention.

FACTS (People v. Souza (1994) 9 Cal.4th 224)

An officer saw a man and a woman standing near a blue Ford, parked at the curb at 3 a.m. The area was almost completely dark due to an inoperable street light. The male (defendant) appeared to be talking with someone in the car. The officer suspected a second degree burglary and pulled behind the car. He shone his spotlight inside the car and saw two people in the front seat bent down. The defendant then began to run. The officer chased down the defendant and pat searched him, resulting in the seizure of 14.5 grams of cocaine.

RATIONALE

The court believed that the time of day, the locality, lighting conditions and the "high crime" area, coupled with Mr. Souza's flight, justified the detention.

The Court of Appeal also upheld a detention based on unprovoked flight in **People v. Britton** (2001) 91 Cal.App.4th 1112.[3]

FACTS (People v. Britton (2001) 91 Cal.App.4th 1112)

Officer Lipton, a 22-year veteran of the Santa Ana Police Department, who had made hundreds of arrests for narcotic related offenses and had received many hours of advanced narcotics training, responded to a dispatched call at a residence on South Daisy Street, Santa Ana. Upon arrival, he noticed the house was vacant based on the absence of furniture in the house, shades or curtains on the windows, or cars in the driveway.

The officer was justified in detaining Mr. Britton in the backyard based on the following factors:

- The residence appeared vacant, based on the absence of window shades, a lack of furniture in the house and no cars in the driveway
- After following a walkway to the rear of the residence, the officer heard voices and saw Mr. Britton and another unidentified male adult seated around an inverted bucket with a white T-shirt table cloth
- The unidentified male, who was facing the officer, fled upon seeing and making eye contact with the officer
- Mr. Britton, who rose to flee, appeared to be holding something in his hand as he attempted to run away
- In plain view on top of the makeshift, inverted bucket table, were items of drug paraphernalia consisting of a glass pipe, a cigarette lighter, a knife, the bottom of an aluminum can, and baking powder in a plastic bag.

[3] The Court also addressed the issue of whether PC §1538.5(f)(3) requires the DA to file a written response to a suppression motion at the preliminary hearing. After a thorough analysis, the Court ruled that it did not.

Officers searched Mr. Britton's person at the scene and found a hypodermic syringe and needle and part of an aluminum can in his hand. They also located a small quantity of tar heroin in Mr. Britton's shirt pocket. A booking search at the station resulted in the seizure of two more small bindles containing heroin.

2.2.2.9 – Vehicle Code Violations

It has long been recognized that an officer's observation of a vehicle code violation by itself justifies the stop and detention of the driver of the offending car.

In **People v. Duncan** (2008) 160 Cal.App.4th 1014, the Court of Appeal ruled, in a case of first impression, that a vehicle displaying a front license plate, mounted upside down, violated California Vehicle Code 2201.

FACTS (People v. Duncan (2008) 160 Cal.App.4th 1014)

Chula Vista Police Officer Szymczak was on patrol on April 24, 2006, when Leonza Duncan drove toward his direction. Officer Szymczak noted that the car displayed a front license plate, but that it was mounted upside down. The officer made a U-turn and then contacted Mr. Duncan shortly after he pulled into a motel parking lot in a high crime area. The officer saw Mr. Duncan getting out of his car and holding a bag of food. The officer asked Mr. Duncan if he was staying at the motel, to which Mr. Duncan replied, "Yes, I am. No. I'm going to get a room later." The officer next asked Mr. Duncan if he possessed a driver's license and if the car belonged to him. Mr. Duncan said "Yes" to both questions and handed the officer his driver's license.

A record check revealed that Mr. Duncan's driver's license was suspended except for driving in the course of employment. Since this errand was clearly not in the course of Mr. Duncan's employment, Officer Szymczak issued Mr. Duncan a citation, impound the car and conducted an inventory search. The encounter lasted three to five minutes up to that point.

During the inventory search, officers found methamphetamine, marijuana, an electronic scale and small baggies. Following the denial of his suppression motion, Mr. Duncan plead guilty to possession of methamphetamine for sale and received a two-year state prison sentence.

RATIONALE

California Vehicle Code 2201 imposed three requirements: 1) that a license plate be securely fastened to the car to prevent it from swinging; 2) that it be clearly visible and 3) that it be clearly legible. The Court found that an upside down displayed license plate was clearly not legible.

In **People v. Colbert** (2007) 157 Cal.App.4th 1068, the 6th District Court of Appeals upheld Santa Clara County Superior Court Judge Pichon's decision denying a motion to suppress evidence seized based on a car stop for an air freshener obstructing a driver's view.

FACTS (People v. Colbert (2007) 157 Cal.App.4th 1068)

On December 1, 2005, at about 12:30 p.m., Los Altos Police Agent McCrossin was on patrol on Foothill Expressway, when he passed an older, white Oldsmobile. He observed that there was an item hanging from the rear view mirror that he believed was large enough to obstruct the driver's view through the windshield. After stopping the car, he learned that the item was a flat air freshener shaped like a tree that was hanging from a string or thread. The tree was 4.75 inches tall, had a 1.75 inch base and was 2.75 inches wide at its widest point. Agent McCrossin knew from personal experience that the tree could obstruct a driver's vision because he removed a similar-sized object from the rear view mirror of his own car because it blocked his view. He found that because of the proximity of the tree to the driver's face, it would actually obstruct the view of larger objects like cars or pedestrians. Agent McCrossin was also personally aware of an accident that occurred within the past year, which was caused by an item hanging from the rear view mirror. He therefore concluded that the air freshener amounted to a violation of California Vehicle Code 26708(a)(2) and stopped the Oldsmobile.

Mark Colbert was the driver of the Oldsmobile and was accompanied by his nephew. While running a license check on Mr. Colbert, Agent McCrossin learned that Mr. Colbert was on active parole for robbery. The officer conducted a parole search of the car and found a Macy's VISA card in the name of a woman under the right front passenger seat and next to the center console. He also found 11 methadone pills that were tied in a plastic bag and tucked behind the center console's armrest. Mr. Colbert claimed the pills were just "vitamin pills." About one-hour after his arrest, Agent McCrossin also determined that Mr. Colbert was under the influence of a controlled substance. The officer also contacted Macy's and learned that the owner of the card had reported it as lost two days earlier and did not know either Mr. Colbert or his nephew.

Prior to the preliminary hearing, Mr. Colbert filed a motion to suppress evidence. He alleged that there was no air freshener hanging from his rear view mirror and that even if there was, it was not "objectively reasonable" for the officer to conclude that it obstructed his view. Judge Pichon denied the motion at the preliminary hearing and the defendant was bound over for trial on a felony charge of possessing methadone and misdemeanor charges of being in possession of lost property and being under the influence of a controlled substance.

Mr. Colbert again raised his claim that the detention was illegal as part of a Penal Code 995 motion, but his motion was again denied. Mr. Colbert then plead no contest to all three charges. The trial court struck the strike prior and the punishment for his prison prior and sentenced him to two years in state prison.

RATIONALE

Contrary to the case of **People v. White** (2003) 107 Cal.App.4th 636, which is discussed in more detail below, Agent ". . . McCrossin explicitly testified that the air freshener was 'large enough to obstruct [the driver's] view through the front windshield.' He described the precise dimensions of the air freshener and related how he had personally experienced the view obstruction that an object of that size could pose when he hung a similar-sized object from the rear view mirror of his personal vehicle. McCrossin explained that the proximity to the driver's face of an object hanging from the rear view mirror resulted in the object 'actually obstruct[ing] the view of larger objects such as vehicles or pedestrians' despite the hanging object's small size." **Colbert**, at 1073. Based on that testimony, the officer supplied sufficient specific and articulable facts justifying the detention. Additionally, and unlike **People v. White**, **supra**, the defense did not produce any evidence rebutting the Agent's claim that the air freshener obstructed Mr. Colbert's view.

However, an appellate court will not always uphold stops based on an alleged violation of the vehicle code. For example, in **People v. White** (2003) 107 Cal.App.4th 636, the Court of Appeal refused to uphold a car stop based on an officer's claim that a very similar air freshener obstructed the driver's view.

FACTS (People v. White (2003) 107 Cal.App.4th 636)

On January 31, 1998, at about 3:30 p.m., CHP Officer Mertz was traveling southbound on Highway 101 when he passed a car with no front license plate. He believed this to be a violation of California Vehicle Code 2200. He also noticed an item hanging from the car's rear view mirror, which he believed also violated the law. The officer made a U-turn and followed the car before stopping it. While following the car, he never saw the item hanging from the rear view mirror move and noticed that the car displayed an Arizona license plate. The officer made a car stop and contacted Jason Fishbain, who was the driver of the car. The right front passenger was identified as Christopher White. The officer saw that the item hanging from the rear view mirror was a very common, tree shaped, flat air freshener.

Upon contact, the officer noticed a very strong odor of marijuana coming from the car. After calling for fill officers, he asked the occupants out of the car and searched it. He found a glass marijuana pipe under the driver's seat and a small glass vial of marijuana. In searching the trunk, he found a backpack containing male clothing, two glass marijuana pipes and $9,230 in cash. A search of a black duffle bag in the trunk yielded over five pounds of marijuana, concealed in 10 heat-sealed packages.

At the motion to suppress evidence, the officer never provided any specific or articulable facts in his testimony regarding hesitant or erratic driving that would have supported a conclusion that the air freshener impaired the driver's vision. However, the defense presented evidence from James Munn, who is a civil engineer, that the air freshener covered less than .05 percent of the windshield's total surface. Based on an experiment he conducted, Mr. Munn rendered an opinion that the air freshener could not obstruct the vision of a six-foot-tall driver. Mr. Fishbain also testified that his vision was not obstructed by the air freshener. The trial court also expressed some difficulty in accepting the conclusion that the air freshener would really be an obstruction to a driver.

After the trial court denied two different motions to suppress evidence, a jury convicted Mr. White of transportation of marijuana, while Mr. Fishbain plead guilty to permitting his car to be used to store marijuana.

RATIONALE

The Court of Appeal noted that California Vehicle Code 26708(a)(2) does not flatly prohibit the hanging of any object on a rearview mirror. Instead, it requires that the object obstruct or reduce a driver's clear view through the windshield or side windows. Based on the facts presented at the suppression hearing, the People did not establish that situation to be present in this case.

With respect to the Arizona license plate, Arizona law clearly requires that only one license plate be displayed and that it be displayed to the rear of the car. The Court assumed that the officer acted in good faith but ruled that the good faith exception could not apply to enforce a non-existent Arizona legal standard.

2.2.3 – Detentions and Vehicle Occupants

In **Pennsylvania v. Mimms** (1977) 434 U.S. 106, the U.S. Supreme Court ruled that officers may lawfully order a driver out of a vehicle during a routine traffic stop, based upon officer safety considerations.

Twenty years later in **Maryland v. Wilson** (1997) 519 U.S. 408, the U.S. Supreme Court extended that decision to cover passengers when it ruled that the police did not violate the Fourth Amendment by ordering passengers out of lawfully stopped cars.

However, in a footnote, the court specifically declined to address the issue of whether an officer may forcibly detain a passenger during a car stop. Specifically, the Supreme Court said, "Maryland urges us to go further and hold that an officer may forcibly detain a passenger for the entire duration of the stop. But respondent was subjected to no detention based on the stopping of the car once he had left it; his arrest was based on probable cause to believe that he was guilty of possession of cocaine with intent to distribute. **The question which Maryland wishes answered, therefore, is not presented by this case, and we express no opinion on it." (Id.** at 415, FN #3. [**Emphasis** added].)

In **Brendlin v. California** (2007) 551 U.S. 249, the U.S. Supreme Court finally addressed the issues of whether a passenger is detained by virtue of a car stop and if so, whether the passenger has standing to object to the lawfulness of the stop. A unanimous Supreme Court held that a passenger, just like the driver, is seized within the meaning of the Fourth Amendment when an officer makes a traffic stop. Accordingly, a passenger has standing to object to the lawfulness of the stop based on that detention.

FACTS (Brendlin v. California (2007) 551 U.S. 249)

On November 27, 2001, Deputy Sheriff Brokenbrough and his partner saw a parked Buick with expired registration tags. Deputy Brokenbrough contacted a police dispatcher and learned that an application for registration renewal was in process. The deputy later saw the same car driving on the roadway and noticed a temporary operating permit with the number "11" affixed to it, which indicated it was legal to drive the car through the end of November. Nevertheless, Deputy Brokenbrough decided to stop the car to verify that the permit matched the car even though there was nothing unusual about the permit or the way the car displayed it.

Deputy Brokenbrough contacted Karen Simeroth, who was the driver of the car and asked for her license. Bruce Brendlin, who the officer recognized as "one of the Brendlin brothers," was the right front passenger. The deputy recalled that either Bruce or Scott had dropped out of parole supervision and asked Mr. Brendlin to identify himself. The deputy called for backup and verified that Mr. Brendlin had an outstanding no bail parole warrant.

The deputy saw the defendant briefly open and then close the passenger side door. Once backup arrived, the deputy ordered the defendant out of the car at gunpoint and arrested him on the warrant. A search of Mr. Brendlin's person incident to that arrest yielded an orange syringe cap. A pat search of the driver yielded syringes and a plastic bag of marijuana. A search of the car incident to the arrest of the occupants resulted in the seizure of tubing, a scale and other things used to manufacture methamphetamine.

Mr. Brendlin brought a motion to suppress the evidence on the ground that the traffic stop resulted in an unlawful seizure of his person. The trial court denied the motion and ruled that Mr. Brendlin was not seized until the deputy ordered him out of the car and arrested him on the warrant. Mr. Brendlin plead guilty and the court sentenced him to four years in state prison.

The Court of Appeal reversed the trial court and ruled that a seizure occurred when the deputy made the unlawful traffic stop. By a narrow majority, the

California Supreme Court reversed the Court of Appeal and held that the traffic stop did not result in Mr. Brendlin's seizure because the driver was the exclusive target of the stop and a passenger cannot submit to an officer's show of authority because the driver controls the car. The U.S. Supreme Court then granted certiorari to decide the issue of whether a traffic stop results in a seizure of both the passenger and driver.

RATIONALE

Justice Souter, writing for the majority, applied the test devised by Justice Stewart in **United States v. Mendenhall** (1980) 446 U.S. 544 (in view of all of the circumstances surrounding the incident, would a reasonable person believed that he or she was free to leave?) as modified by **Florida v. Bostick** (1991) 501 U.S. 429. That test asks "whether a reasonable person in Mr. Brendlin's position when the car stopped would have believed himself free to 'terminate the encounter' between the police and himself." **Brendlin**, at 255. The Court found that "in these circumstances any reasonable passenger would have understood the police officers to be exercising control to the point that no one in the car was free to depart without police permission." (**Id**. at 257.)

"A traffic stop necessarily curtails a passenger's travel just as much as it halts the driver, diverting both from the stream of traffic to the side of the road, and the police activity that normally amounts to intrusion on 'privacy and personal security' does not normally (and did not here) distinguish between passenger and driver. **United States v. Martinez-Fuerte** (1976) 428 U.S. 543 at 554. An officer who orders a particular car to pull over acts with an implicit claim of right based on fault of some sort, and a sensible person would not expect the officer to allow people to come and go freely from the physical focal point of an investigation into faulty behavior or wrongdoing. If the likely wrongdoing is not the driving, the passenger will reasonably feel subject to suspicion owing to close association; but even when the wrongdoing is only bad driving, the passenger will expect to be subject to some scrutiny, and his attempt to leave would be so obviously likely to prompt an objection from the officer that no passenger would feel free to leave in the first place. It is also reasonable for passengers to expect that an officer at the scene of a crime, arrest, or investigation will not let people move around in ways that could jeopardize his safety. See, example, **Maryland v. Wilson** (1997) 519 U.S. 408, 414-415." **Brendlin**, at 250.

The U.S. Supreme Court rejected the California Supreme Court's conclusion that the seizure of Mr. Brendlin came only with his formal arrest and found that it was predicated on three faulty premises:

1. A disregard of the objective test in **Mendenhall**, **supra**, resulting in the faulty conclusion that the deputy's flashing lights were directed only at the driver and therefore did not direct a show of authority toward Mr. Brendlin. That approach injects an analysis of the subjective intentions of

the officer, which the U.S. Supreme Court has repeatedly rejected in favor of an objectively reasonable standard.

2. The California Supreme Court's assumption that the passenger had no ability to submit to the deputy's show of authority because only the driver was in control of the vehicle is flawed because once the car stopped, Mr. Brendlin did submit to the show of authority by remaining inside the car.
3. The impact the rule announced by the U.S. Supreme Court would have on other motorists who are forced to slow down or even stop to accommodate the targeted vehicle's submission to the police's show of authority. The Court found that "[s]uch incidental restrictions on freedom of movement would not tend to affect an individual's 'sense of security and privacy in traveling in an automobile.' [Delaware v.] Prouse, supra, at 662." **Brendlin**, **supra**, at 262.

Finally, the U.S. Supreme Court rejected California's assertion that the rule announced by the U.S. Supreme Court would result in the seizure of all bus and cab passengers when a cab or bus driver is pulled over for a traffic violation. The Court noted, "the relationship between driver and passenger is not the same in a common carrier as it is in a private vehicle, and the expectations of police officers and passengers differ accordingly. In those cases, as here, the crucial question would be whether a reasonable person in the passenger's position would feel free to take steps to terminate the encounter." (**Id**. at 262, fn #6.)

In **United States v. Williams** (9th Cir. 2005) 419 F.3d 1029, which was decided before **Brendlin**, **supra**, the 9th Circuit Court of Appeals considered for the first time whether an officer can order a passenger, who exited a lawfully stopped car, back into the car without violating the passenger's Fourth Amendment rights.

The Court said, "[w]e hold that under the *Fourth Amendment* it is reasonable for an officer to order a passenger back into an automobile that he voluntarily exited because the concerns for officer safety originally announced in *Wilson*, [See **Maryland v. Wilson**, **supra**] and specifically the need for officers to exercise control over individuals encountered during a traffic stop, outweigh the marginal intrusion on the passenger's liberty interest." (**Id**. at 1034.)

The 9th Circuit Court of Appeals agreed with other Circuits (D.C. and 3rd Circuit) and State Courts (Arizona, Colorado, Georgia, Illinois and Virginia) that have addressed the issue and held that officers may detain a passenger during a traffic stop because:

- The intrusion is minimal
- An officer's order to get back into a car merely maintains the status quo by returning the passenger to his original position of occupant inside the car; and

- "Giving officers the authority to control all movement in a traffic encounter is sensibly consistent with the public interest in protecting their safety." (**Id**. at 1034.)

FACTS (United States v. Williams (9th Cir. 2005) 419 F.3d 1029)

Oakland Police Officer Mausz was on patrol alone in the early morning hours of December 20, 2004. He initiated a stop on a car driven by Monica Miller, with a defective rear license plate light. Although Ms. Miller could have pulled over in a number of safe places sooner, she ultimately came to a stop in a parking lot. Before Officer Mausz could approach Ms. Miller, Jamal Williams, who was the right front passenger in the car, opened the passenger door and got out. Officer Mausz immediately ordered Mr. Williams back into the car and he complied.

Officer Mausz contacted Ms. Miller and learned that she did not have a license or ID. He asked her out of the car, handcuffed her and took her back to his patrol car. While doing so, he heard a thud from outside Ms. Miller's car.

Officer Mausz checked the area and located a Taurus revolver about six feet away from the car and lying on top of some recently fallen pine needles.

Mr. Williams was prosecuted in Federal Court. The Court denied his motion to suppress the evidence and he sentenced him to 51 months in prison. Mr. Williams appealed and argued that the officer unlawfully detained him by ordering him back into the car.

A California Court of Appeal reached a similar conclusion in the case of **People v. Castellon** (1999) 76 Cal.App.4th 1369, which was decided six years earlier, when it affirmed the trial court's decision not to suppress the seized evidence. The Court of Appeal ruled that an officer acted reasonably, when he detained the defendant passenger, who he knew to be a gang member, by ordering the defendant to remain in the car during a routine traffic stop. The Court found that the defendant's failure to comply with the officer's commands justified the brief detention, which was not unduly prolonged, and resulted in consent to search the defendant's person and the recovery of two $1 bills with heroin residue.

FACTS (People v. Castellon (1999) 76 Cal.App.4th 1369)

Officer Hibbison was on patrol by himself on October 12, 1995, when he observed a car with expired September registration tags pull away from the curb. Officer Hibbison activated his emergency lights and the car immediately pulled over to the curb and stopped.

Javier Castellon was a passenger in the car and attempted to exit the car just as Officer Hibbison was getting out of his police car. Officer Hibbison recognized the defendant as a member of the Alley Boys gang, with whom he had been "in contact" since 1990. Officer Hibbison once responded to a shooting at the defendant's home, where the defendant was present but not arrested. On another occasion, the officer had conducted a car stop on the defendant. Officer Hibbison never knew the defendant to have weapons on his person.

Officer Hibbison told the defendant not to get out of the car, but the defendant did anyway and stopped about three feet away from the car. The officer did not recall if the defendant stopped on his own or did so in response to the officer's command. The defendant was about 15 to 20 feet away from the officer at that point.

Officer Hibbison asked the defendant if he had any weapons or narcotics on his person. The defendant said, "No". Officer Hibbison obtained the defendant's permission to search his person and found a $1 bill in each of the defendant's front pockets with heroin residue on it. About a minute elapsed between the time the defendant opened the car door and the consent was obtained to search the defendant's person.

RATIONALE

The officer lawfully stopped the car for a vehicle code violation. [CVC 4601]. Because of the defendant's actions, the officer's attention shifted from a routine traffic stop to concerns about the officer's safety.

The Court of Appeal cited **Maryland v. Wilson**, **supra**, and noted that "If the minimal additional intrusion on the personal liberty of the passenger ordered out of the vehicle cannot trump the safety of the officer, then surely the slight inconvenience of ordering the passenger to remain seated can be justified by an officer's concerns." **People v. Castellon**, **supra**, at 1375.

The Court also said, "[i]t is not unreasonable for a lone officer to have concerns for his safety when, upon making a routine traffic stop, he observes there are two people in the car, and then recognizes the passenger as a gang member with whom he has had previous contacts. Hibbison reacted immediately when he saw Castellon start to emerge from the car by ordering him to stay in the car. Hibbison made the judgment that under those circumstances he preferred to have Castellon remain in the car as he approached, and we will not second-guess Hibbison's reasonable in-the-field call; it was for the officer to decide whether his personal safety was better preserved by ordering Castellon to stay inside the car or by ordering him out of the vehicle." (**Id.** at 1375.)

In **People v. Fisher** (1995) 38 Cal.App.4th 338, a motorist was under the influence of a stimulant and told the officer he had a bindle of methamphetamine in the car between the seats. The driver gave the officer permission to search. The court held it was proper to ask the passenger to step out of the car.

The Court said, "[i]t would be unreasonable and unsafe to require the officer to search the car for contraband while the passenger remained seated in the car." (**Id.** at 345.) Additionally, while the passenger's mere presence may not justify his arrest, it furnished an objective manifestation that he may have been involved with methamphetamine and independently justified his detention.

2.2.4 – Detention Examples

2.2.4.1 – Red or Blue Emergency Light Activation

In **People v. Bailey** (1985) 176 Cal.App.3d 402, the Court of Appeal suppressed the seized evidence on the grounds that at the time the officer activated his emergency lights a detention, without a reasonable suspicion of criminal activity, had occurred.

FACTS (People v. Bailey (1985) 176 Cal.App.3d 402)

A San Jose Police Officer drove into a closed Sear's parking lot known for drug use. The officer saw Mr. Bailey sitting in a car and was curious to see what he was doing. While the officer did not block Mr. Bailey in, he did turn on his red and blue lights. As the officer approached the car, he smelled marijuana and told Mr. Bailey of that observation. Mr. Bailey handed over the marijuana. During the officer's search of the car, he located and seized cocaine.

2.2.4.2 – Blocking Person or Vehicle Movement

In **People v. Wilkins** (1986) 186 Cal.App.3d 804, the Court of Appeal suppressed the seized evidence on the grounds that a detention, without a reasonable suspicion of criminal activity, had occurred when the officer blocked the defendant's car from moving.

FACTS (People v. Wilkins (1986) 186 Cal.App.3d 804)

San Jose Police Officer Jeffrey Sun drove into a convenience store parking lot which was known for drug activity, at approximately 10:18 p.m. The officer saw two men in the front seat of a parked car, who crouched down as the officer passed by. The officer circled back and pulled his patrol car in behind the parked car, which effectively blocked the car's ability to move. However, the officer did not activate any lights or sirens.

As the officer approached the car, he smelled marijuana. He then asked for ID, ran a warrant check and learned that the driver was on searchable probation. The officer conducted a search of the car and found PCP.

In **People v. Aldridge** (1984) 35 Cal.3d 473, the Court of Appeal ruled that occupants of a liquor store parking lot were unlawfully detained when a police officer drove into the parking lot intending to conduct "field interviews" of all persons in the lot, per his routine practice. Such action failed to satisfy the requirement of an objective, specific and articulable reasons necessary to justify the detention of the parking lot occupants.

2.2.4.3 – Freeze, Halt or Stop Orders

In **People v. Britton** (2001) 91 Cal.App.4th 1112, the Court of Appeal ruled that a detention occurred when the defendant submitted to the officer's command of "Stop or I'll shoot."

The Court of Appeal ruled in **People v. Jones** (1991) 228 Cal.App.3d 519, that the an illegal detention occurred because the officer directed Mr. Jones to stop after arriving suddenly in the middle of the street, abruptly stopping his patrol car and parking his marked police car in a manner which obstructed traffic.

In **People v. Verin** (1990) 220 Cal.App.3d 551, the Court of Appeal found the officer's use of the phrase, "Hold on, Police," without a legal justification to detain, coupled with the defendant's submission to that show of authority, resulted in an illegal detention.

In **People v. Roth** (1990) 219 Cal.App.3d 211, the Court of Appeal found an officer's command of "Come over here, I want to talk to you." to constitute a detention. Since the only grounds for Mr. Roth's detention was his early morning presence in a deserted shopping center parking lot, with closed businesses, the detention was illegal. The Court of Appeal found that mere presence in the shopping center parking lot, without more, was devoid of indicia showing involvement in criminal activity.

2.2.4.4 – High Crime Areas

In **People v. Green** (1994) 25 Cal.App.4th 1107, the Court of Appeal ruled that the police lawfully attempted to detain suspects leaving a known drug dealers house based on the deputy's expertise regarding drug trafficking activity, the furtive actions of the defendant and the deputy's knowledge that the owner of the home was selling drugs from the home. Therefore, the defendant's subsequent actions in abandoning a handgun and four ounces of cocaine after a 1 ½-mile pursuit were not the result of any illegal action on the part of the police.

FACTS (People v. Green (1994) 25 Cal.App.4th 1107)

On September 3, 1992, Deputy Sheriff Bailey, a highly experienced narcotics officer, served a search warrant at the residence of Adrian Lathan. During the service of the search warrant, Deputy Bailey found cocaine, firearms, a gram scale and a brown paper bag filled with numerous baggies. Mr. Lathan was on probation and later admitted that he sold cocaine from his residence.

On February 3, 1993, and as part of an ongoing investigation, Deputy Bailey was conducting surveillance of Mr. Lathan's house, when he saw a Cadillac pull up to the residence. The Cadillac contained a driver, Mr. Lathan and Derrick Green. All three individuals got out of the Cadillac and rushed into Mr. Lathan's house, but not before hesitating in front of the house and "looking side to side in a hurried manner." The deputy noted that Mr. Lathan was carrying a brown paper bag.

About 10 minutes later, the driver of the Cadillac left the house and departed. A short time later, a fourth man arrived, who also "looked around in a hurried manner" as he hastened to the front door. He was also carrying a brown paper bag when he entered the house and later left with an even larger brown paper bag.

The driver returned and went into the house. Five to ten minutes later, Mr. Lathan, Mr. Green, and the driver came out of the house. Mr. Green was carrying a brown paper bag. Mr. Green and the driver got into the car and left.

Deputy Bailey immediately radioed assisting narcotic units that the Cadillac was leaving Mr. Lathan's residence and that he wanted it stopped, a narcotics investigation conducted and the persons in the car identified. Deputy Sheriff Underdown and his partner attempted to stop the car by activating their emergency lights. The driver initially pulled toward the curb, as if to stop, but instead accelerated away and attempted to elude the deputies. However, he crashed into a stucco wall 1 ½ miles into the pursuit. The driver fled and was never caught.

Mr. Green remained in the car, but opened the passenger door and threw a handgun and brown paper bag underneath the car, thereby abandoning them. The discarded paper bag contained approximately four ounces of cocaine.

In **People v. Limon** (1993) 17 Cal.App.4th 524 the Court of Appeal upheld the detention of a suspect observed in a high crime area who engaged in a hand-to-hand transaction in a carport and exhibited other suspicious activity. The Court found the detention to be lawful based on the officer's expertise and specific knowledge regarding prior drug activity in the carport, the observed hand-to-hand exchange and evidence of a concealing action in connection with the exchange.

2.2.4.5 – Leaving Crime Scenes

In **People v. Conway** (1994) 25 Cal.App.4th 385, the Court of Appeal upheld a deputy sheriff's car stop and detention of its occupants who were driving away from a burglary in progress call, despite the fact the deputy knew nothing about the suspects' descriptions or the use of a car in the burglary.

FACTS (People v. Conway (1994) 25 Cal.App.4th 385)

David McBride lived in Sacramento County on Sawtelle Way. Sawtelle Way is an "L" shaped street that is connected to the main thoroughfare, La Riviera Drive, by Waterton Way.

Mr. McBride got up before 3:00 a.m. to go to work. He looked out his bedroom window and saw that his garage door was open and that two unknown men were leaving his garage. One was dark, one was White, and each had distinctive clothing. Mr. McBride saw that the burglars were carrying tools and fishing poles. Mr. McBride yelled for his wife to call the police and then began a foot pursuit. Approximately four houses down from his, Mr. McBride found his tools on his neighbor's law. Mr. McBride awoke his neighbor and told him about the stolen items on the front law. The victim then ran to the turn in Sawtelle Way and saw a small Chevrolet drive by with the two burglars inside. Mr. McBride yelled for the car to stop, but it did not.

At about that time, Deputy Sheriff Donald Judd, arrived. He had been dispatched to the area on a report of a burglary in progress involving two suspects seen in a garage. He knew nothing about any possible vehicles involved in the burglary. Deputy Judd saw the Chevrolet leaving the immediate area within two minutes of receiving the dispatch and noted that two men were in the car, that it was the only vehicle in the area and that there was no one on foot in the area. The Deputy made a U-turn and followed the car, which was in poor condition and sputtered as it drove away. The Deputy activated the emergency equipment on his car and stopped the car. Both occupants quickly exited the car without being told to do so. Deputy Judd intended to detain the car's occupants, identify them and have the burglary victim look at them.

Mr. McBride arrived at the car stop on foot shortly thereafter and told the Deputy not to let the occupants leave because they had taken property from his garage. He also saw his radio-cassette player in the back of the car.

In **People v. Overton** (1994) 28 Cal.App.4th 1497, the Court of Appeal ruled that an officer stopped a car being driven away from the area of a robbery crime where the robbery had occurred five to seven minutes earlier, the car was traveling away from the crime scene on one of only two logical escape routes out of Coronado [the second route was under surveillance by another police officer] and two black males, who generally matched the description of the robbers (armed, wearing dark clothing with hoods) were in the car. The Court also found it relevant that while following the car onto the Coronado Bridge, the heads of two passengers were popping up and down in an attempt to hide from the police car, after first looking directly at it.

FACTS (People v. Overton (1994) 28 Cal.App.4th 1497)

On January 18, 1993, at approximately 8:00 p.m., two men wearing sweatshirts with hoods over their heads entered the La Avenida Motel on Orange Avenue in Coronado. One man held a gun to the forehead of the live-in manager (Luz Cantwell), while the other went around the counter and put a gun to her temple. She was then shoved to the floor, told she was being robbed, and repeatedly told that she was going to be killed. The robbers pulled the money out of the cash register and fled. Within 30 seconds of their exit, Ms. Cantwell called the police.

Within minutes of the broadcast, Coronado Police Officer Kline saw Maurice Overton driving eastbound onto the Coronado Bridge, which was one of only two exits off Coronado. Mr. Overton was wearing a hooded dark colored jacket. As Officer Kline followed Mr. Overton's car in his marked police car over the Coronado Bridge, he saw two other Black male individuals pop their heads up from the right front passenger and right rear passenger seats.

Mr. Overton continued to drive north onto Interstate 5, during which time the other two occupants popped their heads up two or three times looking at Officer Kline before ducking back down. Officer Kline stopped Mr. Overton at 19th and J Streets in San Diego and ordered him out of the car. After back-up officers arrived, the officers removed the two passengers from the car.

Five to 10 minutes after the car stop, officers brought Ms. Cantwell to the scene and she identified the passengers as the robbers. In plain view on the right front passenger's floorboard was a ripped up register tape and a ripped up personal check taken during the robbery, a black mask and the phone receiver that had been ripped off the wall in the robbery. Coins stolen in the robbery, along with a box of .32-caliber automatic ammunition were found under the left rear passenger seat. A loaded automatic handgun and a second loaded magazine were found on top of a wad of cash stolen in the robbery.

Officers found a black knit watch cap under the left rear passenger seat and wedged to the left of the driver's seat. A second unloaded handgun, a .380-caliber automatic, along with a loaded magazine and a loose .380 caliber round of ammunition were discovered inside a hole in the driver's seat and behind the driver's back.

At trial, Mr. Overton was convicted of first degree residential robbery, with an arming clause pursuant to California Penal Code 22022(a)(1) and sentenced to five years in state prison.

2.2.4.6 – Obscene Gestures

The 9th Circuit Court of Appeals ruled in **Duran v. City of Douglas** (1990) 904 F.2d 1372 that the fact that the passenger in an automobile made obscene gestures and shouted profanity at a police officer did not justify a car stop and detention of the passenger.

2.2.4.7 – Possession of Weapons

Some situations just cry out for police investigation given the unusual circumstances that sometimes confront a police officer. One example of such a case is **People v. Foranyic** (1998) 64 Cal.App.4th 186. In that case, a Huntington Beach Police Officer saw Robert Francis Foranyic standing astride a bicycle at 3 a.m. Attached to the bicycle was a large axe. The officer ordered Mr. Foranyic to dismount and explained that he "wanted to put some distance between him and the ax." During the contact, the defendant had problems following directions and showed classic symptoms of intoxication. The officer ultimately arrested Mr. Foranyic for being drunk in public and, during the booking process, discovered a baggie of methamphetamine taped to the defendant's belt.

The Court of Appeal had lots of fun with this opinion and in pointing out the lunacy of the defendant's position that the officer unlawfully detained him.

> "We conclude that a reasonable police officer, considering the totality of the circumstances, would reasonably suspect criminal activity might be afoot upon viewing someone on a bicycle, with an ax, at 3 in the morning. Certainly we would expect a diligent police officer to investigate such unusual behavior through the relatively unintrusive means of a detention. This is so even though no recent 'ax crime' had been reported. ¶ For while Foranyic insists there was nothing about him which suggested *criminal activity*, he is unable to suggest, and we cannot conceive of, much in the way of *noncriminal* activity which is accomplished with an ax in the dead of night. The officer could reasonably eliminate firefighting and lumberjacking from the list of possible pursuits Foranyic might have been engaged in. And while there are doubtless some reasonable explanations which might be conjured up, 'The possibility of an innocent explanation does not deprive the officer of the capacity to entertain a reasonable suspicion of criminal activity.' (**In re Tony C**., 21 Cal.3d at p. 894.)." (*Italics* in original) **People v. Foranyic**, **supra**, at 189.

The Court of Appeal in **People v. Methey** (1991) 227 Cal.App.3d 349, held that the officer lawfully detained the defendant based on prior contacts with the defendant, the lateness of the hour (3:00 a.m.) and the fact that the defendant was carrying a pry bar.

In **People v. Brown** (1989) 213 Cal.App.3d 187, the Court of Appeal upheld the detention, pat search and subsequent arrest for possession of narcotics by a defendant who was walking down the street in a high crime area while holding a knife and a pair of scissors at his side.

FACTS (People v. Brown (1989) 213 Cal.App.3d 187)

> At 10:30 a.m. on a Sunday morning, Officer Barner was on patrol in a marked police car, when he saw Travis Brown walking in front of a pool hall and bar area known for heavy drug traffic and prostitution activity. The officer saw Mr. Brown holding something in his hand by his side. As the officer slowed down to get a better look at the object, Mr. Brown stared back and then ran. The officer immediately turned his patrol car around to follow him. When the officer regained sight of Mr. Brown, he saw that Mr. Brown was holding a knife and a pair of scissors in his hand. Officer Barner yelled at Mr. Brown to stop and drop the knife and scissors, which Mr. Brown did.

Officer Barner made contact with Mr. Brown and pat searched him for weapons. During the pat search, the officer felt two hard objects in Mr. Brown's pockets and removed them in the belief that they might be weapons. About that time, Officer McKnight arrived as a back-up officer for Officer Barner.

The items were a small cardboard box and an opaque plastic pill bottle. Officer Barner removed all the items from Mr. Brown's pockets and put them on the hood of his patrol car. At some point during the pat search, Officer Barner asked Mr. Brown if he was on parole. Mr. Brown said, "Yes", and provided the name of his parole officer. Officer McKnight opened the cardboard box and plastic pill bottle and found heroin and cocaine inside them.

RATIONALE

The Court of Appeal ruled that the officer's detention was lawful for the following reasons:

- The defendant was in an area for known drug related crime and appeared to be concealing something in his hand
- The defendant fled upon seeing the patrol car
- The defendant was in possession of weapons.

While the first two factors would have been insufficient by themselves to justify a detention, the presence of weapons tipped the scale in favor of the lawfulness of the detention. Since the defendant possessed weapons, the Court of Appeal ruled that the pat search was a reasonable protective measure incident to a lawful detention.

The search of the pill bottle and cardboard box were upheld as a lawful search incident to arrest, since it is illegal for a parolee to possess a knife with a blade over two inches long (Cal. Code Regs., Title. 15, 2512, subd. 5(c)).

2.2.5 – Investigative Stops and Frisks

2.2.5.1 – General

In **Terry v. Ohio** (1968) 392 U.S. 1, the U.S. Supreme Court ruled that with additional factors, an officer may conduct a pat search for weapons during a detention if the officer has a reasonable suspicion that the detained person is presently armed or dangerous. In order to uphold a pat down for weapons, the officer must be able to articulate a reasonable belief that the person may be armed and dangerous. The Court reached a similar result in **Sibron v. New York** (1968) 392 U.S. 40, which was decided the same day as **Terry, supra**.

The Court of Appeal in **People v. Medina** (2003) 110 Cal.App.4th 171, ruled that an officer may not, ". . . as a matter of standard procedure and in the name of 'officer safety,' detain and frisk a driver stopped for an equipment infraction solely on the basis that the stop occurs in a high crime area at night." (**Id.**, at 547.)

FACTS (People v. Medina (2003) 110 Cal.App.4th 171)

At midnight on January 19, 2002, LAPD Officers Lopez and Arroyo stopped 49-year-old Roman Medina near Olympic Blvd and Alvarado Street in Los Angeles, due to a broken taillight.

When the officers activated their overhead lights, Mr. Medina promptly pulled over and remained in the car until the officers ordered him out. The officers ordered Mr. Medina to place his hands behind his head, walk backwards towards the officers and then face a nearby wall. Mr. Medina obeyed these instructions without any problem.

Officer Lopez had no reason to believe that Mr. Medina was armed, but decided to search him because the stop occurred in a high gang area. Officer Lopez grabbed Mr. Medina's hands and asked him if he had any weapons, sharp objects, or "anything he should know about prior to the search". When Mr. Medina disclosed hat he had a rock of cocaine in his pocket, the officer arrested him. A search of the car incident to arrest yielded a small, additional amount of cocaine.

Following the denial of his motion to suppress the evidence, Mr. Medina plead guilty to possession of cocaine and received drug diversion.

RATIONALE

Before conducting a pat down, an officer must have articulable facts justifying a reasonable suspicion that the person is armed and dangerous. None existed in this case. Therefore, any incriminating evidence due to the officer's illegal action, including statements made by the driver, are inadmissible.

2.2.5.2 – Persons

In **People v. Avila** (1997) 58 Cal.App.4th 1069, the Court of Appeal found that the totality of the circumstances confronting the officer justified a weapons pat search of the defendant's person.

FACTS (People v. Avila (1997) 58 Cal.App.4th 1069)

On May 16, 1995, Officer Jones saw Mr. Avila walking across a parking lot at about 4:30 p.m. The officer saw Mr. Avila littering and noted that his actions while littering were suspicious. Mr. Avila ". . . first walked to the passenger side of a truck, then to the driver's side, then back to the front of the truck with his hand directly in front of his body. Finally, he dropped a white envelope from his waist." (**Id.** at 1072.)

Officer Jones contacted Mr. Avila while he was standing in the open driver's side door of the truck. Officer Jones told Mr. Avila of the officer's observations and asked Mr. Avila for ID. Mr. Avila provided a driver's license with the name "Joseph Vargas". While Officer Jones continued to talk to him, the officer noticed two containers of alcohol on the front seat of the truck, but was unable to determine if they were empty or still contained alcohol. Officer Jones also saw a metal object within eight to ten inches of Mr. Avila's left hand, which the officer believed was similar to a "Mag"Flashlight. When Officer Jones asked Mr. Avila about the item, Mr. Avila never turned around, said he did not know what it was and that the truck belonged to a friend of his. It was later determined that the truck did in fact belong to Mr. Avila, who did acknowledge having illegal alcohol in the truck, but no weapons.

Officer Jones told Mr. Avila to walk to the back of the truck. Without being told to do so, Mr. Avila assumed the position for a pat search. While conducting a pat search, Officer Jones ". . . felt a bulky and somewhat hard object at the defendant's ankle. The officer asked what the object was and defendant's reply was unclear. The officer repeated his question and defendant said, " 'It is meth.' " After finding two more bulges, the officer handcuffed the defendant and removed three baggies of methamphetamine." (**Id**. at 1073.) The officer placed Mr. Avila under arrest, and found more methamphetamine and a gun in the truck.

RATIONALE

Officer Jones' question of Mr. Avila regarding the hard object he felt was justified because the officer did not know whether the object was a weapon. The appellate court observed that Mr. Avila told Officer Jones it was "meth" before the officer retrieved the object and that "[t]he Fourth Amendment was not designed to protect a defendant from his own candor." (**Id**. at 1075.)

In **People v. Ritter** (1997) 54 Cal.App.4th 274, the Court of Appeal ruled that the police did not need to obtain a search warrant for the defendant's fanny pack even though they had possession and control of the fanny pack at the time of the search.

FACTS (People v. Ritter (1997) 54 Cal.App.4th 274)

A San Bernardino County Deputy Sheriff responded to a 9-1-1 call regarding a disturbance at 5:07 p.m. The man involved in the disturbance was described as wearing a black fishing-type hat, red shirt, and black jeans, and "was threatening".

The deputy saw Mr. Ritter, who matched that description, walking away from the crime scene. The deputy honked his horn and the defendant stopped and turned around. The deputy approached the defendant on foot and noticed that the defendant had a fanny pack that appeared a bit full. The "nylon top outer compartment was stretched sufficiently tight at that time to reveal to [the deputy] what appeared to be the outline of a small handgun." (**Id**. at 277.)

> The deputy asked the defendant what was in the fanny pack, but the defendant was evasive. The deputy then told the defendant to put the pack on the hood of the police car. The defendant took the fanny pack off, dropped it to the ground and then stepped back. The deputy, based on safety concerns, placed the defendant in the back of his patrol car and then retrieved the fanny pack. When he opened the fanny pack, he found a handgun. The defendant was a third striker.

People v. Dickey (1994) 21 Cal.App.4th 952, the Court of Appeal ruled that a deputy sheriff conducted an illegal pat down of Mr. Dickey. The fact Mr. Dickey lacked written ID, refused consent to search the car, was nervous and sweating, and had baking soda in a film canister, did not justify a pat down of his person for weapons.

The Court also ruled that it was inappropriate for the deputy to reach into Mr. Dickey's pocket to retrieve the soft item he felt because the identity of the contraband was not "immediately apparent."

FACTS (People v. Dickey (1994) 21 Cal.App.4th 952)

> San Luis Obispo County Deputy Sheriff Conway was on routine patrol at 3:40 p.m. with his partner and driving down a one-lane dirt road in rural Nipomo when he saw a 1977 El Camino stopped in the roadway with the engine running. The driver appeared to make ". . . furtive movements, moving around in the driver's seat." The deputy made contact with Warren Douglas Dickey and asked him what he was doing. Mr. Dickey explained that he was just admiring the view of the valley and the sand dunes below. The deputy asked for ID. Mr. Dickey verbally identified himself, but did not have a CDL in his possession. The passenger also failed to produce any ID. The deputy ordered both persons out of the car.
>
> Dispatch confirmed that Mr. Dickey was the registered owner of the car. Mr. Dickey said that the registration might be in a backpack in the car, but the backpack did not belong to him. The deputy asked for permission to search the car two times, and was turned down both times. He then began to get angry and said that Mr. Dickey was "just wasting time or trying to put things off."
>
> The deputy decided just to look for items in plain view. When he found the backpack, both Mr. Dickey and his passenger denied ownership of it, but Mr. Dickey did give the deputy permission to look inside. The deputy opened a film canister and found baking soda.
>
> The deputy then went to the trunk. At this point, Mr. Dickey was sweating profusely so the deputy decided to pat him down for safety reasons. The deputy felt a soft object that was like a bulge. It was elongated and had a texture or "just a good feeling to it." The deputy squeezed it from the outside

> and it had a plastic-like feeling to it. He reached into the pocket and pulled out a baggie of marijuana and a baggie of cocaine.

In **People v. Snyder** (1992) 11 Cal.App.4th 389, the Court of Appeal held that an officer lawfully detained Mr. Snyder and removed a whiskey bottle from the waistband of this panhandler, who was arrested for creating a disturbance in front of the store.

The Court observed, "[a] full liquor bottle carries significant weight and the neck of the bottle may serve as a handle, two characteristics of a club. Once broken, it is effective as a slashing weapon. Both uses make the bottle capable of producing death or great bodily injury, the definition of a "deadly weapon" within the meaning of Penal Code section 245, subdivision (a). Officer Chase testified that, in his experience, people using bottles have inflicted serious injuries upon many victims." (**Id.** at 393.)

FACTS (People v. Snyder (1992) 11 Cal.App.4th 389)

> On September 22, 1991, Bakersfield City Police Officer Chase went to a drugstore to investigate a complaint that a panhandler was causing a disturbance in front of the store. Dispatch described the suspect to Officer Chase as a White male adult, in his 40s and wearing a yellow shirt with brown stripes.
>
> On arrival, the defendant was the only person standing in front of the store and matched the description provided. While talking to Carey Snyder, Officer Chase noticed a large bulge in the front waistband of Mr. Snyder's pants.
>
> For officer safety reasons, Officer Chase pat searched Mr. Snyder and identified the object as a bottle. The officer withdrew the bottle from Mr. Snyder's waistband and noted it to be a fifth of brandy, with the price tag from the drugstore still attached.
>
> Mr. Snyder ultimately plead guilty to a violation Penal Code 666 and the Court sentenced him to two years in a California prison.

In the slightly earlier, but similar case of **People v. Autry** (1991) 232 Cal.App.3d 365, the Court of Appeal upheld the seizure of a syringe from the defendant's person and ruled that a bulge, by itself, authorized a pat down per **Pennsylvania v. Mimms, supra**.

The Court said, "[a] police officer might well prefer to face an assailant armed with a small-caliber pistol rather than a drug addict with a hypodermic needle. The officer might recover from a gunshot wound, but just the merest scratch from the needle could prove fatal. Like Hamlet, who dies from being nicked with a poisoned sword, an officer slashed with a contaminated needle would find no medicine in the world could save him."[**fn1**; See Hamlet, act V, scene II, lines 310-335.] (**Id**. at 369.)

"Moreover, even without the prospect of AIDS, a hypodermic needle and syringe are easily employed as a weapon. If a pin concealed in an apple was a deadly weapon in **In re Jose. R.** (1982) 137 Cal.App.3d 269, a hypodermic needle should be here. It hardly takes the imagination of Alfred Hitchcock to think up any number of nasty ways a hypodermic needle and syringe can do grievous injury, at least in close combat." (**Id**. at 369.)

In **People v. Miles** (1987) 196 Cal.App.3d 612, the Court of Appeals upheld the detention, pat search and subsequent seizure of a firearm from the defendant's person. The Court found that the officer clearly detained the defendant, because a reasonable person would not have felt free to leave. However, it also found that the detention and pat search were almost simultaneous and that the officer was justified in pat searching the defendant based on the officer's observations.

FACTS (People v. Miles (1987) 196 Cal.App.3d 612)

> Oakland Police officers responded to a radio broadcast at about 3:00 p.m., regarding information received by a Taco Bell manager. The manager said there were several persons walking around the parking lot and acting very suspicious. The report stated that the people were looking into the restaurant and were associated with a green Toyota and a brown Chevrolet. The manager was concerned because of a recent shooting in the parking lot.
>
> The two-person unit arrived within a minute. The officers saw two males standing in the parking lot next to a brown vehicle. Officer Fisher exited the patrol car and approached Mr. Miles, who was standing near the brown vehicle. The second officer dealt with the passenger, who is not involved in this case.
>
> As Officer Fisher approached from 20 to 30 feet away, Mr. Miles turned away from the officer. As Officer Fisher came within a few feet of Mr. Miles, he could see an exaggerated bulge in Mr. Mile's jacket pocket. Officer Fisher could tell that the object was heavy and suspected that it might be some kind of weapon. Officer Fisher directed Mr. Miles to put his hands on his head and simultaneously pat searched him for weapons. Officer Fisher discovered a loaded revolver in Mr. Miles' jacket pocket.

In **People v. Valdez** (1987) 196 Cal.App.3d 799, the Court of Appeal ruled that the officer illegally removed a 35mm film canister from the defendant's pocket, which was located during a weapons patdown. Although the officer knew such containers might contain drugs, there was no evidence that the item was a weapon and therefore he was not entitled to enter the pocket and retrieve the object.

The Court observed that ". . . a film canister is not a distinctive drug-carrying item equivalent to a heroin balloon, a paper bindle, or a marijuana-smelling brick-shaped package, which may be seized upon observation. [Citations] Rather, the canister is akin to a common product like a pill bottle, a pack of cigarettes, or a plastic bag which may *not* be seized merely because it may also be commonly used to store narcotics. [Citations]" (**Id**. at 806-807.)

2.2.5.3 – Vehicles

In **Michigan v. Long** (1983) 463 U.S. 1032, the U.S. Supreme Court applied the holding of **Terry v. Ohio**, **supra**, to the passenger compartment of a car and ruled that it is permissible for a police officer to search the passenger compartment of an automobile when the following two factors are present:

- The search is limited to those areas where a weapon may be placed or hidden
- The police officer possesses a reasonable belief, based on "specific and articulable facts which, taken together with the rational inferences from those facts, reasonably warrant" the police officer in believing that the suspect is dangerous and may gain immediate control of weapons.

FACTS (Michigan v. Long (1983) 463 U.S. 1032)

Deputies Howell and Lewis were on patrol in a rural area when, shortly after midnight, they saw a car speeding and driving in an erratic manner. The deputies saw the car turn down a side road and went off the road into a shallow ditch. The deputies stopped to investigate the situation.

David Long was the driver and sole occupant of the car. He met the deputies at the rear of his car, which was protruding into the roadway. The driver's side door of the car remained open. Deputy Howell asked Mr. Long for a driver's license. After repeating the request, Mr. Long produced a driver's license. Deputy Howell then requested to see the car's registration. Mr. Long again had to be asked a second time. Deputy Howell thought that Mr. Long might be under the influence of something.

Mr. Long turned away from the deputies and began to walk towards the open driver's side door of his car. Both officers followed Mr. Long and saw a large hunting knife in plain view on the driver's side of the car. The deputies stopped Mr. Long and pat searched him for weapons, with negative results. While Deputy Lewis and Mr. Long stayed by the rear of the car, Deputy Howell shone his flashlight into the passenger compartment of the car to search for other weapons. He did not enter the car at that time.

Deputy Howell saw something protruding from under the armrest of the front seat. He entered the vehicle, knelt down and lifted the armrest. He saw an open leather pouch and, after shining his flashlight on it, saw marijuana inside the pouch. The deputies arrested Mr. Long for possession of marijuana. A further search of the car's interior revealed no more contraband or the vehicle's registration.

The deputies impounded the vehicle and searched it. Deputy Howell opened the trunk, which did not have a lock, and found approximately 75 pounds of marijuana.

The Barry County Circuit Court denied Mr. Long's motion to suppress the evidence and he was convicted of possession of marijuana. The Michigan Court of Appeal affirmed the conviction and the search of the passenger compartment under **Terry v. Ohio**, **supra**. The trunk search was upheld under **South Dakota v. Opperman**, **infra**.

The Michigan Supreme Court reversed that holding and ruled that the passenger compartment search was not justified by the holding in **Terry v. Ohio**.

The U.S. Supreme Court granted certiorari and reversed. It also remanded the case to the Michigan Supreme Court to reconsider the trunk search in light of the rule announced in this case.

In a 6 to 3 decision in **Adams v. Williams** (1972) 407 U.S. 143, the Supreme Court held that, pursuant to **Terry v. Ohio**, a police officer lawfully reached into a car window to seize a firearm that an informant advised him was hidden in Robert William's waistband, even though the officer had not seen the gun himself.

FACTS (Adams v. Williams (1972) 407 U.S. 143)

Bridgeport Connecticut Sergeant Connolly was patrolling alone in the early morning hours. At about 2:15 a.m., an informant known to Sergeant Connolly approached him and advised the sergeant that someone seated in a nearby car was carrying narcotics and had a gun in his waistband.

Sergeant Connolly called for assistance and then approached the car to investigate the informant's report. Robert Williams was seated in the front passenger seat of the car, which was parked in a high crime area. The car's engine was off and there was no indication Mr. Williams was about to leave.

Sergeant Connolly tapped on the car's window and asked Mr. Williams to open the door. Instead of opening the door, Mr. Williams rolled down his window. Sergeant Connolly reached into the car and removed a fully loaded revolver from Mr. William's waistband, which was located exactly where the informant said it would be. Sergeant Connolly had not seen the gun from outside the car.

Sergeant Connolly arrested Mr. Williams for unlawful possession of the firearm. A search incident to his arrest resulted in the seizure of substantial quantities of heroin from Mr. William's person and car. Also seized from the car were a machete and a second revolver.

Mr. Williams was convicted in Connecticut state court of the illegal possession of a firearm and possession of heroin.

In his dissenting opinion in **Adams v. Williams**, Justice Marshall stated his belief that the informant's information was not credible since the record below established that the informant's prior information to Sergeant Connolly concerned homosexual conduct in the local railroad station, which failed to result in any substantiating information or an arrest. Justice Marshall also found that the record below failed to establish the following facts:

- If or when the informant had ever seen the gun
- Whether the gun was carried legally
- What kind of narcotics Mr. Williams was carrying
- Whether they were legally possessed
- The informant's basis for knowledge about the narcotics
- The informant's ability to distinguish narcotics from other substances that one could lawfully possess under Connecticut's law with a doctor's prescription

Those factors were relevant to Justice Marshall's analysis because when this case happened, **Aguilar v. Texas**, **supra**, and **Spinelli v. United States**, **supra**, were the standards that governed the assessment of the reliability of tips from informants. The Supreme Court later changed those standards by its decision in **Illinois v. Gates** (1983) 462 U.S. 213.

Justice Marshall also pointed out that Connecticut residents could legally carry firearms if they had a permit, so the mere fact Mr. Williams had a firearm in his waistband in a high crime area did not constitute a crime in and of itself. Therefore, he concluded that unlike the facts in **Terry v. Ohio** there was no evidence of criminal activity afoot justifying the "stop and frisk" that happened in this case.

2.2.5.4 – Plain Feel Doctrine

In **Minnesota v. Dickerson** (1993) 508 U.S. 366, the U.S. Supreme Court enunciated what has become known as the "plain feel" doctrine. If during a lawful weapons patdown the officer feels a hard object, which he\she reasonably believes could be used as a weapon he\she may remove it. If the officer feels an item "whose contour or mass" makes its identity as contraband immediately apparent, the object may also be lawfully removed.

In **People v. Lee** (1987) 194 Cal.App.3d 979, the Court of Appeal upheld the weapons pat search and subsequent seizure of about 100 heroin balloons from the defendant's jacket pocket. The Court found that, based on his training and experience, the officer was clearly able to determine that the object in the pocket consisted of heroin filled balloons.

FACTS (People v. Lee (1987) 194 Cal.App.3d 979)

On February 1, 1986, Officer Dunbar and Roberston were on foot patrol near the intersection of 7th and Pine Streets in Oakland, asking citizens about possible drug sales in the area. A woman told the officers that within the last five minutes she had been walking past a park on the west side of Wood Street, between 8th and Goss when a man offered to sell her heroin. Officer Dunbar knew that area to be one known for high amounts of narcotic activity. The woman said that the man was in the company of a second man and said that there was a third man standing at the northeast corner of 8th and Wood.

The officers drove to the location in separate patrol cars. As the officers approached, one of the two men standing together called out "rollers, rollers", which is a common expression used to warn of approaching police. The only other person in the vicinity was Floyd Lee.

Immediately after the warning was given, Mr. Lee turned and began to walk westbound across Wood Street. Officer Dunbar drove to within 15 to 20 feet of Mr. Lee, but had yet to give any commands or signals, or even exit his patrol car. Mr. Lee turned toward the police car and reached inside his jacket. Officer Dunbar was concerned that Mr. Lee might be going for a weapon, so he told Mr. Lee to remove his hand from his jacket and he complied.

Officer Dunbar pat searched the chest area of Mr. Lee's jacket and felt a clump of small resilient objects. He knew the item was not a weapon and felt he had just touched heroin-filled balloons. He arrested Mr. Lee and retrieved two transparent bags from inside the jacket, each containing 50 rolled heroin balloons.

2.2.6 – While Serving Arrest and Search Warrants

A search warrant, absent express authorization to the contrary, does not authorize a search of each individual in the searched location. For example, in **Ybarra v. Illinois** (1979) 44 U.S. 90, the U.S. Supreme Court ruled that a search warrant for evidence of heroin, as well as the bartender's person at a one-room tavern, did not authorize or justify the pat search of 9 of 13 patrons present at the scene at the time of the service of the search warrant.

In **Michigan v. Summers** (1981) 452 U.S. 692, the U.S. Supreme Court upheld the detention of a person as he left a house about to be searched for narcotics on the theory that it prevents flight of the person if incriminating evidence is found, minimizes risks to officers and facilitates the orderly completion of the search. The critical point of this case is that the person detained was an occupant as evidenced by exiting the residence as police approached and indicating that he left his keys to the house inside and therefore could not open the door for the officers.

In a more recent case, the U.S. Supreme Court ruled in **Muehler v. Mena** (2005) 544 U.S. 93, that an officer's detention of the occupants of a Los Angeles residence in handcuffs, for two to three hours during the service of a gang shooting related search warrant, did not violate the Fourth Amendment. The officers also did not violate the occupant's Fourth Amendment rights by asking her questions about her immigration status during the detention.

In **People v. Glaser** (1995) 11 Cal.4th 354, the California Supreme Court ruled that during the service of a search warrant, officers are allowed to briefly detain persons on the premises for purposes of officer safety, ID and to establish the person's connection to the premises.

The U.S. Supreme Court revisited its 1981 decision in **Michigan v. Summers**, **supra**, in 2013 in the case of **United States v. Bailey** (2013)___ U.S. ___; 133 S.Ct. 1031; 185 L.Ed. 19 In **Bailey**, **supra**, the court ruled 6 to 3 that the Summers rule was spatially constrained and limited to the immediate vicinity of the premises to be searched.

FACTS (United States v. Bailey (2013)___ U.S. ___; 133 S.Ct. 1031)

On July 28, 2005, at approximately 8:45 PM, police obtained a search warrant to search a basement apartment in the residence at 103 Lake Drive, Wyandanch, New York. A confidential informant had informed the police that he had observed a gun when he was at the apartment to purchase drugs from a heavyset black male with short hair. The person was known to the informant as "Polo." Detectives Sneider and Gorbecki were in an unmarked car outside the residence conducting pre-search warrant service surveillance.

About 9:56 PM, the detectives saw two men, one of which was later identified as Chunon Bailey, leave the gated area above the basement apartment and enter a car parked in the driveway. Both individuals matched the general description of "Polo". There was no indication that either individual was aware of the detectives' presence or knew about the search that was about to occur. The detectives followed the car once it was a few hundred yards down the street and away from the residence. The search team executed the search warrant while the detectives followed the car.

After following the car for approximately five minutes and 7/10ths of a mile, the detectives pulled the car over in a parking lot by a fire station. They ordered both men out of the car and conducted a weapons pat search. No weapons were found, but Mr. Bailey was found to have a ring of keys, one of which later fit the front door to the basement apartment. Mr. Bailey's driver's license showed his address to be in Bayshore, New York, which is where the informant told the police that "Polo" used to live. The passenger, later identified as Bryant Middleton, told the detectives that Mr. Bailey was giving him a ride home and confirmed that they were coming from the residence at 103 Lake Drive. The detectives placed both men in handcuffs. In response to Mr. Bailey's question as to why he was being placed in handcuffs, Detective Gorbecki said that they were being detained incident to the service of a search warrant at the Lake Drive residence. Mr. Bailey said,"

I don't live there. Anything you find there ain't mine, and I'm not cooperating with your investigation." **Id.** at 1036.

Detective Gorbecki used Mr. Bailey's keys to drive Mr. Bailey's car back to the scene. When the group arrived, the search team had already discovered a gun and drugs in plain view inside the apartment.

Mr. Bailey was charged with three federal offenses involving weapons and drug trafficking activity. His motion to suppress the apartment key and the statements he made when stopped by the detectives was denied by the trial court. The District Court found Mr. Bailey's detention was permissible under the rule announced in **Michigan v. Summers**, **supra**. A jury found Mr. Bailey guilty of all three-felony counts. The 2nd Circuit Court of Appeals affirmed his conviction and upheld the District Court's denial of his suppression motion. The U.S. Supreme Court granted certiorari and ultimately reversed the denial of the motion to suppress evidence.

RATIONALE

Justice Kennedy wrote the majority opinion and framed the issue as one of whether or not the **Michigan v. Summers** rule could justify detentions beyond the immediate vicinity of the premises being searched.

Justice Kennedy stated that the Supreme Court recognized three important law enforcement interests that, taken together justified the detention in **Summers**. He identified these as 1) minimizing the risk of harm to the officers serving the search warrant; 2) the orderly completion of the search would be facilitated if occupants of the premises were present; and 3) law enforcement's legitimate interest in preventing flight in the event incriminating evidence was found. After discussing those three justifications, Justice Kennedy observed,

> In sum, of the three law enforcement interests identified to justify the detention in **Summers**, none applies with the same or similar force to the detention of recent occupants beyond the immediate vicinity of the premises to be searched. Any of the individual interests is also insufficient, on its own, to justify an expansion of the rule in **Summers** to permit the detention of a former occupant, wherever he may be found away from the scene of the search. This would give officers too much discretion. The categorical authority to detain incident to the execution of a search warrant must be limited to the immediate vicinity of the premises to be searched. **Id.** at 1041.

Justice Kennedy also stated that "the detention here was more intrusive than a usual detention at the search scene. Bailey's car was stopped; he was ordered to step out and was detained in full public view; he was handcuffed, transported in a marked patrol car, and detained further outside the apartment. These facts illustrate that detention away from a premises

> where police are already present often will be more intrusive than detentions at the scene." **Id.** at 1041.
>
> Finally, he noted that "[d]etentions incident to the execution of a search warrant are reasonable under the Fourth Amendment because the limited intrusion on personal liberty is outweighed by the special law enforcement interests at stake. Once an individual has left the immediate vicinity of a premises to be searched, however, detentions must be justified by some other rationale." **Id.** at 1042.

In **People v. Hannah** (1996) 51 Cal.App.4th 1335, the Court of Appeal ruled that the brief detention of occupants of a residence during the service of an arrest warrant is permissible pursuant to **People v. Glaser**, **supra**, and **Michigan v. Summers**, **supra**.

FACTS (People v. Hannah (1996) 51 Cal.App.4th 1335)

> Police received information that a juvenile, with an outstanding arrest warrant, might be located at a certain apartment in Fresno. The police went to the apartment and were admitted inside by a female resident. After entering the apartment, the police saw two males seated in the living room, later identified as Mr. Hannah and Mr. DeSoto.
>
> The police asked them "if they could just stay seated where they were at" while they searched the apartment for the juvenile. The Court of Appeal ruled that the police clearly detained Mr. Hannah when he complied with the officer's command to remain seated.
>
> Within a few minutes, the police noticed that Mr. Hannah had dilated pupils and, after further investigation, arrested him for being under the influence of narcotics. Mr. Hannah unsuccessfully resisted arrest. A search of his person incident to arrest revealed rock cocaine.

In **People v. Samples** (1996) 48 Cal.App.4th 1197, the Court of Appeal upheld the detention and pat search of Mr. Samples, pursuant to **Michigan v. Summers**, **supra**, and **People v. Glaser**, **supra**, because he was in close association with subjects of a narcotics search warrant. The Court found that officer safety concerns were reasonable given the association of weapons and drugs, and the detention was minimally intrusive.

The Court of Appeal found the pat-search to be a closer question, but upheld it based on a totality of the circumstances standard. The Court found the officer's actions to be reasonable because the stop was at night, there were five people in the car and only four officers and Mr. Samples was in close association with persons who were the subject of a narcotics search warrant.

FACTS (People v. Samples (1996) 48 Cal.App.4th 1197)

> The Mendocino Countywide Narcotics Task Force had a search warrant authorizing the search of a Ukiah apartment for methamphetamine and two identified occupants: Dawn Carlesen and Freddie Barnett.

When the police arrived at the apartment to serve the search warrant on June 15, 1994, other occupants told them that Ms. Carlesen and Mr. Barnett had gone to the store and would return shortly in a white colored, Ford Mustang. Agents shortly thereafter saw a car matching that description pulling up and parking some distance away from the apartment. As the police approached the car, they recognized Mr. Barnett as being a passenger in the back seat of the car. Mr. Samples was driving the car with his wife Karen next to him in the front seat of the car. Mr. Renfro, who is Mrs. Samples' son was in the backseat along with her nephew Mr. Barnett and his girlfriend, Ms. Carlesen. The police ordered all of the car's occupants out of the car.

Mr. Samples was pat searched by Officer McQueary, who found a knife case attached to Mr. Samples' belt. Inside the case, an officer found a glass pipe he suspected was used for smoking methamphetamine. Officer McQueary also found a plastic container containing approximately .4 grams of suspected methamphetamine, a plastic Ziploc bag containing approximately .1 grams of suspected methamphetamine, approximately 10 Ziploc bags of assorted sizes, a large baby bottle liner and a short straw in Mr. Samples' right shirt pocket. In Mr. Samples' left shirt pocket, Officer McQueary found $553 in cash.

Another officer found a brown paper bag behind the driver's seat and on the floorboard near Charles Refro, the third backseat passenger. Inside the bag was a Ziploc bag with a small amount of suspected methamphetamine inside, a grinding device, a set of scales, three different sizes of packaging materials, metal instruments and another methamphetamine pipe.

In **People v. Matelski** (2000) 82 Cal.App.4th 837, the Court of Appeal ruled that under the totality of the circumstances, police officers who were going to a residence to conduct a probation search, lawfully detained the defendants who were leaving the residence, to determine if they were convicted felons. If the probationer were associating with felons, that would have been a violation of the terms of the probation grant. Upon learning their identity, the officers properly arrested the defendants for the outstanding warrants and lawfully seized contraband from Mrs. Matelski's purse.

FACTS (People v. Matelski (2000) 82 Cal.App.4th 837)

On September 8, 1998, Officer Henry and two other officers went to the residence of Michael Mitchell in Twenty-Nine Palms, to conduct a probation search on Mr. Mitchell, who had failed a drug test. As the officers approached the residence, they saw Raymond and Herminia Matelski leaving the residence. One of the officers ordered the defendants to "Come over here". The defendants complied with that command.

The officers explained Mr. Mitchell's probation condition that prevented him from associating with convicted felons. The officers asked the defendants for their names and dates of birth and then ran a criminal history and warrant check through police dispatch. Both defendants were arrested when outstanding warrants were discovered.

During the search of their persons incident to their arrest, the police found methamphetamine and two marijuana pipes in Mrs. Matelski's purse. Both defendants said that the methamphetamine belonged to Mr. Matelski.

Both defendants were charged with violating Health and Safety Code 21377(a). At a motion to suppress the evidence, the trial court found that the initial detention was illegal and suppressed the evidence. The People appealed and the Court of Appeal reversed the trial court.

RATIONALE

Looking at the totality of the circumstances, the Court of Appeal ruled in a split decision that the officers acted reasonably in detaining the defendants because there was no other way to determine if the defendants were convicted felons. The majority of the court specifically applied the rationale of **People v. Glaser, supra**, and **People v. Hannah**, **supra**, to the facts of this case.

The court reasoned that the probation condition could only be enforced if the officers could identify the probationer's associates and determine if they were felons. In balancing the defendants' privacy interests against the governmental interest in enforcing a valid probation condition, the governmental interest outweighed the brief and minimally intrusive detention of the defendants. Upon learning of the warrants, the defendants were properly arrested and the contraband was lawfully seized.

In **People v. Gallant** (1990) 225 Cal.App.3d 200, Riverside police officers served a search warrant at a Riverside residence and seized several baggies of methamphetamine. While serving the warrant, Mr. Gallant drove up to the house with a truck pulling a boat. He approached the house, knocked on the front door and was greeted by officers at gunpoint. The officers ordered Mr. Gallant inside and pat searched him for weapons. No weapons were found, but Mr. Gallant did have approximately $3,000.00 in cash on his person. The officers then obtained Mr. Gallant's consent to search his vehicle and boat and seized approximately one-half pound of methamphetamine.

The Court of Appeal ruled that the officer's initial contact with Mr. Gallant constituted an unjustified detention and that the initial illegal detention tainted Mr. Gallant's consent to search his vehicle and boat.

The Court found the initial detention illegal for the following reasons:

- There were no males named in the search warrant
- There were no males in the house
- The officers did not know the defendant
- There was nothing about the appearance\manner of the defendant's approach to the house to make him a suspect of criminal activity

- It was not until after the police illegally detained Mr. Gallant, pat searched him and seized $3,000 in cash from his person that the police suspected he was involved in criminal activity.

The Court observed that "[f]rom the fact that drugs in a saleable quantity have been found in a house, police may reasonably assume that *some* people come to that house to either deliver or buy drugs. However, a police officer may *not* reasonably conclude from that same fact that *everyone* approaching that house is involved in the drug trade. In the absence of evidence of their particular involvement in the illegal activity, friends, family, and the Fuller Brush man should be free to knock on the door without being ordered inside at gunpoint and frisked." (**Id.** at 208. [*Italics* in original].)

In **People v. Reyes** (1990) 223 Cal.App.3d 1218, the Court of Appeals upheld the pat search of the clothes of a person taking a shower when officers served a search warrant at the residence, and before the person put the clothes on after the shower. However, the Court found the search of the interior of the pockets of those same clothes to be illegal. The Court of Appeal ruled that the search warrant did not cover the defendant's clothing, which was an extension of the defendant's person.

FACTS (People v. Reyes (1990) 223 Cal.App.3d 1218)

> Bakersfield Police detectives served a search warrant on a house, based on CRI information that "Santio" was selling PCP. The search warrant authorized the search of the residence and Santio for PCP. Mr. Reyes, who was not Santio, was in the shower. The officers ordered Mr. Reyes out of the shower. Mr. Reyes attempted to put his pants and shirt on, which were laying nearby. The officer searched the shirt pocket and found heroin.

In contrast, in **People v. Thurman** (1989) 209 Cal.App.3d 817, the Court of Appeal upheld the pat search of outer clothing of the defendant who was found at the scene of a search warrant, and the officer's actions in reaching into the jacket pocket to see if the item was in fact a weapon. Upon reaching into the pocket, the officer determined that the hard object was not a weapon, but was rock cocaine.

FACTS (People v. Thurman (1989) 209 Cal.App.3d 817)

> On October 9, 1987, City of Vallejo police officers served a narcotics search warrant on the residence at 949 B Grant Street. The warrant did not authorize the search of James Thurman's person.
>
> Officer Azuar was one of four officers who served the search warrant and, after entry was made, saw Mr. Thurman sitting silently and passively on the sofa by himself in the front room. Two females were also in the room. Officer Azuar approached Mr. Thurman and pat searched him for weapons out of concern for safety. During the pat search, Officer Azuar felt a large bulge in Mr. Thurman's jacket pocket. It felt like it could be a gun, but he was not sure.

Because he believed it might be a gun, Officer Azuar reached into the pocket and squeezed the object. He realized it was not a weapon, but instead felt like pieces of rock or rock cocaine in a baggie. Officer Azuar had 10 years of experience and had felt rock cocaine on 10 to 15 occasions. He had also patted down about 50 people for rock cocaine and knew the object "felt like a rock". However, he had never seen rock cocaine that large. He removed the baggie, which contained 12 large rocks of cocaine and arrested Mr. Thurman.

RATIONALE

"We hold that where police officers are called upon to execute a warranted search for narcotics within a private residence they have the lawful right to conduct a limited **Terry** patdown search for weapons upon the occupants present while the search is in progress. Such protective action in the circumstances defined is, in our judgment, manifestly reasonable." (**Id**. at 824.)

"We hold that where an outside clothing pat search reveals the presence of an object of a size and density that reasonably suggests the object might be a weapon, the searching officer is entitled to continue the search of the inner garments where the object is located in order to determine whether the object is in fact a weapon. Weapon verification is essential if safety is to be preserved and potentially volatile situation neutralized. We cannot impose a condition of certainty that the object is a weapon before allowing an officer to continue the pat search to the inner clothing site where the object is located. To do so would frustrate the objective of the pat search. We can impose a condition that an officer's belief that the object is a weapon be reasonably grounded and not a mere subterfuge for a random search." (**Id**. at 825-826.)

2.2.7 – Prolonged Detentions

In **People v. McGaughran** (1979) 25 Cal.3d 577, the California Supreme Court ruled that when a police officer stops a person for a non-custodial traffic offense, the officer may make a check for outstanding arrest warrants, provided that check can be completed in the time necessary for the officer to discharge the officer's duties related to the traffic stop. Because the officer had decided against issuing Mr. McGraughran a traffic citation within the first four minutes of the car stop, the additional ten-minute detention to run a warrant check amounted to a prolonged illegal detention. Since the evidence seized was a poisonous fruit derived from that illegal detention, the Supreme Court suppressed the seized evidence and reversed the defendant's burglary conviction.

FACTS (People v. McGaughran (1979) 25 Cal.3d 577)

Larkspur Police Officer Thomas made a car stop on a Plymouth for driving in the wrong direction on a one-way street that crosses the Redwood High School parking lot. As the officer drove up behind the car and activated his emergency lights, the right front passenger turned around and reached over the back of the front seat towards the rear floorboard. Officer Fischer later found a brown paper

> bag in that location containing the remains of a meal, which Mr. Acosta had placed there.
>
> Officer Thomas approached Larry McGaughran, explained why he stopped him, and asked for ID. The officer also obtained ID from the front passenger, who was identified as Walter Acosta. Both of those IDs listed San Francisco addresses. Mr. McGaughran and Mr. Acosta each told the officer that they were lost and were looking for the Marin County Juvenile Hall, which the officer knew to be several miles away. This discussion took between three and four minutes.
>
> Officer Thomas then returned to his patrol car, relayed the information to his dispatcher, and requested a record check for outstanding warrants. Ten minutes later the dispatcher called back and reported that Mr. McGaughran had an outstanding Alameda County warrant for burglary and that Mr. Acosta had two outstanding traffic warrants.
>
> Officer Thomas then called for assistance and requested a confirmation of the warrants. Officer Fischer arrived about five minutes later. The officer confirmed the warrants via radio between 20 to 25 minutes later. After Mr. McGaughran was arrested, he was pat-searched and seated in Officer Fischer's patrol car. The defendant then asked Officer Fischer to retrieve Mr. McGaughran's jacket and wallet from the Plymouth. Officer Fischer complied with that request and found the wallet lying open on the dashboard, with a methadone treatment card from San Francisco in plain view. On the back seat of the car, Officer Fischer noted an open canvas bag containing several screwdrivers, a set of small wrenches, and a pair of pliers.
>
> Officer Thomas questioned Mr. Acosta about his outstanding traffic warrants. Mr. Acosta told the officer that if he could make a phone call he could raise the necessary bail. Mr. McGaughran told the officer that if that happened he would like to have the Plymouth released to Mr. Acosta so he could return to San Francisco.
>
> After a quick inspection of the car, officers allowed Mr. Acosta to drive it to the Larkspur Police station, while being escorted by the officers in their respective patrol cars. After arriving at the police station, Officer Fischer searched under the front seat of the Plymouth and found a citizen band radio that had been stolen earlier that day from a car parked approximately one mile from the scene of Mr. McGaughran's arrest. The thief entered the burglarized car by breaking open a door and the defendant's fingerprints were later located on that door.
>
> Officer Thomas later testified at a motion to suppress that he did not intend to issue the defendant a citation for driving on the wrong side of the street. He testified that the traffic pattern is confusing in that area and many people had made the same mistake the defendant did and he never cited any of them.

It was not until 1985 in **United States v. Sharpe** (1985) 470 U.S. 675, that the U.S. Supreme Court addressed the issue of prolonged detentions. In that case, the

Supreme Court rejected the defense's contention that a 20-minute stop was unreasonable where the police acted diligently and the suspect's own actions contributed to the added delay.

The Supreme Court issued the following guideline regarding prolonged detentions: "In assessing whether a detention is too long in duration to be justified as an investigative stop, we consider it appropriate to examine whether the police diligently pursued a means of investigation that was likely to confirm or dispel their suspicions quickly, during which time it was necessary to detain the defendant. [Citations]. A court making this assessment should take care to consider whether the police are acting in a swiftly developing situation, and in such cases the court should not indulge in unrealistic second-guessing. See generally *post*, at 712-716 (BRENNAN, J., dissenting). A creative judge engaged in *post hoc* evaluation of police conduct can almost always imagine some alternative means by which the objectives of the police might have been accomplished. But "[the] fact that the protection of the public might, in the abstract, have been accomplished by 'less intrusive' means does not, by itself, render the search unreasonable." **Cady v. Dombrowski**, 413 U.S. 433, 447 (1973); see also **United States v. Martinez-Fuerte**, 428 U.S. 543, 55, n. 12 (1976). The question is not simply whether some other alternative was available, but whether the police acted unreasonably in failing to recognize or to pursue it." **United States v. Sharpe**, at 486-487.

In **Illinois v. Caballes** (2005) 543 U.S. 405, the U.S. Supreme Court reversed the Illinois Supreme Court's reversal of Mr. Caballes' marijuana conviction. The Illinois Supreme Court held that the use of a canine unjustifiably enlarged a routine traffic stop into a drug investigation because there were no specific and articulable facts to suggest drug activity.

The U.S. Supreme Court held that the Fourth Amendment does not require a reasonable, articulable suspicion to justify using a canine to sniff the exterior of a car during a legitimate traffic stop. However, in this case, the fill officer was a member of the Illinois State Police Drug Interdiction Team and responded to the car stop with his drug sniffing canine. While the first officer was issuing the motorist a ticket, the fill officer walked the dog around the car. The dog alerted to the trunk of the car where the police found the marijuana. In his 5-3 majority opinion, Justice Stevens made the following observation:

> "Here, the initial seizure of respondent when he was stopped on the highway was based on probable cause, and was concededly lawful. It is nevertheless clear that a seizure that is lawful at its inception can violate the *Fourth Amendment* if its manner of execution unreasonably infringes interests protected by the Constitution. *United States v. Jacobsen, 466 U.S. 109, 124, 80 L. Ed. 2d 85, 104 S. Ct. 1652 (1984).* **A seizure that is justified solely by the interest in issuing a warning ticket to the driver can become unlawful if it is prolonged beyond the time reasonably required to complete that mission.** In an earlier case involving a dog sniff that occurred during an unreasonably prolonged traffic stop, the

Illinois Supreme Court held that use of the dog and the subsequent discovery of contraband were the product of an unconstitutional seizure. *People v. Cox, 202 Ill. 2d 462, 782 N.E.2d 275, 270 Ill. Dec. 81 (2002).* We may assume that a similar result would be warranted in this case if the dog sniff had been conducted while respondent was being unlawfully detained." (**Id**. at 407-408. [**Emphasis** added].)

In **United States v. Chavez-Valenzuela** (9th Cir. 2001) 268 F.3d 719, the 9th Circuit Court of Appeals ruled that a CHP Officer, who stopped the defendant for following too closely on Interstate 40, unlawfully prolonged the defendant's detention when he held him for seven additional minutes to conduct a warrant check and after he had already decided in the first three minutes that he was not going to issue the defendant a citation. The Court ruled that the defendant's subsequent consent to search his SUV, and the recovery of 10.5 kilograms of methamphetamine (9.4 pounds of which were pure), were illegally seized due to that prolonged detention.

The 9th Circuit also held that the defendant's extreme shaking and avoidance of eye conduct were insufficient to justify an extension of the initial detention and inquire about other possible criminal activity. The 9th Circuit stated that all other Circuits agree that nervousness alone does not constitute enough under the Fourth Amendment to arouse an officer's suspicion. The court observed that "[e]ncounters with police officers are necessarily stressful for law-abiders and criminals alike. We therefore hold today that nervousness during a traffic stop – even the extreme nervousness of Chavez-Valenzuela exhibited here – in the absence of other particularized, objective factors, does not support a reasonable suspicion of criminal activity, and does not justify an officer's continued detention of a suspect after he has satisfied the purpose of the stop." (**Id**. at 726.)

FACTS (United States v. Chavez-Valenzuela (9th Cir. 2001) 268 F.3d 719)

On February 24, 1999, at approximately 8:00 a.m., CHP Officer David saw the defendant driving eastbound on Interstate 40. Mr. Chavez-Valenzuela passed a slower moving car before approaching another car and slowing down. After pacing the defendant for about two tenths of a mile, Officer David initiated a traffic stop for a violation of CVC 21703.

The officer left his patrol car and motioned for the defendant to approach him. Officer David notice that Mr. Chavez-Valenzuela's hands were severely shaking as he handed over his license and vehicle registration. The officer asked Mr. Chavez-Valenzuela if he was on any medication or suffered from any medical problems and was told "No" in response to both questions.

At 8:04 a.m., Officer David radioed the CHP dispatcher for a license and registration check. However, he had already decided not to cite Mr. Chavez-Valenzuela. During the seven-minute wait, Officer David asked Mr. Chavez-Valenzuela a series of questions about his starting point, travel destination, whom he was visiting, and where he worked. During the entire conversation, the defendant's entire body was trembling and he continued to avoid eye contact.

At 8:11 a.m., CHP dispatch told Officer David that there were no wants or warrants for the defendant and that his CDL and registration were valid. Officer David then asked Mr. Chavez-Valenzuela if he had any drugs in his car and was told, "No". Mr. Chavez-Valenzuela consented to a search of his car and even signed a consent to search form. Upon opening the back of the SUV, Officer David found a nylon bag contained six package of methamphetamine, wrapped in black electrical tape.

After his suppression motion was denied, the defendant plead guilty to possessing methamphetamine with an intent to distribute it, and received a 14-year prison sentence.

RATIONALE

The Court characterized the seven-minute conversation as a fishing expedition into the defendant's travel and work and found that given the factual situation of this case, no reasonable motorist would have believed he was free to leave, even after the license and registration were returned to him. Therefore, the illegal prolonged detention tainted the defendant's consent to search the SUV.

In **People v. Russell** (2000) 81 Cal.App.4th 96, the Court of Appeal ruled that the officer's detention of the occupants of a car stopped for weaving was not unduly prolonged, but was justified based on observations that led the officer to believe the car might currently be used to transport narcotics. The subsequent consent to search the car was therefore valid and not the product of an unreasonably prolonged detention.

FACTS (People v. Russell (2000) 81 Cal.App.4th 96)

At about 7 a.m. on February 28, 1998, California Highway Patrol (CHP) Officer Lapthorne was on patrol on Highway 5 in Shasta County. He observed a black colored Ford Taurus traveling between 53 to 58 miles an hour in an area with a posted 65 mph speed limit. Officer Lapthorne followed the Taurus for about three miles and noticed that it repeatedly drifted around and within its lane. Officer Lapthorne thought that the driver might be either sleepy or intoxicated, so he initiated a traffic stop.

As Officer Lapthorne approached the car, he smelled an "overwhelming strong" odor that was similar to the type of masking odors used to conceal narcotics. Louis Burks was the driver of the car and immediately volunteered, without first being asked, that the odor was from a Vicks tablet he had taken for a cold. Although there was a package of Vicks in the car, Officer Lapthorne did not believe the odor he smelled was Vicks.

Mr. Burks produced a CDL bearing the name "Larry Johnson" and said he could not produce the car registration because the car did not belong to him. Robert Russell, who was the right front and only other passenger in the car, said that the car belonged to his niece. Officer Lapthorne noticed that Mr. Burks had red and watery eyes, but nothing in his manner or speech led the officer to believe Mr. Burks was intoxicated. His eyes could be consistent with someone who had been drinking or was sleepy.

Officer Lapthorne also made the following observations which in their totality suggested drug activity:

- The overwhelming odor coming from the car which could be used to mask drugs
- Mr. Burks' unsolicited claim that the odor was from a Vicks tablet, which could suggest possible drug paranoia
- The absence of the registered owner of the car, which is sometimes done by drug dealers to distance themselves from drugs found inside a car
- One of the occupants was wearing a pager and there was a cell phone in the car
- There were worn screws on the dashboard and the upholstery did not appear to be original, which suggested that the car might have been taken apart
- The occupants of the car were two men from Los Angeles, where large quantities of drugs are brought into the country, and they were headed north, having apparently driven through the night. The officer noted that when the car came to a stop Mr. Russell bolted upright, which would be consistent with having been asleep.

Officer Lapthorne asked Mr. Burks to step out of the car so he could investigate his condition for driving and the possibility of drug activity. Officer Lapthorne conducted no field sobriety tests, but did conclude that Mr. Burks' red eyes and slow gait were due to a cold.

Mr. Burks appeared nervous and was hesitant in giving answers to the officer's questions. Mr. Burks said that he and his passenger were brothers and were headed for a weekend vacation in Portland, with no plans to visit anyone. Officer Lapthorne knew Portland was a major distribution point for illegal drugs. Mr. Burks said that he was cold and sick so the officer asked him if he wanted to sit in the patrol car. Mr. Burks accepted the offer and sat in the backseat of the patrol car. The officer closed the back door, which the occupants could not open from the inside, but Mr. Burks was not handcuffed or placed under arrest. However, he was not free to leave.

Officer Lapthorne next spoke to Mr. Russell who said he was Mr. Burks' brother and produced a CDL bearing the name "Robert Bangston". Mr. Russell provided three inconsistent stories to the officer:

- They were going to visit Mr. Russell's niece in Portland, but he could not provide an address or phone number for the niece
- Mr. Russell first said he and Mr. Burks lived in Los Angeles, then said they lived in both Portland and Los Angeles

- Mr. Russell later said Mr. Burks and his niece had driven the car to Los Angeles, and the niece had flown back to Portland.

Mr. Russell said he was responsible for the car and its contents. The officer asked for and obtained Mr. Russell's consent to search the car. The officer then placed Mr. Russell in the back of the patrol car with Mr. Burks. The entire discussion with Mr. Russell took between three to five minutes.

During the car search, Officer Lapthorne found a locked, non-factory manufactured compartment between the rear seat and trunk wall. Both defendants were arrested for violating Health and Safety Code 21366.8 (False compartment for drugs in a vehicle). Officers later forced open the compartment and found it to contain guns, two large bricks of cocaine, numerous wax-type Glade brand air fresheners and a towel smeared with wax air freshener. The arrest occurred about 25 minutes after the officer's first contact with the suspect.

After the trial court denied the defense's suppression motion, both defendants plead guilty to transportation of controlled substances. Mr. Russell received a three-year prison term, while Mr. Burks received a 10-year prison term based on prior drug convictions and a prison prior.

RATIONALE

Officer Lapthorne lawfully stopped the car based on Mr. Burks' erratic driving. The officer was not required to accept Mr. Burks' statement that he had a cold without further inquiry.

The officer had encountered further information during his contact that led him to believe drug activity might be occurring in his presence. This justified a further detention. Before Officer Lapthorne had concluded that Mr. Burks was fit to drive, he had observed enough to justify a drug investigation.

In **People v. Brown** (1998) 62 Cal.App.4th 493, the Court of Appeal affirmed the trial court's denial of the defendant's motion to suppress the seized evidence. The appellate court ruled that during a routine traffic stop (bicyclist here) an officer may run a warrant check and ask for permission to search while awaiting the results of the warrant check, provided the check does not unreasonably prolong the detention. An officer may temporarily detain a traffic violator for the time necessary to discharge the duties incurred by virtue of the traffic stop.

FACTS (People v. Brown (1998) 62 Cal.App.4th 493)

On Nov. 30, 1996, Officer Bolinger stopped Michael Dean Brown for riding a bicycle without a light or reflectors (CVC 21201(d)) on Robertson Road in Stanislaus County. Officer Bolinger asked the defendant for ID in case he decided to issue Mr. Brown a citation for the traffic infraction. The defendant produced a California ID card.

Officer Bolinger ran a warrant check, which is common practice when the officer stops someone. The warrant check took about a minute. During the minute, Officer Bolinger asked the defendant some questions. The defendant responded to those questions and said that he was on searchable probation. He denied having any guns or anything else illegal in his fanny pack. Officer Bolinger asked for permission to search the defendant's fanny pack. Mr. Brown said, "Go ahead".

Inside the fanny pack, Officer Bolinger found a film canister containing a useable amount of methamphetamine. The defendant brought a motion to suppress the evidence alleging an illegal prolonged detention and that the consent was therefore the result of an illegal detention. The trial court denied the motion.

The defendant was convicted of violating Health and Safety Code 21377(a) (Possession of Methamphetamine), placed on probation and sentenced to 150 days in the county jail.

RATIONALE

"Questioning during the routine traffic stop on a subject unrelated to the purpose of the stop is not itself a Fourth Amendment violation. Mere questioning is neither a search nor a seizure. [Citations.] . . . While the traffic detainee is under no obligation to answer unrelated questions, the Constitution does not prohibit law enforcement officers from asking questions. ([Citations.], **Id.**, at 499.)

Officer Bolinger requested permission to search the fanny pack while waiting for the results of the warrant check, which took about one minute. Therefore, the request to search the fanny pack did not unduly prolong the detention or extend the period justified by the valid traffic stop.

2.2.8 – Arrests

An arrest is a seizure not limited in duration, scope and purpose. An officer is required to have probable cause that a person committed a crime or is committing a crime before the officer can make an arrest. In assessing the existence of probable cause, courts look at the totality of the circumstances in a given case. Some of the factors to consider are whether the person was moved from the scene of the detention or if the restraint used exceeded that reasonably necessary for investigation, such as handcuffing a person or stopping a car at gunpoint.

In **People v. Campbell** (1981) 118 Cal.App.3d 588, the Court of Appeal ruled that the officer's actions in handcuffing a suspect in an airport amounted to an arrest.

The Court of Appeal reached a similar result in the case of **In re Antonio B.** 166 Cal.App.4th 435. In that case, the Court of Appeal overruled the trial court's decision that handcuffing Antonio B. was lawful under the circumstances of this case.

FACTS (In re Antonio B. 166 Cal.App.4th 435.)

Los Angeles Police Detective Hugo Cepeida worked as a juvenile narcotics enforcement officer. On the day in question, he and two of his partners were driving westbound on Sixth Street near Chicago Avenue, when they saw 16-year-old Antonio B. walking eastbound on Sixth Street. Antonio B. was in the company of a second minor, who was approximately two feet away, and was walking side-by-side with Antonio B. An officer saw the second minor smoking what he believed to be a hand-rolled marijuana cigarette. The officers made a U-turn in their unmarked car and parked in an alley.

The officers got out of the car and approached the minors. They identified themselves as police officers, at which point the second minor with the cigarette threw it to the ground. One of the officers retrieved the discarded cigarette and identified it as a marijuana joint. The officers arrested the minor who was in possession of the cigarette moments earlier. Because Detective Cepeida believed, based on his training and experience, that marijuana was a communal drug, he believed that when one person is smoking it, his companions usually join in smoking. The Detective handcuffed Antonio B. and asked if he could search him. Antonio B. gave his consent. Detective Cepeida asked Antonio B. if he had anything sharp or anything that might hurt the Detective in his possession. Antonio B. said he did not. The Detective then asked Antonio B. if he had anything he was not supposed to have. Antonio B. stated that he had cocaine in his left front pocket. The Detective reached in the pocket and removed a baggie containing four small baggies of cocaine. A second officer searched Antonio B. further and found a sock in Antonio B's groin area that contained six baggies of suspected marijuana.

When asked at a suppression hearing by the defense attorney why the detective handcuffed Antonio B. before asking for permission to search, the Detective said, "We always handcuff people if were going to detain him [sic]. For further investigation, it's our procedure and our policy to handcuff people." **Id.** at 439. The prosecutor followed up on this in subsequent questioning of the Detective, who elaborated further and said, "It's our procedure that if anybody is going to be detained for [a] period of time, and we know we're going to arrest them, we handcuff them." **Id.** at 439.

After the trial court denied the motion to suppress evidence, Antonio B. plead guilty to a felony violation of Health & Safety Code 11359, while the felony violation of Health & Safety Code 11351 was dismissed as part of a negotiated settlement. Antonio B. was found to be a ward of the court under Welfare & Institution 602, placed on probation and returned to the custody of his parents.

RATIONALE

The appellate court noted that when a detention exceeds the boundaries of a permissible investigative stop, the detention becomes a de facto arrest requiring probable cause. The appellate court did not dispute that the police officers had cause to conduct an investigate detention of Antonio B., but found that they did not have probable cause to arrest him at the time they stopped him. The appellate court found that the officer's conduct in handcuffing Antonio B. transformed the valid detention into an invalid arrest.

The court found that the issue was whether the use of handcuffs during the detention was reasonably necessary under all of the circumstances. The appellate court then cited several California Supreme Court and federal cases in which handcuffing a suspect did not convert a detention into an arrest. However, in all of the cases cited, the court (both the California Supreme Court and the federal courts), found that at the time of the detention, the officers had a reasonable basis to believe that the detainee presented a physical threat to the officer or would flee.

In the present case, no such circumstances existed. "The officers outnumbered the suspects, one of whom was in handcuffs incident to his valid arrest, there was no one else in the vicinity, and appellant [Antonio B.] did not attempt to flee. In short, there is no evidence to suggest that the officers had any basis to believe that appellant [Antonio B.] posed a danger to them or that handcuffing him was necessary to effectuate the purpose of the stop, i.e., to determine whether appellant [Antonio B.] had been smoking marijuana." **Id**. at 442.

The appellate court ruled that "[b]ecause the use of handcuffs on appellant [Antonio B.] during the stop was not warranted under the circumstances, the seizure constituted an arrest rather than a detention. As there was no probable cause to arrest appellant [Antonio B.] at the time he was handcuffed, the arrest was illegal, and the consent to be searched, which on this record flowed directly from the illegal arrest, was not voluntary. Therefore, the evidence discovered must be suppressed." **Id**. at 442.

2.2.8.1 – Fine-Only Misdemeanor Offenses

In a 5 to 4 decision in **Atwater v. City of Lago Vista** (2001) 532 U.S. 318, the U.S. Supreme Court ruled that "[i]f an officer has probable cause to believe that an individual has committed even a very minor criminal offense in his presence, he may, without violating the Fourth Amendment, arrest the offender." (**Id**., at 354.)

"We confirm today what our prior cases have intimated: the standard of probable cause 'applies to all arrests, without the need to "balance" the interests and circumstances involved in particular situations.' If an officer has probable cause to believe that an individual has committed even a very minor criminal offense in his presence, he may, without violating the Fourth Amendment, arrest the offender." (**Id**., at 354.)

FACTS (<u>Atwater v. City of Lago Vista</u> (2001) 532 U.S. 318)

In March 1997, Gail Atwater was driving her pick-up truck in Lago Vista, Texas, with her three-year-old son and five-year-old daughter in the truck. She was traveling 15 mph in broad daylight on a residential street with no other traffic. No one was wearing a seatbelt, which is a direct violation of Texas law. It is punishable by a fine of not less than $25 or more than $50. Ms. Atwater had received only one ticket 10 years earlier, which was for a failure to signal for a lane change. Texas law allows a peace officer to arrest anyone committing a seatbelt violation, although it also allows the issuance of a citation in lieu of arrest.

Lago Vista Police Officer Bart Turek saw the seatbelt violation and made a car stop. Officer Turek approached the car and told Ms. Atwater something to effect that they had met before and that she was going to jail. Three months earlier Officer Turek had stopped Ms. Atwater because he believed her son was not wearing a seatbelt. While the child was wearing a seatbelt, he was seated on the armrest. Ms. Atwater acknowledged the child's seating position was unsafe and received only a verbal warning.

Officer Turek asked Ms. Atwater for her driver's license and insurance documentation. Ms. Atwater told the officer that she did not have the papers with her because her purse had been stolen the day before, which was the truth. Officer Turek replied that he had heard that story two hundred times. However, Ms. Atwater did orally give the officer her license number and residence address.

A nearby friend came and took custody of the children. The officer handcuffed Ms. Atwater and placed her in a police car. Ironically, he did not fasten her seatbelt on the ride to the station. At the police station, she had to remove her shoes, jewelry, and eyeglasses and empty her pockets. A mug shot was taken and she was placed in a cell alone, for about one hour. She was then taken before a magistrate, who released her on a $310 bond. Her car was towed while she was at the police station. Ms. Atwater ultimately plead no contest to the misdemeanor seatbelt offense and paid a $50 fine.

Ms. Atwater then filed a civil rights suit in Texas state court against the city, the officer and the Chief of Police for violating her Fourth Amendment right against unreasonable searches and seizure. The City removed the case to Federal court, where the District Court granted the City's summary judgment motion and dismissed the claim as meritless. The City contended that two interests were served by the arrest: (1) It was necessary to ensure Ms. Atwater's court appearance. However, she was a 16 year resident of a town with 2,486 residents and (2) enforcing child safety laws.

The Court of Appeals, 5th Circuit reversed and held that Officer Turek was not entitled to qualified immunity. An en banc panel of the 5th Circuit Court of

Appeals reversed that decision. The Supreme Court then granted the City's request for certiorari.

RATIONALE

The Supreme Court rejected Ms. Atwater's historical contention that the Fourth Amendment, as originally understood, forbade police officers from arresting someone for a misdemeanor without a warrant that did not amount to or involve a breach of the peace. However, the Court did note that "[i]n her case, the physical incidents of arrest were merely gratuitous humiliation imposed by a police officer who was (at best) exercising extremely poor judgment. Atwater's claim to live free of pointless indignity and confinement clearly outweighs anything the City can raise against it specific to her case." (**Id.**, at 346.)

In **People v. Patterson** (2001) 92 Cal.App.4th 561, the Court of Appeal applied the holding in **Atwater**, **supra**, and upheld the confession of the defendant to a robbery murder, following his custodial arrest for the misdemeanor violation of California Health and Safety Code 21357(b) (Possession of < 1 oz. of Marijuana).

In the published portion of the opinion, the appellate court specifically held that "a custodial arrest for a fine-only misdemeanor offense, even if it violates California law, does not require the suppression of evidence obtained as a product of that arrest." (**Id**. at 898.)

FACTS (People v. Patterson (2001) 92 Cal.App.4th 561)

The defendant and three other accomplices robbed a Long Beach jewelry and music store. During the robbery, one of the accomplices shot and killed the storeowner. The police shortly thereafter determined that Kenny Buckner was one of the robbers and planned to arrest him inconspicuously so as not to alert his co-conspirators.

Two days after the robbery, the police conducted surveillance on Mr. Buckner and saw him in the company of Trynun Patterson, who they had not yet identified as a suspect. During the surveillance, Mr. Bucker and Mr. Patterson left Mr. Buckner's residence and entered a car that Mr. Patterson drove away. After a few blocks, Mr. Patterson stopped so Mr. Buckner could talk with a pedestrian. While Mr. Buckner talked to the pedestrian, Mr. Patterson remained in the car, rolled a marijuana joint and smoked it. After Mr. Buckner returned to the car, the pair drove off.

The officers stopped the car because of a missing mirror and noticed the odor of marijuana. An officer asked for and obtained Mr. Patterson's permission to search the car. The officer located a partially smoked marijuana cigarette in the ashtray and found Mr. Patterson to be in possession of five grams of marijuana.

Police took Mr. Patterson into custody, where homicide detectives questioned him for six hours at the police station. He eventually provided a detailed confession to the robbery murder.

The defendant was convicted at trial of robbery murder, with a special circumstances allegation, and received a life sentence, without the possibility of parole. He appealed the denial of his suppression motion.

2.2.8.2 – California Arrests for Infractions

Infraction arrests are governed by California Penal Code 853.5. Penal Code 853.5(a) states in part that "[o]nly if the arrestee refuses to sign a written promise [to appear], has no satisfactory identification, or refuses to provide a thumbprint or fingerprint may the arrestee be taken into custody."

2.2.8.3 – Officer Probable Cause Mistakes

Where an officer has probable cause for the arrest of a suspect, the fact the officer pronounces an arrest for an additional offense does not make the arrest unlawful or require suppression of the fruits of the arrest even if there is no probable cause for the offense named by the officer.

The Court of Appeal held in **In re Donald L.** (1978) 81 Cal.App.3d 770 that even if the officer lacked probable cause to arrest the defendant for burglary, he still had probable cause to arrest the defendant for carrying a spiked billy club.

FACTS (In re Donald L. (1978) 81 Cal.App.3d 770)

Martinez Police Officer Walmsley responded to a report of a suspicious person in the 1000 block of Arreba Street. The officer saw the defendant about five blocks from the residence and detained him because he matched the suspect's description. At the time, the officer noticed that the defendant was carrying a billy type club, and told him to drop it. Possession of the weapon violated California Penal Code 22020(a).

During a pat search of the defendant, several items of jewelry were recovered from his person. The officer arrested the defendant on suspicion of burglary because the officer was aware of several burglaries that had occurred in the area, including one with stolen jewelry.

In **People v. Lewis** (1980) 109 Cal.App.3d 599, the appellate court ruled that even if the officers lacked probable cause to arrest the defendant for burglary and grand theft, they did have probable cause to arrest him for defrauding an innkeeper in violation of California Penal Code 237. Accordingly, the trial court properly denied the defendant's motion to suppress the seized evidence.

FACTS (People v. Lewis (1980) 109 Cal.App.3d 599)

Officers arrested the defendant after he was found inside a motel room at the Hollywood Hills Motel that he had not rented and where it appeared entry to the room might have been made through a broken bathroom

> window. The defendant also did not possess any ID documents. Following his arrest, the officers seized a key from Mr. Lewis' person, which fit a stolen 1977 Mercury Monarch located in the motel's parking lot.

The Court of Appeals in **People v. Goldberg** (1984) 161 Cal.App.3d 170, affirmed the trial court's denial of the defendant's motion to suppress the evidence and held that even though it was doubtful that the police had probable cause to arrest the co-defendant Mr. Mendez for attempted extortion, they did have probable cause to arrest him for receiving stolen property. Therefore, "[T]he fact Mendez was arrested for extortion, as well as receiving, is of no consequence." (**Id**. at 179.)

FACTS (People v. Goldberg (1984) 161 Cal.App.3d 170)

> The defendant and three co-defendants were convicted of several crimes related to the burglary and assault of a wealthy elderly woman. One of the co-defendants, Hector Mendez, contacted the victim a few months after the crime and offered to return some of the stolen jewelry in exchange for the money needed to retrieve it from a pawnshop.
>
> The victim contacted the police who met with Mr. Mendez in an undercover capacity. As soon as Mr. Mendez produced a pawn ticket, he was arrested for extortion and receiving stolen property. Like the links in the chain, the arrest of Mendez led to the issuance of a *Ramey* warrant [**People v. Ramey** (1976) 16 Cal.3d 263] for Mr. Goldberg. Mr. Goldberg unsuccessfully moved to suppress the information in the *Ramey* warrant claiming that the arrest of Mr. Mendez was illegal and therefore the fruits of that illegal arrest could not be used in the *Ramey* affidavits.

The Court of Appeal in **People v. Rodriguez** (1997) 53 Cal.App.4th 1250 ruled that it was irrelevant whether the officer arrested the defendant on the Contreras or Moore homicide cases, since he had probable cause to believe the defendant committed a homicide.

2.3 – Bodily Intrusion Searches

Bodily intrusion searches are searches of a person where law enforcement either obtains bodily fluid samples or conducts internal body searches. These searches implicate Fourth Amendment rights but do not implicate Fifth Amendment rights and, with few exceptions, usually require a search warrant.

Issues arise in the context of obtaining blood and other bodily fluid samples from suspects, removing bullets, and other objects from someone's body. Based on prior U.S. Supreme Court precedent, law enforcement generally believed that a forced blood draw was allowed from an arrestee in a typical driving under the influence (DUI) refusal case without a search warrant. However, in 2013, the U.S. Supreme Court made it clear that its prior precedent did not allow for obtaining a blood sample absent exigent circumstances and specifically ruled that the dissipation of alcohol alone from one's system did not create sufficient exigent circumstances to justify the warrantless obtaining of a forced blood sample in a typical, driving under the influence refusal case.

While Fourth Amendment issues also arise where law enforcement officers prevent suspects from swallowing contraband, warrantless action is allowed when law enforcement officers do not use excessive force or choke the suspect when they retrieve the contraband the suspect is attempting to swallow.

Finally, bodily intrusion searches may occur in the context of strip searches. California statutory provisions govern strip searches involving misdemeanor and infraction arrests and are discussed in section 5.3.9.

2.3.1 -- The Fifth Amendment and Bodily Intrusion Searches

The Fifth Amendment's protection against self-incrimination does not apply to any physical evidence that a person may possess in their body.

2.3.2 – Bodily Intrusion Searches Based on Arrest Warrants

In **People v. Bracamonte** (1975) 15 Cal.3d 394, the California Supreme Court ruled that although probable cause existed to believe Mrs. Bracamonte swallowed narcotics, the search warrant authorizing a search of her person did not authorize the intrusion of Mrs. Bracamonte's body. The California Supreme Court cautioned that

> We are not confronted with, nor do we decide, the issue of when, if at all, a search warrant may issue authorizing an intrusion into a suspect's body. (**Bracamonte**, **supra**, fn. 3, at p. 400.)

FACTS (People v. Bracamonte (1975) 15 Cal.3d 394)

On March 10, 1972, BNE Field Supervisor William Miller obtained a search warrant for the search of the Fresno residence of Rita Bracamonte and her husband, their cars and persons. The warrant was based on information obtained from two confidential informants and observations made by Agent Miller and other BNE agents.

On the morning of March 15, 1972, a surveillance agent saw Mrs. Bracamonte enter one of the cars described in the search warrant and drive away. Two BNE agents in a nearby car spotted Mrs. Bracamonte and attempted a car stop. The BNE car stopped in front of Mrs. Bracamonte's car, with one of the agents exiting the BNE car and walking back to Mrs. Bracamonte's car.

Mrs. Bracamonte looked at the agent, put the car in reverse, and accelerated backwards. The agent saw Mrs. Bracamonte reach down with her right hand toward the automobile seat and then rapidly place two balloons in her mouth, and appear to swallow. As Mrs. Bracamonte's car continued backward, the agent saw Mrs. Bracamonte repeat the mouth stuffing motion two more times.

Other agents arrested Mrs. Bracamonte a short distance away and took her back to her house. Twenty minutes later, the agents transported Mrs. Bracamonte to a local hospital to retrieve the items they believed she had swallowed.

At the hospital, BNE Agent Walley showed the search warrant to the emergency room attending doctor and requested he pump Mrs. Bracamonte's stomach. Based solely on the authority of the search warrant, the doctor ordered two nurses to prepare and administer a Syrup of Ipecac emetic solution. A still handcuffed and struggling Mrs. Bracamonte refused to drink the solution so the nurses forced her on her back and strapped her to a table. The nurses then inserted a rubber tube through one of Mrs. Bracamonte's nostrils, down her esophagus and into her stomach. The syrup was to be delivered through this tube.

Mrs. Bracamonte continued to struggle and after about five minutes said that the tube was "too painful" and agreed to drink the emetic. Shortly thereafter, Mrs. Bracamonte regurgitated seven balloons of heroin, continued vomiting for about 10 minutes and remained nauseated for an additional 15 minutes.

RATIONALE

This warrantless bodily intrusion search of her stomach was not justified by either exigent circumstances or Mrs. Bracamonte's consent. The California Supreme Court ruled that no emergency existed because:

- Agent Walley did not take Mrs. Bracamonte directly to the hospital
- It was stipulated that if the attending physician was called as a witness at the suppression motion he would have stated:
- The balloons would have safely passed through Mrs. Bracamonte's digestive tract without the need for an emetic
- The procedure was not necessary to protect Mrs. Bracamonte's life or health
- He would have recommended regurgitation as a medical precaution.

2.2.4.5 -- Blood Samples

In Breithaupt v. Abram (1957) 352 U.S. 432, the U.S. Supreme Court ruled that blood test evidence, even if involuntarily seized from an unconscious patient, is admissible and does not violate the United States Constitution.

FACTS (Breithaupt v. Abram (1957) 352 U.S. 432)

Paul H. Breithaupt, while driving a pick-up truck on a New Mexico highway, collided with a passenger car. Mr. Breithaupt was seriously injured and killed three occupants in the car. Police found an almost empty pint of whiskey in the glove compartment of the truck.

Emergency personnel took Mr. Breithaupt to the hospital. While lying unconscious in the emergency room, a state patrolman smelled the odor of alcohol on Mr. Breithaupt's breath. The officer requested that the attending doctor obtain a sample of Mr. Breithaupt's blood. While Mr. Breithaupt lay unconscious, the attending physician withdrew 20ccs of blood in a medically approved manner. Subsequent laboratory analysis revealed a blood alcohol level of .17 percent. Over Mr. Breithaupt objections, the trial court admitted testimony regarding the blood test result and an expert's opinion that a .17 percent blood alcohol level showed that the defendant was under the influence of alcohol at the time of the accident.

A jury convicted Mr. Breithaupt of involuntary manslaughter, which he did not appeal. Mr. Breithaupt sought a writ of habeas corpus to the New Mexico Supreme Court, alleging a violation of the Due Process clause. The Court denied that request after argument on the issues. The U.S.S.C. granted a writ of certiorari to address the issue of whether a conviction based on an involuntary blood test result deprived the defendant of his liberty interest, which is guaranteed to him by the Due Process clause of the Fourteenth Amendment to the United States Constitution.

RATIONALE

There is nothing "brutal" or "offensive" in the taking of blood when done under the watchful eye of a physician.

> The blood test procedure has become routine in our everyday life. It is a ritual for those going into the military service as well as those applying for marriage licenses. Many colleges require such tests before permitting entrance and literally millions of us have voluntarily gone through the same, though a longer, routine in becoming blood donors. (**Id**. at 410-411.)
>
> A blood test taken by a skilled technician is not such "conduct that shocks the conscience," **Rochin v. California** (1952) 342 U.S. 165, at 172, nor such a method of obtaining evidence that it offends a "sense of justice," **Brown v. Mississippi** (1936) 297 U.S. 278, at 285-286. This is not to say that the indiscriminate taking of blood under different conditions or by those not

> competent to do so may not amount to such "brutality" as would come under the Rochin rule. (**Breithaupt**, **supra**, at 436-438.)

Nine years later, in **Schmerber v. California** (1966) 384 U.S. 757, the U.S. Supreme Court ruled that the state may, over the objection of a defendant, have a physician extract blood from a person suspected of driving under the influence of alcohol or drugs, without violating the Fourth Amendment. In reaching this ruling, the Court cautioned

> It bears repeating, however, that we reach this judgment only on the facts of the present record. The integrity of an individual's person is a cherished value of our society. That we today hold that the Constitution does not forbid the States minor intrusions into an individual's body under stringently limited conditions in no way indicates that it permits more substantial intrusions, or intrusions under other conditions.
>
> (**Id.** at 772 [Emphasis added].)

FACTS (Schmerber v. California (1966) 384 U.S. 757)

Armando Schmerber, the defendant in this action, and a companion were drinking at a tavern and bowling alley earlier in the evening. Mr. Schmerber left the bowling alley at about midnight on November 12, 1964. While driving away from the bowling alley with his companion, Mr. Schmerber's car skidded, crossed the road and struck a tree. Both were injured and taken to a hospital for treatment.

At the accident scene, the officer noticed the smell of alcohol on Mr. Schmerber's breath and that his eyes were bloodshot, watery and somewhat glassy in appearance. While Mr. Schmerber was being treated at the hospital, and within two hours of the accident, the officer again noticed the symptoms of alcohol intoxication and arrested Mr. Schmerber.

The officer, without first obtaining a search warrant, ordered the doctor to obtain a blood sample from Mr. Schmerber. A jury convicted Mr. Schmerber in Los Angeles Municipal Court of driving under the influence of alcohol based in part on the results of the blood test.

RATIONALE

- There was probable cause to believe Mr. Schmerber was driving under the influence of alcohol
- Exigent circumstances were present for the warrantless seizure of the blood sample given the body's efforts to eliminate the alcohol from its system
- The test was performed in a reasonable manner by a doctor in a hospital setting and done in accordance with accepted medical practices
- The blood extracted was minimal, there was virtually no risk involved in the procedure, and no trauma or pain to Mr. Schmerber.

It was this decision that caused law enforcement to believe that a warrantless forced blood draw was allowed in routine, driving under the influence cases. However, as we will see in **Missouri v. McNeeley** (2013) ___U.S.___; 133 S.Ct. 1552 , the U.S. Supreme Court made it crystal clear that the **Schmerber**, **supra**, decision did not stand for that proposition.

In **McNeely**, **supra**, the U. S. Supreme Court addressed the issue of whether or not the natural metabolization of alcohol in one's bloodstream presented a per se exigency that justified an exception to the Fourth Amendment's search warrant requirement for nonconsensual blood testing in all drunk driving cases. The Court held that the exigency in the context of a DUI case must be determined on a case-by-case basis, based on the totality of the circumstances presented, and declined the invitation to establish a *per se* rule.

FACTS (Missouri v. McNeely, (2013) ___ U.S.___)

At approximately 2:08 AM, a Missouri police officer stopped Mr. McNeely's truck after observing it exceed the posted speed limit and repeatedly crossing the centerline. The officer noted several signs that Mr. McNeely was intoxicated; bloodshot eyes, slurred speech, the smell of alcohol on Mr. McNeely's breath and his unsteadiness when he exited the truck. Mr. McNeely admitted that he had consumed "a couple of beers" at a bar." Mr. McNeely failed the field sobriety tests the officer administered and declined to use a portable breath test device to measure the alcohol content in his blood. The officer arrested Mr. McNeely for driving under the influence of alcohol.

As the officer transported Mr. McNeely to the station house, Mr. McNeely indicated that he would again refuse to provide a breath sample. The officer then changed course and took Mr. McNeely to a nearby hospital for a blood test. The officer did not first attempt to secure a search warrant believing none was required. The officer read from a standard implied consent form and explained to Mr. McNeely that under Missouri law refusal to submit voluntarily to a test would lead to the immediate revocation of his driver's license for one year and that it could be used against him in a future prosecution. Despite this admonition, Mr. McNeely still refused to submit to a test. The officer then directed a hospital lab technician to take a blood sample, which was obtained approximately 27 minutes after the car stop, in a medically approved manner. A later analysis of that blood sample revealed that Mr. McNeely had a blood alcohol concentration (BAC) of 0.154 percent. The legal limit allowed under Missouri law is 0.08 percent.

Mr. McNeely was charged with driving while intoxicated and moved to suppress the blood test arguing that taking his blood for chemical testing, without first obtaining a search warrant, violated his rights under the Fourth Amendment. The trial court agreed with him and ruled that there were no circumstances suggesting the officer faced an emergency in which she could not practicably obtain a search warrant.

On appeal, a Missouri Court of Appeals stated its intention to reverse the trial court's ruling, but then transfered the case directly to the Missouri Supreme Court. The Missouri Supreme Court held that **Schmerber, supra**, required:

- lower courts to engage in a totality of circumstances analysis when determining whether exigent circumstances permitted a nonconsensual, warrantless blood draw; and
- more than the mere dissipation of blood-alcohol evidence in order to allow a warrantless blood draw in alcohol related cases.

The Missouri Supreme Court ruled that exigency depended heavily on the existence of additional special facts, such as whether an officer was delayed by the need to investigate an accident and transport an injured suspect to the hospital, as was the case in **Schmerber, supra**. The court therefore found that the facts in McNeely's case were consistent with a routine driving under the influence case and that other than the natural dissipation of blood-alcohol, there was no emergency present. Accordingly, the Missouri Supreme Court ruled that the nonconsensual warrantless taking of a blood sample for Mr. McNeely violated his Fourth Amendment rights to be free from unreasonable searches. The U.S. Supreme Court affirmed that decision.

RATIONALE

The U.S. Supreme Court explained that in the case of **Schmerber, supra**, time had to be taken to bring the accused to a hospital and to investigate the scene of the accident, thereby creating no time to seek out a magistrate and secure a warrant. Given those special facts, the court explained that they found it appropriate for the police to act without warrant.

The Court noted:

Regardless of the exact [alcohol] elimination rate, it is sufficient for our purposes to note that because an individual's alcohol level gradually declines soon after he stops drinking, a significant delay in testing will negatively affect the probative value of the results. This fact was essential to our holding in **Schmerber**, as we recognized that, under the circumstances, further delay in order to secure a warrant after the time spent investigating the scene of the accident and transporting the injured suspect to the hospital to receive treatment would have threatened the destruction of evidence. [**Schmerber**] 384 U.S., at 770-771, 86 S.Ct. 1826, 16 L.Ed.2d 908. ¶ But it does not follow that we should depart from careful case-by-case assessment of exigency and adopt the categorical rule proposed by the State and its *amici*. In those drunk driving investigations where police officers can reasonably obtain a warrant before a blood sample can be drawn without significantly undermining the efficacy of the search, the Fourth Amendment mandates that they do so."

McNeely, supra, at 1560-1561 [italics in original].

The Court observed

> ...because a police officer must typically transport a drunk driving suspect to a medical facility and obtain the assistance of someone with appropriate medical training before conducting a blood test, some delay between the time of the arrest or accident and the time of the test is inevitable regardless of whether police officers are required to obtain a warrant.

(**Id.** at 1561.)

The Court further stated:

> The State's proposed *per se* rule also fails to account for advances in the 47 years since **Schmerber** was decided that allow for the more expeditious processing of warrant applications, particularly in contexts like drunk driving investigations where the evidence offered to establish probable cause is simple.
>
> **Id.**
>
> The court specifically referenced telephonic and other reliable electronic means of obtaining search warrants, and also noted that in addition to technology-based developments, jurisdictions have found other ways to streamline their search warrant process such as by using standard forms for search warrant applications for drunk-driving investigations. The court observed that while warrants inevitably take some time for police officers or prosecutors to complete and for magistrates to review, technological developments do enable police officers to obtain search warrants more quickly, and not support a neutral magistrate's central role as a check on police discretion.

The majority U.S. Supreme Court opinion stated:

> In short, while the natural dissipation of alcohol in the blood may support a finding of exigency in a specific case, as it did in **Schmerber**, it does not do so categorically. Whether a warrantless blood test of a drunk-driving suspect is reasonable must be determined case-by-case based on the totality of the circumstances."

Id. at 1536.

In response to the U.S. Supreme Court's 2013 decision in **Missouri v McNeely**, **infra**, the California Legislature enacted a 13th ground for issuance of a search warrant. On September 20, 2013, the Governor of California signed into law that legislation, which unanimously passed both houses of the California Legislature and, since it was classified as urgency legislation, took effect immediately upon obtaining the Governor's signature. The statute requires that the person from whom the sample is being sought refuse an officer's request to submit to, or has failed to complete, a blood test as required by California Vehicle Code 23612 (Implied Consent Law) and that the sample be drawn in a reasonable, medically approved manner.

That provision reads as follows:

> "When a sample of the blood of a person constitutes evidence that tends to show a violation of Section 23140, 23152, or 23153 of the Vehicle Code and the person from whom the sample is being sought has refused an officer's request to submit to, or has failed to complete, a blood test as required by Section 23612 of the Vehicle Code, and the sample will be drawn from the person in a reasonable, medically approved manner. This paragraph is not intended to abrogate a court's mandate to determine the propriety of the issuance of a search warrant on a case-by case basis."

Notice that the statue is only limited to driving under the influence cases, as opposed to being under the influence of drugs in violation of California Health & Safety Code 11550(a). The section also requires that an officer has first requested that the arrestee submit to a blood test and that the arrestee has refused to provide a sample, before an officer can obtain a search warrant for a force blood draw. The blood also must be taken in a reasonable, medically approved manner.

2.3.4 – Buccal Swab Samples

The U.S. Supreme Court ruled in a 5-4 decision in **Maryland v. King** (2013) ___ U.S. ___; 133 S.Ct. 1958; 186 L.Ed.2d 1, that Maryland's law allowing for the taking of a buccal swab[4] from a person arrested based on probable cause that they committed a serious offense, did not violate the Fourth Amendment. The Court noted that a buccal swab was a quick and painless procedure, required no surgical intrusions beneath one's skin and posed no threat to the arrestee's health or safety.

FACTS (Maryland v. King (2013) ___ U.S. ___; 133 S.Ct. 1958; 186 L.Ed.2d 1)

In 2003, a woman was raped at gunpoint in her home in Salisbury, Maryland. The assailant concealed his face, but the investigating officers did obtain from the victim a sample of the perpetrator's DNA. In 2009, Alonzo King was arrested in Wicomico County, Maryland, and charged with first and second degree assault for menacing a group of people with a shotgun. As part of a routine booking procedure for serious offenses, a buccal swab was taken from the inside of his mouth cheeks. That DNA sample was found to match the sample recovered from the rape victim in 2003.

Mr. King was tried and convicted for the rape and sentenced to life in prison without the possibility of parole. It was this initial buccal sample taken during his booking in 2009 that led to his being linked to the rape and charged with the commission of that crime.

A divided Maryland Court of Appeals ruled that the 2009 DNA sample was unlawfully seized from Mr. King because it amounted to an unreasonable search

[4] As explained in the Court's opinion, the procedure involves wiping a small piece of filter paper or a cotton swap, similar to a Q-tip, against the inside of the mouth cheek of an individual to collect some skin cells. **Id.** at 1967-1968.

of his person and Mr. King's expectation of privacy was greater than the State's interest in using his DNA to identify him. It therefore set aside the rape conviction. The U.S. Supreme Court granted certiorari and ultimately reversed that decision.

RATIONALE

After a thorough discussion of DNA, as well as the Maryland statute in question, Justice Kennedy, writing for the majority, observed that "[a] buccal swab is a far more gentle process than a venipuncture to draw blood. It involves but a light touch on the inside of the cheek; and although it can be deemed a search within the body of the arrestee, it requires no 'surgical intrusions beneath the skin.' **Winston**, 470 U.S., at 760. The fact tha[t] intrusion is negligible is of central relevance to determining reasonableness, although it is still a search as the law defines that term." **Id.** at 1969.

Justice Kennedy said that "[w]hen probable cause exists to remove an individual from the normal channels of society and hold him in legal custody, DNA identification plays a critical role in serving those interests." **Id.** at 1971. He identified four specific instances that identification was important. First, he noted that in every criminal case it must be known who's been arrested and who is being tried. He observed that identity has never been considered limited to the name on the arrestee's birth certificate and that a suspect's criminal history is a critical part of an arrestee's identification that officers need to know when they are processing the arrestee. Justice Kennedy noted that "[a] DNA profile is useful to the police because it gives them a form of identification to search the records already in their valid possession. In this respect the use of DNA for identification is no different than matching an arrestee face to a wanted poster of a previously unidentifed suspect; or matching tattoos to known gang symbols to reveal a criminal affiliation; or matching the arrestee's fingerprints to those recovered from a crime scene." **Id.** at 1972.

Second, Justice Kennedy said that law enforcement officers bear a responsibility for ensuring that the custody of an arrestee doesn't create inordinate risks for either the facility staff, the existing detained population, or for the new detainee.

Third, Justice Kennedy said that looking forward to future stages of criminal prosecution, "'the Government has a substantial interest in ensuring that persons accused of crimes are available for trials.' **Bell v. Wolfish**, 441 U.S. 520 (1979), 534. A person who is arrested for one offense but knows that he has yet to answer for some past crime may be more inclined to flee the instant charges, lest continued contact with the criminal justice system expose one or more other serious offenses." **Id.** at 1972-1973.

Fourth, Justice Kennedy said that "an arrestee's past conduct is essential to an assessment of the danger he poses to the public, and this will inform a court's determination whether the individual should be released on bail." **Id.** at 1973.

In summarizing the Court's opinion, Justice Kennedy said that "[i]n light of the context of a valid arrest supported by probable cause respondent's expectations of privacy were not offended by the minor intrusion of a brief swab of his cheeks. ... the Court concludes that DNA identification of arrestees is a reasonable search that can be considered part of a routine booking procedure. When officers make an arrest supported by probable cause to hold for a serious offense and they bring the suspect to the station to be detained in custody, taking and analyzing a cheek swab of the arrestee's DNA is, like fingerprinting and photographing, a legitimate police booking procedure that is reasonable under the Fourth Amendment." **Id.** at 1979.

Justice Scalia, joined by three other justices, wrote a scathing dissent. Justice Scalia stated that the Court's assertion that DNA was being taken not to solve crimes but to identify those in custody, "taxes the credulity of the credulous." **Id.** at 1980. Justice Scalia observed that "DNA testing does not even begin until after arraignment and bail decisions are already made. The sample sits in storage for months, and take weeks to test. When they are tested, they are checked against the Unsolved Crimes Collection– rather than the Convict and Arrestee Collection, which could be used to identify them. The Act forbids the Court's purpose (identification) but prescribes as its purpose what our suspicionless–search cases forbid ('official investigation into a crime'). Against all of that, it is safe to say that if the Court's identification theory is not wrong, there is no such thing as error." **Id.** at 1986.

In a decision issued after the ruling issued in **Maryland v. King**, **supra**, the California Fourth District Court of Appeal upheld the constitutionality of California's law regarding the obtaining of buccal swabs from all persons arrested for felony charges. In the case of **People v. Lowe** (2013) 221 Cal.App.4th 1276, Mr. Lowe was convicted of 13 felony counts involving rapes, other sex crimes, residential burglaries, and robberies. His motion to suppress the buccal swab taken from him at his arrest in 2006, which linked him to several of the crimes that occurred before his arrest, was denied. After a jury trial, he received a prison sentence in excess of 100 years to life. The court of appeal specifically held that the 2004 Amendment to the California statute authorizing the mandatory and warrantless collection and analysis of buccal swab DNA samples from felony arrestees did not violated the Fourth Amendment.

In upholding the trial court's denial of Mr. Lowe's motion to suppress the buccal swab, the appellate court said

> We conclude that the legitimate governmental interests promoted by the warrantless collection of buccal swab DNA samples from felony arrestees who are taken into custody upon probable cause, far outweigh the arrestees' privacy concerns. Our conclusion is based on the following five reasons: The felony arrestee's diminished privacy interests; the de minimis nature of the physical

> intrusion involved in the collection of a buccal swab DNA sample; the carefully limited scope of the DNA information that is extracted; the strict limits on the range of permissible uses of the DNA information obtained and the significant criminal penalties imposed upon those who violate those limitations; and the strong law enforcement interests in obtaining arrestees' identifying information, solving past and future crimes, deterring future criminal acts, and exonerating the innocent.

Id. at 1296 to 1297.

2.3.5 -- Non-Blood, Bodily Fluid Samples

In reversing the conviction in **People v. Scott** (1978) 21 Cal.3d 284, the California Supreme Court ruled that when a bodily intrusion warrant is sought, the magistrate is required to find probable cause and conduct an additional balancing test. The test balances whether the character of the requested search is appropriate.

The Court required that the following factors must be balanced against the severity of the proposed intrusion:

- The reliability of the method to be employed
- The seriousness of the underlying criminal offense and society's consequent interest in obtaining a conviction
- The strength of law enforcement suspicions that evidence of a crime will be revealed
- The importance of the evidence sought and
- The possibility that evidence may be recovered by alternative means less violative of Fourth Amendment freedoms.

FACTS (People v. Scott (1978) 21 Cal.3d 284)

In June or July 1974, the 13-year-old victim went to live with her parents, who were the defendant and his wife. An affectionate relationship developed between the defendant and the victim, which soon developed into child molestation and incest.

In August 1974, the victim engaged in a "French kissing" episode with the defendant. Between September 1974 and January 1975, the defendant and the victim engaged in four episodes of sexual intercourse.

In May 1975, and while living with her grandmother, a doctor examined the victim to learn the cause of a vaginal discharge. The pediatrician diagnosed a non-specific vaginal infection.

In June 1975, another doctor's examination revealed the presence of trichomoniasis, which is an infection transmitted primarily through intercourse. The victim admitted having sexual intercourse with her father to the doctor.

In September 1975, and just prior to the start of trial, the People moved to have the defendant tested for trichomoniasis. The test involves a manual massage of the prostate gland, via the rectum, resulting in a semen sample discharge. The exam takes about 15 minutes, is not painful and has a 70 percent probability of revealing if a male has trichomoniasis. Over the defendant's objection, the court ordered the test. It revealed a chronic prostate inflammation, of which trichomoniasis was one of three possible causes.

A jury convicted the defendant of four counts of child molestation and four counts of incest.

RATIONALE

The argument offered by the People to support their request for the test was inadequate to justify the bodily intrusion because:

- The intrusion was very substantial
- The intrusion constituted a very significant invasion of dignity and privacy
- The intrusion sought was not a routine procedure
- The evidence sought was highly circumstantial and speculative.

In **People v. Fulton** (2012) 205 Cal.App.4th 1546; 14 Cal.Rptr.3d 374 (**Depublished**), the court of appeal found in a unanimous decision that the warrantless seizure of Mr. Fulton's DNA from a sample of his pubic hair and a penile swab violated his Fourth Amendment rights, but by a 2 to 1 decision that it was harmless beyond a reasonable doubt given the evidence in the case.

FACTS (People v. Fulton (2012) 205 Cal.App.4th 1546; 14 Cal.Rptr.3d 374 (Depublished)

In July 2008, the 14-year-old victim was visiting her stepbrother (28-year-old Dion Fulton). The victim lived in Oak Grove and Mr. Fulton lived in Sacramento with his wife and three children at the time of the crime. On July 15, 2008, Mr. Fulton picked up the victim at her house in the afternoon with the intention that she would babysit his children at his house. That evening, the children, as well as Mr. Fulton's wife, went to bed. The victim was lying on the couch and watching television in the family room, while Mr. Fulton was sitting at a nearby computer. Mr. Fulton approached the victim and began tickling her, which he had done on previous occasions. This time, however, Mr. Fulton began touching the victim's chest and buttocks. The victim told him to get off her, but he told her to be quiet. When the victim tried to get up, Mr. Fulton grabbed her arm and told her to go to sleep. Mr. Fulton put his hand down the victim's pants and touched her vagina. Mr. Fulton also pulled the victim's pants down, lay down behind her, and put his penis in her vagina. The victim did not call out for anyone or try to get up because she was scared.

Mr. Fulton heard his daughter call for him from her bedroom, and he jumped up off the couch. The victim took the opportunity to pull up her pants and stood up. Mr. Fulton went to his daughter's bedroom while the victim went into a bathroom. In the bathroom, the victim called her boyfriend, but did not tell him what was wrong. The victim urinated and wiped herself. The victim left the bathroom and went into one of the bedrooms, and again called her boyfriend. During this second call she told him generally what had happened. This call was made after 1:00 a.m. Her boyfriend encouraged her to call her mother. After finishing the call to her boyfriend, the victim called her mother and told her what had happened. Her mother yelled at her.

The victim went back into the bathroom and locked the door. Mrs. Fulton knocked on the door of the bathroom and the victim let her in. Mrs. Fulton spoke on the phone to the victim's mother and victim's mother asked Mrs. Fulton to bring the victim home. Mrs. Fulton yelled at the victim and asked her what had happened, but the victim did not respond.

Mr. Fulton and his wife took the victim home but nothing was said during the car ride on the way to the victim's house. Upon arriving at the victim's house, the victim's mother grabbed her and hugged her and Mr. Fulton kept saying he was sorry. About 20 minutes after the victim arrived home, the victim's mother took her to U.C. Davis Medical Center. Once at that location, the victim told a police officer what happened. The victim also lied, telling the officer that she had not had sex with her boyfriend for several months when she had actually had sex two days earlier. The victim lied because she knew her mother would be angry if she found out about it.

A nurse conducted a rape examination on the victim but did not observe any injuries. The nurse also collected the victim's clothing.

Police officers arrested Mr. Fulton between 5 and 6 a.m. that morning. At the jail, he was taken into a room where pubic hair was collected from him and a swab was taken of his penis. His clothing was also collected as evidence. A criminalist later found DNA from both Mr. Fulton and the victim. The criminalist found sperm on the victim's underwear but was unable to get a DNA sample from the sperm on the underwear.

A second criminalist later retested the penile swabs and underwear. She also found Mr. Fulton's and the victim's DNA on the penile swabs. She was able to obtain DNA samples from the victim's underwear and found both Mr. Fulton's and the victim's DNA to be present.

Mr. Fulton was charged with one count of rape and a second count of a lewd act on a 14-year-old by a person at least 10 years older than the victim.

Prior to trial, Mr. Fulton moved to suppress the pubic hair and penile swab taken from him without a search warrant after his arrest. At that hearing, the parties stipulated to the following facts:

- "The defendant was at the county jail.
- The defendant was taken to a private room with the arresting officer and a female nurse.
- The officer stood in front of the window in the door, the only window in the room.

- The defendant pulled down his pants far enough to expose his genital area.
- The nurse combed his pubic hair and wiped the outside of his penis with a swab. (If there were a foreskin, it would have been pulled back. However, there is no evidence concerning whether the defendant was circumcised.)
- The swab was put in a rape kit and turned over to the officer.
- The evidence was seized because the defendant had been arrested for rape and the victim had alleged that he penetrated her vagina with his penis.
- The alleged rape occurred around midnight, the defendant was arrested about 4:00 or 4:30 that morning, and the evidence was seized at approximately 6:50, two or more hours after he was arrested." **Id**. at 378.

At trial, the defense claimed that there was no sexual act and the victim was lying. The defense attempted to discredit the victim's testimony by showing discrepancies in her statements. Mrs. Fulton's testified that she did not hear her daughter call out to Mr. Fulton in the night and that when she approached the victim in the bathroom, the victim told her that Mr. Fulton had touched her leg and she wanted to go home. Mrs. Fulton also testified that she did not hear Mr. Fulton apologizing when they arrived at the victim's house.

Despite Mr. Fulton's attempts to discredit the victim, a jury convicted him of both counts and the trial court sentenced him to the upper term of eight years in state prison for the rape charge and a concurrent middle term of two years for the lewd act with a 14-year-old child.

On appeal, Mr. Fulton contended that the evidence seized from his penis without a warrant should have been suppressed because it violated the Fourth Amendment. The Attorney General argued that the seizure did not violate the Fourth Amendment because it was incident to a lawful arrest and justified by exigent circumstances. The court agreed with Mr. Fulton that the warrantless seizure violated the Fourth Amendment and the evidence should have been suppressed, but found any error to be harmless beyond a reasonable doubt, based on the facts of this case.

RATIONALE

The appellate court found the seizure of the evidence from Mr. Fulton's penis to be problematic. It found that the collection of the evidence was a major intrusion on Mr. Fulton's dignity. The appellate court pointed out that the prosecution bears the burden of justifying the warrantless seizure and it made no attempt to establish the evidence would have been destroyed absent the warrantless seizure. The court found that the stipulation entered into by the parties at the suppression hearing in the trial court established only what had happened. Specifically, the evidence was taken from Mr. Fulton's penis without a warrant. At the suppression hearing, the prosecution did not put on any evidence concerning the destructibility of the evidence or even that the police had a good faith belief, or any kind of belief for that matter, that the evidence could be destroyed, absent the warrantless seizure.

The appellate court also rejected the Attorney General's argument that the search was lawful as incident to an arrest. The court found that the seizure of evidence from an arrestee's genitalia is a major intrusion on the arrestee's dignity. The court ruled that to justify such a seizure there must be an exigency justifying the seizure, such as officer safety or the imminent destruction of evidence. In this case, the court found no such showing to have been presented.

The court found the error to be harmless in this case for the following reasons: "this was not a simple he-said-she-said case. Disregarding the evidence of D's [the victim's] DNA on the defendant's penis, D's [the victim's] rape allegation was supported by the presence of the defendant's DNA and sperm on D's [the victim's] underwear. The defendant presented evidence concerning transfer of DNA, but only bare speculation supports the view that the defendant's DNA somehow got deposited on D's [the victim's] underwear by some means other than the rape." **Id**. at 379-380. The appellate court then concluded that the jury would have convicted Mr. Fulton even without the evidence collected from his penis, and therefore rejected his contention that his conviction should be reversed for a violation of his Fourth Amendment rights.

Justice Duarte agreed with the majority's decision that no evidence was produced at the suppression hearing showing that there was any risk that the evidence on the defendant's penis would be contaminated during the time it would take to obtain a warrant. However, he disagreed with the majority's position that the error was harmless beyond a reasonable doubt. Justice Duarte believed that it was DNA from Mr. Fulton's penis that undermined the defense case and the jury found the victim credible based in part on evidence and argument regarding the highly persuasive but illegally seized evidence that substantiated the victim's claim of a sexual assault.

2.3.5 -- Bullets in Live Bodies

In **Winston v. Lee** (1985) 470 U.S. 753, the U.S. Supreme Court ruled that the reasonableness of beneath the skin surgical intrusions depends on a case by case analysis. This analysis weighs the individual's privacy and security interests against society's interest in conducting the procedure to obtain evidence for fairly determining the guilt or innocence of the accused. In this case, the Court found that the proposed surgery would violate the defendant's right to be secure in his person and the search would be "unreasonable" under the Fourth Amendment.

In reaching this decision, the Supreme Court ruled that the factors to consider in that balancing test include:

- The presence of probable cause
- The extent that the procedure may threaten the safety or health of the suspect
- The extent of the intrusion upon the individual's dignitary interests in personal privacy and bodily integrity
- The community's interest in fairly and accurately determining guilt or innocence.

FACTS (<u>Winston v. Lee</u> (1985) 470 U.S. 753)

At about 1:00 a.m. on July 18, 1982, Ralph Watkinson was closing his shop for the night. As Mr. Watkinson was locking the door, he saw someone who was armed with a gun coming towards him from across the street. Mr. Watkinson drew his own gun and was told by the suspect to freeze. Mr. Watkinson fired at the suspect, who fired back at him. Mr. Watkinson was hit in the legs. The suspect, who appeared to be wounded in the left side, ran away.

The police were called and Mr. Watkinson was taken by ambulance to the Medical College of Virginia (MCV) Hospital emergency room. About 20 minutes later, the police responded to another call about eight blocks away from the shooting. The defendant, Rudolph Lee, was found to be suffering from a gunshot wound to the left chest area that he claimed was done by two individuals who attempted to rob him. Mr. Lee was taken to MCV by ambulance. When Mr. Lee entered the emergency room, Mr. Watkinson saw him and said, "That's the man that shot me." Further police investigation led them to reject Mr. Lee's story and arrest him for attempted robbery, malicious wounding and two counts of using a firearm in the commission of a felony.

The Commonwealth of Virginia moved in state court for an order directing Mr. Lee to undergo surgery to remove an object, believed to be a bullet from the victim's gun, from under Mr. Lee's left collarbone. The court held several evidentiary hearings.

At the first hearing, the State's expert said that the surgical procedure would take 45 minutes, involve a 3 to 4 percent chance of temporary nerve damage, a 1 percent chance of permanent nerve damage, and a one tenth of one percent chance of death.

At the second hearing, the State's expert said that after re-examining Mr. Lee, the expert discovered that the bullet was not "back inside close to the nerves and arteries," but "just beneath the skin." The surgery would now only require an incision slightly bigger than an inch, could be performed under local anesthesia, and would result in "no danger on the basis that there's no general anesthesia employed." The trial judge granted the motion to compel surgery.

Mr. Lee sought a Writ from the Virginia Supreme Court, which was denied. The Federal Court also refused to issue a preliminary injunction.

On October 18, 1982, just before the surgery was scheduled, the surgeon ordered X-rays, which now revealed that the bullet was in fact lodged approximately one inch deep in muscular tissue in Mr. Lee's chest. This was substantially deeper than was thought when the State Court issued the removal order. The surgeon now thought that a general anesthetic would be desirable for medical reasons.

Mr. Lee moved the trial court for a rehearing based on new evidence. The trial court denied a new hearing and the Virginia Supreme Court affirmed that denial. Mr. Lee returned to Federal Court, where the District Court held an evidentiary hearing and then issued an order enjoining the surgery. A divided panel of the 4th Circuit affirmed the denial. The U.S. Supreme Court granted a writ of certiorari to resolve the issue.

RATIONALE

> A compelled surgical intrusion into an individual's body for evidence, however, implicates expectations of privacy and security of such magnitude that the intrusion may be 'unreasonable' even if likely to produce evidence of a crime. (**Winston v. Lee** at 759.)

The Court found that the medical risks were uncertain, that the intrusion into Mr. Lee's privacy interests and bodily integrity were severe, and that the State had substantial evidence to prove that Mr. Lee had assaulted Mr. Watkinson.

2.3.6 -- Stomach Pumping

In **Rochin v. California** (1952) 342 U.S. 165, the U.S. Supreme Court unanimously ruled that the forced pumping of Mr. Rochin's stomach to recover narcotics violated the Fourth Amendment.

FACTS (Rochin v. California (1952) 342 U.S. 165)

Three Los Angeles County Deputy Sheriffs had information that Antonio Rochin was selling narcotics. On the morning of July 1, 1949, the deputies went to Rochin's house, where he lived with his mother, common-law wife, brothers and sisters. Upon arrival, the Deputies found the outside door open.

After entering the house, the deputies forced open the door on Mr. Rochin's second floor room. Mr. Rochin was partially dressed and sitting on the side of the bed, while his wife was lying on the bed. On the nightstand next to the bed, the deputies saw two capsules, which later turned out to be morphine. When the deputies saw the capsules, they asked, "Whose stuff is this?" Mr. Rochin seized the capsules, put them in his mouth, and despite the efforts of the three deputies who pounced on him, ultimately swallowed them.

Mr. Rochin was handcuffed and taken to the hospital. Acting under the direction of one of the deputies, a doctor forced an emetic solution through a tube into Mr. Rochin's stomach against his will. The forced "stomach pumping" produced vomiting, which led to the recovery of the two morphine capsules. The Court convicted Mr. Rochin after a trial and sentenced him to 60 days in jail for possessing morphine.

The California Court of Appeal upheld the conviction, but noted that the deputies were guilty of unlawfully breaking into Mr. Rochin's room, assaulting and battering him both in his room and at the hospital, and of falsely imprisoning him and torturing him at the hospital. While the California Supreme Court refused to grant a hearing, the U.S. Supreme Court granted certiorari to address the issues raised.

RATIONALE

The Court found that the conduct of the police "shocked the conscience" of the community and offended the Due Process Clause of the U.S. Constitution. (**Rochin** at 172.)

The Court found the conduct so brutal and offensive that it violated traditional ideas of fair play and decency.

The Court noted that:

> Illegally breaking into the privacy of the petitioner, the struggle to open his mouth and remove what was there, the forcible extraction of his stomach's contents – this course of proceeding by agents of government to obtain evidence is bound to offend even hardened sensibilities. They are methods too close to the rack and the screw to permit of constitutional differentiation. (**Rochin** at 172.)

2.3.7 -- Choking and the Use of Force

Law enforcement can use reasonable force to prevent a suspect from destroying contraband by swallowing it.

In **People v. Cappellia** (1989) 208 Cal.App.3d 1331, the Court of Appeal upheld the search and seizure of contraband from the defendant's mouth because the police used minimal force to prevent the defendant from swallowing the evidence and did not choke the defendant.

FACTS (People v. Cappellia (1989) 208 Cal.App.3d 1331)

On December 19, 1985, undercover Huntington Police Department Officer Gildea met with defendant Richard Cappellia to buy heroin. The defendant agreed to sell heroin to the officer the next day if the officer would "slam" or inject the drug in front of him.

On December 20, 1985, when Officer Gildea returned, the defendant repeated that he did not trust Officer Gildea and wanted to see him "slam." He knew police officers would not inject drugs. Officer Gildea agreed to do so, but only at his house in Santa Ana.

As they prepared to leave for the officer's home, the defendant returned to his barbershop and removed a toilet paper roll from a shelf. Officer Gildea saw "the plunger and the body of the syringe protruding from the . . . open end of the toilet paper roll" on the ride towards Santa Ana. While enroute, the defendant also opened up a small cardboard box and showed Officer Gildea three small bindles of tar heroin wrapped in cellophane, which the officer thought were not sealed, but merely twisted closed.

After arriving at a house on 9th Street in Santa Ana, the defendant saw a man, later identified as Officer Poe, on a fence in front of the house, and asked Officer Gildea about him. The defendant commented that he did not like "fixing" in front of strangers. Officer Gildea told the defendant that the man, actually undercover Officer Poe, was merely a friend who was there to drop merchandise off and then leave. Officer Gildea observed the defendant putting the three bindles in his mouth, which he had removed from a matchbox, then, put the toilet paper roll in the glove compartment. Officer Gildea and the defendant got out of the car, and began to walk along the driveway, with Officer Gildea in front. Officer Poe joined in behind him.

Officer Gildea abruptly turned around, identified himself as a police officer and yelled to Officer Poe that the defendant "had it in his mouth." As the defendant tried to run away, both officers grabbed him around the neck being careful not to use a carotid restraint or a choke hold. Officer Gildea grabbed the lower part of the neck with his right hand "to prevent him [the defendant] from swallowing and to keep his Adam's apple from going down." Officer Gildea's hand was in a V-shape, with the thumb on one side of the defendant's throat and the rest of his fingers on the other side.

A struggle ensued, with all parties going to the ground. Officer Gildea noted that the defendant appeared to be chewing something and was trying to get the object to the back of his mouth so he could swallow it. Officer Gildea reached into the defendant's mouth to retrieve the object(s), but the defendant bit him.

After a two minute struggle, the officers subdued the defendant and handcuffed him. Officer Gildea then let go of the defendant's throat and told him to open his mouth. The defendant complied and Officer Gildea retrieved two bindles of heroin. Upon examination, the officers found chew marks and blood on the inside and outside of the bindles.

The defendant neither stopped breathing nor lost consciousness during the struggle nor did he faint, gasp for air or groan in pain after the throat hold was released. However, he did suffer a bloody nose which was due largely to his efforts to destroy the evidence and elude arrest.

Officer Poe testified that he did not put pressure on the carotid artery, but did place his thumbs on the back of the defendant's neck and his fingers around the front of the defendant's Adam's apple.

After a jury trial, the defendant was found guilty of offering to sell heroin.

RATIONALE

The officers had probable cause for the search since they saw the defendant put the narcotics in his mouth.

Exigent circumstances existed such that an immediate search was necessary to prevent destruction of the evidence and to protect the defendant's safety.

In **People v. Fulkman** (1991) 235 Cal.App.3d 555, the Court of Appeal ruled that the police lawfully removed a wad of masking tape from the defendant's mouth and did not choke him in the course of retrieving that object.

FACTS (People v. Fulkman (1991) 235 Cal.App.3d 555)

In January 1988, Riverside Police Officers arrived at the residence of Michael Fulkman for the purpose of serving a drug search warrant. The police observed the defendant, with amputated legs, seated in a wheelchair in the rear patio of the residence. They saw him place a two-inch wad of masking tape into his mouth, which was a little bigger than a golf ball.

During a struggle to remove the masking tape, the defendant fell out of his chair and landed on the cement. To prevent the defendant from swallowing the masking tape, Detective Meier applied pressure to the defendant's chin and throat with his hand, placing two or three fingers on either side of the defendant's neck, without choking him.

The officers yelled at the defendant on three or four occasions to spit out the wad of masking tape, which he refused to do. Officer Delarosa assisted the other officer by inserting the capped end of a Bic brand pen into the corner of the defendant's mouth and he used a sweeping motion to pry the object out of the defendant's mouth. Officer Delarosa retrieved a wad of masking tape which contained 16 balloons with a total of 3.5 grams of heroin.

The defendant later testified that he was trying to swallow the wad of tape and that it was partially down his throat when the officers tried to retrieve it. After the court denied the defendant's suppression motion he changed his plea to guilty of possession for sale of heroin and was placed on probation and given two days credit for time served.

RATIONALE

The officers did not apply a choke hold to the defendant and used no more force than was necessary to overcome the defendant's resistance. The police procedure did not threaten the defendant's health or safety.

2.3.8 -- Strip Searches for Misdemeanor and Infraction Offenses

In 1984, the California Legislature enacted Penal Code 4030, which is entitled "Strip and body cavity searches; limitation; application; definitions; conditions; damages." The section has not been amended since its enactment.

In subsection (a), the Legislature unmistakably stated its concerns and intentions:

> The Legislature finds and declares that law enforcement policies and practices for conducting strip or body cavity searches of detained persons vary widely throughout California. Consequently, some people have been arbitrarily subjected to unnecessary strip and body cavity searches after arrests for minor misdemeanor and infraction offenses. Some present search practices violate state and federal constitutional rights to privacy and freedom from unreasonable searches and seizures.
>
> It is the intent of the Legislature in enacting this section to protect the state and federal constitutional rights of the people of California by establishing a statewide policy strictly limiting strip and body cavity searches.

2.3.8.1 – Application of Penal Code 4030

Subsection (b) limits the provisions of this statute to cases involving strip searches of "prearraignment detainees arrested for infraction or misdemeanor offenses and to any minor detained prior to a detention hearing on the grounds that he or she is a person described in" California Welfare and Institutions Sections 300, 601 or 602, and "alleged to have committed a misdemeanor or infraction offense."

Section 4030 does "not apply to any person in the custody of the Director of the Department of Corrections or the Director of the Youth Authority."

Subsection (e) specifically states that when a person is arrested and taken into custody, that person may be subjected to the following types of searches "in order to discover and retrieve concealed weapons and contraband substances prior to being placed in a booking cell":

- Patdown searches
- Metal detector searches
- Thorough clothing searches.

2.3.8.2 – Definitions

Subsection (c) states that "'[s]trip search' means a search which requires a person to remove or arrange some or all of his or her clothing so as to permit a visual inspection of the underclothing, breasts, buttocks, or genitalia of such person."

Subsection (d) contains definitions of the terms "body cavity," visual body cavity search" and "physical body cavity search."

Subsection (d)(1) states that "'[b]ody cavity' only means the stomach or rectal cavity of a person, and vagina of a female person."

Subsection (d)(2) states that a "'[v]isual body cavity search' means visual inspection of a body cavity."

Subsection (d)(3) states that a "'[p]hysical body cavity search' means physical intrusion into a body cavity for the purpose of discovering any object concealed in the body cavity."

2.3.8.3 – Physical Body Cavity Searches Require a Search Warrant

Penal Code 4030(h) specifically prohibits any person arrested for a misdemeanor or infraction offense, including a minor as defined in California Welfare and Institutions Sections 300, 601 or 602, from being

> subjected to a physical body cavity search except under the authority of a search warrant issued by a magistrate specifically authorizing the physical body cavity search.

Penal Code 4030(f) does allow for a strip search or visual body cavity search (but not a physical body cavity search) prior to placement in the general jail population of a person arrested and held in custody on a misdemeanor or infraction offense or a juvenile as defined in California Welfare and Institutions Sections 300, 601 or 602 if

> a peace officer has determined there is reasonable suspicion based on specific and articulable facts to believe such person is concealing a weapon or contraband, and a strip search will result in the discovery of the weapon or contraband.

Before a strip search or visual body cavity search or both can occur, prior written authorization of the supervising officer on duty is required.

> The authorization shall include the specific and articulable facts and circumstances upon which the reasonable suspicion determination was made by the supervisor.

Penal Code 4030(f) provides an exception to the rule governing strip searches or visual body cavity searches (but not a physical body cavity search) for both adults and minors if the misdemeanor or infraction offense involves weapons, controlled substances or violence. An exception to the rule also exists if the minor is alleged to have committed felonies.

2.3.8.4 – Rules Regarding the Performance of the Strip Search

Per Penal Code 4030(j), "Persons conducting a strip search or a visual body cavity search shall not touch the breasts, buttocks, or genitalia of the person being searched."

Penal Code 4030(k) requires that

> [a] physical body cavity search shall be conducted under sanitary conditions, and only by a physician, nurse practitioner, registered nurse, licensed vocational nurse or emergency medical technician Level II licensed to practice in this state. Any physician engaged in providing health care to detainees and inmates of the facility may conduct physical body cavity searches.

Penal Code 4030(l) requires that

> [a]ll persons conducting or otherwise present during a strip search or visual or physical body cavity search shall be of the same sex as the person being searched, except for physicians or licensed medical personnel.

Penal Code 4030(m) requires that

> [a]ll strip, visual and physical body cavity searches shall be conducted in an area of privacy so that the search cannot be observed by persons not participating in the search. Persons are considered to be participating in the search if their official duties relative to search procedure require them to be present at the time the search is conducted.

2.3.8.5 – Record Keeping

Penal Code 4030(i) requires that a copy of the written authorizations required by subsections (f) and 4030(g) and the search warrant required under subsection (h) "shall be placed in the agency's records and made available on request, to the person searched or his or her authorized representative."

Subsection (i) also requires that if a strip, visual or body search is conducted, the following information be recorded and "placed in the agency's records and made available, upon request, to the person searched or his or her authorized representative":

- "The time, date and place of the search"
- "The name and sex of the person conducting the search"
- "A statement of the results of the search, including a list of any items removed from the person searched."

2.3.8.6 – Placement in the General Jail Population

Penal Code 4030(g)(1) prohibits any one "arrested and held in custody" for "a misdemeanor or infraction offense not involving weapons, controlled substances or violence" from being confined in the general jail population unless all the below listed factors are true:

1. "The person is not cited and released"
2. The person is not released on his or her own recognizance pursuant to" Penal Code 1318 through 1319.5.
3. "The person is not able to post bail within a reasonable time not less than three hours."

The Legislature created an exception to this jail housing rule in 4030(g)(2) if "a documented emergency exists and there is no reasonable alternative to such placement." However, a person can only be placed in the general jail population "upon prior written authorization documenting the specific facts and circumstances of the emergency. The written authorization shall be signed by the uniformed supervisor of the facility or by a uniformed watch commander."

Additionally, "[a]ny person confined in the general jail population [under this exception] shall retain all rights to release on citation, his or her own recognizance, or bail which were preempted as a consequence of the emergency."

2.3.8.7 – Civil and Criminal Liability

Subsection (n) commands that

> [a] person who knowingly and willfully authorizes or conducts a strip, visual or physical body cavity search in violation of this section is guilty of a misdemeanor.

The Legislature explicitly stated in subsection (o) that it was not limiting criminal prosecution or civil liability for violating this section only to the provisions of Penal Code 4030 when it stated:

> [n]othing in this section shall be construed as limiting any common law or statutory rights of any person regarding any action for damages or injunctive relief, or as precluding the prosecution under another provision of law of any peace officer or other person who has violated this section.

The Legislature also stated in subsection (p) that

> [a]ny person who suffers damage or harm as a result of a violation of this section may bring a civil action to recover actual damages, or one thousand dollars ($1,000), whichever is greater. In addition, the court may, in its discretion, award punitive damages, equitable relief as it deems necessary and proper, and costs, including reasonable attorney's fees.

2.4 – Cell Phones

On June 25, 2014, the U.S. Supreme Court handed down its landmark decision in **Riley v. California** (2014) 573 U.S. ___; 134 S.Ct. 2473 (companion case **United States v. Wurie** (2013) 728 F.3d 1), in which it addressed—for the first time—the Fourth Amendment and cell phone searches. The Supreme Court reached the same result in both *Riley* and *Wurie*. Chief Justice John Roberts wrote the Court's opinion, with Justice Alito writing a separate, concurring opinion.

The rule unanimously enunciated by the U.S. Supreme Court is that the police **may not** generally search through digital information on a seized cell phone, incident to a lawful arrest, without first obtaining a search warrant. The holding specifically rejected the rationale put forth by some lower courts that allowed the search of a cell phone, incident to a lawful arrest. In reaching its decision, the Court decided that one's privacy interests in the material stored on a cell phone outweighed any justification put forth by the United States and California governments in support of a warrantless search exception.

The Court noted in the context of privacy issues how unique cell phones are in the digital age compared to other physical items people normally carry on their person:

> The storage capacity of cell phones has several interrelated consequences for privacy. First, a cell phone collects in one place many distinct types of information—an address, a note, a prescription, a bank statement, a video—that reveal much more in combination than any isolated record. Second, a cell phone's capacity allows even just one type of information to convey far more than previously possible. The sum of an individual's private life can be reconstructed through a thousand photographs labeled with dates, locations, and descriptions; the same cannot be said of a photograph or two of loved ones tucked into a wallet. Third, the data on a phone can date back to the purchase of the phone, or even earlier. A person might carry in his pocket a slip of paper reminding him to call Mr. Jones; he would not carry a record of all his communications with Mr. Jones for the past several months as would routinely be kept on a phone.
>
> Finally, there is an element of pervasiveness that characterizes cell phones but not physical records. Prior to the digital age, people did not typically carry a cache of sensitive personal information with them as they went about their day. Now it is the person who is not carrying a cell phone, with all that it contains, who is the exception. According to one poll, nearly three-quarters

> of smart phone[5] users report being within five feet of their phones most of the time, with 12% admitting that they even use their phones in the shower. [Citation.] . . .Today, by contrast, it is no exaggeration to say that many of the more than 90% of American adults who own a cell phone keep on their person a digital record of nearly every aspect of their lives—from the mundane to the intimate. [Citation.] Allowing the police to scrutinize such records on a routine basis is quite different from allowing them to search a personal item or two in the occasional case.
>
> Although the data stored on a cell phone is distinguished from physical records by quantity alone, certain types of data are also qualitatively different. An Internet search and browsing history, for example, can be found on an Internet-enabled phone and could reveal an individual's private interests or concerns—perhaps a search for certain symptoms of disease, coupled with frequent visits to WebMD. Data on a cell phone can also reveal where a person has been. Historic location information is a standard feature on many smart phones and can reconstruct someone's specific movements down to the minute, not only around town but also within a particular building. [Citation.] . . .
>
> Indeed, a cell phone search would typically expose to the government far *more* than the most exhaustive search of a house: A phone not only contains in digital form many sensitive records previously found in the home; it also contains a broad array of private information never found in a home in any form—unless the phone is.

(**Riley**, **supra**, at 2489–2491.)

Chief Justice Roberts acknowledged the impact the Court's ruling would have on law enforcement, but explained why the rule announced was necessary:

> We cannot deny that our decision today will have an impact on the ability of law enforcement to combat crime. Cell phones have become important tools in facilitating coordination and communication among members of criminal enterprises, and can provide valuable incriminating information about dangerous criminals. Privacy comes at a cost.
>
> Our holding, of course, is not that the information on a cell phone is immune from search; it is instead that a warrant is generally

[5] **Riley**, **supra**, at 2480. The Court defined a "smart phone" as "a cell phone with a broad range of other functions based on advanced computing capability, large storage capacity, and Internet connectivity."

> required before such a search, even when a cell phone is seized incident to arrest.

(**Id**. at 2493.)

In his concurring opinion, Justice Alito emphasized that he was not convinced that the search incident to arrest doctrine was based exclusively or primarily on the need to protect the arresting officer's safety and the need to prevent the destruction of evidence. He also said that while he agreed with the Court's decision, he would reconsider the issue if either Congress or state legislatures enacted legislation that drew reasonable distinctions based on categories of information or other variables. He cited the example of Title III of the Omnibus Crime Control and Safe Streets Act of 1968 passed by Congress, in response to the Court's decision in **Katz v. United States** (1967) 389 U.S. 347, holding that electronic surveillance constituted a search even when no property interest was invaded.

FACTS (Riley v. California (2014) 573 U.S. ___; 134 S.Ct. 2473 [companion case United States v. Wurie (2013) 728 F.3d])

A police officer stopped David Riley for driving with expired registration tags. In the course of the stop, the officer learned that Mr. Riley's license had been suspended. Accordingly, the officer impounded Mr. Riley's car pursuant to departmental policy. The officer conducted an inventory search of the car. During that search, the officer found two loaded handguns concealed under the car's hood.

Mr. Riley's person was searched incident to arrest and the officer found evidence associating him with the "Bloods" street gang. The officer also seized a "smart" cell phone from Mr. Riley's pants pocket. The officer accessed information on the phone and saw that the letters "CK" preceded some words—a label the officer believed stood for "Crip Killers," as well as a slang term for members of the Bloods gang.

At the police station, approximately two hours after Mr. Riley's arrest, a detective specializing in gangs conducted a further examination of the phone's contents. The detective testified at the suppression hearing that he "went through" the phone "looking for evidence, because . . . gang members will often video themselves with guns or take pictures of themselves with the guns." (*Riley, supra,* at 2480–2481.) Although there were a lot of things on the cell phone, the detective's attention was attracted to particular files including videos of young men sparring while someone yelled encouragement using the moniker "Blood." On the phone, officers found photographs of Mr. Riley standing in front of a car that they suspected had been involved in a shooting a few weeks earlier.

Mr. Riley was ultimately charged—in connection with that earlier shooting—with firing at an occupied vehicle, assault with a semiautomatic firearm, and attempted murder. The charging document also alleged that those crimes had been committed for the benefit of a criminal street gang, which is an aggravating factor under California law and carries an enhanced sentence.

Mr. Riley asked the trial court to suppress all the evidence obtained from his cell phone, arguing that the search of the cell phone violated his Fourth Amendment rights because the search had been conducted without a warrant and was not otherwise justified by exigent circumstances. The trial court rejected Mr. Riley's argument and denied his motion to suppress the evidence. At his trial, officers testified about the photographs and videos found on the cell phone, with some of the photographs even being admitted into evidence. A jury convicted Mr. Riley on all counts, and the court sentenced him to an enhanced sentence of 15 years to life.

Mr. Riley appealed that verdict to the California Court of Appeal, which affirmed the case relying on the California Supreme Court's decision in **People v. Diaz** (2011) 51 Cal.4th 84. The California Supreme Court denied Mr. Riley's petition for review, but the U.S. Supreme Court granted certiorari.

In the **Wurie** case, officers were performing routine surveillance when they saw Brima Wurie make an apparent drug sale from a car. Mr. Wurie was arrested and taken to the police station. At the station, officers seized two cell phones from his person. The cell phone that formed the basis of the appeal was a "flip phone."[6]

Approximately five to ten minutes after arriving at the station, the officers noticed that the phone was repeatedly receiving calls from a source identified as "my house" on the phone's external screen. A few minutes later, the officers opened the phone and saw a photograph of a woman and a baby set as the phone's wallpaper. The officers pressed one button on the phone to access the call log, then another button to determine the phone number associated with the "my house" label. The officers then used an online phone directory to trace that phone number to an apartment building.

When the officers went to the apartment building, they saw Mr. Wurie's name on a mailbox and observed a woman, through a window, who resembled the woman in the photograph on Mr. Wurie's phone. The officers secured the apartment and obtained a search warrant. During the service of the search warrant, the officers seized 215 grams of crack cocaine (approximately 7.5 ounces), marijuana, drug paraphernalia, a firearm and ammunition, and a sum of cash. Mr. Wurie was charged with distributing crack cocaine, possessing crack cocaine with the intent to distribute it, and being a felon in possession of a firearm and ammunition. Mr. Wurie moved to suppress the evidence in the district court, but the court denied his

[6] **Id**. at 2481. The Court defined a flip phone as "a kind of phone that is flipped open for use and that generally has a smaller range of features than a smart phone."

motion. At trial, a jury convicted Mr. Wurie of all three counts and the court sentenced him to 262 months (approximately 21 years and 9 months) in federal prison.

A divided panel of the First Circuit Court of Appeal reversed the denial of the suppression motion. The First Circuit ruled that "cell phones are distinct from other physical possessions that may be searched incident to arrest without a warrant, because of the amount of personal data cell phones contain and the negligible threat they pose to law enforcement interests." (**Riley**, **supra**, at 2482, citing **Wurie**, **supra**, at 8–11.) The United States appealed and the Supreme Court granted certiorari.

RATIONALE

In reaching its decision that the search was unlawful in both cases, the Court relied on three precedents: **Chimel v. California** (1969) 395 U.S. 752; **United States v. Robinson** (1973) 414 U.S. 218; and **Arizona v. Gant** (2009) 556 U.S. 332.[7] Chief Justice Roberts observed:

> When an arrest is made, it is reasonable for the arresting officer to search the person arrested in order to remove any weapons that the latter might seek to use in order to resist arrest or affect his escape. Otherwise, the officer's safety might well be endangered, and the arrest itself frustrated. In addition, it is entirely reasonable for the arresting officer to search for and seize any evidence on the arrestee's person in order to prevent its concealment or destruction . . .

(**Riley**, **supra**, at 2483, quoting **Chimel**, **supra**, at 762–763.)

In **Robinson**, the Supreme Court applied the **Chimel** analysis in the context of the search of an arrestee's person. The court concluded in that case that the search of Mr. Robinson was reasonable even though there was no concern about the loss of evidence, and the arresting officer had no specific concern that Mr. Robinson might be armed.

Chief Justice Roberts observed that the search incident to arrest doctrine now required the Court to apply that doctrine to modern cell phones, which

---

[7] In a 5–4 decision in **Arizona v. Gant** (2009) 556 U.S. 332, whose facts are similar to those in **New York v. Belton** (1981) 453 U.S. 454, the U.S. Supreme Court modified its earlier holding in **Belton** in two significant ways: First, it ruled that "**Belton** does not authorize a vehicle search incident to a recent occupant's arrest after the arrestee has been secured and cannot access the interior of the vehicle." **Gant**, **supra**, at 355. By comparison, when the arrestee is unsecured and within reaching distance of a car's passenger compartment, such a search is allowed under the twin rationales of **Chimel v. California** (1969) 395 U.S. 752. In so ruling, the Court effectively ended law enforcement's common practice of automatically searching the passenger compartment of a vehicle incident to an occupant's lawful custodial arrest. Second, it held that "circumstances unique to the automobile context justify a search incident to arrest when it *is reasonable to believe that evidence of the offense of arrest might be found in the vehicle*." **Gant**, **supra**, at 335 [italics added].

he observed were "such a pervasive and insistent part of daily life that the proverbial visitor from Mars might conclude they were an important feature of human anatomy." (*Riley, supra,* at 2484.)

Chief Justice Roberts observed,

> Absent more precise guidance from the founding era, we generally determine whether to exempt a given type of search from the warrant requirement "by assessing, on the one hand, the degree to which it intrudes upon an individual's privacy and, on the other, the degree to which it is needed for the promotion of legitimate governmental interests." **Wyoming v. Houghton** (1999) 526 U.S. 295, 300.
>
> While **Robinson's** categorical rule strikes the appropriate balance in the context of physical objects, neither of its rationales has much force with respect to digital content on cell phones.

(**Riley**, **supra**, at 2484.)

While the two risks identified in **Chimel** are present in all custodial arrests, there are no comparable risks when the search is of digital data. **Robinson** regarded any privacy interest retained by an individual after arrest as significantly diminished due to the arrest itself. "Cell phones, however, place vast quantities of personal information literally in the hands of individuals. A search of the information on a cell phone bears little resemblance to the type of brief physical search considered in **Robinson**." (**Riley**, **supra**, at 2485.)

The Court therefore declined to extend the **Robinson** rule to cell phone data searches and instead held that officers must generally secure a warrant before they conduct a cell phone search.

Chief Justice Roberts observed,

> Digital data stored on a cell phone cannot itself be used as a weapon to harm an arresting officer or to effectuate the arrestee's escape. Law enforcement officers remain free to examine the physical aspects of a phone to ensure that it will not be used as a weapon—say, to determine whether there is a razor blade hidden between the phone and its case. Once an officer has secured a phone and eliminated any potential physical threats, however, data on the phone can endanger no one.

(Riley, **supra**, at 2485.)

In the Court's view, the interest in protecting officers' safety does not justify dispensing with the warrant requirement across the board as it relates to cell phones.

Chief Justice Roberts stated that "once law enforcement officers have secured a cell phone, there is no longer any risk that the arrestee himself will be able to delete incriminating data from the phone." (**Id.** at 2486.)

The Supreme Court rejected the United States and California's argument that information on the cell phone may nevertheless be vulnerable to two types of evidence destruction unique to digital data: remote wiping and data encryption.

> With respect to remote wiping, the Government's primary concern turns on the actions of third parties who are not present at the scene of the arrest. And data encryption is even further afield. There, the government focuses on the ordinary operation of a phone's security features, apart from *any* active attempt by a defendant or his associates to conceal or destroy evidence upon arrest.

(**Id.**)

Chief Justice Roberts noted that the Court had been given little reason to believe that either problem was a prevalent one, and stated:

> [I]n situations in which an arrest might trigger a remote-wipe attempt or an officer discovers an unlocked phone, it is not clear that the ability to conduct a warrantless search would make much of a difference. The need to effect the arrest, secure the scene, and tend to other pressing matters means that law enforcement officers may well not be able to turn their attention to a cell phone right away.

(**Id**. at 2487.)

With respect to remote wiping of a cell phone, the Chief Justice pointed out that,

> . . . law enforcement is not without specific means to address the threat. Remote wiping can be fully prevented by disconnecting a phone from the network. There are at least two simple ways to do this: First, law enforcement officers can turn the phone off or remove its battery. Second, if they are concerned about encryption or other potential problems, they can leave a phone powered on and place it in an enclosure that isolates the phone from radio waves.

(**Id.**)

The Court also specifically referred to "Faraday bags":[8]

---

[8] **Riley**, **supra**, at 2487. The Court described Faraday bags as "essentially sandwich bags made of aluminum foil: cheap, lightweight, and easy to use."

> If "the police are truly confronted with a 'now or never' situation,"—for example, circumstances suggesting that a defendant's phone will be the target of an imminent remote-wipe attempt—they may be able to rely on exigent circumstances to search the phone immediately. [Citation] Or, if officers happen to seize a phone in an unlocked state, they may be able to disable a phone's automatic-lock feature in order to prevent the phone from locking and encrypting data. [Citation] Such a preventive measure could be analyzed under the principles set forth in our decision in [**Illinois v.**] **McArthur** [(2001)] 531 U.S. 326,[9] which approved officers' reasonable steps to secure a scene to preserve evidence while they awaited a warrant.

(**Riley**, **supra**, at 2487–2488.)

The Court also rejected the United States' argument that a search of all data stored on a cell phone is "materially indistinguishable" from searches of physical items. Chief Justice Roberts responded to the argument by noting that the argument was

> . . . like saying a ride on horseback is materially indistinguishable from a flight to the moon. Both are ways of getting from point A to point B, but little else justifies lumping them together. Modern cell phones, as a category, implicate privacy concerns far beyond those implicated by the search of a cigarette pack, a wallet, or a purse. A conclusion that inspecting the contents of an arrestee's pockets works no substantial additional intrusion on privacy beyond the arrest itself may make sense as applied to physical items, but any extension of that reasoning to digital data has to rest on its own bottom.

(**Id**. at 2488–2489.)

> Cell phones differ in both a quantitative and qualitative sense from other objects that might be kept on an arrestee's person. The term "cell phone" is itself misleading shorthand; many of these devices are in fact minicomputers that also happen to have the capacity to be used as a telephone. They could just as easily be called cameras, video players, rolodexes, calendars, tape

[9] In an 8–1 opinion by the U.S. Supreme Court in **Illinois v. McArthur** (2001) 531 U.S. 326, with only Justice Stevens dissenting, the Court ruled that it was reasonable for the police to prohibit the defendant from re-entering his trailer without the police accompanying him, while a search warrant was being sought for the trailer. The Supreme Court ruled that the Fourth Amendment did not prohibit the type of seizure done by the police in this case. Rather than adopting a per se rule of unreasonableness, the court balanced the privacy-related interests of the individual and the law enforcement-related interests to determine if the intrusion was unreasonable.

recorders, libraries, diaries, albums, televisions, maps, or newspapers.

One of the most notable distinguishing features of modern cell phones is their immense storage capacity. Before cell phones, a search of a person was limited by physical realities and tended as a general matter to constitute only a narrow intrusion on privacy. [Citation]

But the possible intrusion on privacy is not physically limited in the same way when it comes to cell phones. The current top-selling smart phone has a standard capacity of 16 gigabytes (and is available with up to 64 gigabytes). Sixteen gigabytes translates to millions of pages of text, thousands of pictures, or hundreds of videos. ... [Citation] Even the most basic phones that sell for less than $20 might hold photographs, picture messages, text messages, Internet browsing history, a calendar, a thousand-entry phone book, and so on. [Citation] We expect that the gulf between physical practicability and digital capacity will only continue to widen in the future.

(**Id**. at 2489.)

To further complicate the scope of the privacy interests at stake, the data a user views on many modern cell phones may not in fact be stored on the device itself. Treating a cell phone as a container whose contents may be searched incident to an arrest is a bit strained as an initial matter. ... [Citation] Cloud computing is the capacity of Internet-connected devices to display data stored on remote servers rather than on the device itself. Cell phone users often may not know whether particular information is stored on the device or in the cloud, and it generally makes little difference. [Citation] Moreover, the same type of data may be stored locally on the device for one user and in the cloud for another.

The United States concedes that the search incident to arrest exception may not be stretched to cover a search of files accessed remotely—that is, a search of files stored in the cloud. [Citation] Such a search would be like finding a key in a suspect's pocket and arguing that it allowed law enforcement to unlock and search a house. But officers searching a phone's data would not typically know whether the information they are viewing was stored locally at the time of the arrest or has been pulled from the cloud.

(**Id**. at 2491.)

The Court further rejected several fallback positions of the United States and California that would have allowed a warrantless search of a cell phone under certain circumstances. The Court reasoned, "[e]ach of the proposals is flawed and contravenes our general preference to provide clear guidance to law enforcement through categorical rules." (**Id**.)

The first proposal was based on **Arizona v. Gant**, and would allow for a search of a cell phone whenever it is reasonable to believe that the phone contains evidence of the crime for which a suspect has been arrested. An example would be the arrest of a drug dealer who was driving a vehicle at the time of the arrest and was in possession of a cell phone. This proposal—and the reasons for its rejection—will be discussed in more detail in Section 2.4.1, Probable Cause and Vehicle Searches.

The United States also proposed a rule that would restrict the scope of a cell phone search to those areas of the phone where an officer reasonably believes that information relevant to the crime, the arrestee's identity, or officer safety will be discovered.

In rejecting that proposed rule, the Court stated:

> This approach would again impose few meaningful constraints on officers. The proposed categories would sweep in a great deal of information, and officers would not always be able to discern in advance what information would be found where.

(**Id**. at 2492.)

The final proposal put forth by the United States and rejected by the Court was that officers should always be allowed to search a phone's call log. In rejecting this proposal, Chief Justice Roberts observed:

> [C]all logs typically contain more than just phone numbers; they include any identifying information that an individual might add, such as the label "my house" in Wurie's case.

(**Id**. at 2493.)

At oral argument, California suggested a different limiting principle where officers could search cell phone data if they could have obtained the same information from a pre-digital counterpart. In rejecting this approach, the Court stated:

> [T]he fact that a search in the pre-digital era could have turned up a photograph or two in a wallet does not justify a search of thousands of photos in a digital gallery. The fact that someone could have tucked a paper bank statement in a pocket does not justify a search of every bank statement from the last five years. And to make matters worse, such an analogue test would allow law enforcement to search a range of items contained on a phone, even though people would be unlikely to carry such a variety of information in physical form. In Riley's case, for

> example, it is implausible that he would have strolled around with video tapes, photo albums, and an address book all crammed into his pockets. But because each of those items has a pre-digital analogue, police under California's proposal would be able to search a phone for all of those items—a significant diminution of privacy.
>
> In addition, an analogue test would launch courts on a difficult line-drawing expedition to determine which digital files are comparable to physical records. Is an email equivalent to a letter? Is a voicemail equivalent to a phone message slip? It is not clear how officers could make these kinds of decisions before conducting a search, or how courts would apply the proposed rule after the fact.

(**Id**.)

In a 5-2 decision in the case of **People v. Diaz** (2011) 51 Cal.4th 84, the California Supreme Court affirmed the Court of Appeal decision allowing the admissibility of evidence obtained from a cell phone 90 minutes after the defendant's arrest on drug charges. However, in upholding the admissibility of the evidence derived from a search of the cell phone under the "search incident to arrest" theory, that decision is now in direct conflict with the U.S. Supreme Court's decision in Riley v. California, and therefore, is no longer valid.

Since some California searches of cell phones that occurred before *Riley* will be justified based on the decision in **People v. Diaz**, it is important to know the facts of the case and the California Supreme Court's rationale. Those searches should be upheld by reviewing courts based on the U.S. Supreme Court's decision in **Davis v. United States** (2011) 564 U.S. ___; 131 S.Ct. 2419, which held that when the police conduct a search in objectively reasonable reliance on binding appellate precedent, the exclusionary rule does not apply.

Prior to the Supreme Court's landmark decision in **Riley**, the only valid, legal precedent regarding cell phone searches in California was the California Supreme Court's decision in **People v. Diaz**, which was fully applicable and binding on all California law enforcement officers.

FACTS (People v. Diaz (2011) 51 Cal.4th 84)

On April 25, 2007, at about 2:50 p.m., senior Ventura County Deputy Sheriff Victor Fazio saw Gregory Diaz participate in an informant-related, controlled purchase of Ecstasy. Mr. Diaz drove the Ecstasy seller to the location of the sale, which then took place in the backseat of the car Mr. Diaz was driving. Immediately after the sale, Deputy Fazio, who had listened in on the transaction via a wireless transmitter worn by the informant, stopped Mr. Diaz's car and arrested him for being a conspirator in the sale of drugs. Deputy Fazio seized six tabs of Ecstasy in connection with Mr. Diaz's arrest and a small amount of marijuana from Mr. Diaz's pocket. Mr. Diaz also had a cell phone on his person. A detective seized the cell phone from Mr. Diaz and gave it to Deputy Fazio.

Deputy Fazio interviewed Mr. Diaz at the Sheriff's station at 4:18 p.m., but Mr. Diaz denied having any knowledge of the drug transaction. At approximately 4.23 p.m.—after the interview was concluded—Deputy Fazio looked at the cell phone's text message folder and discovered a message that read "6 4 80." Based on his training and experience, Deputy Fazio interpreted the message to mean "six pills of Ecstasy for $80." Deputy Fazio showed the message to Mr. Diaz within minutes of discovering it, and Mr. Diaz then admitted participating in the sale of Ecstasy.

The district attorney charged Mr. Diaz with a violation of Health and Safety Code section 11379(a). Mr. Diaz entered a not guilty plea and moved to suppress the evidence derived from the cell phone text message search. After losing his motion in the trial court, Mr. Diaz changed his plea to guilty of transportation of a controlled substance. Sentence was suspended, and the trial court placed him on probation for three years.

The Court of Appeal affirmed that conviction and held that since the cell phone
"was immediately associated with [defendant's] person at the time of his arrest," it was "properly subjected to a delayed warrantless search." (*Id.* at 89.)

The California Supreme Court granted the defendant's petition for review,

> to decide whether the Fourth Amendment to the United States Constitution permits law enforcement officers, approximately 90 minutes after lawfully arresting a suspect and transporting him to a detention facility, to conduct a warrantless search of the text message folder of a cell phone they take from his person after the arrest. (**Id**. at 88.)

RATIONALE

In reaching its decision upholding the search of the text message folder in the cell phone, the Court stated that

> the key question in this case is whether defendant's cell phone was "personal property . . . immediately associated with [his] person" (**Chadwick**, **supra**, 433 U.S. at p. 15)[10] like the cigarette package in **Robinson** and the clothes in **Edwards**.[11] If it was, then

[10] **United States v. Chadwick** (1971) 433 U.S. 1, involved a 200-pound, double-locked footlocker that had been removed from a train and placed in a waiting car. Federal agents had probable cause to believe it contained marijuana prior to it being placed in the car. The Supreme Court held that a warrant was required to search the luggage, even though it had been transferred to an automobile.

[11] In **United States v. Edwards** (1974) 415 U.S. 800, the Supreme Court upheld the seizure of Eugene

> the delayed warrantless search was a valid search incident to defendant's lawful custodial arrest. If it was not, then the search, because it was "remote in time [and] place from the arrest," "cannot be justified as incident to that arrest" unless an "exigency exist[ed]." (**Chadwick**, **supra**, at p. 15.)

(**Diaz**, *supra*, at 93.)

The Court then said:

> We hold that the cell phone was "immediately associated with [defendant's] person" (**Chadwick**, *supra*, 433 U.S. at p. 15), and that the warrantless search of the cell phone therefore was valid. As the People explain, the cell phone "was an item [of personal property] on [defendant's] person at the time of his arrest and during the administrative processing at the police station." In this regard, it was like the clothing taken from the defendant in **Edwards** and the cigarette package taken from the defendant's coat pocket in **Robinson**, and it was unlike the footlocker in **Chadwick,** which was separate from the defendants' persons and was merely within the "area" of their "immediate control." (**Chadwick**, **supra**, 433 U.S. at p. 15.) Because the cell phone was immediately associated with defendant's person, Fazio was "entitled to inspect" its contents without a warrant (**Robinson**, **supra**, 414 U.S. at p. 236) at the sheriff's station 90 minutes after defendant's arrest, whether or not an exigency existed.

(*Diaz, supra*, at 94.)

Our Founding Fathers wrote the Fourth Amendment with the intention of preventing a general rummaging search of one's possessions by government authorities. Indeed, the decision in *Arizona v. Gant* reinforces this position by allowing a search of a vehicle only if a recent arrestee can gain access to a weapon, or if there is evidence of a crime that might be in the vehicle for which the person is arrested.

Justice Werdegar correctly observes in her dissent that the majority's holding allows

> police carte blanche, with no showing of exigency, to rummage at leisure through the wealth of personal and business information that can be carried on a mobile phone or handheld computer merely because the device was

---

Edwards' clothing 10 hours after his 11:00 p.m. arrest and the subsequent seizure from them of paint chips originating from a Lebanon, Ohio, post office window that he attempted to pry open to break into the post office. The Court ruled that the normal process incident to arrest and custody had not been completed, and the delay in seizing Mr. Edwards' clothing was reasonable since substitute clothing could not be found at the late hour of his arrest.

> taken from an arrestee's person. The majority thus sanctions a highly intrusive and unjustified type of search, one meeting neither the warrant requirement nor the reasonableness requirement of the Fourth Amendment to the United States Constitution.

(**Diaz**, **supra**, at 111.)

In **People v. Macabeo** (2014) 229 Cal.App.4th 486 [2014 Cal.App. Lexis 793] (Review granted by California Supreme Court on 11-25-2014), the Court of Appeal found that while the case was on appeal, the U.S. Supreme Court ruled in **Riley**: Absent an emergency, law enforcement was required to obtain a search warrant before searching through the digital contents of a cell phone incident to arrest. However, the appellate court held that based on the U.S. Supreme Court's ruling in **Davis v. United States** (2011) 564 U.S. ___; 131 S.Ct. 2419, and because **Diaz**, was applicable at the time of the search, the officer's actions in conducting a warrantless search of a seized cell phone, incident to a lawful traffic infraction arrest were done in good faith and therefore, the trial court did **not** err by refusing to exclude 18 images of child pornography found on the cell phone.

Another case that is commonly cited as justifying a cell phone search incident to arrest is **United States v. Finley** (5th Cir. 2007) 477 F.3d 250. But like **Diaz**, this case is no longer of any value after the **Riley** decision. **Finley**. also involved the sale of narcotics in a vehicle, but by someone other than Mr. Finley.

FACTS (United States v. Finley (5th Cir. 2007) 477 F.3d 250)

> On August 19, 2005, Midland Texas Police officers were working with the DEA regarding a controlled purchase of methamphetamine from Mark Brown. Amy Stratton was working as an informant with the police on that date. Under the direction of the Midland Police Department (MPD), Ms. Stratton called Mr. Brown and arranged to purchase $600 worth of methamphetamine. Mr. Brown requested that Ms. Stratton travel to his residence to buy the drugs, but pursuant to MPD instructions, she told Mr. Brown that she was at a truck stop in Midland and that she had no transportation to get to his house. Mr. Brown agreed to meet Ms. Stratton at the truck stop. Mr. Brown asked Jacob Pierce Finley for a ride to the truck stop, which Mr. Finley agreed to do. Mr. Finley drove his white-colored, Southwest Plumbing van to the meeting. Mr. Finley's uncle, who also employed Mr. Finley, owned the Southwest Plumbing Company.
>
> Once at the truck stop, Ms. Stratton approached the van's passenger side where Mr. Brown was sitting, and gave him $600 in pre-recorded MPD bills. Mr. Brown gave Ms. Stratton a cigarette package containing a plastic baggie of methamphetamine. According to the lab, 3.1 grams were located inside the cigarette pack, with 1.4 grams being pure methamphetamine. Neither Mr. Brown nor Mr. Finley ever got out of the van.

Mr. Finley drove away from the truck stop, and MPD officers stopped him three to five miles away and searched the van. During the search, they found MPD-marked bills used in the transaction in a trash can between the driver's and passenger seats. They also found two medicine bottles in the trash can. One bottle had an orange top and contained five small plastic bags, two of which contained methamphetamine. The white-capped bottle had a label with the name "Finley" on it. Inside that bottle was a homemade, glass, smoking pipe with methamphetamine residue in it, and a small piece of straw commonly used to snort narcotics. Also inside the bottle was a plastic bag containing approximately 1.6 grams of a methamphetamine-cutting agent. Both Mr. Finley and Mr. Brown were arrested. A search of Mr. Finley's person yielded a cell phone in his pocket. The phone belonged to Southwest Plumbing and was issued to Mr. Finley for his work; he was allowed to use the phone for personal purposes as well.

During his interview with the police, Mr. Finley admitted to some past cocaine and methamphetamine use, including using the methamphetamine he received from Mr. Brown three days earlier. He admitted to getting his friends marijuana from Mr. Brown on multiple occasions but denied any involvement in the sale of methamphetamine to Ms. Stratton. An MPD officer handed Mr. Finley's cell phone to Special Agent Cook. The agent looked through the phone and found call records and text messages consistent with narcotics trafficking activity. When confronted with these text messages, Mr. Finley claimed that they referred to sales of marijuana and not methamphetamine.

Both Mr. Finley and Mr. Brown were indicted and charged with one count of possession with intent to distribute methamphetamine. Mr. Brown pled guilty and became a cooperating witness in the prosecution of Mr. Finley. Mr. Finley claimed at trial that although he aided and abetted Mr. Brown, he did not know that the purpose of the trip was to sell methamphetamine to Ms. Stratton. Mr. Brown disputed that in his testimony. The jury ultimately convicted Mr. Finley, and he appealed the conviction.

RATIONALE

The Court found that Mr. Finley did, in fact, have standing to object to the search of his cell phone, but concluded that the search was lawful nevertheless. The court found that the search of the cell phone was allowed incident to Mr. Finley's lawful arrest.

2.4.1 - Standing to Challenge a Search of Stolen Cell Phones

In **People v. Barnes** (2013) 216 Cal.App.4th 1508, the appellate court addressed the issue of whether or not a thief has standing under the Fourth Amendment to challenge the use of a Global Positioning System (GPS) to locate a stolen cell phone and detain the thief. The court ruled that there is no Fourth Amendment violation when the information generated by the GPS, with the owner's consent, is only part of the police's objective reasons leading to their decision to detain a suspect.

FACTS (People v. Barnes (2013) 216 Cal.App.4th 1508)

Shortly after midnight on November 5, 2009, Charles Parce and Carolyn Fey were walking near Fort Mason in San Francisco when a Black male adult (later identified as Lorenzo Barnes) approached them, brandished a handgun, and demanded their belongings. Mr. Parce handed over his wallet, but Ms. Fey ran across the street and threw her turquoise Prada purse under a parked car. Mr. Barnes retrieved the purse and fled on foot. Both Mr. Parce and Ms. Fey provided a physical description of Mr. Barnes to the police. Ms. Fey told the police that her wallet and a "Palm pre-smart phone" were inside her purse. Ms. Fey also told the police that her cell phone "had GPS on it."

Officer Zelster contacted Ms. Fey's phone service carrier, Sprint PCS, and spoke to their corporate security people. The officer was advised that if Ms. Fey would sign a release form, they would be able to ping the cell phone. What this meant is that they would be able to send a signal to the cell phone and find a general location within either 15 yards or 15 meters of the phone's location. Ms. Fey signed a release, which was faxed back to Sprint. The officer then asked Sprint to ping the cell phone and they advised the officer that the phone was stationary at 16th and Mission Street. This was approximately 45 minutes after the robbery occurred. Officer Zeltser handed the phone over to Officer Hamilton so that he could continue speaking with Sprint, while Officer Zeltser went to 16th and Mission. Enroute, Officer Zeltser learned that the ping was now "between 16th and 17th and Mission."

Officers Clifford and Tannenbaum were in the area and saw a person matching the robber's description enter a car and drive down Mission Street. While the car was stopped at a red light at 15th and Mission, the cell phone was re-pinged by Sprint and shown to be at 15th and Mission. Officer Zeltser arrived on the scene, which was now at 13th and Mission, just as Officer Tannenbaum made a car stop. As Officer Zeltser approached the car, he had his flashlight out. He looked in the rear seat of the car and saw a purse that matched Ms. Fey's description on the backseat of the car. On the front seat of the car, he saw a cell phone. It was now approximately one hour after the robbery. Once Mr. Barnes exited the car, the officers immediately noticed a gun tucked in his waistband. Ms. Fey was brought to the scene and identified Mr. Barnes as the robber. Later, at the police station, Ms. Fey identified both the purse and cell phone as her property.

Mr. Barnes brought a suppression motion challenging the legality of the initial car stop. Through his attorney, he claimed the prosecution was merely relying on a hunch and based their car stop on that hunch. He also attempted to analogize that idea to the reliability of a confidential informant and said, "I would submit that there really is not enough evidence to justify the stop of this individual miles away from where the crime occurred based upon the GPS and the clothing description, which could have fit anybody." (**Id**. at 1512.)

The trial court agreed with the prosecution's argument and stated:

> I think Ms. Fey had every right to utilize her phone company to find her phone, and I think that's what happened here. I don't believe that the defendant has a privacy interest in that regard. [¶] I don't think that there was a particular action on the part of the police . . . to intrude on the defendant's privacy. They were in pursuit of a phone that they have consent from the owner of the phone to pursue; so they went to the area where the phone was located. [¶] ... [¶] I don't feel that there was an unreasonable intrusion . . . [with] . . . the stop of the defendant. [¶] Motion to suppress is denied.

(**Id**. at 1513.)

The appellate case was heard after the United States Supreme Court's decision in **United States v. Jones**. Mr. Barnes changed his argument in light of that decision and no longer saw the use of GPS technology as a per se violation of the Fourth Amendment. However, he continued to raise the issue of "reliability" and the confidential informant analogy. He also argued that even assuming that Sprint provided reliable information, "it merely established the location of the stolen phone, not the location of the suspected robber." (**Id**. at 1521.) Mr. Barnes also argued, "without the GPS information, Officers Clifford and Tannenbaum had only 'pedestrian facts—i.e., 'the suspects race, gender and attire'—'which did not support reasonable suspicion for the stop.'" (**Id**. at 1512.)

RATIONALE

After a lengthy discussion of *United States v. Jones*, the Court of Appeal said that since there was no physical trespass or intrusion, as was the case in ***Jones***, the question became one of how Mr. Barnes fared under the **Katz** [Katz v. United States (1967) 389 U.S. 347] "reasonable expectation of privacy test." In essence, the question before the court was did Mr. Barnes have a legitimate expectation of privacy in the stolen cell phone and was it one that society was prepared to recognize as reasonable. The court answered no to both questions. The court also referred to Penal Code section 637.7, which prevents law enforcement from using an electronic tracking device without the person's knowledge unless the owner of the property in question consented to the search. The court noted, "If California is willing to have police and the owner cooperate in tracking a motor vehicle, it seems unlikely state policy would be outraged by such cooperation employed to apprehend armed robbers in possession of stolen property."

(**Barnes**, **supra**, at 1519.) The Court of Appeal therefore concluded that the use of GPS technology to find the location of the stolen cell phone, which assisted in locating the robber, did not violate the Fourth Amendment.

The Court of Appeal observed:

> Unlike an informant, Sprint did not initiate contact with the police. Instead, it was police, with the active assistance of the property owner, who approached Sprint. . . . The officers could verify the information passed on from Sprint if in the pinged areas the officers encountered a person matching the description provided by the victims. . . . ¶ [T]he officers could certainly infer a reasonable possibility that if they could locate the phone they would also locate the robber.

(**Id**. at 1520.)

Finally, the court concluded "[C]orrelating defendant's observed movements with both the GPS location *and* the victims' description provided Officers Tannenbaum and Clifford with ample reasonable suspicion for detention." [Citation] (**Id**.) [Italics in original.]

2.4.2 - Probable Cause and Vehicle Searches

In **Riley**, the United States proposed that the U.S. Supreme Court allow a cell phone search whenever it is reasonable to believe that the phone contains evidence of the crime for which a suspect has been arrested, based on the Court's reasoning in **Arizona v. Gant**. For example, a drug dealer who was driving a vehicle at the time of the arrest and was in possession of a cell phone.

The Court rejected this proposal and stated:

> . . . a **Gant** standard would prove no practical limit at all when it comes to cell phone searches. In the vehicle context, **Gant** generally protects against searches for evidence of past crimes. [Citation] In the cell phone context, however, it is reasonable to expect that incriminating information will be found on a phone regardless of when the crime occurred. Similarly, in the vehicle context **Gant** restricts broad searches resulting from minor crimes such as traffic violations. [Citation] That would not necessarily be true for cell phones. It would be a particularly inexperienced or unimaginative law enforcement officer who could not come up with several reasons to suppose evidence of just about any crime could be found on a cell phone. Even an individual pulled over for something as basic as speeding might well have locational data dispositive of guilt on his phone. An individual pulled over for reckless driving might have evidence on the phone that shows whether he was texting while driving. The sources of potential pertinent information are virtually unlimited, so applying the **Gant** standard to cell phones would in

> effect give "police officers unbridled discretion to rummage at will among a person's private effects. ([**Gant**, **supra**,] 556 U.S. at 345.)

(**Riley**, **supra**, at 2492.)

2.4.3 - Inventory Searches

Inventory searches commonly arise in the context of impounded cars, backpacks, or even luggage. However, the issue can also arise when inventorying a suspect's property at the jail prior to booking it under a suspect's name for safekeeping.

When an officer finds a cell phone inside an impounded car, and the phone is turned off—once again, given the **Riley** decision —it would be an impermissible search if the officer turned on the cell phone and examined its contents. All that is required for inventory is a notation of the cell phone make, model, and serial number. That information is usually stored in the phone's battery compartment under the battery. The contents of the cell phone would be irrelevant to the inventory search objective, and a court might view any search of those contents as a general rummaging search, which would lead to any seized evidence being suppressed.

By way of analogy, an officer who finds a briefcase in an impounded car would not be justified in reading the contents of all of the documents found in the briefcase if he was merely filling out a simple inventory sheet. An entry of "a briefcase containing miscellaneous documents" would be sufficient.

2.4.4 - Exigent Circumstances

Even though the search incident to arrest exception does not apply to cell phones, other case-specific exceptions might still justify a warrantless search of a *particular* phone. In **Riley**, the Supreme Court observed:

> One well-recognized exception applies when 'the exigencies of the situation' make the needs of law enforcement so compelling that [a] warrantless search is objectively reasonable under the Fourth Amendment." [Citations.] Such exigencies could include the need to prevent the imminent destruction of evidence in individual cases, to pursue a fleeing suspect, and to assist persons who are seriously injured or are threatened with imminent injury. [Citation.]
>
> In light of the availability of the exigent circumstances exception, there is no reason to believe that law enforcement officers will not be able to address some of the more extreme hypotheticals that have been suggested: a suspect texting an accomplice who, it is feared, is preparing to detonate a bomb, or a child abductor who may have information about the child's location on his cell phone. The defendants here recognize—indeed, they stress—that such fact-specific threats may justify a warrantless search of cell phone data. See Reply Brief in No. 13–132, at 8–9; Brief for Respondent in No. 13–212, at 30, 41. The critical point is that, unlike the search incident to

arrest exception, the exigent circumstances exception requires a court to examine whether an emergency justified a warrantless search in each particular case. [Citation.]

(**Riley**, **supra**, at 2494.)

2.4.5 - Abandonment

If a person abandons his or her reasonable expectation of privacy in a cell phone, even while committing a crime, then a warrantless search of the cell phone for identifying information about the owner **is permissible**. In **People v. Daggs** (2005) 133 Cal.App.4th 361, the Court of Appeal upheld the trial court's finding that the defendant had abandoned his cell phone when he left it behind at a robbery crime scene, and that the subsequent warrantless search of the cell phone by the police, which led back to the defendant, did not violate the defendant's Fourth Amendment rights.

FACTS (**People v. Daggs** (2005) 133 Cal.App.4th 361)

On December 7, 2003, the clerk at a Walgreens store in San Mateo County saw James Daggs go behind a counter and grab several cartons of cigarettes. The clerk grabbed Mr. Daggs' arm to try to stop him, but Mr. Daggs turned around, sprayed the clerk in the eyes with pepper spray, and then fled the store with the merchandise. When the police arrived, they found a cell phone near the cash register where the clerk confronted Mr. Daggs. The clerk told the police that he had used the register 10–15 minutes before the robbery and had not seen the phone in the area. During the 20–30 minutes the police were on the premises, no one tried to claim the cell phone, so the police booked it into evidence at the police station.

One week after the robbery, no one had yet come forward to reclaim the cell phone. Detective Moran obtained the cell phone from evidence and, without a search warrant, removed the battery from the cell phone and obtained the electronic serial number, hex number, and decimal number, which were all located on the cell phone itself. Using these numbers, Detective Moran obtained a search warrant for the telephone company for the cell phone subscriber's name, phone number, and records. The documents revealed that Charles Daggs, the defendant's brother, was the subscriber. The police interviewed Charles, who told them that he had given the cell phone to his brother in August 2003, a fact that was also confirmed by the defendant's mother.

James Daggs was ultimately arrested and charged with robbery. He brought a motion to suppress the information obtained from the cell phone claiming that he had a reasonable expectation of privacy in the cell phone and that Detective Moran's search of the cell phone violated Mr. Daggs' Fourth Amendment rights. He also sought to suppress the information obtained from the search warrant on the phone company and the statements of his brother and mother as fruits of the illegal search. Mr. Daggs testified at the suppression motion that a few hours after the crime, he realized that he might have lost his cell phone at Walgreens, but decided not to try to retrieve it because he believed the police might have it and would connect him with the robbery. However, before the phone was lost, he had locked it to prevent anyone else from using it or accessing the information he stored on the cell phone.

After the trial court denied Mr. Daggs' motion, he pled no contest to one count of robbery. The court placed him on three years formal probation and sentenced him to eight months in the county jail. The Court of Appeal later upheld the trial court's decision not to suppress the seized evidence.

RATIONALE

The Court of Appeal rejected Mr. Daggs' argument and legal conclusion that because "he accidentally left his cell phone at Walgreens, and would have reclaimed it had he not feared arrest, . . . he did not voluntarily discard the phone, and therefore he did not abandon it, but merely 'lost it.'" (**Id**. at 365.) Instead, it specifically ruled that the "[d]efendant abandoned the cell phone when he left it unattended in a public place of business, at the scene of a crime, fled, and made no attempt to reclaim it." (**Id**. at 365.)

In reaching that conclusion, the court observed that the intent to abandon is determined by objective factors, and not based on a defendant's subjective intent. The Walgreens clerk

> informed the officers who found the phone at the scene that he had not seen the cell phone in that area prior to his confrontation with the robber. No one else at the scene claimed the phone, nor did anyone assert a claim to it in the week after the robbery. It was inferable that the telephone belonged to, or had been in the possession of, the robber who had fled the scene, thereby evincing his intent not to reclaim it. Therefore, when the police seized the phone, and certainly by the time Detective Moran finally performed the challenged search, these circumstances were all objective indications that defendant had discarded the phone, and would not reclaim it.

(**Id**. at 366.)

The court went on to explain that what was abandoned was the defendant's reasonable expectation of privacy in the cell phone, not necessarily the property itself. "Indeed, were it not for the incriminating circumstances, defendant, and any other reasonable person, would no doubt have hoped and expected that someone would examine the phone to ascertain the owner, and would have been grateful if someone had done so, and returned it to him." (**Id**. at 369.)

2.4.6 - Plain View Observations

Suppose an officer manipulates a cell phone to turn it off or place it in airplane mode, and in the process makes a plain view observation of something inappropriate on the cell phone such as child pornography or pictures of narcotics. Should that information be disclosed to the magistrate in a search warrant affidavit requesting authorization to search the cell phone?

The author suggests that it should not be included in the affidavit. This conclusion is based on **Segura v. United States** (1984) 468 U.S. 796, where the U.S. Supreme Court ruled that an illegal entry to secure a private residence while a search warrant was sought (it took 19 hours to get the warrant!) did not result in the suppression of evidence because the search warrant was based on independent probable cause and not on anything observed during the "freezing" of the residence. Hence, the evidence in the apartment was discovered through a lawful "independent source," that is, the search warrant.

In the context of a cell phone search warrant request, the affiant should tell the magistrate in the supporting affidavit that the cell phone was turned off, placed in airplane mode, or otherwise disconnected from the cellular network, but not told about any observations about the phone's contents the officer might have made while doing so. By not seeking a finding of probable cause based on anything observed during the possibly inappropriate manipulating of the cell phone, a strong argument can be made that the search warrant is based on independent grounds and not on anything observed while "freezing" the cell phone. This would therefore allow one to analogize the pending case to **Segura**.

2.4.7 - Riley and the Future of Cell Phone Searches

Technology continues to evolve and converge in this area, as cell phones become more like handheld computers and less like traditional phones. Because of this evolving situation, the day may arise when a court rules that cell phone searches should be governed by alternative statutory schemes (e.g., the PPA), rather than by traditional Fourth Amendment analysis. (See Justice Alito's concurring opinion in **Riley**.) Officers should always remember that bad facts can create bad rules of law, and that it is prudent to carefully consider a situation before searching through information stored on a cell phone. **When in doubt, always get a search warrant.**

2.4.8 - Consent

Warrantless searches based on consent are almost always legal. However, there are four basic questions to consider when analyzing the lawfulness of a search based on consent:

1. Was there consent?

2. Was the consent freely and voluntarily given?
3. Did the consenting party have the authority to give consent?
4. What was the scope of the consent?

2.4.8.1 - General Rules

The U.S. Supreme Court ruled in **Schneckloth v. Bustamonte** (1973) 412 U.S. 218, that the police do not have to tell a subject who voluntarily consents to a search that he or she has the right to withhold consent. However, it is a proper factor to look at when considering whether the person freely and voluntarily consented to the search.

In **United States v. Matlock** (1974) 415 U.S. 164, 171, the U.S. Supreme Court ruled that no warrant is needed if a competent individual who "possessed common authority over or other sufficient relationship to the premises or effects sought to be inspected. . ." consents to the search.

Under **Matlock**, common authority rests on mutual use of the property by persons generally having joint access or control for most purposes. The burden for proving that common authority rests on the State.

However, in a 5–3 decision written by Justice Souter in **Georgia v. Randolph** (2006) 547 U.S. 103, the U.S. Supreme Court ruled that the Fourth Amendment provisions against unreasonable searches and seizure are violated when police conduct a warrantless search of a residence based on the consent of one occupant when a co-occupant is present and objects to the search. The Court ruled that the fruits of such a warrantless search are inadmissible against the physically present, non-consenting party. In reaching this decision, the Court observed,

> [T]here is no common understanding that one co-tenant generally has a right or authority to prevail over the express wishes of another, whether the issue is the color of the curtains or invitations to outsiders.

(**Id**. at 114.)

In reaching this conclusion, the majority had to justify its decision in light of its own precedent in **Matlock**, where it upheld the entry to a residence based on the consent of one co-occupant in the absence of the other. Justice Souter referred to this as "two loose ends," which he characterized as:

1. The explanation "for the constitutional sufficiency of a co-tenant's consent to enter and search" in **Matlock**.
2. The significance of **Matlock** and **Illinois v. Rodriguez** (1990) 497 U.S. 177 after the U.S. Supreme Court's decision in this case.

Justice Souter explained away the first issue by stating that the **Matlock** Court did not address the issue of "whether customary social understanding accords the consenting tenant authority powerful enough to prevail over the co-tenant's objection."

(**Randolph**, **supra**, at 121.)

With respect to the second issue, Justice Souter said:

> If those cases are not to be undercut by today's holding, we have to admit that we are drawing a fine line; if a potential defendant with self-interest in objecting is in fact at the door and objects, the co-tenant's permission does not suffice for a reasonable search, whereas the potential objector, nearby but not invited to take part in the threshold colloquy, loses out.
>
> This is the line we draw, and we think the formalism is justified. So long as there is no evidence that the police have removed the potentially objecting tenant from the entrance for the sake of avoiding a possible objection, there is practical value in the simple clarity of complementary rules, one recognizing the co-tenant's permission when there is no fellow occupant on hand, the other according dispositive weight to the fellow occupant's contrary indication when he expresses it.

(**Id**. at 121.)

In a strong dissent, Chief Justice Roberts disagreed with the majority rule and stated:

> A wide variety of often subtle social conventions may shape expectations about how we act when another shares with us what is otherwise private, and those conventions go by a variety of labels—courtesy, good manners, custom, protocol, even honor among thieves. The Constitution, however, protects not these but privacy, and once privacy has been shared, the shared information, documents, or places remain private only at the discretion of the confidant.

(**Id**. at 131.)

The Chief Justice expressed his belief that the majority's decision did not protect privacy nearly as much as the good luck of a co-owner who just happened to be present when the police arrived at the door.

Finally, the Chief Justice argued:

> [T]he more reasonable approach is to adopt a rule acknowledging that shared living space entails a limited yielding of privacy to others, and that the law historically permits those to whom we have yielded our privacy to in turn cooperate with the government. Such a rule flows more naturally from our cases concerning Fourth Amendment reasonableness and is logically grounded in the concept of privacy underlying that Amendment.

(**Id**. at 137.)

In **Fernandez v. California** (2014) ___ U.S. ___; 134 S.Ct. 1126; 188 L.Ed.2d 25, the U.S Supreme Court followed the holding in **Georgia v. Randolph**, **supra**, and upheld the co-tenants' consent to search the apartment despite the fact that Mr.

Fernandez objected to such a search before he was lawfully arrested and removed from the premises.

In the case of **In re D.C.** (2010) 188 Cal.App.4th 978, the Court of Appeal concluded that "[b]ecause of the unique nature of the rights and duties of parents with respect to their children, **Randolph** does not require the police to defer to an objecting minor child over a consent to search by his or her parent." (**Id**. at 989.)

Officers need to proceed with extreme caution when attempting to search a cell phone or even a computer in a **Georgia v. Randolph** type of situation. The consent of a spouse or co-occupant who has joint access and control over a cell phone or computer will not be sufficient if the other spouse or co-occupant is present and objects to the search. A search done over the objections of a present spouse or co-occupants could lead to the suppression of any evidence obtained during that cell phone or computer search.

2.4.8.2 - Parents and Children

In **In re Scott K.** (1979) 24 Cal.3d 395, the California Supreme Court ruled that the minor's father could not lawfully give the police consent to search a locked toolbox inside the room of his 17-year-old son because the father claimed no interest in the son's locked tool box or its contents and acknowledged that the toolbox belonged to his son.

In reaching that conclusion, the California Supreme Court rejected the following arguments put forth by the People in support of the police search:

- Because a parent is responsible for minor children and may inspect their property on their own, the police search was lawfully based on the parental consent.
- The father's consent fell within a third party exception to the warrant requirement based on the combined circumstances of ownership of the home and the nature of the parent-child relationship.

The Court of Appeal ruled in **People v. Daniels** (1971) 16 Cal.App.3d 36, that Mr. Daniels's mother could properly give the police consent to search her adult son's bedroom for evidence of bomb making materials when the son resided at the house rent free. However, she could not give the police consent to search a suitcase in the bedroom that belonged to her son.

With respect to cell phone searches, a parent who has no access to or right of control over a minor child's cell phone would not be able to lawfully consent to a search. Likewise, even if a parent pays the cell phone bill for an adult child, but otherwise does not share or use that adult child's cell phone, the parent would not have the authority to give law enforcement consent to search it.

2.4.8.3 - Third Parties

In a 6–3 decision in **Illinois v. Rodriguez** (1990) 497 U.S. 177, the Supreme Court ruled that a warrantless entry does not violate the Fourth Amendment proscription against unreasonable searches and seizures where such entry is based upon the consent of a third party, whom the police, at the time of entry, reasonably believe to possess common authority over the premises, but who in fact does not possess such authority.

The Court applied the following objective test:

> Whether the facts available at the moment would warrant a person of reasonable caution in the belief that the consenting party had authority over the premises. If not, then warrantless entry without further inquiry is unlawful unless authority actually exists. But if so, the search is valid.

(**Id**. at 178.)

In the context of cell phone searches, if the officers reasonably believe that the consenting party has sole control, ownership, and use of the cell phone, but it later turns out that they were lied to, the search should be upheld based on the holding in **Illinois v. Rodriguez**.

2.4.8.4 - Landlords

In **Chapman v. United States** (1961) 365 U.S. 610, the U.S. Supreme Court ruled in an 8–1 decision that a landlord cannot give the police consent to enter a tenant's residence. By way of analogy, a landlord also cannot give police consent to search a tenant's cell phone.

2.4.9 - Probation Searches

2.4.9.1 - General Principles

Probation searches—when there is a search and seizure clause associated with the grant of probation—are generally going to be upheld by the courts' under the "special needs" doctrine articulated by the 5–4 U.S. Supreme Court decision in *Griffin v. Wisconsin* (1987) 483 U.S. 868. It does not matter if the search is for investigatory purposes or probationary purposes. Furthermore, a probation search conducted pursuant to a known probation condition, even without a reasonable suspicion of criminal activity, will be upheld, provided the search is not done for arbitrary, capricious, or harassment purposes.

In recognizing the validity of warrantless probation searches in **Griffin, *supra,*** at 876, the Court stated,

> [a] warrant requirement would interfere to an appreciable degree with the probation system, setting up a magistrate rather than the probation officer as the judge of how close a supervision the probationer requires. Moreover, the delay inherent in obtaining a warrant would make it more difficult for probation officials to respond quickly to evidence of misconduct, see **New**

> **Jersey v. T.L.O**. (1985) 469 U.S. 325, at 340, and would reduce the deterrent effect that the possibility of expeditious searches would otherwise create, [citations]. By way of analogy, one might contemplate how parental custodial authority would be impaired by requiring judicial approval for [the] search of a minor child's room.

In reaching this decision, the U.S. Supreme Court declined to embrace the Wisconsin Supreme Court's new principle of law that "... any search of a probationer's home by a probation officer satisfies the Fourth Amendment as long as the information possessed by the officer satisfies a federal 'reasonable grounds' standard." (**Id**. at 872.) Instead, the U.S. Supreme Court upheld the constitutionality of the search based on "special needs" beyond normal law enforcement. Those "special needs" justified a departure from the usual probable cause and warrant requirements.

In **United States v. Knights** (2001) 534 U.S. 112, the U.S. Supreme Court unanimously reversed the Ninth Circuit Court of Appeals and held that the search of Mr. Knights pursuant to his probation condition and supported by reasonable suspicion, did not violate the Fourth Amendment. In doing so, the Supreme Court specifically rejected the Ninth Circuit's distinction that the search was illegal because it was done for an investigatory purpose rather than a probationary purpose.

In **People v. Medina** (2007) 158 Cal.App.4th 1571, the Court of Appeal reversed the trial court's decision and explicitly ruled that under California law and the California Supreme Court's decision in **People v. Bravo** (1987) 43 Cal.3d 600,

> ... a search conducted pursuant to a known probation search condition, even if conducted without reasonable suspicion of criminal activity, does not violate the Fourth Amendment as long as the search is not undertaken for harassment or for arbitrary or capricious reasons or in an unreasonable manner.

(**Medina**, **supra**, at 1577.)

The Court of Appeal also noted that

> [the] ... ***Knights*** court expressly declined to reach the issue whether "acceptance of the search condition constituted consent in the ***Schneckloth*** sense of a complete waiver of his Fourth Amendment rights." (**Knights**, **supra**, 534 U.S. at p. 118.) Moreover, the court expressly declined to decide whether a probation search *without* reasonable suspicion satisfies the reasonableness requirement of the Fourth Amendment. (**Knights**, **supra** at p. 120, fn. 6.) Thus, **Knights** did not consider the question relevant to the present case: whether reasonable suspicion is *required* (and not just sufficient) for a search pursuant to a probation condition. [Italics in original.]

(**Medina**, **supra**, at 1578.)

There is no reasonableness requirement before an officer can conduct a probation search. All that is required is that the search is not arbitrary, capricious, or done for harassment purposes (see **In re Anthony S.** (1992) 4 Cal.App.4th 1000, 1004) and an officer's subjective intentions play no role in determining the lawfulness of a probation or parole search.

> As explained in **People v. Clower** (1993) 16 Cal.App.4th 1737 [21 Cal.Rptr. 2d 38], "a parole search could become constitutionally 'unreasonable' if made too often, or at an unreasonable hour, or if unreasonably prolonged or for other reasons establishing arbitrary or oppressive conduct by the searching officer." (*Id.* at 1741; **United States v. Follette** (S.D.N.Y. 1968) 282 F.Supp.10, 13; see **In re Anthony S**., (1992) 4 Cal.App.4th 1000, 1004 [6 Cal.Rptr.2d 214] [a search is arbitrary and capricious when the motivation for the search is unrelated to rehabilitative, reformative or legitimate law enforcement purposes, or when the search is motivated by personal animosity toward the parolee]; **People v. Bremmer** (1973) 30 Cal.App.3d 1058, 1062 [106 Cal.Rptr. 797] [unrestricted search of a probationer or parolee by law enforcement officers at their whim or caprice is a form of harassment].)

People v. Reyes (1998) 19 Cal.4th 743, at 753–754.

In **People v. Sardinas** (2009) 170 Cal.App.4th 488, the Court of Appeal rejected Mr. Sardinas's contention that the two searches occurring within 24 hours of each other, combined with the officer's prior six or seven contacts with him over a five-year period, belied any legitimate purpose for the second search that resulted in the seizure of cocaine from his person, and compelled the conclusion that the search was done for harassment or other arbitrary purpose.

In **People v. Gomez** (2005) 130 Cal.App.4th 1008, the Court of Appeal ruled that an " officer's subjective intent has no role to play in determining the lawfulness of a probation or parole search."

(**Id**. at 1015.)

2.4.9.2 - Scope of Search

In **People v. Ermi**, (2013) 216 Cal.App.4th 277, the Court of Appeal addressed the issue of whether a probationer's search condition authorized the search of a purse belonging to the probationer's girlfriend that the officer found on a chair in a shared bedroom. The Court of Appeal upheld the trial court's ruling that the officer properly searched the purse because the probationer had access and control over the purse.

Likewise, if a probationer has access and control over a cell phone, a probation search of the cell phone under these circumstances should be upheld by the courts.

2.4.9.3 - Cohabitant Search Conditions

In a 6–1 decision, **People v. Sanders** (2003) 31 Cal.4th 318, 335, with only Associate Justice Baxter dissenting, the California Supreme Court repudiated the rationale of **In re Tyrell J.**, **supra**, in the context of parole searches. The Court held that

> . . . an otherwise unlawful search of the residence of an adult parolee may not be justified by the circumstance that the suspect was subject to a search condition of which the law enforcement officers were unaware when the search was conducted.

In his majority opinion, Justice Moreno stated,

> [p]ermitting evidence that has been suppressed as to a cohabitant to be used against the parolee would encourage searches that violate the rights of cohabitants and guests by rewarding police for conducting an unlawful search of a residence.

Sanders, **supra**, at 335.

A search that violates a cohabitant's reasonable expectation of privacy also violates a parolee's expectation of privacy. While "... a parolee's expectation of privacy is certainly diminished, it is not eliminated." **Sanders**, **supra**, at 332.

By suppressing the evidence against both defendants, the Supreme Court sent a clear signal to law enforcement that it did not want to legitimize the police's illegal actions.

The California Supreme Court later applied the same rule to probation searches for their decision in **In re Jaime P**. (2006) 40 Cal.4th 128.

In **People v. Pleasant** (2004) 123 Cal.App.4th 194, the Court of Appeal upheld the search of a locked bedroom in a probationer's (mom) house and the subsequent seizure of firearms used against her adult son in a criminal prosecution. Even though the son resided in that bedroom, the probationer possessed keys to that locked bedroom.

The majority observed:

> Persons who live with probationers cannot reasonably expect privacy in areas of a residence that they share with probationers. (**People v. Woods** (1999) 21 Cal.4th 668, 675–676.) Since Ms. Pleasant gave a search waiver as a condition of probation, law enforcement authorities could, without a warrant or probable cause, search areas used exclusively by Ms. Pleasant, areas within "common authority" . . . of the probationer and fellow occupants and areas which she "normally had access." [Citations.] Since Ms. Pleasant had access to the keys to the room in which the gun was found, [Mr.] Pleasant could not reasonably expect privacy in the room and the

> officers reasonably entered the room under the authority of Ms. Pleasant's probation waiver.
>
> (**Pleasant**, **supra**, at 197–198.)

In this 2–1 decision, the dissenting justice noted that the officers were told the room belonged to the probationer's son and that he kept the door locked. Based on this information, the dissenting Justice believed the officers could not reasonably believe Ms. Pleasant had access to this clearly "differentiated private living space."

2.4.9.4 - Probation Searches and Electronic Devices

Given our technological society and the proliferation of computers, electronic storage devices such as cell phones, personal digital assistants (PDAs) and thumb drives, the issue often arises as to whether an officer can conduct a warrantless search of a probationer's computer and other electronic items as part of a probation search. The answer to this question is a qualified maybe.

If a probationer is on probation for a crime involving the use of a computer, the trial court may have ordered restrictions on the probationer's use and possession of computer equipment. For example, Penal Code section 1203.047 mandates that a person convicted of a violation of certain subdivisions of Penal Code sections 502 or 502.7 be placed on not less than three years of probation unless the ends of justice would be served by a shorter term. Section 1203.047 also mandates that

> During the period of probation, that person shall not accept employment where that person would use a computer connected by any means to any other computer, except upon approval of the court and notice to and opportunity to be heard by the prosecuting attorney, probation department, prospective employer, and the convicted person. Court approval shall not be given unless the court finds that the proposed employment would not pose a risk to the public.

A probationer's mere possession of a computer under those circumstances would be a violation of the terms of probation and would justify its search and seizure by law enforcement.

A sentencing court may also impose other restrictions such as specific terms allowing search and seizure of all digital devices in a probationer's possession, including both on-site and off-site analysis by a forensic lab. Such a condition would obviously justify the warrantless seizure, removal, and off-site forensic analysis by a lab of a computer or cell phone and its contents.

However, if the sentencing court did not go so far in issuing probation conditions, but instead issued terms of probation that included stay away orders from online computer chat rooms, a prohibition against the use of pseudonyms in online communications, no credit card use over the Internet, and no participation in Internet-based auctions or e-commerce, then the situation moves into a gray area.

Once law enforcement verifies some or all of the above probation conditions, a probationer's Fourth Amendment rights would not be violated if an officer conducted a warrantless search of a probationer's computer files, cell phone information, or PDA either at or away from the location of the probation search.

In the absence of those conditions, a very cursory search of electronic items for evidence of dominion and control of the property would be appropriate. For a more detailed search, including removing the computer or cell phone for analysis at a forensic lab, the better practice is to freeze the device and promptly obtain a search warrant allowing it to be removed from the location. For example, if the court prohibits a probationer from possessing child pornography and a probation officer's cursory search of a computer or cell phone yields evidence of the presence of picture files containing such items, the officer should seize the device and suspend any further search pending the issuance of a search warrant authorizing a more detailed off-site forensic analysis of its information.

2.4.10 - Parole Searches

Parole searches are very similar to probation searches, but almost always include a search and seizure clause. Penal Code section 3067, when enacted in 1996, initially required an inmate to consent to a search and seizure condition in exchange for being released from prison. However, in 2012, the California Legislature amended the section in response to prison overcrowding and the enactment of Penal Code section 1170(h), which allows prison sentences to be served in local county jails. Under the revised formulation, a parolee was only required to be advised that he or she is subject to search and seizure by probation, parole, or peace officers at any time of the day or night, with or without a search warrant or with or without probable cause. In 2006, the U.S. Supreme Court ruled that a suspicionless search of a parolee did not violate the Fourth Amendment prohibition against unreasonable searches and seizures.

The California Legislature added Penal Code section 3067 in 1996. At that time, subdivision (a) mandated that

> Any inmate who is eligible for release on parole pursuant to this chapter shall agree in writing to be subject to search or seizure by a parole officer or other peace officer at any time of the day or night, with or without a search warrant and with or without cause.

Subdivision (b) stated that "Any inmate who does not comply with the provision of subdivision (a) . . . shall not be released until he or she either complies with the provision of subdivision (a) or has no remaining worktime credit, whichever occurs earlier."

In passing this legislation, the California Legislature limited its application in subsection (c) "This section shall only apply to an inmate who is eligible for release on parole for an *offense committed on or after January 1, 1997.*"

In 2012, the California Legislature amended Penal Code section 3067 to eliminate the language in subdivision (a) requiring an inmate to agree in writing to be subject to search or seizure by a parole officer or other peace officer at any time of the day or night. The amendment added paragraphs (1), (2), and (3) to subdivision (b). The amended statute now reads in part as follows:[12]

> (a) Any inmate who is eligible for release on parole pursuant to this chapter or postrelease community supervision pursuant to Title 2.05 (commencing with Section 3450) of Part 3 shall be given notice that he or she is subject to terms and conditions of his or her release from prison.
>
> (b) The notice shall include all of the following:
>
> (1) The person's release date and the maximum period the person may be subject to supervision under this title.
>
> (2) An advisement that if the person violates any law or violates any condition of his or her release that he or she may be incarcerated in a county jail or, if previously paroled pursuant to Section 3000.1 or paragraph (4) of subdivision (b) of Section 3000, returned to state prison, regardless of whether new charges are filed.
>
> (3) An advisement that he or she is subject to search or seizure by a probation or parole officer or other peace officer at any time of the day or night, with or without a search warrant or with or without cause.
>
> (c) This section shall only apply to an inmate who is eligible for release on parole for an offense committed on or after January 1, 1997.
>
> (d) It is not the intent of the Legislature to authorize law enforcement officers to conduct searches for the sole purpose of harassment.

The California Supreme Court initially applied its decision in **In re Tyrell J.**, supra, to parole searches in a 4–3 decision in **Reyes**, **supra**, 19 Cal.4th 743 and in so doing, disapproved its earlier decisions in **In re Ralph Martinez** (1970) 1 Cal.3d 641, which held that a warrantless search of a residence could not be upheld as a parole search, if the officers were unaware of the parole condition at the time

[12] All new additions are shown as underlined text. Additionally, only subsection (e), which relates to the power of the Secretary of Department of Corrections and Rehabilitation to prescribe and amend rules and regulations, is omitted above.

they conducted the search— and **People v. Burgener** (1986) 41 Cal.3d. 505, which held that a warrantless search of a parolee must be justified by at least a reasonable suspicion that the parolee had violated a condition of his parole or a law, or was planning to do so. However, as stated earlier, the California Supreme Court reversed itself in *Sanders, supra,* 31 Cal.4th 318, just five years later, which means that **In re Ralph Martinez** and **People v. Burgener** are once again valid California law.

In **People v. Middleton** (2005) 131 Cal.App.4th 732, the Court of Appeal ruled that an officer's awareness that a third party was a parolee was sufficient to inform the officer of the existence of a search and seizure clause (see Penal Code 3067(a)) and provide the officer with authority to conduct a warrantless search of a motel room.

In a 6–3 opinion in **Samson v. California** (2006) 547 U.S. 843, the U.S. Supreme Court resolved the question it left open in **United States v. Knights** (2001) 534 U.S. 112:

> whether a condition of release can so diminish or eliminate a released prisoner's reasonable expectation of privacy that a suspicionless search by a law enforcement officer would not offend the Fourth Amendment.

Samson, **supra**, at 847.

The Court ruled that suspicionless searches of a parolee do not violate the Fourth Amendment prohibition against unreasonable searches and seizures. Based on Proposition 8, California courts are bound to follow this decision. This means that **Samson** supersedes the California Supreme Court's decision in **Burgener**, **supra**, requiring a "reasonable suspicion" standard before an officer can search a parolee.

2.4.10.1 - Invalidity of Parole Search Conditions

The issue often arises as to when a suspect, who is on parole, can no longer be searched based on the parole conditions because the parolee has been incarcerated for a parole violation. In **People v. Hunter** (2006) 140 Cal.App.4th 1147 (cert. denied, March 19, 2007, 127 S.Ct. 1838), the Court of Appeal held that a parole officer retained authority to conduct a parole search of Mr. Hunter before the court formally revoked his parole.

2.5 – Exceptions to the Need for a Search Warrant

2.5.1 – Exigency

2.5.1.1 – General Principles

Exigent circumstances apply anytime an officer is concerned about escapes, destruction of evidence or safety issues. The necessity needed is a substantial threat to life, health or property. Courts have held that the knock-notice rules are applicable to the warrantless entry of a residence for investigative purposes. Knock-notice rules may not apply if circumstances requiring instantaneous entry exist or if such notice will increase the danger of a violent confrontation.

In **People v. Miller** (1999) 69 Cal.App.4th 190, the Court of Appeal ruled that exigent circumstances existed for the warrantless entry of a residence given the need to return the child to his home and the possibility that other children might have been inside unattended.

FACTS (People v. Miller (1999) 69 Cal.App.4th 190)

On the morning of August 6, 1995, Randy Raines saw a small child wandering around the neighborhood unattended. His wife, Jona Bowen-Raines approached the child, who was calling out for his mother. Mrs. Bowen-Raines and the child were observed by Lywinda Brittain Keast, who approached and told her that the child's name was Jeffrey and where he lived. Ms. Keast also stated that she had found the boy alone in the street 10 days earlier and returned him to the Miller residence. Mrs. Bowen-Raines took the child to her house and phoned the police.

Bakersfield Police Officer Grady arrived at the Raines' house around 11 a.m. He spoke with both women and listened to their concerns about the Millers leaving the children unattended on other occasions. Officer Grady took the child back to the Miller residence. The front door to the residence was open about two inches. Officer Grady knocked on the door, rang the bell and announced himself. He yelled that he was from the Bakersfield Police Department and asked if anyone was home. After receiving no response, he knocked several more times and again stated that he was from the police department. Still receiving no response, Officer Grady pushed the door open and again announced himself before entering the residence. Officer Grady was holding Jeffrey's hand when he entered the residence.

Once inside the house, Officer Grady saw Brian Jeffrey Miller in the hallway near the kitchen. Officer Grady asked Mr. Miller if the child was his and if he lived at the residence. Mr. Miller answered both questions affirmatively. Mr. Miller said he had been asleep and did not know the whereabouts of his wife or other children. Officer Grady asked Mr. Miller for ID, but Mr. Miller was not able to produce any. Officer Grady noted that Mr. Miller seemed very nervous, was slow to respond to questions, had dilated pupils and repeatedly stated that he was thirsty. These observations caused Officer Grady to believe that Mr. Miller might be under the influence of cocaine or methamphetamine. However, when asked, Mr. Miller denied being under the influence of drugs.

Officer Grady asked for permission to search for other children and narcotics. Mr. Miller said, "Sure, go ahead. I don't have anything." During the search, the officer found numerous firearms, explosives, ammunition and dangerous chemicals in the house and garage. Literature discussing bomb making, sniper fire and the Oklahoma City bombing were found in the house.

A similar result was reached in **People v. Seminoff** (2008) 159 Cal.App.4th 518, where the Court of Appeal upheld the trial court's ruling that exigent circumstances justified the police's initial entry into a hotel room without a warrant. The **Seminoff** Court also upheld a search warrant that the police later obtained for the room and resulted in the seizure of 46 pounds of marijuana. The police initially responded to the room after a four-year-old child came to the hotel lobby and told the clerk that he was unable to awaken his mother. The Court observed that "[i]f there is one thing four-year-old boys are usually good at, it is waking their parents. So, the report of Timothy walking into the hotel lobby and reporting he couldn't wake his mother would have been enough to put any reasonable person on notice that something might be seriously wrong with Bassett. It was, after all, the middle of the day, not the time that most parents of young children are at luxury to doze off." (**Id**. at 529.) For the officer to fail to enter the room on these facts and after receiving no response to his repeated knocking and announcements would have constituted a "dereliction of duty."

FACTS (People v. Seminoff (2008) 159 Cal.App.4th 518)

On the morning of March 27, 2005, four-year-old Timothy, the child of Anthony Seminoff's girlfriend, (Ms. Bassett) went to the lobby of the Holiday Inn in Placentia where they were all staying and reported that he was unable to wake up his mother. A hotel employee went up to the room and was also unsuccessful in waking up Timothy's mother. Placentia Police Officer Butts was sent to the hotel "to assist the fire department with the possible medical aid of a female." He arrived at 11:52 a.m., and went to Bassett's room with three fire department paramedics. The officer gave knock notice outside the room by saying, "Placentia Police Department. Come to the door or make your presence known." After about 30 seconds and upon failing to receive a response from the room, Officer Butts used the passkey and entered the room.

Once inside the room, Officer Butts continued to announce his presence. He noted that the room was dark and smelled heavily of marijuana. While holding his gun and a flashlight, Officer Butts checked the area around the doorway. When he opened the closet door behind the front door, the odor of marijuana became even stronger. In the living room area, Officer Butts found a couple of hunting knives and a loaded handgun magazine in plain view. The officer continued to announce his presence as he entered the bedroom area. In that area, he saw a baggie of methamphetamine on a desk and Ms. Bassett lying on the bed. Officer Butts opened the curtains, holstered his gun and tried unsuccessfully to awaken Ms. Bassett. Officer Butts then called the paramedics into the room.

The paramedics were able to awaken Ms. Bassett. Although groggy, Ms. Bassett told the paramedics she was fine and was just a heavy sleeper. Officer Butts asked Ms. Bassett if there were any guns in the room and she said there were two and gave the officer permission to look. She also directed him to a few locations where they might be located, including the nightstand, a dresser and a briefcase. Officer Butts searched for the guns while the paramedics continued to tend to Ms. Bassett. Officer Butts found a pipe and baggie of methamphetamine in a nightstand drawer. He found a .357 revolver, a digital scale and pouch full of baggies inside the briefcase. One of the paramedics found a 9 mm pistol under a pillow near Ms. Bassett. Officer Butts also found some paperwork belonging to Mr. Seminoff in the room.

Officers brought Timothy back to the room and reunited him with his mother. Officer Butts asked Ms. Bassett to sign a consent to search form for the room, but she refused. The officers obtained a search warrant and found a duffel bag with 46 pounds of marijuana inside the closet by the front door.

It is important that the police not create the exigency by which they are seeking to justify their warrantless entry because that will result in the suppression of any evidence seized. For example, the Court of Appeal ruled that exigent circumstances did not exist for a warrantless hotel room entry in **People v. Bellizzi** (1995) 34 Cal.App.4th 1849, because the plain-clothes officers who burst into the hotel room with guns drawn, illegally created any exigency that might have existed.

FACTS (People v. Bellizzi (1995) 34 Cal.App.4th 1849)

A maid at the Radisson Hotel in South San Francisco saw several clear baggies with white powder in them while cleaning Mr. Bellizzi's room. Mr. Bellizzi was not in the room at the time. The maid contacted the manager, who contacted the police.

The police discussed the situation with a DDA, who did not believe a search warrant was appropriate and encouraged the officers to do a "knock and talk." Two plain-clothes officers and the hotel manager went to the room. The manager knocked on the door, while the officers remained out of sight. Mr. Bellizzi asked who was there and the manager said "housekeeping." Mr. Bellizzi opened the chained door a bit, looked out, and then closed the door.

There was a silent interval and the officers and manager began to leave when Mr. Bellizzi again opened the door.

One of the Officers drew his gun at this point and Mr. Bellizzi put his arms over his head and began to yell words like "Oh, no. Oh, Shit. Oh, God." Mr. Bellizzi retreated into the room and began to close the door. The officers followed with drawn guns and identified themselves. Large amounts of cocaine were scattered about the room.

2.5.1.2 – Nature of the Crime

In **Welsh v. Wisconsin** (1984) 466 U.S. 740, the U.S. Supreme Court ruled that a warrantless entry into a house to arrest someone for driving under the influence (DUI) of alcohol did not constitute an exigent circumstances. The Supreme Court, in looking at the gravity of the underlying offense said that such an entry was not justified when driving under the influence amounted to a nonjailable, civil offense, involving a 60-day license suspension under Wisconsin law.

In **People v. Hua** (2008) 158 Cal.App.4th 1027, the Court of Appeal reversed a trial court decision and suppressed evidence seized when officers made a warrantless entry into the defendant's apartment to make an arrest for misdemeanor possession of marijuana. In reaching this conclusion, the Court of Appeal found the rationale of **Welsh v. Wisconsin** (1984) 446 U.S. 740, applicable to the People's claim that the warrantless entry was justified by exigent circumstances.

FACTS (People v. Hua (2008) 158 Cal.App.4th 1027)

On March 27, 2005, at 11:08 p.m., uniformed Pacifica Police Officers Mostasisia and Corporal Mix responded to an apartment residence regarding a report of a "noise disturbance." As they approached the apartment, they noticed the "distinct odor" of burnt marijuana coming from it. Officer Mix was standing in a common area in front of a window next to the front door. From that vantage point, she could see through the open vertical blinds and saw a group of people socializing in the living room. Corporal Mix also saw someone put an object to his lips and smoke from it. Based on her experience and training, she testified that the action was consistent with someone smoking marijuana.

Officer Mostasisia knocked on the front door for about 45 seconds before John Hua answered the door. The officers remained outside and explained why they were at the apartment. Mr. Hua said he had been using a drill earlier that evening. When asked about the marijuana odor, Mr. Hua denied smoking marijuana but implied other people were smoking it in the apartment. However, when told by Corporal Mix of her observations, Mr. Hua denied anyone was smoking marijuana in the apartment.

Given the amount of smoke in the apartment and their concern about the possible destruction of evidence, the officers asked for consent to enter the apartment, which Mr. Hua declined to give. Corporal Mix then asked if Mr. Hua had a medical marijuana card and he answered "No." The officers again asked for permission to enter and Mr. Hua stepped aside and allowed them in the apartment. However, "[O]n cross-examination, Officer Mostasisia conceded that he made it clear to appellant that the officers wanted to enter the apartment and that in his report he stated, '[Appellant] succumbed to our request and stepped aside.'" (**Id**. at 1031.)

After entering the apartment, Officer Mostasisia observed the smell of marijuana and a cloud of smoke in the living room. He also saw two used marijuana cigarettes on a coffee table in the living room. The officer asked if anyone else was in the apartment and a few of the guests said, "No." No one had a medical marijuana card and no one claimed ownership of the used marijuana joints. The officer next asked if there were any weapons or animals in the apartment and someone said, "No." All of the living room occupants consented to a search of their persons, but the officers discovered no contraband. Corporal Mix then did a 30 to 45 second protective sweep of the apartment for officer safety and to ensure no animals or other persons were present.

During the protective sweep, Corporal Mix opened no drawers or closets, but did find 46 marijuana plants growing in plastic, dirt-filled tubs in Mr. Hua's bedroom. Mr. Hua was detained and said there was a letter allowing him to cultivate the marijuana. Officer Mostasisia believed that Mr. Hua was giving the officers permission to find the letter, so Corporal Mix retrieved it from an open safe. In and around the safe were a large quantity of empty plastic baggies. The letter did not give Mr. Hua permission, but named someone else who was not present in the apartment. Mr. Hua was placed in handcuffs and told he was being detained but not under arrest.

"Aside from the plants, the police observed, in plain view, a bag of potting soil in the hallway, three bottles of liquid plant food in the living room, and a small digital scale. Inside the bathroom, a 'Cannabis Grow Bible' and plastic planter trays were found. A cane sword was found on the top bookshelf in the living room. Each of these items was seized. Sometime after Mix conducted her protective sweep of the apartment, other officers arrived and took control of the scene." (**Id**. at 1032.)

At the police station, Mr. Hua waived his rights and claimed that he grew marijuana as a hobby and for use as wallpaper. Mr. Hua also admitted to smoking marijuana with his friends, but not to selling it. However, no such wallpaper was found in his apartment. Mr. Hua was not arrested that night.

Following the denial of his motion to suppress, he plead guilty to felony cultivation of marijuana and misdemeanor possession of a cane sword. He then appealed the denial of his motion.

RATIONALE

"California has chosen to treat the offense of possession of less than 28.5 grams of marijuana as a minor offense that is nonjailable even for repeat offenders. Under *Welsh, McArthur* **[Illinois v McArthur** (2001) 531 U.S. 326] and *Thompson*, one consequence of that decision is to preclude officers who see this offense being committed from entering a home without a warrant or consent to seize the offender or the contraband, in order to prevent the imminent destruction of evidence of the offense." (**Id**. at 1037.)

A similar result was reached by the appellate court in **People v. Torres et al**. (2012) 205 Cal.App.4th 989.[13]

FACTS (People v. Torres et al. (2012) 205 Cal.App.4th 989)

On December 21, 2010, Los Angeles hotel security personnel contacted the police about a hotel guest who reported several items were missing from her room, including a laptop computer and a Blackberry cell phone. Hotel personnel determined that a hotel engineer had unlocked the victim's room door for two women. The security officer believed that the suspects were staying in a particular room and informed the police of that fact. The hotel security officer also believed that he had previously helped the two women enter a different hotel room with their key. LAPD officers went to the hotel room where the women were staying. At the door, they noticed a "strong smell" of marijuana coming from the room. The officers could smell the marijuana from two to three feet away from the room door. An officer knocked on the hotel room door and a woman opened the door. When she opened the door, the smell of marijuana was even stronger. The police asked everyone in the room to step into the hallway. The defendant and two men came out of the room. The police ultimately released two men after questioning them. The police did a "protective sweep" of the room. During the sweep, the officers noticed a Blackberry cell phone in plain view. The police saw a purse on the bed that was open at the top. Inside the purse, the officer saw a credit card bearing the victim's name. The officer then looked in the purse to locate an ID card, and found identification inside the purse. The officer saw what looked like and smelled like marijuana ashes in an ashtray. The police also found a black laptop underneath a mattress in the room.

[13] After **People v. Hua** (2008) 158 Cal.App.4th 1027 was decided, and completely unrelated to the holding in the case, in 2009 the California Legislature further decreased the penalty for possession of less than one ounce of marijuana (H&S 11357(b)) by reducing it from a misdemeanor to an infraction and eliminating drug diversion as an sentencing option for a conviction of that offense.

The defendants moved to suppress the evidence found in the room. The defendants argued that there were no exigent circumstances permitting a warrantless entry of the hotel room, and there was no evidence a protective sweep was necessary. The trial court concluded that a protective sweep rationale did not permit the warrantless entry. However, the court found that there were exigent circumstances to justify the entry. The trial court found that the police officers could lawfully enter the hotel room to prevent marijuana from being destroyed or from "going up in smoke." The trial court then concluded that the items in plain view were admissible, but suppressed the evidence seized that was not in plain view, which included the laptop computer found under the mattress.

The defendants eventually pled no contest to burglary and grand theft charges. The trial court sentenced them to three years formal probation.

The appellate court overruled the trial court and found that the warrantless entry to the hotel room was not lawful.

RATIONALE

In reaching its decision, the appellate court relied on the case of **People v. Hua** (2008) 158 Cal.App.4th 1027. The appellate court found that the officers had even less reason than the police in the **Hua** case to believe that the defendants possessed more than 28.5 grams of marijuana. The appellate court stated that "Where, as here, police articulated no basis to believe a jailable offense was occurring, there were no exigent circumstances justifying a warrantless entry to prevent destruction of evidence that would prove the offense." **Id**., at 997.

The appellate court also adopted the **Hua** court's statement that "California has chosen to treat the offense of possession of less than 28.5 grams of marijuana as a minor offense that is nonjailable even for repeat offenders. Under *Welsh, McArthur* **[Illinois v McArthur** (2001) 531 U.S. 326] and *Thompson*, one consequence of that decision is to preclude officers who see this offense being committed from entering a home without a warrant or consent to seize the offender or the contraband, in order to prevent the imminent destruction of evidence of the offense." (**Hua**, at 1037. Torres et al., at 997).

2.5.1.3 – Driving Under the Influence Offenses

In a 6 to 1 decision in **People v. Thompson** (2006) 38 Cal.4th 811, the California Supreme Court reached a different result than the U.S. Supreme Court in **Welsh**, when it ruled that exigent circumstances justified the warrantless entry of Mr. Thompson's home to arrest him for driving under the influence of alcohol. The Court explained that "[i]n short, the state's intrusion into the home was the minimum necessary to effect the arrest and extended only to areas already exposed to public view. Under these circumstances, it was reasonable for the police to enter the home without a warrant in order to arrest defendant and thereby prevent the imminent destruction of evidence of his crime." **Thompson**, at 828.

In a cautionary note, the California Supreme Court said, "[i]n holding that exigent circumstances justified the warrantless entry here, we need not decide-and do not hold-that the police may enter a home without a warrant to effect an arrest of a DUI suspect in *every* case. We hold merely that the police conduct here, taking into account all of the circumstances, was reasonable – with reasonableness measured as 'a balance between the public interest and the individual's right to personal security free from arbitrary interference by law officers.' (*Pennsylvania v. Mimms* (1977) 434 U.S. 106, 109, 98 S.Ct. 330, 54 L.Ed.2d 331; accord, *People v. Ramey* (1976) 16 Cal.3d 263, 276, 127 Cal.Rptr. 629, 545 P.2d 1333 . . .)" **Thompson**, at 827.

FACTS (People v. Thompson (2006) 38 Cal.4th 811)

Early in the evening on July 21, 2003 Madelene Orvos returned to her Santa Barbara apartment complex after walking with her dogs on the beach. Ms. Orvos saw Daniel Lyon Thompson passed out in a white Bronco that was parked in her assigned parking space. A neighbor came outside, woke up Mr. Thompson and asked him to leave. Before he left, Ms. Orvos saw Mr. Thompson stumble around and throw an empty bottle of Vodka out of the Bronco. He then passed out a second time. She believed he was intoxicated.

Ms. Orvos saw Mr. Thompson in this condition on several prior occasions and decided this time to follow Mr. Thompson when he drove away and to call 9-1-1 and report the situation. As she followed Mr. Thompson, she saw him run a red light, drive about 70 mph on the freeway and drive close to the concrete side of the roadway. When he exited the freeway, he turned right and began running stop signs and speeding in a neighborhood where children were present. Officer Gutierrez arrived just as Ms. Orvos lost track of the Bronco. After obtaining the license number of the Bronco, he instructed her to wait in the parking lot of a nearby golf course while he picked up the pursuit.

Officer Gutierrez went to the address for the registered owner of the Bronco and saw the Bronco parked in front. After Officer Dejohn arrived to assist, Officer Gutierrez went back and had Ms. Orvos follow him back to Mr. Thompson's residence to identify the Bronco, which she did. Officer Gutierrez also found the hood of the Bronco warm when he touched it.

The officers approached the wide open front door and rang the doorbell. Slavka Kovarick answered the door and was asked who had been driving the Bronco. Ms. Kovarick said Daniel owned the Bronco. When asked if the officers could speak to him, she said he was asleep. Officer Dejohn asked her to wake him up, so she entered a bedroom to the left of the front door and returned a few moments later and said she could not wake up Mr. Thompson. Ms. Kovarick refused to let the officers enter the residence and walked away.

Officer Dejohn heard people speaking softly down the hall and then saw Mr. Thompson, who was shirtless, leave the house and go into the backyard. Upon turning around, Mr. Thompson made eye contact with Officer Dejohn, who motioned for him to come to the front door. As Mr. Thompson approached the officers, he was staggering slightly, had slurred speech and had an odor of alcohol emanating from his person. Officer Dejohn explained that the officers suspected he was driving under the influence of alcohol and wanted to talk to him and have him perform some field sobriety test, but Mr. Thompson refused to cooperate and began to walk away. Officer Dejohn entered the house and arrested Mr. Thompson with the assistance of Officer Gutierrez. After his arrest, Ms. Orvos identified Mr. Thompson as the driver and a later blood test revealed a blood alcohol level of .21 percent. Enroute to jail, Mr. Thompson told Officer Dejohn, "I'll kick your ass."

After the denial of his motion to suppress evidence, Mr. Thompson pled guilty to driving under the influence of alcohol, resisting arrest and to two prior convictions for driving under the influence of alcohol. The trial court sentenced him to 24 months in jail, but suspended execution during a three year probationary period. A divided Superior Court appellate panel affirmed the trial court's ruling, but the Court of Appeal reversed the trial court citing **Welsh v Wisconsin**, **supra,** which it believed was the controlling authority in the case. The People then sought review before the California Supreme Court.

RATIONALE

The California Supreme Court distinguished the U.S. Supreme Court decision in **Welsh** by noting that California "classifies a first offense for driving under the influence as a *criminal* act that is punishable by no more than six months and no less than 96 hours in jail. (Veh.Code, 23536(a)) The possibility of imprisonment distinguishes DUI in California from DUI in Wisconsin." (*Italics* in original) **Thompson**, at 821. Therefore, and unlike the situation in **Welsh**, a California DUI is not an "extremely minor" offense.

The California Supreme Court then concluded that "[w]e therefore believe *Welsh* was limited to Wisconsin's "amazing" decision to classify DUI as a civil nonjailable offense (*Welsh, supra,* 466 U.S. at p. 755, 104 S.Ct. 2091 (conc. opn. of Blackmun, J.)) and not as a categorical bar on warrantless arrests in the home for DUI in the vast majority of states that, like California, classify it as a crime with the possibility of imprisonment." **Thompson**, at 821.

The Court upheld the warrantless entry of the residence based on the exigent circumstances that Mr. Thompson's blood alcohol would diminish while the police sought a search warrant and based on a concern that Mr. Thompson could have masked his true blood alcohol level by ingesting additional quantities of alcohol while the police sought a search warrant.

In **People v. Schofield** (2001) 90 Cal.App.4th 968, the Court of Appeal upheld a DUI arrest outside Mr. Schofield's residence where an Atascadero Police Officer went to the residence following a liquor store clerk's observations that Mr. Schofield was intoxicated and drove away from the liquor store. It is important to note that nothing in this case's holding authorizes a police officer to force entry into a residence to effect a DUI arrest.

FACTS (People v. Schofield (2001) 90 Cal.App.4th 968)

At approximately 2:30 p.m., on February 8, 2002, Atascadero Fire Department personnel were dispatched to Chalk Mountain Liquor Store based on a report of a person passed out near the side entrance of a liquor store. Atascadero Peace Officer McCray also responded and was the first to arrive.

Officer McCray spoke with Stephen Bolin, a store employee. Mr. Bolin said that he saw the defendant passed out near the side entrance to the liquor store, thought the defendant had a medical problem, and therefore called 9-1-1. Another customer helped the defendant stand. Mr. Bolin told Officer McCray that he saw the defendant enter a green colored Karman Ghia. Mr. Bolin approached the car to check on the defendant's welfare and noticed a strong odor of alcohol emanating from the defendant's breath. Since he believed the defendant was too intoxicated to drive, he tried to pull the keys out of the ignition. The defendant pulled them out and threw them on the passenger floorboard. Believing that the defendant was not going to drive, Mr. Bolin returned to the liquor store and then saw the defendant drive away southbound on El Camino Real.

Mr. Bolin gave the officer a physical description of the defendant and identified the defendant as a regular customer of the liquor store. He then pulled out a piece of paper with the license number "1EMS119" written on it. A check with police dispatch revealed that the car was registered to Mr. Schofield at 9371 Musselman Avenue, Atascadero. Upon arrival at that address, the officer saw the car parked in front of the residence and noted that the hood felt warm.

Officer McCrary contacted the defendant at the residence and had a discussion with him at his doorway. Officer McCrary asked the defendant to perform some field sobriety tests and the defendant voluntarily, but with some balance problems, walked outside of the residence. After failing those sobriety tests, the officer arrested Mr. Schofield.

RATIONALE

The police conducted their investigation from Mr. Schofield's doorway. The officer acted courteously and did not assert the right to enter the premises or secure the answers to his questions. Mr. Schofield voluntarily stepped outside of his residence and took field sobriety tests, which he failed.

The Court of Appeal in **People v. Keltie** (1983) 148 Cal.App.3d 773. found the dissipation of alcohol from the suspect's system sufficient exigent circumstances to allow the warrantless entry of a residence to arrest the defendant who was suspected of committing a felony DUI, and a felony hit and run, one and one half (1½) hours earlier and a few blocks away.

The Court ruled that in order to justify an entry based on decreasing blood alcohol level, the following four factors must be present:

1. Probable cause to believe the suspect was under the influence
2. That the suspect had committed a felony in which being under the influence of alcohol was an element
3. That the suspect was presently in the home
4. The time interval between the offense and the entry must be brief enough so that evidence of drinking could still be found in the blood.

FACTS (People v. Keltie (1983) 148 Cal.App.3d 773)

At about 10 p.m., on August 14, 1981, Yoko Toda was struck and killed by a car on Beverly Glen Boulevard in Los Angeles. No one saw the accident but several people looked out their window after hearing the impact and saw George Keltie's van and a sports car stopped parallel to each other in the two northbound lanes of traffic. The van was in the right lane near where Ms. Toda lay by the curb. The driver of the van, who witnesses identified as being a male, was seen to briefly exit his car and stagger for no apparent reason, and then drive away. The officers had probable cause to believe a violation of California Vehicle Code 23101 had occurred.

About one hour later, officers came upon Mr. Keltie's van, which was parked in his driveway a few blocks away from the crime scene. The right side of the van was damaged and was smeared with blood and human tissue. The driver's compartment of the van smelled strongly of alcohol. The officers knocked on the front door to the residence and were greeted by Mrs. Keltie. She told them that the van belonged to her and that her husband was not home. She exhibited no signs of intoxication.

Although the wife claimed the husband was not at home, the officers had observed more than one person looking out the window before making contact. Therefore, it was reasonable to believe the husband might be in the house. The officers entered Mr. Keltie's home, found him intoxicated and arrested him. At 12:48 a.m., he had a blood-alcohol level of .24%.

At trial, Mr. Keltie was convicted of felony DUI and felony hit and run. The court placed him on probation and sentenced him to nine months in the county jail.

2.5.1.4 – Homicides

In **Mincey v. Arizona** (1978) 437 U.S. 385, the U.S. Supreme Court ruled that there is no homicide scene exception to the search warrant requirement. The Supreme Court ruled that a warrantless, very thorough search of a murder scene, which lasted for four days and followed the death of an undercover narcotics officer, did not fall within the exigent circumstances exception to the warrant requirement.

The Court observed that "[t]here was no indication that evidence would be lost, destroyed, or removed during the time required to obtain a search warrant. Indeed, the police guard at the apartment minimized that possibility. And there is no suggestion that a search warrant could not easily and conveniently have been obtained. We decline to hold that the seriousness of the offense under investigation itself creates exigent circumstances of the kind that under the Fourth Amendment justify a warrantless search." (**Id.** at 394.)

Six years later in **Thompson v. Louisiana** (1984) 469 U.S. 17, the Supreme Court reaffirmed its earlier decision in **Mincey v. Arizona**, and again suppressed evidence seized without the benefit of a search warrant from a homicide scene.

FACTS (Thompson v. Louisiana (1984) 469 U.S. 17)

On May 18, 1982, several Jefferson Parish Sheriff Department's deputies went to the defendant's home in response to the daughter's call regarding a homicide at the residence. According to the daughter, the mother had shot her husband, taken an overdose in an attempt to kill herself and, after reconsideration, called her daughter to tell her what had happened and to request help.

When the police arrived, the daughter admitted them into the house and directed them to the victims' respective rooms. The officers made a cursory search and found the defendant's husband, who had been shot and killed, in a bedroom in the house. The defendant was found lying unconscious from a drug overdose, in another bedroom.

The deputies immediately secured the crime scene and had the victims transported to the hospital. Approximately 35 minutes later, two members of the sheriff's department's homicide team arrived to conduct a follow-up investigation.

Deputies then began a two-hour, warrantless, general exploratory search of the residence for evidence of the crime. Based on the evidence seized, the defendant was charged with the second-degree murder of her husband and moved to suppress the following items:

- A pistol found inside a chest of drawers in the same room as the husband's body
- A torn up suicide note in a wastepaper basket in an adjoining bathroom
- A suicide type letter, folded inside an envelope containing a Christmas card, found on top of a chest of drawers.

In **Flippo v. West Virginia** (1999) 528 U.S. 11, the U.S. Supreme Court again reiterated its holding in **Mincey v. Arizona**, and reversed a lower court ruling upholding the warrantless search of a homicide crime scene. The Supreme Court issued a Per Curium opinion based on the defendant's petition for a writ of certiorari and to proceed in forma paupeis.

FACTS (Flippo v. West Virginia (1999) 528 U.S. 11)

One night in 1996, James Flippo, who is a minister, and his wife were vacationing at cabin #13 in a state park. Mr. Flippo called 9-1-1 to report that he and his wife had been attacked. When the police arrived, they found Mr. Flippo waiting outside the cabin for them. He had head and leg injuries. After questioning him, the officer entered the cabin and found the body of Mrs. Flippo, who had suffered fatal head wounds.

The officers secured the scene, took Mr. Flippo to the hospital and searched the exterior and surrounding area of the cabin for footprints or signs of forced entry. A police photographer arrived at about 5:30 a.m., whereupon the officers re-entered the cabin and proceeded to "process the crime scene" without first obtaining a search warrant authorizing their actions.

For over 16 hours, the police took photographs, collected evidence, and searched through the contents of the cabin. On a table in the cabin, the police found and opened a briefcase. Inside the briefcase was an envelope containing various photographs and negatives of a man, later identified as Joel Boggess, who appeared to be removing his jeans. Mr. Boggess is a friend of Mr. Flippo and a member of Mr. Flippo's congregation.

The defendant was indicted for murder and moved to suppress the illegally seized photographs and negatives. The trial court denied the motion and approved of the search under the non-existent "homicide crime scene" exception to the warrant requirement.

At trial, the DA introduced these photographs against Mr. Flippo to show the relationship between the defendant and Mr. Boggess. The DA argued that Mr. Flippo might have killed his wife because of her displeasure over this relationship. A jury returned a guilty verdict and Mr. Flippo appealed his conviction to the Supreme Court of Appeals of West Virginia, which denied discretionary review of case.

2.5.1.5 – Sick or Injured Parties

The California Supreme Court ruled in **Tamborino v. Superior Court** (1986) 41 Cal.3d 919, that an officer was justified in making a warrantless re-entry of an apartment to see if other victims of a robbery were inside. The Court found that the officer's actions were justified even though he had no facts indicating that a second victim was inside the apartment and Mr. Tamborino was outside the apartment bleeding from his wounds.

The California Supreme Court found that the observations of Mr. Tamborino's injuries, coupled with the earlier report of a robbery, justified the immediate brief search of the apartment for other victims. The Court said, "Officer Klein had no prior information indicating that only *one* victim was involved in the robbery, and in light of the situation he confronted, ordinary, routine common sense and a reasonable concern for human life justified him in conducting a walk-through search truly limited in scope to determining the presence of other victims. Nothing in the record suggests that the officer had any hidden additional motive, such as searching for drugs or contraband. . ." **Tamborino**, **supra**, at 923.

FACTS (Tamborino v. Superior Court (1986) 41 Cal.3d 919)

On November 12, 1983, Newport Police Officer Klein, a four-year veteran of the police force, received a radio report of a robbery at a particular address. The report said that there was a belief of the existence of an injured and bleeding victim. The officer received no description of either the robbery or victim(s).

Officer Klein and a second officer went to the reported location and saw some blood spots outside the building and on the walkway outside of Danny Tamborino's apartment. Alvino Johnson, who was a neighbor, confirmed that an injured person was inside the apartment. Officer Klein knocked on the door of the apartment and loudly identified himself as a police officer. After waiting one to two minutes and hearing no response, he knocked again. Officer Klein now heard some movement inside the apartment. Believing prompt action was necessary, Officer Klein kicked in the door and saw Mr. Tamborino in the living room walking toward the front door.

Mr. Tamborino was barefoot and wearing a bathrobe. He also had quite a bit of blood on his head, neck and hands. Mr. Tamborino was holding his head and appeared to be bleeding from the right side of his face, although not profusely. Because Officer Klein was unsure if Mr. Tamborino was the victim or the suspect, he brought him outside the apartment and handcuffed him. After first checking to see that the wound was not serious, Officer Klein re-entered the apartment to see if any other injured person might need assistance. He did not first ask Mr. Tamborino if anyone else was in the apartment.

> As Office Klein walked through the apartment, he saw cocaine residue in plain view on a coffee table in the living room, along with some narcotic paraphernalia. He also saw some marijuana, a weighing scale and a cocaine cutting agent.
>
> Officer Klein brought Mr. Tamborino back into the apartment and questioned him about the incident. Mr. Tamborino said that the attacker entered the apartment, asked for Mr. Tamborino's roommate Joe Smith, and then attacked him with a knife. The officer found a bloody knife on the sofa in the living room. The officer summoned paramedics to assist Mr. Tamborino.
>
> Mr. Smith arrived a short time later. The officers requested permission to search, but were initially refused. Mr. Smith and Mr. Tamborino later consented when they learned that the officers sought a search warrant. The police found several bindles of cocaine under Mr. Smith's mattress.

In **<u>People v. Zabelle</u>** (1996) 50 Cal.App.4th 1282, the Court of Appeal upheld the warrantless entry of a hotel room based on exigent circumstances, which included the observation of the defendant passed out in a fetal position near balls of heroin. In so doing, the Court explicitly rejected the defendant's contention that he was merely sleeping and that the welfare check was a ruse on the part of the officers.

FACTS (<u>People v. Zabelle</u> (1996) 50 Cal.App.4th 1282)

> Experienced narcotics officers were walking down the common hallway of a hotel when they passed by an open doorway. Inside the room, they could see the defendant seated on the bed with his face lying on a dresser at the foot of the bed. The defendant was in a fetal position, had his eyes closed and his hands were not visible.
>
> The officers could see a jagged mirror on the dresser with several dark balls of heroin on it. The officers entered the room to check on the defendant's welfare and confirmed that the dark balls were indeed heroin.

The Court of Appeal upheld the warrantless entry of a residence based on the exigent circumstances of a possible in progress domestic violence in **<u>People v. Higgins</u>** (1994) 26 Cal.App.4th 247.

FACTS (<u>People v. Higgins</u> (1994) 26 Cal.App.4th 247)

> Police received an anonymous call of a domestic violence incident at a particular address. Officers went to the scene and knocked on the back door. When they received no response, they went to the front door. During the walk to the front door, the officers saw a man inside the house and heard shouting.
>
> A woman answered the door and appeared "extremely frightened." She had a small red mark under one eye and slight darkness under both. She claimed

the red mark was a birthmark. The woman said her boyfriend was home earlier, but had left. The officers believed she was lying and entered.

The officers met Mr. Higgins as he came down the stairs. While talking to him, the officers smelled marijuana and saw a triple beam balance scale on the floor. Near the scale was a plastic bag with marijuana. Inside the bag was a bindle of cocaine. Mr. Higgins consented to a house search and the police found more contraband.

In **People v. Poulson** (1998) 69 Cal.App.4th Supp. 1, the San Luis Obispo Superior Court Appellate Department ruled that an officer's warrantless entry of a residence through a kitchen window was justified by exigent circumstances after finding a severely damaged car, which was streaked with blood around the passenger side of the car, and which contained the name and address of the defendant's wife. Upon going to the house, the police also observed the wife inside the residence bleeding from a cut above her eye. The Court found that despite the wife's claim that she did not need assistance, the police acted reasonably in believing she needed medical attention.

FACTS (People v. Poulson (1998) 69 Cal.App.4th Supp. 1)

At approximately 7:30 p.m., on May 18, 1997, Arroyo Grande Police Officer Berry was dispatched to a traffic accident. On arrival, Officer Berry found an abandoned Chevrolet, straddling the sidewalk, at the end of a trail of about 125 feet of skid marks and debris consisting of trees, shrubbery, dirt and fences that the car passed through before coming to a stop. The heavily damaged Chevrolet was resting against a brick wall and both front seat air bags were deployed. Blood streaked the passenger side air bag and was smeared on the fractured passenger-side windshield and on an armrest in the right door panel. There were droplets of blood on the passenger-side seat cushion and on the right-side floor mat. There were also droplets of blood on the driver's seat and smeared blood on the driver's seat belt webbing.

Officer Berry retrieved either a notebook or a ring binder from the car, which contained the name, address and telephone number of Patricia Poulson, who is the defendant's wife. Officer Berry told Officer Sanchez to go to the Poulson's residence and contact whoever might be there.

Officer Sanchez went to the residence and later told Officer Berry that he observed blood on a walkway leading to the front door, and saw blood smeared on the doorframe. Officer Sanchez knocked on the front door but no one answered his knock. Officer Sanchez also telephoned the residence twice. The first time the phone was answered by a male who hung-up. The second time the phone was answered by the answering machine.

When Officer Berry arrived at the residence, he also knocked on the front door but received no answer. At this point, Officer Berry called for an ambulance and fire department EMTs. He then began to look for a way into the house. Officer Berry found a window on the front of the house that afforded him a view into the kitchen of the house. He yelled, "Police", but still received no response.

Shortly after he yelled, "Police", he heard a woman's voice and Mrs. Poulson walked into view. Mrs. Poulson had blood on her face from a cut over her right eye. Officer Berry told her to meet him at the front door, but she refused and said either "Everything is all right" or "I'm perfectly all right." Mrs. Poulson also told Officer Berry, "Do not come in." Officer Berry testified that given the accident scene, the blood and the obvious impact with the windshield he decided to enter the residence because he did not feel safe leaving Mrs. Poulson alone at the residence.

Officer Berry climbed through the kitchen window and let the EMTs in through the front door. The police arrested Mr. Poulson, who was also in the house, for driving under the influence of alcohol, causing an accident with injury and hit and run.

2.5.1.6 – Evidence Destruction

In **People v. Ortiz** (1995) 32 Cal.App.4th 286, two officers were walking down a hotel hallway when they saw the defendant and a woman in a hotel room. The door was open and the woman was counting out tinfoil bindles and placing them on a table. The officers believed that the bindles contained heroin, so they entered and arrested the defendant and the woman.

The Court of Appeal ruled that it was reasonable for the officers to believe that the evidence would have been destroyed but for their warrantless entry into the room. It did not matter that there was no evidence that the defendant or the woman saw the officers in the hallway; it was reasonable for the officers to believe the occupants might have seen them.

While the defendant was being booked for possession of cocaine in **People v. Bullock** (1990) 226 Cal.App.3d 380, his pager continued to go off. The officer pushed the button and collected the numbers. Several of the phone calls received were requests for the delivery of rock cocaine. The Court of Appeal ruled that exigent circumstances existed for the warrantless search because the numbers in the pager's memory would be lost if the officer did not activate the pager and retrieve them.

In **People v. Hull** (1995) 34 Cal.App.4th 1448, the Court of Appeal upheld the warrantless entry of a residence occupied by recent bait car stereo thieves based on the exigent circumstances of destruction of evidence and the loss of florescent powder on the thieves' hands.

FACTS (People v. Hull (1995) 34 Cal.App.4th 1448)

Roseville police set up a "bait" vehicle with stereo speakers inside. The speakers were dusted with a florescent green power and contained a tracking device. At about 12:52 a.m., an alarm went off and Officer Herring responded. He discovered that the car had been broken into and the speakers taken. The officer used the tracking device and followed the speakers to a residence that was between three and four miles away.

While waiting for back-up, Officer Herring saw two males in a lighted back bedroom. When a second officer arrived, someone in the bedroom looked out the window and saw the police car. The person then moved to the front porch of the residence.

Officer Herring made contact with the person at the front porch and detained him. He then saw Mr. Hull sitting on the couch in the living room, with one of the stolen speakers on the coffee table. Officer Herring entered the residence and arrested Mr. Hull.

While searching the rest of the house for other suspects, Officer Herring located a second speaker in plain view in a back bedroom. With the assistance of an ultraviolet light, the officer found the green powder on Mr. Hull's hands.

RATIONALE

Exigent circumstances existed for the warrantless entry and arrest of Mr. Hull because the occupants could have attempted to destroy or hide the speakers while the officer obtained a search warrant. While the officers waited for a search warrant, Mr. Hull could have also removed the florescent powder from his hands.

2.5.1.7 – Fires

In **Michigan v. Tyler** (1978) 436 U.S. 499, the U.S. Supreme Court ruled that the Fourth Amendment applies to the actions of firefighters. "Searches for administrative purposes, like searches for evidence of crime, are encompassed by the Fourth Amendment." **Tyler**, at 506.

The high Court took a very thoughtful and reasoned approach to deciding this case. The Court noted that a burning building creates an exigency to make a warrantless entry "reasonable". "It would defy reason to suppose that firemen must secure a warrant or consent before entering a burning structure to put out the blaze." **Tyler**, at 509. Once in the building to put out the fire, firefighters may seize evidence of arson that is in plain view. The Court therefore found the initial entry to put out the fire lawful as well as Chief See's removal of two plastic containers of flammable liquid.

The Supreme Court ruled that "[o]fficials need no warrant to remain in a building for a reasonable time to investigate the cause of a blaze after it has been extinguished." **Tyler**, at 510. This is so for the following reasons:

- Prompt determination of a fire's cause may be necessary to prevent a reoccurrence
- Immediate investigation might also be necessary to preserve evidence from either accidental or intentional destruction
- The sooner officials complete their duties the less likely will be their future interference with the victim's privacy and recovery efforts.

However, the Supreme Court ruled that additional entries to investigate the cause of the fire must be made pursuant to administrative search warrants. When evidence of arson is discovered during those administrative searches, the evidence is admissible at trial. If investigating officials find probable cause to believe arson has occurred and require further access to the premises to gather evidence for criminal prosecution, they must obtain a warrant based on the traditional showing of probable cause.

In order "[t]o secure a warrant to investigate the cause of a fire, an official must show more than the bare fact that a fire has occurred." **Tyler**, at 507. Relevant factors might include the following:

- The number of prior entries
- The scope of the search
- The time of day when the search is proposed to be made
- The lapse of time since the fire occurred
- The continued use of the building
- The owner's efforts to secure it against intruders.

FACTS (Michigan v. Tyler (1978) 436 U.S. 499)

Around midnight on January 21, 1970, a fire broke out at Tyler's Auction, which was a furniture store in Oakland County, Michigan. Loren Tyler leased the building and ran the business with Robert Tompkins. The fire department responded to the furniture store. Fire Chief See arrived at about 2 a.m., and while firefighters were still watering down the fire's smoldering embers. It was the Chief's responsibility to make out all the reports and determine the cause of the fire.

Lieutenant Lawson met Chief See and told him about two plastic containers of flammable liquid that he found inside the building. Using portable lights, the two entered the gutted smoke and steam filled building to examine the containers. Upon concluding that the fire could have its origins in arson, Chief See called for Police Detective Webb, who arrived at about 3:30 a.m.

Detective Webb took several pictures of the containers and the store's interior, but was forced to cease his activities because of the smoke and steam. Chief See had also briefly looked through the rest of the building to see if there was any further evidence regarding the fire's origin. By 4 a.m., the fire was out and the firefighters had left the scene. Chief See and Detective Webb took the containers to the fire station where they were released to Detective Webb for safekeeping.

At approximately 8 a.m., Chief See returned to the fire scene with Assistant Chief Somerville, whose job involved determining the origin of all fires that happened in the township. The fire was now out and the building was empty. Following a cursory examination, the pair left.

At about 9 a.m., Assistant Chief Somerville returned to the furniture store with Detective Webb. At that time, they discovered suspicious burn marks in the carpet, which were not observable earlier in the morning due to darkness and the smoke and steam. They also found a piece of tape with burn marks on the stairway, which could be consistent with the remains of a fuse trail.

After briefly leaving the building to get some tools, the two returned and removed pieces of the carpet and sections of the stairs to preserve for evidence. Assistant Chief Somerville also continued looking through the rubble for evidence of how the fire began.

On February 16, or approximately 26 days after the fire, Michigan State Police Sergeant Hoffman, who was assigned to the arson section, returned to the building to take some photographs. He entered the building without a warrant on January 26th and 29th with other officials, but they obtained no physical evidence during those entries.

On February 16, Sergeant Hoffman checked the building's circuit breakers, had someone check out the furnace and had a TV repairman look at several TVs found in the building's ashes. He also found and seized a piece of a fuse. Based on several visits to the furniture warehouse, Sergeant Hoffman seized evidence and formed opinions that helped prove arson at the trial. The sole purpose of his entries into the building was to "make an investigation and seize evidence".

Both Ms. Tyler and Mr. Tompkins were charged with arson and objected to much of the seized evidence at trial. A jury convicted both parties of conspiracy to burn the furniture store.

The Michigan Appellate Court affirmed the convictions, but the Michigan Supreme Court reversed the convictions and remanded the case for a new trial, ruling that once the fire was out, a warrant was required to re-enter the premises, absent the owner's consent or evidence that the property had been abandoned. The U.S. Supreme Court granted certiorari and affirmed the Michigan Supreme Court's order regarding a new trial.

2.5.2 – Search Incident to Arrest

2.5.2.1 – Person

The U.S. Supreme Court created a "bright-line" rule in **United States v. Robinson** (1973) 414 U.S. 218, when it held that officers could conduct a warrantless person search incident to a lawful custodial arrest. The Court based its decision on the need to disarm a suspect in order to take him into custody and the need to preserve evidence for later use at trial.

FACTS (United States v. Robinson (1973) 414 U.S. 218)

Washington D.C. Police Officer Jenks, a 15-year veteran of the force, was on duty on April 23, 1968. Officer Jenks saw Willie Robinson, Jr. driving a 1965 Cadillac. Officer Jenks, based on a prior contact with Mr. Robinson, knew he was driving on a suspended license and stopped him.

Following Mr. Robinson's arrest, Officer Jenks conducted a pat search of Mr. Robinson's person and felt an object in his left breast coat pocket. Because the officer could not determine what it was, he reached into the pocket and pulled out a crumpled cigarette pack. The officer fondled the package and could feel objects inside, but still could not identify them. Upon opening the package, Officer Jenks found 14 gelatin capsules containing heroin.

The Supreme Court reached the same result in **Gustafson v. Florida** (1973) 414 U.S. 260, which is a companion case to **Robinson**. In reaching its decision in **Gustafson**, the U.S. Supreme Court ruled that it was immaterial that:

- There were no police department policies that required that the defendant be taken into custody or that that a full scale body search be conducted
- There were no mandatory minimum sanctions for the offense of driving without having a driver's license in one's possession
- Lieutenant Smith did not have any subjective fear of the defendant or suspect that he was armed
- The search could have had no evidentiary purpose with regard to the offense of driving without being in possession of a driver's license.

FACTS (Gustafson v. Florida (1973) 414 U.S. 260)

Lieutenant Smith of the Eau Gallie, Florida Police Department was driving an unmarked patrol car at about 2 a.m., on January 12, 1969. He saw the defendant driving a 1953 white Cadillac, bearing New York license plates, weave across the center line and back to the right side of the road three or four times. Mr. Gustafson and his passenger looked back at the officer and then drove across the highway and behind a grocery store, before heading south on another city street.

Lieutenant Smith activated the emergency equipment on his unmarked car and pulled the Cadillac over. After the stop, Lieutenant Smith asked Mr.

Gustafson for his driver's license. Mr. Gustafson said that he had left it in his dorm room in the neighboring city of Melbourne, Florida. The lieutenant then arrested Mr. Gustafson for failure to have his operator's license in his possession.

Lieutenant Smith conducted a pat down search of Mr. Gustafson's clothing and found a "long chain" and a Benson and Hedges cigarette pack inside the left front pocket of Mr. Gustafson's coat. When the Lieutenant opened the package, he found what appeared to be hand rolled marijuana cigarettes.

The Florida trial court denied the defendant's motion to suppress the seized evidence, but the 4th District Florida Court of Appeal reversed the lower court and held that the search was unreasonable. The Florida Supreme Court then reversed the District Court's ruling. The U.S. Supreme Court granted certiorari and affirmed the Florida Supreme Court's decision.

2.5.2.1.1 – Minors and Curfew Centers

An issue has arisen as to whether a minor could be lawfully searched incident to a curfew violation arrest, especially when the minor was going to be taken to a curfew center and not admitted into a custodial facility. The cases cited below indicate that a limited, cursory search of a minor and the property in his immediate control is lawful.

For example, the Court of Appeal ruled in **In re Ian C**. (2001) 87 Cal.App.4th 856, that the police lawfully took the minor to a SJPD local curfew center after he was found in violation of the City of San Jose's curfew ordinance. The SJPD officer lawfully pat searched the minor for weapons incident to that temporary custody\arrest and properly asked the minor to raise the pant legs on a pair of long and baggy pants he was wearing. When the minor raised his pant legs, the officer lawfully discovered four small packets of marijuana in a bulge in the minor's sock and $515 in cash in his shoe.

FACTS (In re Ian C. (2001) 87 Cal.App.4th 856)

On July 11, 1999, shortly after midnight, SJPD Officer Mark Efigenio and another officer stopped a group of seven young people, who were loitering in a known drug trafficking area. The 16-year-old minor was part of the group detained for violating the local curfew law. The officers took all the minors to the local curfew center for parental notification and release.

Minors are not booked, photographed, fingerprinted or strip-searched at the curfew center. However, officers do pat search the minors before releasing them into the detention room in order to insure the safety of all minors at the facility and to insure that no weapons or contraband goes into the main population.

At the curfew center, the officer told the minor to raise his long and baggy pant legs. The officer saw a suspicious bulge in the minor's sock and removed four small baggies of marijuana from the sock. The minor also had $515 in his shoe, in $5, $10 and $20 denominations. The marijuana was packaged in several one-gram bags and included a single ½-gram bag. The minor possessed a pager that received five pages with the number "420." This apparently signified an inquiry from a potential buyer.

The Alameda County Superior Court adjudged the minor, who was a Hayward resident, a ward of the court and sent him home on probation.

The Court of Appeal ruled in **In re Charles C.** (1999) 76 Cal.App.4th 420, that the police lawfully searched a minor's person, which resulted in the seizure of methamphetamine, following his arrest for a curfew violation.

In reaching that conclusion, the 4th District, Div. 3, of the Court of Appeal believes that the Court of Appeal for the 2nd District, Division 4, wrongly decided **In re Justin B**. (1999) 69 Cal.App.4th 879. This is based on the 4th District's interpretation of the effect of the passage of Article 1, 28(d), of the California Constitution. The 4th District explains that conclusion by stating that because evidence can no longer be excluded in California unless exclusion is mandated by the United States Constitution, a violation of California Welfare & Institutions Code 625.5 by the police does not violate the United States Constitution and therefore any evidence seized cannot be suppressed. The Court also believes that based on U.S. Supreme Court precedent, an officer can lawfully search a minor's person incident to a curfew violation.

Nothing in the holding of this case authorizes a minor to be strip-searched and **In re Charles C.**, **supra**, does not even discuss the issue.

FACTS (In re Charles C. (1999) 76 Cal.App.4th 420)

On July 24, 1997, Orange Police Officer Schaffer received a call regarding juveniles loitering in front of a Ralph's supermarket on Chapman Avenue and possibly soliciting others to buy them alcohol. Officer Schaffer responded to that location and saw Charles C. and another youngster standing in front of the store at around 12:45 a.m.

Officer Schaffer detained the youngsters and ascertained during a 20-minute discussion that Charles C., the other youngster, and two youths who had been brought across the street by another officer were all under 18 years of age and in violation of the City of Orange's curfew ordinance. However, there was insufficient evidence regarding the solicitation of adults to buy alcohol. Orange Municipal Ordinance 9.28.010 in essence prohibits persons under 18 from being in a public place between 10:00 p.m. and 5:00 a.m., unless in the company of an adult.

Officer Schaffer made numerous attempts via a police dispatcher to contact Charles C's parents, and arrange for him to be picked up at Ralph's market. However, all attempts proved fruitless. Officer Schaffer then conducted a cursory weapons search, handcuffed the minors and took them to the police station.

Once at the police station, the minors were taken to an interview room in the detective bureau, where their handcuffs were removed and officers filled out a "juvenile contact report." Following the completion of the paperwork, the minors were read their *Miranda* rights and an officer conducted an inventory search. Officer Schaffer located a .6-gram baggie of methamphetamine in Charles C.'s right upper coin pocket. When asked by the officer what it was, Charles C. said, "Speed."

At approximately 1:45 a.m., officers finally made contact with Charles C.'s relatives and he was released around 3:00 a.m.

RATIONALE

There was probable cause to arrest the minor for a curfew violation. Following a lawful arrest, a full search of Charles C's person could be lawfully performed.

The lawfulness of the search does not turn on whether the officer intended to release the minor after taking him into custody, but on whether the officer was justified in arresting him and taking him into custody in the first place. In this case, that justification clearly existed.

2.5.2.2 – Arrestee's Immediate Area

In **Chimel v. California** (1969) 395 U.S. 752, the U.S. Supreme Court created a bright line rule that allows police to search the immediate area under an arrestee's control where the arrestee might gain control of a weapon or destroy evidence.

The Court of Appeal ruled in **In re Humberto O.** (2000) 80 Cal.App.4th 237, that the police lawfully searched the backpack of a minor who was arrested for a truancy violation pursuant to California Education Code 48264 and 48265, and thereby lawfully seized a dagger found inside of the backpack.

FACTS (In re Humberto O. (2000) 80 Cal.App.4th 237)

On Thursday, February 26, 1998, at about 9:15 a.m., three LAPD officers were on juvenile patrol in Hollywood when they saw the minor walking down the street. He was several miles away from Hollywood High School. Based on the minor's youthful appearance, his backpack and the proximity to school during school hours, the officers detained him to investigate a possible truancy violation.

The officers determined that the minor was supposed to be in school and told him that they would cite him for truancy and then take him to school. When the officers asked for a school ID, the minor could only produce a bus pass with the name and photograph of someone else.

In accordance with standard police procedure, the officers planned to handcuff the minor's hands behind his back, place him in the patrol car and drive him to school. Before doing so, the officers conducted a pat search of the defendant's person with negative results. A search of the minor's backpack resulted in the seizure of a dagger.

A petition was subsequently filed against the minor alleging a felony violation of California Penal Code 22020(a). During his suppression motion, the juvenile trial court explicitly found, and contrary to the officers' version of events, that the minor did not consent to a search of his backpack. The trial court granted the motion and dismissed the petition with prejudice. The Court of Appeal reversed that decision.

RATIONALE

The Court of Appeal ruled that the police properly detained the minor to investigate the possible truancy violation. Once the officers verified the minor's truancy, they had probable cause to "arrest" him under 48264. Even though the purpose of the 48264 arrest, unlike a typical criminal arrest, was to return the minor to school, the police could lawfully search the backpack incident to the truancy arrest.

In **<u>People v. Summers</u>** (1999) 73 Cal.App.4th 288, the Court of Appeal ruled that officers lawfully seized a shotgun from inside a trailer, which was hidden between the mattress and the headboard of a bed where the defendant was sleeping just prior to his arrest. The seizure was lawful even though the seizure occurred after the defendant was out of the trailer but while the scene was still under police control. The Court observed that "[t]his was not a cold arrest scene with a long-gone suspect. He was still being removed from the cramped premises; one roommate was present and free of police control, and another was unaccounted for when the weapon was chanced upon. This was a fluid situation in close quarters, and a court could properly find, as we do, that the circumstances justified reasonable precautions for the safety of everyone involved." (**<u>Id</u>.** at 291.)

FACTS (<u>People v. Summers</u> (1999) 73 Cal.App.4th 288)

The defendant lived in a small trailer. Anaheim police officers went to his trailer to serve an arrest warrant. As they approached the trailer, they encountered Selena Poer, who was on her way out of the trailer. Ms. Poer admitted to living in the trailer with the defendant and another man, who she said was nearby in the trailer park laundromat. Ms. Poer agreed to go with the officers while they talked to the defendant.

The defendant was asleep inside the trailer and awakened. After identifying himself, the police told him that they had a warrant for his arrest. The defendant stood up, put on his pants and was handcuffed. While one officer handcuffed the defendant, the second officer watched Ms. Poer and also kept an eye out for the other roommate.

While one officer escorted the defendant to the trailer door, the second officer patted down the bed. As he moved the pillow, he saw a sawed-off shotgun between the mattress and the headboard. It is not clear from the facts if the defendant was inside or outside the trailer when the shotgun was first observed, but the defendant was less than 10 feet away in any event.

The officers held both Ms. Poer and the defendant outside for a few minutes while they waited for backup. Once backup arrived, the police located the second man in the laundromat about 50 to 100 feet away from the trailer. The officers then re-entered the trailer, photographed, fingerprinted and seized the shotgun. About 10 minutes elapsed between Mr. Summers arrest and the seizure of the shotgun.

The Court of Appeal in **People v. Rege** (2005) 130 Cal.App.4th 1584 ruled that the police properly searched under a mattress in the motel room because it was within the defendant's grabbing area at the time she was arrested and the search was contemporaneous with that arrest. However, the court did suppress the scales seized in the nightstand, because the Court deemed them to be outside the defendant's grabbing area.

FACTS (People v. Rege (2005) 130 Cal.App.4th 1584)

San Bernardino County Deputy Sheriff Roe received information from a citizen informant on June 25, 2003, that a woman named Alison was selling methamphetamine from a motel room in Victorville. The CI provided a description of Alison and said she drove a brown Honda Accord.

Deputy Roe went to the motel and saw the brown Honda in the parking lot. A Department of Motor Vehicles (DMV) check on the license plate revealed that it was registered to the defendant and that she had an outstanding arrest warrant. The motel manager told Deputy Roe that the defendant was in room 220 and gave the Deputy a passkey.

Deputy Roe and other officers went to the door, identified themselves and their purpose and demanded entry. The defendant agreed to open the door as soon as she got dressed, but later refused to open the door. The motel manager went to the adjacent room and told the defendant that the police had an arrest warrant, but the defendant said she did not believe they had such a warrant and they needed a search warrant to enter her room. About 20 minutes later, the police gained entry via a battering ram.

When the officers entered the room, the defendant was standing just inside the 12-foot by 15-foot room and her 11-year old daughter was crying in the corner of the room by the bed. Deputy Roe noted that the bathroom window was open and thought that a weapon or other object might have been thrown out the window. When he checked the area below the window, he found pieces of a broken glass pipe and a glass vial with methamphetamine.

Although the defendant was lying on the floor at the foot of the bed in handcuffs, a second officer lifted the mattress and located a black pouch, which was three feet from the defendant. Inside the pouch were scales, packaging material, drug paraphernalia, approximately 14.43 gram of methamphetamine, and 1.52 grams of marijuana. Inside the nightstand, officers' located another set of scales. The defendant claimed she was a methamphetamine user and used the scales to weigh her purchases.

After denial of her motion to suppress the evidence, the defendant plead guilty to simple possession of methamphetamine.

2.5.2.3 – Cell Phones

As more fully explained in section 2.4, on June 25, 2014, the U.S. Supreme Court unanimously ruled in **Riley v. California** (2014) 573 U.S. ___ ; 134 S.Ct. 2473 (companion case **United States v. Wurie** (2013) 728 F.3d 1), that the police **may not** generally search through digital information on a seized cell phone, incident to a lawful arrest, without first obtaining a search warrant. The holding specifically rejected the rationale put forth by some lower courts that allowed the search of a cell phone, incident to a lawful arrest.

2.5.2.4 – Vehicles

In **New York v. Belton** (1981) 453 U.S. 454, the United States Supreme Court ("U.S. Supreme Court") applied its prior ruling in **Chimel v. California** (1969) 395 U.S. 752, to vehicle searches. **Chimel** held that when police make a custodial arrest in a residence, the police could search the arrestee's person and an area within an arrestee's "immediate control" based on the twin rationales of officer safety and evidence destruction.

In **Belton**, an officer stopped the defendant's car for speeding. Upon contacting Mr. Belton, the officer noticed the odor of marijuana coming from the car's interior. The officer was alone, but there were four occupants in the car. The officer ordered all four occupants out of the car and did not arrest anyone at that point. Once outside the car, the Officer pat searched all the occupants for weapons. After separating the unhandcuffed occupants into four separate areas so they would not be close enough to touch each other, the officer searched the passenger compartment based on probable cause regarding a drug offense. The search resulted in the seizure of a marijuana envelope from the floorboard of the car. Following his arrest, the officer seized Mr. Belton's jacket from the backseat of the car and searched it, which resulted in the seizure of cocaine from within a pocket. Based on those facts, and its application of the **Chimel** rule to cars, the U.S. Supreme Court created a bright line rule that incident to the lawful "*custodial arrest*," officers could search the passenger compartment of a car, and any containers therein, without a warrant.

On April 21, 2009, the U.S. Supreme Court fundamentally changed the **Belton** rule and in so doing, eliminated the bright line that has existed for 28 years.[14] In a 5 to 4 decision in **Arizona v. Gant** (2009) 556 U.S. 332, whose facts are similar to those in **Belton**, the Court modified its earlier holding in **Belton** in two significant ways; *First*, it ruled that "**Belton** does not authorize a vehicle search incident to a recent occupant's arrest after the arrestee has been secured and cannot access the interior of the vehicle." **Gant**, at 1714. By implication, when the arrestee is unsecured and within reaching distance of a car's passenger compartment, such a search is allowed under the twin rationales of **Chimel**, **supra**. In so ruling, the Court effectively ended law enforcement's common practice of automatically searching the passenger compartment of a car incident to an occupant's lawful custodial arrest.[15] *Second*, it held "that circumstances unique to the automobile context justify a search incident to arrest when it *is reasonable to believe that evidence of the offense of arrest might be found in the vehicle*." [*Italics*, added] **Gant**, at 1714.

This means that officers can no longer make a custodial arrest of a suspect in a vehicle, place the suspect in the back of a patrol car and then routinely search the interior of the suspect's vehicle incident to that arrest. For example, when an officer arrests someone for driving on a suspended driver's license and places the arrestee in such a position that the arrestee cannot access the interior of the car, the officer cannot then search the car incident to that arrest. Because there would be no further evidence of the offense of driving on a suspended driver's license, an officer also cannot search the car's interior on an incident to arrest theory.[16] However, other automobile search theories such as consent, probable cause, and the impound and inventory exception remain available as viable options depending on the facts of a given case.

FACTS (Arizona v. Gant (2009) 556 U.S. 332)

[14] In his majority opinion, Justice Stevens in essence stated that law enforcement and many lower courts have misinterpreted the ruling in **Belton** and this decision partially corrects that misinterpretation, refines the **Belton** rule and narrows its application.

[15] Justice Stevens noted that while the previous interpretation of **Belton** has been taught in police academies and officers have relied on that rule to conduct vehicle searches over the past 28 years, "may of these searches were not justified by the reasons underlying the **Chimel** exceptions." **Gant**, at 1727. He also noted in FN. 11 that "because a broad reading of **Belton** has been widely accepted, the doctrine of qualified immunity will shield officers from liability for searches conducted in reasonable reliance on that understanding." **Gant**, at 1723.

[16] See **Knowles v. Iowa** (1998) 525 U.S. 113, where the U.S. Supreme Court ruled that there is no such thing as a "search incident to citation" exception to the Fourth Amendment.

On August 25, 1999, and pursuant to an anonymous tip that a residence was being used to sell drugs, two Tucson police officers knocked on the front door of the residence and asked to speak to the owner. Mr. Gant answered the door, identified himself and said that he expected the owner to return later. The officers then left the residence and did a records check on Mr. Gant, which revealed that he had a suspended driver's license and an outstanding arrest warrant for driving with a suspended license.

Later that evening, the officers returned to the residence and found a man near the back of the house and a woman in a car parked in front of the residence. After a third officer arrived, the officers arrested the man for providing a false name and the woman for possessing drug paraphernalia. The officers handcuffed both arrestees and placed them in separate patrol cars. Mr. Gant then arrived at the residence and officers recognized his car as it entered the driveway.

Officer Griffith confirmed that Mr. Gant was the driver of the car by shining a flashlight inside the car as it drove passed him. Mr. Gant parked the car at the end of the driveway, left his car and shut the door. Officer Griffith, who was about 30 feet away, called out to Mr. Gant, who walked towards the officer and met with him about 10 to 12 feet from the car. Officer Griffith immediately arrested Mr. Gant and handcuffed him. After two more officers arrived, bringing the total on scene to five, officers placed Mr. Gant in the back of a patrol car. Two officers then searched his car, with one of them finding a gun. The other officer found a bag of cocaine inside the pocket of a jacket on the backseat.

Mr. Gant was charged with possession of cocaine and drug paraphernalia. [17] He brought a motion in the trial court to suppress the evidence. Mr. Gant argued in his motion that "**Belton** did not authorize the search of his vehicle because he posed no threat to the officers after he was handcuffed in the patrol car and because no further evidence of the traffic offense could be found in his vehicle." **Gant**, at 336. When Officer Griffith was asked at the suppression hearing why he searched the car, he replied, "Because the law says we can do it." **Gant**, at 337. The trial court denied the suppression motion and ruled that the search was lawful incident to Mr. Gant's arrest. At trial, a jury convicted Mr. Gant of both charges and the judge sentenced him to a three-year prison term.

The Arizona Supreme Court overturned the conviction. After a thorough analysis of **Belton**, the court concluded that **Belton** did not answer ". . . the threshold question whether the police may conduct a search incident to arrest at all once the scene is secure." **Gant**, at 337. The Arizona Supreme Court then ruled that "[w]hen 'the justifications underlying **Chimel** no longer

[17] The paraphernalia charge was based on the possession of the plastic bag containing the cocaine.

exist because the scene is secure and the arrestee is handcuffed, secured in the back of a patrol car, and under the supervision of an officer' . . . 'a warrantless search of the arrestee's car cannot be justified as necessary to protect the officers at the scene or prevent the destruction of evidence.'" **Gant**, at 338. The U.S. Supreme Court granted certiorari in order to revisit the **Belton** decision based on the courts, scholars and U.S. Supreme Court Justices (including sitting Justices Scalia and Ginsberg) who questioned the "decision's clarity and its fidelity to Fourth Amendment principles." **Gant**, at 338.

RATIONALE

Justice Stevens observed in his majority opinion that "[i]f there is no possibility that an arrestee could reach into the area that law enforcement officers seek to search, both justifications for the search-incident-to-arrest exception are absent and the rule does not apply." **Gant**, at 339.

The Court noted that its decision in **Belton** has been widely understood to allow a search of a vehicle's interior incident to the arrest of a recent occupant even if there was no possibility that an arrestee could gain access to the car at the time of the search. Justice Stevens opined that such a reading was attributable to statements made by Justice Brennan in his dissent in **Belton**. In rejecting such an interpretation, Justice Stevens observed that "[u]nder this broad reading of **Belton**, a vehicle search would be authorized incident to every arrest of a recent occupant notwithstanding that in most cases the vehicle's passenger compartment will not be within the arrestee's reach at the time of the search. To read **Belton** as authorizing a vehicle search incident to every recent occupant's arrest would thus untether the rule from the justifications underlying the **Chimel** exception – a result clearly incompatible with our statement in **Belton** that it 'in no way alters the fundamental principles established in the **Chimel** case regarding the basic scope of searches incident to lawful custodial arrests.' **Chimel**, 453 U.S., at 460, n.3." **Gant**, at 363.

In a unanimous opinion by the U.S. Supreme Court in **Knowles v. Iowa** (1998) 525 U.S. 113, the Court ruled that there is no such thing as a "search incident to citation" exception to the Fourth Amendment.

The Supreme Court specifically rejected Iowa's invitation to extend the search incident to arrest bright line rule " . . . to a situation where the concern for officer safety is not present to the same extent and the concern for destruction or loss of evidence is not present at all." (**Id**. at 119.) The Court said that the justification of **United States v. Robinson**, **supra**, does not apply to this type of situation and added that "[o]nce Knowles was stopped for speeding and issued a citation, all the evidence necessary to prosecute the offense had been obtained. No further evidence of excessive speed was going to be found either on the person of the offender or in the passenger compartment of the car." (**Id.**, at 118.)

FACTS (Knowles v. Iowa (1998) 525 U.S. 113)

> A Newton, Iowa, police officer stopped Patrick Knowles for doing 43 mph in a 25 mph zone. Iowa law allowed an officer to either issue a motorist a citation or arrest the motorist and immediately bring the motorist before a magistrate if a motorist violated any Iowa traffic or motor vehicle equipment law. Following the issuance of the citation, an in accordance with an Iowa statute, the officer conducted a full search of the car and found a bag of marijuana and a "pot pipe" under the front seat.

In **Thornton v. United States** (2004) 541 U.S. 615, the U.S. Supreme Court held for the first time that **Belton**, **supra**, applies even when the officer does not make contact until the person arrested has left the vehicle. "So long as an arrestee is the sort of 'recent occupant' of a vehicle such as petitioner was here, Officers may search that vehicle incident to the arrest." **Thornton**, at 623-624.

In his dissenting opinion, Justice Scalia, who is joined by Justice Ginsburg, stated that he was unhappy with the current **Belton** rule. Justice Scalia stated that he would ". . . limit *Belton* searches to cases where it is reasonable to believe evidence relevant to the crime of arrest might be found in the vehicle." **Thornton**, at 632. In **Gant**, **supra**, he got that opportunity and cast the deciding vote.

Justice Scalia explained his decision to support Justice Stevens' opinion by stating the following:

> No other Justice, however, shares my view that application of *Chimel* in this context should be entirely abandoned. It seems to me unacceptable for the Court to come forth with a 4-to-1-to-4 opinion that leaves the governing rule uncertain. I am therefore confronted with the choice of either leaving the current understanding of *Belton* and *Thornton* in effect, or acceding to what seems to me the artificial narrowing of those cases adopted by Justice Stevens. The latter, as I have said, does not provide the degree of certainty I think desirable in this field; but the former opens the field to what I think are plainly unconstitutional searches-which is the greater evil. I therefore join the opinion of the Court. **Gant**, at 354.

In her concurring opinion in **Thornton** Justice O'Connor also indicated that she agreed with Justice Scalia's concerns and believed that ". . . lower court decisions seem now to treat the ability to search a vehicle incident to the arrest of a recent occupant as a police entitlement rather than as an exception justified by the twin rationales of *Chimel v. California, 395 U.S. 752, 23 L. Ed. 2d 685, 89 S. Ct. 2034 (1969)*. That erosion is a direct consequence of *Belton*'s shaky foundation." **Thornton**, at 624.

FACTS (<u>Thornton v. United States</u> (2004) 541 U.S. 615)

Norfolk, Virginia Officer Deion Nichols was in uniform, but driving an unmarked police car. He first noticed Mr. Thornton when Mr. Thornton slowed down to avoid driving next to the officer. Officer Nichols suspected that Mr. Thornton realized he was a police officer and pulled off onto a side street so that Mr. Thornton would pass him.

After he passed Officer Nichols, the officer ran a check on Mr. Thornton's license tags, which revealed that the tags belonged to a different car. Before Officer Nichols could initiate a stop on Mr. Thornton, the suspect drove into a parking lot, parked and exited his car.

Officer Nichols saw Mr. Thornton get out of his car and stopped him. Officer Nichols explained why he had stopped him and noticed that Mr. Thornton was nervous, rambling, sweating and licking his lips. Out of concern for his safety, Officer Nichols asked if he had any drugs or weapons on him or in the car. Mr. Thornton said, "No" and agreed to let the officer pat search him. Officer Nichols felt a bulge in Mr. Thornton's left front pocket and again asked if he had any drugs on him. This time Mr. Thornton stated that he did. Officer Nichols reached into the pocket and pulled out two individual bags. One contained three bags of marijuana and the other contained a large amount of crack cocaine. The officer arrested Mr. Thornton and searched his car. Officer Nichols found a BryCo .9-millimeter handgun under the driver's seat.

Mr. Thornton was convicted of possessing cocaine with the intent to distribute, being a felon with a gun and in possession of a firearm in furtherance of a drug trafficking crime. He received a 15-year prison sentence with eight years of supervised release.

Mr. Thornton appealed his conviction arguing that the search of the car violated **<u>Belton</u>**, **<u>supra</u>**.

2.5.3 – Consent

Warrantless searches based on consent are legal. However, there are four basic questions to consider in analyzing the lawfulness of a search based on consent:

- Was there consent?
- Is the consent freely and voluntarily given?
- Does the consenting party have the authority to give consent?
- What is the scope of the consent?

2.5.3.1 – General Rules

In **<u>Schneckloth v. Bustamonte</u>** (1973) 412 U.S. 218, the U.S. Supreme Court ruled that the police don't have to tell someone that they have the right to say no. However, it is a proper factor to look at in considering whether the person has freely and voluntarily consented to the search.

In **United States v. Matlock** (1974) 415 U.S. 164, 171, the U.S. Supreme Court ruled that no warrant is needed if a competent individual who owns or "possesses common authority over or other sufficient relationship to the premises or effects sought to be inspected. . ." consents to the search.

Under **Matlock**, common authority rests on mutual use of the property by persons generally having joint access or control for most purposes. The burden for proving that common authority rests on the State.

In **United States v. Drayton et al**. (2002) 536 U.S. 194, the Court extended it holding in **Schneckloth, supra**, and ruled that the police are not required to advise bus passengers of their right not to cooperate during a routine drug and weapon interdiction effort provided a reasonable person would feel free to decline the request or otherwise terminate the encounter.

A California Court of Appeal ruled in **People v. Harwood** (1977) 74 Cal.App.3d 460, that a person's consent to search a residence does not include authority to answer the telephone during that search. The Court explicitly said, "[w]e hold, therefore, that neither a general consent to search particular premises nor a consent to search for specific items includes the right to intercept telephone calls to the premises involved." (**Id**. at 468.)

2.5.3.2 – Spouses

In **People v. Bishop** (1996) 44 Cal.App.4th 220, the Court of Appeal ruled that despite the fact that the wife had not resided at the house for the last month, and had to climb through a kitchen window to gain entrance to the house, she still had dominion and control over the premises, still had property inside and was liable for any accidents that might have befallen visitors. Therefore, the wife could reasonably believe she could give officers consent to search the house. The Court observed that the fact the defendant changed the locks "is indicative of the level of antagonism between [wife] and appellant but is not determinative of [her] continuing authority in her own right to consent to a search of the house." (**Id**. at 238.)

FACTS (People v. Bishop (1996) 44 Cal.App.4th 220)

Mr. Bishop worked as a security guard and told his wife Heather that he and a friend intended to rob a certain business and would probably have to kill the manager. In February 1992, that plan was carried out. Thereafter, Heather began to fear for her safety.

On October 10, 1992, she took her children, and a number of their belongings, and moved to a shelter. On November 1, 1992, she went to the police and told them all that she knew. The police arrested Mr. Bishop at his home and he consented to a search of the house, which resulted in the seizure of items linking him to the murder\robbery, including a white canvas moneybag.

Five days later, Heather and the police returned to the house so that she could retrieve additional items. The police also wanted to conduct a more thorough search. Mr. Bishop had changed the locks and Heather had to gain entry to the house via a kitchen window. The police found and seized additional evidence.

The Court of Appeal ruled in **People v. Wilkins** (1993) 14 Cal.App.4th 761, that the victim of spousal abuse could give police consent to enter the house to arrest her husband.

2.5.2.4.5 – Parents and Children

In **In re Scott K.** (1979) 24 Cal.3d 395, the California Supreme Court ruled that the minor's father could not lawfully give the police consent to search a locked toolbox inside the room of his 17-year-old son because the father claimed no interest in the son's locked tool box or its contents and acknowledged that the toolbox belonged to his son.

In reaching that conclusion, the California Supreme Court rejected the following arguments put forth by the People in support of the police search:

- Because a parent is responsible for minor children and may inspect their property on their own, the police search was lawful based on the parental consent
- The father's consent fell within a third party exception to the warrant requirement based on the combined circumstances of ownership of the home and the nature of the parent-child relationship.

FACTS (In re Scott K. (1979) 24 Cal.3d 395)

The minor's mother found marijuana in his desk drawer and gave it to an off-duty police officer who lived in the neighborhood. She also said that based on discussions with other parents she believed that her 17-year-old son might be selling marijuana. One week later, the information was turned over to Narcotics Officer Schian for a follow-up investigation.

Officer Schian called the minor's father and advised him that he intended to arrest his son for the marijuana that the minor's mother had turned over to the police. The father told the officer that his son was working on a motorcycle in the garage. Officer Schian received the father's permission to enter the garage to arrest his son and was told to enter the house after the son was arrested.

Officer Schian went to the residence, arrested the minor in the garage, and then entered the house. Once inside the house, the father gave the officer permission to search the son's bedroom. While searching the bedroom, Officer Schian came across a locked toolbox. The father told the officer that he did not have a key to the box and that the box belonged to his son.

Officer Schian asked the minor for the key to the toolbox and the minor told him that he had lost it. The officer told the minor, "Your father already told me I could break the toolbox open if I couldn't find a key, but it's not my interest to destroy the lock. Let me see the keys you have in your pocket." The minor gave the officer his keys, including one that opened the toolbox. Inside the toolbox were nine baggies of marijuana.

The trial court found the entry of the garage illegal because of the lack of an arrest warrant, but denied the motion to suppress the evidence in the toolbox based on the conclusion that the box search was independent of the arrest and based on a valid consent. The Supreme Court reversed and held that the minor did not consent to the search of the toolbox.

In **People v. Hoxter** (1999) 75 Cal.App.4th 406, the Court of Appeal ruled that the police lawfully relied on the consent of the defendant's 16-year-old daughter before entering the house to arrest the defendant. Because the daughter consented to the officer's entry, there was no breaking within the meaning of Penal Code 844, and therefore no knock-notice violation by the police.

FACTS (People v. Hoxter (1999) 75 Cal.App.4th 406)

Donald Hoxter failed to appear in court on a case unrelated to his current charges, so the court issued an arrest warrant. On September 24, 1996, at approximately 8 p.m., two plain clothes Laguna Beach police officers went to his residence to serve the warrant.

As the officers approached the front door, they encountered an approximately 30-year-old man and asked him if he was named "Don." The man said "No" and stated "Don is inside."

The officers approached the front door and one of them knocked. Amy, the defendant's 16-year-old daughter, told her younger sister to open the door. As the young girl answered the door, Amy told the officers, "Come on in." One of the officers yelled back, "What?", and Amy again invited the officers inside.

The officers believed that Amy was between 14 to 16 years old, entered the residence and walked into the living room where Amy was located. The officers did not state their purpose, but simply told her they were looking for "Don." Amy pointed to a nearby bedroom. The door opened and the defendant stepped out to see who the visitors were.

After confirming that the defendant was "Don," the officers identified themselves, showed their badges, and announced that they had a warrant for the defendant's arrest. As the officers took the defendant into custody, they saw in plain view a portable propane tank and torch, a pipe, and a plastic baggie containing white power.

The officers explained the difference between an arrest warrant and a search warrant to the defendant and then obtained his consent to search the entire bedroom. During the bedroom search, the officers found a gram scale, methamphetamine and additional drug paraphernalia.

The trial court denied the defendant's motion to suppress the evidence. The defendant then plead guilty to possession for sale of methamphetamine [Health & Safety Code 21378] and admitted a strike prior.

RATIONALE

Amy appeared to be in her middle teens and acted in a manner consistent with one who had authority to exercise some control over the premises, which was demonstrated by her supervision of her sister and twice inviting the officers to enter the residence.

When Mr. Hoxter was confronted by the fact that Amy had allowed the officers to enter the residence, he did not object to their entry and made no attempt to revoke his consent.

"We are convinced that one of the characteristics of the end of the 20th century is that many California 16-year-olds are mature enough to be left in charge of their homes. **[FN. 4 applies here]**. Certainly police officers confronted by a young woman of that age who appears to have such authority may reasonably forego knock-notice in reliance upon the likelihood her parents have made that decision. But we hasten to express our recognition that not *all* 16 year olds will either have or appear to have such authority, and that the reasonableness of reliance upon their consent is initially a matter of fact for the trial court to resolve. (**Id**., at 412. [*Italics* in original.].)

The court facetiously notes in footnote 4 to the paragraph, "It is impossible to contemplate this fact without wondering just how close to the Apocalypse we have come. But to fail to recognize it is to blink at reality." (**Id**., at 412.)

The Court of Appeal ruled in **People v. Daniels** (1971) 16 Cal.App.3d 36, that Mr. Daniels' mother could properly give the police consent to search her adult son's bedroom for evidence of bomb making materials when the son resided at the house rent free. However, she could not give the police consent to search a suitcase in the bedroom that belonged to her son.

FACTS (People v. Daniels (1971) 16 Cal.App.3d 36)

On October 12, 1969, at approximately 2:15 a.m., Mrs. Daniels was driving an automobile on a public roadway when a bomb went off underneath the driver's compartment. Mrs. Daniels and her companion, Mrs. Washington, were ejected from the car. Mrs. Daniels lost both legs, while Mrs. Washington suffered burns and cuts about her face, hands and legs. The bomb was made of dynamite, a blasting cap, batteries and a triggering device activated by a timer.

On March 10, 1969, and while the defendant was a student at New Mexico State University, a maintenance worker saw a book entitled "Explosives and Homemade Bombs", authored by Major Joseph Stoffel in the defendant's dormitory. The book was indexed in the university card catalogue and had not been checked out by anyone, but was missing. The maintenance worker noted that pieces of scrap paper were used as bookmarks and noted one of the bookmarks was to a photograph of an automobile engine with an explosive device electrically attached to it. A second photograph showed how to hook up an explosive device with a mechanical device.

An expert testified that a grade school student could build a bomb using the book. The book also explained how to use mousetraps, clocks and a variety of other easily available materials to set off any type of explosive device.

On three occasions before the explosion, the defendant had physically abused his wife, which supported the conclusions that he would kill her if she ever divorced him. On April 20, 1968, he chased his wife with a knife, knocked her down and plunged it down toward her. She received a cut to the hand during that incident.

In late May 1968, he pointed a loaded gun at her head and said, "If I can't have you, nobody else can." The victim's sister got between the two of them and prevented the shooting, while another person got the defendant to turn the gun over to him.

On August 25, 1968, the defendant drove a car with the victim as a passenger and got into an argument with her. He was driving 30 mph and headed the car to a steep embankment before he jumped out of the car. Mrs. Daniels was able to stop the car safely and free herself, even though she was wearing a seatbelt. Mrs. Daniels reported the incident to the police. The defendant went to New Mexico, but was still charged with assault to commit murder. Mr. Daniels, following extradition proceedings, voluntarily returned from New Mexico. He was arrested and pled guilty to assault by means of force likely to produce great bodily injury. On October 10, 1969, which was just two days before the bombing in this case, the court placed him on probation.

An investigator at the car explosion found fragments of small flashlight batteries attached to bits of masking tape. Two days before the explosion, the defendant was in a friend's garage. After the explosion, the police found a clock in the garage with a severed electrical cord and some masking tape. The owner of the garage said that the clock still had its cord attached when she last saw it. She also said she had not previously seen the masking tape.

On the morning of the explosion, the police went to the defendant's mother's residence where he was staying. The police entered the house with her permission and asked for the defendant. The mother told them he was asleep in his bedroom. The mother got the defendant and he came into the living room with the police. While the police questioned the defendant about his whereabouts, Officer Schilder asked to speak to the defendant's mother privately and they went into another room.

Officer Schilder asked the mother if the defendant had any batteries, wires or other such equipment in the house. The mother said no and added, "The officers were certainly welcome to look in the room where he slept to see if there was anything like that there." Officer Schilder questioned the defendant's mother and learned that the defendant did not pay rent, that the house belonged to her and that the son was merely staying at the house.

During the search of the defendant's bedroom, the police found four .30 caliber shells without gunpowder in them, a prescription bottle containing what appeared to be black powder and a pair of surgical scissors. Inside various dresser drawers were several dry-cell batteries of different sizes and voltages, a small electric motor, an 8-inch piece of red wire and a pair of wire cutters. A broken down .30 caliber rifle was found between the bed mattresses.

The police located defendant's suitcase in a corner of the room and opened it. Papers, books and bottles containing quantities of saltpeter, sulfur and charcoal, which are the ingredients of black powder, were in the bottles.

After the police arrested the defendant, the police told him that his wife had been badly hurt, was in the hospital, and might not live. He was asked if he cared and said, "Hurray, hurray, hurray; hurray if she lives and hurray if she dies. Doesn't make any difference if she lives or if she dies."

2.5.3.4 – Third Parties

In a 6 to 3 decision in **Illinois v. Rodriguez** (1990) 497 U.S. 177, the Supreme Court ruled that a warrantless entry does not violate the Fourth Amendment proscription against unreasonable searches and seizures where such entry is based upon the consent of a third party, whom the police, at the time of entry, reasonably believe to possess common authority over the premises, but who in fact does not possess such authority.

The Court applied the following objective test: "whether the facts available at the moment would warrant a person of reasonable caution in the belief that the consenting party had authority over the premises. If not, then warrantless entry without further inquiry is unlawful unless authority actually exists. But if so, the search is valid." (**Id**. at 178.)

In a 5 to 3 decision written by Justice Souter in **Georgia v. Randolph** (2006) 547 U.S. 103, the U.S. Supreme Court ruled that the Fourth Amendment provisions against unreasonable searches and seizure are violated when police conduct a warrantless search of a residence based on the consent of one occupant when a co-occupant is present and objects to the search. The Court ruled that the fruits of such a warrantless search are inadmissible against the physically present, non-consenting party. In reaching this decision the Court observed, ". . . [T]here is no common understanding that one co-tenant generally has a right or authority to prevail over the express wishes of another, whether the issue is the color of the curtains or invitations to outsiders." (**Id**. at 114.)

In reaching this conclusion, the majority had to justify its decision in light of its own precedent of **United States v. Matlock** (1974) 415 U.S. 164, where it upheld the entry of a residence based on the consent of one co-occupant in the absence of the other. Justice Souter referred to this as "two loose ends", which he characterized as one, the explanation "for the constitutional sufficiency of a co-tenant's consent to enter and search" in **Matlock**, and two, the significance of **Matlock** and **Rodriguez** [**Illinois v. Rodriguez** (1990) 497 U.S. 177] after the U.S. Supreme Court's decision in this case.

Justice Souter explained away the first issue by stating that the **Matlock** Court did not address the issue of "whether customary social understanding accords the consenting tenant authority powerful enough to prevail over the co-tenant's objection." **Georgia v. Randolph**, **supra**, at 121.

With respect to the second issue, Justice Souter said,

> "If those cases are not to be undercut by today's holding, we have to admit that we are drawing a fine line; if a potential defendant with self-interest in objecting is in fact at the door and objects, the co-tenant's permission does not suffice for a reasonable search, whereas the potential objector, nearby but not invited to take part in the threshold colloquy, loses out. ¶
>
> This is the line we draw, and we think the formalism is justified. So long as there is no evidence that the police have removed the potentially objecting tenant from the entrance for the sake of avoiding a possible objection, there is practical value in the simple clarity of complementary rules, one recognizing the co-tenant's permission when there is no fellow occupant on hand, the other according dispositive weight to the fellow occupant's contrary indication when he expresses it." (**Id**. at 121.)

In a strong dissent, Chief Justice Roberts disagreed with the majority rule and stated, "[a] wide variety of often subtle social conventions may shape expectations about how we act when another shares with us what is otherwise private, and those conventions go by a variety of labels – courtesy, good manners, custom, protocol, even honor among thieves. The Constitution, however, protects not these but privacy, and once privacy has been shared, the shared information, documents, or places remain private only at the discretion of the confidant." (**Id**. at 131.)

The Chief Justice expressed his belief that the majority's decision did not protect privacy nearly as much as the good luck of a co-owner who just happened to be present when the police arrived at the door.

Finally, the Chief Justice argued that ". . . the more reasonable approach is to adopt a rule acknowledging that shared living space entails a limited yielding of privacy to others, and that the law historically permits those to whom we have yielded our privacy to in turn cooperate with the government. Such a rule flows more naturally from our cases concerning *Fourth Amendment* reasonableness and is logically grounded in the concept of privacy underlying that Amendment." (**Id**. at 137.)

FACTS (Georgia v. Randolph (2006) 547 U.S. 103)

Janet and Scott Randolph separated in late May 2001, when she left their home in Americus, Georgia, and went to stay with her parents in Canada. When she left, she took their son and some belongings. In July 2001, Mrs. Randolph returned to the family home with the child, although it is not clear from the record whether this was due to reconciliation or a desire to retrieve the rest of her belongings.

On the morning of July 6, 2001, Mrs. Randolph complained to the police that her husband took their son away after a domestic dispute. When officers arrived at the house, she also told them that her husband was a cocaine user and that his use caused financial problems for the family. Shortly after the police arrived, Mr. Randolph returned to the house and told the police that he took his son to a neighbor's house because he was afraid that his wife would again take his son out of the country. The police questioned him about his wife's allegations of cocaine use, but he denied them and said that it was his wife who abused drugs and alcohol.

Sergeant Murray and Mrs. Randolph went to the neighbor's house and picked up the child. Upon their return, Mrs. Randolph renewed her complaint about her husband's cocaine use and told Sergeant Murray that "items of drug evidence" were in the house. Sergeant Murray asked Mr. Randolph for permission to search the house, but he unequivocally refused to consent to the search. The sergeant then asked Mrs. Randolph for consent to search the house, which she gave. She led the officer upstairs to a bedroom she identified as Mr. Randolph's. In plain view, Sergeant Murray saw a drinking straw with what he suspected contained cocaine residue.

The sergeant left the house to obtain an evidence bag from his car and to consult with the district attorney's office, which instructed the sergeant to stop the search and seek a search warrant. Upon returning to the house, Mrs. Randolph now withdrew her consent to search the residence.

Officers took the Randolphs to the police station and obtained a search warrant. Upon returning to the house, they found more evidence of drug use which led to the indictment of Mr. Randolph for possession of cocaine.

Mr. Randolph moved to suppress the evidence in the trial court, but the court denied his motion. He then appealed to the Georgia Court of Appeals, which reversed the denial of the motion. The Georgia Supreme Court affirmed the Court of Appeals decision and ruled, "the consent to conduct a warrantless search of a residence given by one occupant is not valid in face of the refusal of another occupant who is physically present at the scene to permit a warrantless search." (**Id**. at 108.) The U.S. Supreme Court granted certiorari to resolve a split in authority in the circuit's and affirmed the Georgia Supreme Court's decision.

In **Fernandez v. California** (2014) ___ U.S. ___; 134 S.Ct. 1126; 188 L.Ed.2d 25, the U.S Supreme Court followed the holding in **Georgia v. Randolph**, **supra**, and upheld the co-tenants consent to search the apartment despite the fact that Mr. Fernandez objected to such a search before he was lawfully arrested and removed from the premises.

FACTS (Fernandez v. California (2014) ___ U.S. ___; 134 S.Ct. 1126; 188 L.Ed.2d 25)

On October 12, 2009, at approximately 11 a.m., Abel Lopez (hereinafter referred to as "victim") was approached by Walter Fernandez after he cashed a $400 check near the corner of 14th Street and Magnolia in Los Angeles. Mr. Fernandez asked the victim what neighborhood he was from and the victim said, "I'm from Mexico." Mr. Fernandez laughed and told the victim that the victim was in his territory and he should give him his money. Mr. Fernandez then said, "The D.F.S. rules here. They rule here." Mr. Fernandez then took a knife out of his pocket and pointed it towards the victim's chest. The victim put up his hands to protect himself and Mr. Fernandez cut the victim's wrist. The victim tried to run away, and while running, took out his cell phone and called 9-1-1. He told the operator that he needed help because someone was trying to kill him. Mr. Fernandez then whistled loudly and four men ran out of the building on 14th Street and Magnolia. They attacked the victim by hitting him in the face and all over his body. They knocked the victim to the ground, where they continued to hit and kick him. When the victim got up, he did not have his cell phone or wallet with him. The victim estimated that he had approximately $400 in his wallet as well as his Mexican ID. The victim suffered a deep cut on his left wrist and bruising and swelling all over his body.

Detective Clark and Officer Cirrito responded to the police dispatch and stood in an alley where they knew the Drifters street gang hung out. While in the alley, two men walked by and one said, "The guy is in the apartment." The speaker appeared scared and walked away quickly. When he again returned, he said, "He's in there. He's in the apartment." Immediately thereafter, the officers saw a tall, light-skinned, Hispanic or White male wearing a light blue T-shirt and khaki pants run through the alley and into the house that had previously been pointed out by the witness. A minute or two later, the officers heard the sounds of screaming and fighting coming from the apartment building into which the suspect had run.

After calling for backup, and waiting for its arrival, the officers knocked on the door of the unit and heard screaming. The door was opened by Roxanne Rojas, who was holding her two-month old daughter and appeared to be crying. Her face was red and she had a big bump on her nose that looked fresh. Ms. Rojas also had blood on her shirt and hand that appeared to come from a fresh injury. Ms. Rojas said she had been in a fight. Officer Cirrito asked if anyone else was in the apartment, and Ms. Rojas said that her four-year-old son was the only other person present.

When Officer Cirrito asked her to step outside so he could conduct a protective sweep of the apartment, Mr. Fernandez stepped forward. He seemed very agitated and was only wearing boxer shorts. He said, "You don't have any right to come in here. I know my rights." Officer Cirrito removed Mr. Fernandez from the residence and place him in custody, suspecting that he had assaulted Ms. Rojas.

Approximately one hour after Mr. Fernandez's arrest, Detective Clark went back to Ms. Rojas at the apartment and told her that Mr. Fernandez had been identified as a robbery suspect and asked for her consent to search the apartment. She gave her consent both orally and in writing. During the search, officers found Drifters gang paraphernalia, a butterfly knife, boxing gloves, and clothing. None of the items stolen from the victim were found in the residence.

The officers interviewed Ms. Rojas about her injuries. She said that when Mr. Fernandez entered the apartment, she confronted him about his relationship with a woman named "Vanessa." They argued, and Mr. Fernandez struck her in the face. The officers also interviewed Ms. Rojas's four-year-old son, Christian, who told him that Mr. Fernandez had a gun. Christian told the officers where it was hidden and the officers recovered a sawed off shotgun from a heating unit. Two days later, Officer Cirrito re-interviewed Ms. Rojas, who stated several times that she did not want to be a "rat" and recanted her earlier statement.

Mr. Fernandez brought a motion to suppress in the trial court, seeking to suppress the following items: "(1) a Mossberg New Haven 20–gauge shotgun, (2) Remington 20–gauge shotgun ammunition, (3) a knife with a four and a half-inch stainless steel blade, (4) any currency seized during the search, and (5) any other evidence seized, including clothing, notebooks, and boxing gloves." **Fernandez**, **supra** at 112. After losing that motion, Mr. Fernandez entered a nolo contendere plea to firearm and felon with ammunition possession charges, and went to trial on the robbery, spousal abuse and gang enhancement allegations. The jury returned a guilty verdict on those charges and he was sentenced to 14-years in prison for all of his crimes.

The California Court of Appeal affirmed the denial of the suppression motion, and the California Supreme Court denied Mr. Fernandez's petition for review, but the U.S. Supreme Court granted certiorari.

In the case of **In re D.C.** (2010) 188 Cal.App.4th 978, the Court of Appeal concluded that "[b]ecause of the unique nature of the rights and duties of parents with respect to their children, *Randolph* [**Georgia v. Randolph** (2006) 547 U.S. 103] does not require the police to defer to an objecting minor child over a consent to search by his or her parent." **Id**. at 989.

FACTS (In re D.C (2010) 188 Cal.App.4th 978)

On October 26, 2009, Oakland Housing Authority Officer Morris, and other officers, were called to an apartment building regarding a report of possible narcotics activity. After they arrived, they detained the juveniles' adult brother, suspecting he was involved in the reported criminal activity. In the meantime, a building resident reported to another officer that his apartment had been burglarized. The officers ran a check on the juvenile's brother and learned that he was on probation and subject to warrantless searches. Officer Morris escorted the brother to the apartment where he lived with the juvenile and their mother, intending to conduct a probation search. On the way, they met the juvenile's mother who was in a wheelchair, and explained to her that they wanted to search the apartment to confirm that the juvenile's brother was not involved in narcotics activity or the burglary. She consented to the search both verbally and in writing. At the time, the juvenile was lingering nearby and barred the officers as they attempted to enter the apartment. The juvenile said, "You're not going to enter the apartment." **Id**. at 982. The juvenile's mother told him to "Get out of the way." **Id**. at 982. The juvenile complied with his mother's command and stepped aside, but remained outside the apartment while the officers entered and began to search. During the search of the juvenile's bedroom, the officers found some of the items reportedly taken in the burglary. By the time the officers completed their search, the juvenile was no longer outside of the apartment

On November 25, 2009, the Alameda County District Attorney filed a wardship petition alleging that the juvenile, then age 15, had received stolen property in violation of Penal Code 496(a). The juvenile court denied the juvenile's motion to suppress the evidence and found the petition true. The court then continued the juvenile on probation[18] and released him to the custody of his mother.

RATIONALE

The courts have held that adults sharing a residence but maintaining separate bedrooms do not have the apparent authority to consent to the search of one another's bedroom, at least when the officers have no information about the living arrangements. The Court of Appeal declined to apply the rationale of **Georgia v. Randolph** (2006) 547 U.S. 103 to the facts of the present case.

The court found that the mere fact that the son is permitted to use a particular bedroom does not confer upon him exclusive control of the residence, and his occupancy is subservient to the control of the parents. "When the child is a minor, there is an even stronger case for apparent authority in a parent to consent to the search of the child's bedroom." **Id** at 984.

The Court reasoned that:

> Given the legal rights and obligations of parents toward their minor children, common authority over the child's bedroom is inherent in the parental role. Carrying out their duty of supervision and control requires a parent to have the ability to monitor their child's activities whenever the parent deems it appropriate, even when the child is in a bedroom nominally regarded as private. Proper exercise of parental duties therefore demands that the parent have 'joint access or control' of a minor child's bedroom. This is true regardless of whether the parent finds it necessary to exercise that privilege frequently. Further, given the parental duty of control and supervision, it is reasonable 'to recognize that [the parent] has the right to permit the inspection in his own right . . . .' **Matlock**, **supra**, 415 U.S. at p. 171, fn. 7. In the absence of evidence suggesting a parent has abdicated this role toward his or her child, police officers may reasonably conclude that a parent can validly consent to the search of a minor child's bedroom. **Id** at fn. 3.

The Court explained that the mere fact that a son is permitted to use a particular bedroom does not confer upon him some exclusive control of the bedroom. The son's occupancy is subservient to the control of his parents. The court noted that when the child is a minor, as opposed to an adult child living at home, there is an even stronger case for apparent authority in a parent's consent to the search of the child's bedroom.

The court explained that Randolph only governs a disagreement between joint adult occupants having apparent equal authority over a residence and

[18] He was apparently already on probation for a violation of Penal Code §140 (Threatening a witness).

not to the situation in the present case involving the rights and duties of parents with respect to their children.

"To fulfill their duty of supervision, parents must be empowered to authorize police to search the family home, even over the objection of their minor children. While a minor child's Fourth Amendment rights may be narrower in these circumstances than those of an adult cohabiting with another, the difference is not great; police will still be required to obtain the consent of a person with common authority over the home – the parent – before the requirement of a search warrant is excused." **In re D.C.,** at 990.

Officers need to proceed with extreme caution when attempting to search a computer in a **Georgia v. Randolph** type of situation. The consent of a spouse or co-occupant who has joint access and control over a computer will not be sufficient if the other spouse or co-occupant is present and objects to the search. A search done over the objections of a spouse or co-occupants could lead to the suppression of any evidence obtained during that computer search.

2.5.3.5 – Landlords

In **Chapman v. United States** (1961) 365 U.S. 610, the U.S. Supreme Court ruled in an 8 to 1 decision that a landlord cannot give the police consent to enter a tenant's residence.

FACTS (Chapman v. United States (1961) 365 U.S. 610)

Mr. Bridgaman and another owned a house in a wooded area, near the airport in Macon, Georgia. They commonly rented the house out with the assistance of a rental agency. Mr. Chapman recently rented the house and Mr. Bridgaman went by on Sunday, February 16, 1958, with the intention of inviting the tenants to attend church with him. Upon arriving at the house, he knocked on the door and found no one home. He did notice the strong odor of whiskey mash coming from the residence, but could not see into the residence because the shades were closed.

Mr. Bridgaman returned home, called the local police department, and advised them of his observations. Officers Harbin and Chance met Mr. Bridgaman at his home and the three returned to the rented house. The officers also noted the strong odor of whiskey mash coming from the house and received no response to their knock at the front door. The officers walked around the exterior of the house, but the shades were still down and all the windows, except for a bathroom window, were locked.

Mr. Bridgaman gave the officer's permission to enter the house by climbing thru the bathroom window. He later testified that he said, "If it's what I think it is, what it smells like, you, you can have my permission to go in." (**Id**. at 612.) Upon entering the house through the bathroom window, Officer Harbin found the house to contain a sizable distillery and 1,300 gallons of mash in the living room. The house lacked household furniture or any other evidence of residential occupancy. Except for some accessories, containers and firewood, the house was empty inside.

Officer Harbin remained behind while Mr. Bridgaman and Officer Chance left to get assistance. Mr. Bridgaman called federal officers from his home and while they were enroute, Mr. Chapman returned to the house. Officer Harbin immediately arrested him and turned him over to the federal officers when they arrived. Without a search warrant, the federal officers took a sample of the mash, photographs of the scene and then destroyed the still and its contents.

A jury convicted the defendant at trial and the court sentenced him to one year and one day in prison. The Fifth Circuit Court of Appeals affirmed the conviction, but the U.S. Supreme Court granted certiorari and reversed the conviction.

The Court of Appeal reached a similar conclusion in **People v. Roman** (1991) 227 Cal.App.3d 674, when it ruled that a landlord cannot lawfully consent to a police search of premises the landlord rented to the tenant.

FACTS (People v. Roman (1991) 227 Cal.App.3d 674)

On Friday, August 4, 1989, Mr. Roman spoke to Vincente Medrano about leasing commercial warehouse space so that Mr. Roman could replace an engine on his truck. Mr. Medrano agreed to let them have space in "the big room" of a warehouse for $200 for the weekend or Mr. Roman and his associates could rent a garage in the warehouse for $600 a month. Mr. Medrano lent Mr. Roman two locks for the doors for the garage he desired to rent and allowed Mr. Roman and his associates to take immediate possession of the garage.

Over the weekend, Mr. Medrano looked through a hole in the garage and saw wheels inside. This led him to the conclusion that Mr. Roman had moved property into the garage. On Monday, August 7, 1989, Mr. Roman brought Mr. Medrano $200 as a down payment for a month's rent and promised to provide the rest of the money later that week.

Mr. Roman failed to pay the remaining $400 to Mr. Medrano. Mr. Medrano and Mr. King, who owned the warehouse, entered the garage on the 21st to ascertain if Mr. Roman and his associates were still using the garage. They observed truck parts and tools scattered throughout the room. Mr. King called CHP vehicle theft Officer Guzik regarding the discovery of the vehicle parts. Mr. King explained that he rented the garage to Mr. Roman and his associates to repair their truck and that Mr. Roman had failed to pay the remainder of his rent. Mr. King asked Officer Guzik to come by and inspect the premises to make sure nothing illegal was happening.

Mr. King pointed out to Officer Guzik fiberglass fenders and a truck hood that were outside the building. Mr. King also unlocked the garage and admitted Officer Guzik inside. Officer Guzik discovered VINs from parts stolen off a 1989 Peterbilt truck earlier in the month. After conducting surveillance of the garage for several days, Officer Guzik arrested Mr. Roman and three others.

RATIONALE

California Vehicle Code 2805 does not authorize a warrantless entry on property rented for private use. Mr. Roman's rental of the enclosed space in a commercial building did not diminish his expectation of privacy or somehow transform the rented premises into a public garage.

"The general rule is that a landlord has no authority to consent to a police entry of premises occupied by a tenant." (**Id.**, at 680.) In this case, the landlord has not evicted the tenants and the tenants did not abandon the property. Therefore, the landlord had no authority to grant Officer Guzik consent to enter the premises. The Court stated, "the officer was told that the owner entered the garage to see if anyone was still there and saw parts and tools scattered about. Although Mr. King unlocked the door with a key, the officer never inquired whether the landlord retained authority to do so. The officer's assumption that an owner had the right to have law enforcement inspect his property was not reasonable." (**Id.**, at 680.)

2.5.3.6 – Office Computer Searches

In **United States v. Ziegler** (9th Cir. 2007) 474 F.3d 1184, the Court of Appeals upheld the trial court's ruling that Mr. Ziegler had a legitimate expectation of privacy in the company supplied office computer based on the use of a password on his computer and the lock on his private office. Therefore, he had standing to object to the search of his office computer for evidence of child pornography.

Despite the Court of Appeals ruling that two of Frontline's employees were de facto government agents and were engaged in a search when they entered Mr. Ziegler's office and made a copy of his hard drive, the Court affirmed the District Court's order denying suppression of the evidence and ruled that Frontline exercised common authority over the office and work place computer and therefore could and did validly consent to the search of the hard drive. The Court found that ". . . the computer is the type of workplace property that remains within the control of the employer 'even if the employee has placed personal items in [it].' [*O'Connor v.*] *Ortega* (1987) 480 U.S. 709 at 716." **Ziegler**, at 1191.

As the Court of Appeals explained, "[a]lthough use of each Frontline computer was subject to an individual log-in, Schneider and other IT-department employees 'had complete administrative access to anybody's machine.' The company had also installed a firewall, which, according to Schneider, is 'a program that monitors Internet traffic . . . from within the organization to make sure nobody is visiting any sites that might be unprofessional.' Monitoring was routine, and the IT department reviewed the log created by the firewall '[o]n a regular basis,' sometimes daily if Internet traffic was high enough to warrant it. Finally, upon their hiring, Frontline employees were apprised of the company's monitoring efforts through training and an employment manual, and they were told that the computers were company-owned and not to be used for activities of a personal nature. In this context, Ziegler could not reasonably have expected that the computer was his personal property, free from any type of control by his employer." (**Id**. at 1191-1192.)

FACTS (United States v. Ziegler (9th Cir. 2007) 474 F.3d 1184)

Frontline Processing is a company that services Internet merchants by processing on-line electronic payments. Its offices are located in Bozeman, Montana. On January 30, 2001, Anthony Cochenour, who is the owner of the company and the fiancé of a Frontline employee, contacted FBI Special Agent James Kennedy, Jr. and provided him with a tip that a Frontline employee had accessed child pornographic websites from his work place computer.

Agent Kennedy followed up on that tip the same day and contacted Frontline Internet Technology (IT) Administrator John Softich. One of Mr. Softich's duties was to monitor employee work place Internet use of company computers. Frontline's employees were aware of the IT department's monitoring capabilities. Mr. Softich told Agent Kennedy that the company had a firewall in place, which permitted constant monitoring of a Frontline employee's Internet use. Mr. Softich confirmed the accuracy of the tip and told Agent Kennedy that he had personally viewed the sites and found them to depict "very, very young girls in various states of undress." According to the company's Internet Protocol and log-in information, Jeffrey Brian Ziegler, who was the company's Director of Operations since August 2000, had accessed those sites. Mr. Softich also told Agent Kennedy that the company had placed a monitor on Mr. Ziegler's computer to record his Internet traffic by copying his computer's cache files.

Agent Kennedy next interviewed William Schneider, who was Mr. Softich's subordinate in the IT department. Mr. Schneider confirmed that the IT department had placed a monitor on Mr. Ziegler's computer and that he "spot checked" the cache files and found several images of child pornography. He also reviewed Mr. Ziegler's search engine cache files and found searches for "preteen girls" and "underage girls".

There is some dispute whether Frontline acted on its own or under Agent Kennedy's direction, but in any event, around 10 p.m. on January 30, 2001, Mr. Softich and Mr. Schneider obtained a pass key to Mr. Ziegler's private office from Ronald Reavis, who is Frontline's Chief Financial Officer. The two entered Mr. Ziegler's office, opened up his computer case and made two copies of his hard drive.

On February 5, 2001, Mr. Reavis delivered Mr. Ziegler's computer tower, which contained the original hard drive, to Agent Kennedy. He also provided Agent Kennedy with one of the hard drive copies. Mr. Schneider delivered the second copy on another occasion.

FBI forensic examiners searched the hard drive and located several child pornography images. On May 23, 2003, a federal grand jury issued a three count indictment against Mr. Ziegler charging him with violating 18 U.S.C. 2252A(a)(2) (Receipt of Child Pornography), 18 U.S.C. 2252A(5)(B) (Possession of Child Pornography) and 18 U.S.C. 2462 (Receipt of Obscene Material).

On September 8, 2004, the District Court issued an order denying Mr. Ziegler's suppression motion, but found that Agent Kennedy directed Frontline employees to make a backup copy of Mr. Zeigler's computer files. The court also ruled that Mr. Ziegler had no reasonable expectation of privacy in the Internet files he accessed with the company's computer.

Following the denial of Mr. Ziegler's suppression motion, he pled guilty to receiving obscene materials and the other charges were dismissed. As part of the plea agreement, Mr. Ziegler was allowed to appeal the denial of his suppression motion. On March 4, 2005, the District Court placed Mr. Ziegler on two years of probation and fined him $1,000.

2.5.3.7 – Computers and Exceeding the Scope of Consent

In **United States v. Turner** (1st Cir. 1999) 169 F. 3d 84, the Court of Appeal affirmed the District Court's order granting the defendant's motion to suppress child pornography seized from his computer by law enforcement during a consent search of his apartment. The Court of Appeal held that the search of the defendant's computer files exceeded the scope of the defendant's consent to search the apartment for evidence in connection with an intruder's attempted assault on a next door neighbor.

FACTS (United States v. Turner (1st Cir. 1999) 169 F. 3d 84)

Twenty six year old Megan Thomas was at home and asleep in her bedroom at 2:00 a.m. on July 28, 1997, when a masked intruder, wielding a knife, awakened her. During the struggle, Ms. Thomas cut her hands when she grabbed for the knife and the intruder fled. Daniel Turner lived next door to the victim and called the Bangor, Maine police, who responded to the scene. Mr. Turner told them that while he was seated at his computer upstairs he saw an intruder fleeing the apartment and called the police.

The next morning, Detectives Reagan and Gould returned to the crime scene for further investigation. They noticed that the window screens on both Ms. Thomas' and Mr. Turner's apartments were ajar and that blood was smeared on Mr. Turner's windowsill. The Detectives awakened Mr. Turner, told him of their observation, and expressed concern that the intruder might have also entered Mr. Turner's apartment. Mr. Turner responded by handing the detectives a knife which fit the description of the one used on the victim. Mr. Turner claimed he found it near the kitchen sink but didn't recall placing it there.

Mr. Turner then gave the detectives verbal consent to look around the apartment. The detectives did not consider Mr. Turner a suspect at that time. During the initial tour of the apartment with Mr. Turner, the detectives saw blood stains on the stairway walls leading to the second floor and on a trash can lid in the second floor computer room. Mr. Turner could not explain the origin of these blood stains.

At that point, the detectives began to suspect that Mr. Turner was somehow involved in the assault of his neighbor and obtained his written consent to search the apartment, his car and his personal property for "any signs the suspect had been inside the apartment" or left anything behind and for "evidence of the assault itself."

Mr. Turner and a detective remained on the first floor while other officers began a 90-minute search of the second floor. In the computer room closet, Detective Gould found several videotapes containing sexually explicit material. As he removed several boxes from the closet, he stacked them next to the computer. Detective Gould saw that Mr. Turner's computer monitor screen suddenly activated and displayed a photograph of a nude woman with light colored hair, similar to Ms. Thomas' hair color.

Detective Gould sat down at the computer and used the computer mouse to access the documents index in the Windows 95 task bar. Detective Gould saw several indexed files with a ".jpg" file extension, which denoted the presence of a photographic image. The detective clicked on these files and found a photograph of a nude blond woman in bondage. He also noted several text files under the document listing which had titles suggesting rape and or bondage. Detective Gould called the district attorney's office for guidance and copied the adult pornographic files onto a floppy disk.

Detective Gould next searched the computer hard drive for more incriminating files. When he opened the "My Computer" icon he found a folder labeled "G-Images." Several of the files had names such as "young" and "young with breasts". The detective opened one of those files and found what he believed to be child pornography. He then shut down the computer and seized it. At this point, Mr. Turner came upstairs and learned for the first time that the police had searched his computer.

The government charged Mr. Turner with a single count of possessing child pornography. He successfully moved to suppress the seized evidence in the District Court and the government appealed.

RATIONALE

> ". . . [A]ggravated assault is neither akin to so-called 'paper trail' crimes like bank or mail fraud, nor to possession of child pornography, wherein the suspect might be expected to retain evidence of the offense itself among personal papers or in a computer hard drive. *See* *United States v. Hall*, 142 F.3d 988, 995-97 (7th Cir. 1998) (noting that child pornographers often download photographic images from the Internet, and store them on hard drives). Thus, we believe that an objective observer, witnessing in context the pre-consent exchange between Turner and the investigating detectives, reasonably would construe 'evidence of the assault itself" to mean physical evidence linked to the crime scene, rather than documentary or photographic evidence." **Turner**, at 88-89.

2.5.4 – Probation Searches

2.5.4.1 – General Principles

In a 5 to 4 decision, the U.S. Supreme Court recognized the validity of warrantless probation searches in **Griffin v. Wisconsin** (1987) 483 U.S. 868, and stated, "[a] warrant requirement would interfere to an appreciable degree with the probation system, setting up a magistrate rather than the probation officer as the judge of how close a supervision the probationer requires. Moreover, the delay inherent in obtaining a warrant would make it more difficult for probation officials to respond quickly to evidence of misconduct, see *New Jersey v. T.L.O. (1985) 469 U.S. 325, at 340, 105 S.Ct., at 743*, and would reduce the deterrent effect that the possibility of expeditious searches would otherwise create, [Citations] By way of analogy, one might contemplate how parental custodial authority would be impaired by requiring judicial approval for [the] search of a minor child's room. . . ." (**Id**. at 876.)

In reaching this decision, the U.S. Supreme Court declined to embrace the Wisconsin Supreme Court's new principle of law that ". . . any search of a probationer's home by a probation officer satisfies the Fourth Amendment as long as the information possessed by the officer satisfies a federal 'reasonable grounds' standard." (**Id**. at 872.) Instead, the U.S. Supreme Court upheld the constitutionality of the search based on "special needs" beyond normal law enforcement. Those "special needs" justified a departure from the usual probable cause and warrant requirements.

FACTS (Griffin v. Wisconsin (1987) 483 U.S. 868)

> On September 4, 1980, Mr. Griffin was convicted in a Wisconsin state court of resisting arrest, disorderly conduct and obstructing an officer. The court placed him on probation. He was also previously convicted of a felony in Wisconsin. Under Wisconsin law, a probationer is under the legal custody of the state Department of Health and Social Services and is subject to the conditions imposed by the court and the department's rules and regulations.

One regulation allows a probation officer to conduct a warrantless search of the probationer's residence as long as the probation officer's supervisor approves and there are "reasonable grounds" to believe that contraband is present, including items that the probationer is prohibited from possessing.

In determining whether "reasonable grounds" exist, the rule requires an officer to consider a variety of factors such as "information provided by an informant, the reliability and specificity of that information, the reliability of the informant (including whether the informant has any incentive to supply inaccurate information), the officer's own experience with the probationer, and the 'need to verify compliance with rules of supervision and state and federal law.' HSS 328.21(7). Another regulation makes it a violation of the terms of probation to refuse to consent to a home search. HSS 328.04(3)(k). And still another forbids a probationer to possess a firearm without advance approval from a probation officer. HSS 328.04(3)(j)." (**Id**. at 871.)

On April 5, 1983, Michael Lew, who was the supervisor of Mr. Griffin's probation officer, received information from a Beloit Police Department detective that Mr. Griffin might be in possession of guns at his apartment. Supervisor Lew, who was unable to obtain the assistance of Mr. Griffin's probation officer, went to Mr. Griffin's apartment with another probation officer and three plain-clothes police officers. When Mr. Griffin answered the door, Supervisor Lew told him why they were present and that they intended to conduct a probation search of his home. During the search, the officers found a handgun and arrested Mr. Griffin for being a felon in possession of a firearm.

Following the denial of his motion to suppress the firearm, a jury convicted Mr. Griffin of the firearm violation and the court sentenced him to two years in prison. Mr. Griffin appealed, but the Wisconsin Supreme Court affirmed the conviction and ruled that probation diminishes a probationer's reasonable expectation of privacy such that a warrantless search of a probationer's home based on "reasonable grounds" (and not probable cause) that contraband is present is permissible.

RATIONALE

"To a greater or lesser degree, it is always true of probationers (as we have said it to be true of parolees) that they do not enjoy 'the absolute liberty to which every citizen is entitled, but only . . . conditional liberty properly dependent on observance of special [probation] restrictions.' *Morrissey v. Brewer (1972) 408 U.S. 471, 480, 92 S.Ct. 2593, 2600, 33 L.Ed.2d 484 (1972).*" (**Id**. at 874.)

"We think it clear that the special needs of [the] Wisconsin's probation system make the warrant requirement impracticable and justify replacement of the standard of probable cause by 'reasonable grounds,' as defined by the Wisconsin Supreme Court." (**Id**. at 876.)

In **United States v. Knights** (2001) 534 U.S. 112, the U.S. Supreme Court unanimously reversed the 9th Circuit Court of Appeals and held that the search of Mr. Knight pursuant to his probation condition and supported by reasonable suspicion, did not violate the Fourth Amendment. In doing so, the Supreme Court specifically rejected the 9th Circuit's distinction that the search was illegal because it was done for an investigatory purpose rather than a probationary purpose.

In **People v. Medina** (2007) 158 Cal.App.4th 1571, the Court of Appeal reversed the trial court and explicitly ruled that under California law and the California Supreme Court's decision in **People v. Bravo** (1987) 43 Cal.3d 600, ". . . a search conducted pursuant to a known probation search condition, even if conducted without reasonable suspicion of criminal activity, does not violate the Fourth Amendment as long as the search is not undertaken for harassment or for arbitrary or capricious reasons or in an unreasonable manner." (**Id**. at 1577.)

The Court of Appeal also noted that the ". . . **Knights** [(2001) 534 U.S. 112] court expressly declined to reach the issue whether 'acceptance of the search condition constituted consent in the **Schneckloth** [**Schneckloth v. Bustamonte** (1973) 412 U.S. 218] sense of a complete waiver of his Fourth Amendment rights.' (*Knights, supra,* 534 U.S. at p. 118, 122 S. Ct. 587.) Moreover, the court expressly declined to decide whether a probation search *without* reasonable suspicion satisfies the reasonableness requirement of the Fourth Amendment. (*Id.* at p. 120, fn. 6, 122 S.Ct. 587). Thus, *Knights* did not consider the question relevant to the present case: whether reasonable suspicion is *required* (and not just sufficient) for a search pursuant to a probation condition." (**Id**. at 1578.)

FACTS (People v. Medina (2007) 158 Cal.App.4th 1571)

A Bakersfield police officer stopped John Medina Jr. due to an inoperable taillight. At the time of the stop, Mr. Medina had just pulled into the driveway of his house and stopped. Mr. Medina informed the officer that it was his house and provided his identification. A records check revealed that Mr. Medina was on felony probation and subject to a search and seizure clause for narcotics and paraphernalia. A search of Mr. Medina and his car revealed no contraband. The officer then asked Mr. Medina for his house keys and rang the doorbell to the house. Mr. Medina's father answered the door and the officer told him he was there to conduct a probation search. The father directed the officer to Mr. Medina's bedroom, where the officer found a small amount of methamphetamine and some ammunition.

The defendant was charged with possession of methamphetamine and possession of ammunition by a felon and filed a motion to suppress the evidence. The trial court granted the motion and dismissed the case citing

United States v. Knights, **supra**, in support of its holding. The trial court said that "[t]here existed no facts which would suggest a search was necessary or reasonable." **Medina**, at 1575.

RATIONALE

In California, probationers consent in advance, as a condition of their probation, to warrantless searches and seizures in exchange for the opportunity to avoid serving a state prison term. (*People v. Bravo* (1987) 43 Cal.3d 600, 609...; *People v. Mason* (1971) 5 Cal.3d 759, 764-766, ...; disapproved on other grounds in *People v. Lent* (1975) 15 Cal.3d 481, 486, fn. 1, ...) Warrantless searches of probationers are justified because they aid in deterring further offenses by the probationer and in monitoring compliance with the terms of probation. (*People v. Mason, supra,* at pp. 763-764, ...see *Bravo, supra,* at p. 610, ...) 'By allowing close supervision of probationers, probation search conditions serve to promote rehabilitation and reduce recidivism while helping to protect the community from potential harm by probationers. [Citation.]' (*People v. Robles (2000) 23 Cal.4th 789, 795*) **Medina**, at 1575-1576.

There is no reasonableness requirement before an officer can conduct a probation search. All that is required is that the search is not arbitrary, capricious or done for harassment purposes (See **In re Anthony S.** (1992) 4 Cal.App.4th 1000, 1015.) and an officer's subjective intentions play no role in determining the lawfulness of a probation or parole search.

"As explained in *People v. Clower* (1993) 16 Cal.App.4th 1737 [21 Cal.Rptr. 2d 38], 'a parole search could become constitutionally "unreasonable" if made too often, or at an unreasonable hour, or if unreasonably prolonged or for other reasons establishing arbitrary or oppressive conduct by the searching officer.' (**Id**. at 1741; *United States v. Follette* (S.D.N.Y. 1968) 282 F.Supp.10, 13; see *In re Anthony S.*, (1992) 4 Cal.App.4th 1000, 1004 [6 Cal.Rptr.2d 214] [a search is arbitrary and capricious when the motivation for the search is unrelated to rehabilitative, reformative or legitimate law enforcement purposes, or when the search is motivated by personal animosity toward the parolee]; *People v. Bremmer* (1973) 30 Cal.App.3d 1058, 1062 [106 Cal.Rptr. 797] [unrestricted search of a probationer or parolee by law enforcement officers at their whim or caprice is a form of harassment].)" **People v. Reyes** 19 Cal.4th 743, at 753-754.

In light of the California Supreme Court's holding in **People v. Sanders**, **infra**, (2003) 31 Cal.4th 318, the Court of Appeal ruled in **People v. Lazalde** (2005) 120 Cal.App.4th 858, that law enforcement officers' attempt to justify a search based on a probation search clause could not be sustained because that clause was unknown to the officers at the time of the search.

FACTS (People v. Lazalde (2005) 120 Cal.App.4th 858)

In October 2002, Watsonville police officers observed the defendant engage in several hand-to-hand transactions at a shopping center over multiple days. Officers followed the defendant to the Economy Inn Motel and obtained a telephonic search warrant for his room. During the search of the defendant's room, the officers located heroin, packaging materials, injecting paraphernalia and almost $600 in cash. Following his arrest, the defendant admitted selling heroin for another person to support his own habit.

At the suppression hearing, the prosecution decided not to justify the search of the motel room based on the telephonic search warrant, which had several problems with it. Instead, the Santa Cruz County DDA sought to justify the search solely on the basis of the defendant's search and seizure clause arising out of his prior misdemeanor convictions for violating Health & Safety Code 21550(a) and Penal Code 248.9. However, the officers did not know about that clause when they searched the defendant's hotel room.

In **People v. Gomez** (2005) 130 Cal.App.4th 1008, the Court of Appeal ruled that a "... officer's subjective intent has no role to play in determining the lawfulness of a probation or parole search." (**Id**. at 1015.)

FACTS (People v. Gomez (2005) 130 Cal.App.4th 1008)

Stockton Police Officer Thomas Walters went to an antiques store on September 16, 2002, after the owner called to report that a man was trying to sell him antiques stolen from another antique store the night before. The officer arrived and contacted Chauncy Washington, who told the officer that he had received the antiques from the defendant, who lived at 1420 North Monroe.

Officer Walters went to Robert Gomez' residence and spoke to him. Mr. Gomez said that he was on probation and subject to a search and seizure clause. The officer told Mr. Gomez that he was looking for stolen antiques that were supposed to be at the defendant's home. After pausing for a moment, Mr. Gomez acknowledged that the antiques were located in a garage behind the house.

Officer Walters detained Mr. Gomez in handcuffs and contacted adult probation to confirm the search clause. Mr. Gomez' search clause required that he "[s]ubmit person, vehicles, place of residence or area over which he has control to search for and seizure of . . . [n]arcotics, drugs and other contraband . . . [w]eapons . . . [or] [f]irearms . . . [a]t any time of day or night, with or without a search warrant, with or without probable cause as directed by probation officer or any peace officer." Another condition of probation was that defendant shall "[o]bey all laws." (**Id.** at 1012.)

After confirming the search clause, Officer Walters checked out the garage and located two storage boxes containing some of the stolen antiques. The police arrested Mr. Gomez and the DA charged him with possession of stolen property.

At the suppression hearing, Mr. Gomez argued that the evidence should be suppressed because Officer Walter's subjective intent was to search for stolen property, which exceeded the scope of Mr. Gomez' search clause.

RATIONALE

"Consistent with the objective standard adopted in *Woods* [**People v. Woods** (1999) 21 Cal.4th 668], in order for a search to be limited in scope to the terms of the search clause, it is only necessary that the search not exceed the areas that could be searched pursuant to the clause. For example, a probation condition permitting a search for firearms would only permit a search of areas under the probationer's control where firearms might be found. Even where the officers are searching for something else, as long as the search is confined to areas where firearms might be found, the scope of the search condition has not been exceeded. (**Id**. at 1017.)

2.5.4.2 – Juveniles

In the case of **In re Tyrell J.** (1994) 8 Cal.4th 68, the California Supreme Court ruled that an otherwise unlawful search of a juvenile was legal because the juvenile, unbeknownst to the officer, was on probation and therefore had a lessened expectation of privacy. The case involved an officer who suspected that gang members, who were at a football game, were carrying weapons. The officer pat searched Tyrell J. and found marijuana.

The principle enunciated in this holding led to some interesting twist and turns until the California Supreme Court *implicitly overruled* itself in **People v. Sanders** (2003) 31 Cal.4th 318, and then *explicitly overruled* itself in **In re Jaime P.** (2006) 40 Cal.4th 128.

2.5.4.3 – Third Party Search Conditions

In **People v. Woods** (1999) 21 Cal.4th 668, the California Supreme Court ruled that a police officer's ulterior motives in using a roommate's probationary search clause to search for evidence against the probationer's live-in boyfriend were irrelevant and that the circumstances presented ample justification to enter and search the residence for narcotics. **People v. Sanders**, **supra**, does not affect the ruling in this case.

In **People v. Robles** (2000) 23 Cal.4th 789, the California Supreme Court signaled its willingness to overrule its decision in **In re Tyrell J.**, **supra**, when it ruled that the warrantless entry of a garage to search for a stolen car violated Mr. Robles' Fourth Amendment reasonable expectation of privacy rights, when the police did not know about the defendant's brother's probation search clause until the next day after the police conducted the warrantless search. The police never suspected or charged the defendant's brother with being involved in the theft of the car.

In a 6 to 1 decision in **People v. Sanders** (2003) 31 Cal.4th 318, with only Associate Justice Baxter dissenting, the California Supreme Court repudiated the rationale of **In re Tyrell J.**, **supra**, in the context of parole searches. The Court held that "an otherwise unlawful search of the residence of an adult parolee may not be justified by the circumstance that the suspect was subject to a search condition of which the law enforcement officers were unaware when the search was conducted." **Sanders**, at 335. The California Supreme Court later applied the same rule to probation searches. (See **In re Jaime P.**, **supra**.)

In his majority opinion, Justice Moreno said, "[p]ermitting evidence that has been suppressed as to a cohabitant to be used against the parolee would encourage searches that violate the rights of cohabitants and guests by rewarding police for conducting an unlawful search of a residence." **Sanders**, at 335. A search that violates a cohabitant's reasonable expectation of privacy also violates a parolee's expectation of privacy. While "a parolee's expectation of privacy is certainly diminished, . . . it is not eliminated." **Sanders**, at 332. By suppressing the evidence against both defendants, the Supreme Court sent a clear signal to law enforcement that it did not want to legitimize the police's illegal actions.

FACTS (People v. Sanders (2003) 31 Cal.4th 318)

> On April 6, 1999, Bakersfield police responded to a report of a domestic disturbance at the defendant's apartment. Arlene Sanders lived with Kenton McDaniel. Mr. McDaniel was on parole, but the officers did not know that when they went to the apartment. The officers heard yelling when they approached the apartment and knocked on the door and demanded entry. A short time later, Ms. Sanders opened the door. She had an abrasion on her face and the officers saw Mr. McDaniel standing near a couch with some kind of metal object in his hand, which he attempted to conceal behind a couch cushion. Mr. McDaniel demanded that the officers leave. Because of their belligerence, the officers handcuffed both occupants and then did a protective sweep of the apartment. During the protective sweep, officers observed plastic bags of cocaine in plain view, which were sticking out of a pair of boots in one of the bedroom closets. After the find, one of the officers contacted the police department and learned that Mr. McDaniel was on parole. The police then conducted a parole search of the apartment and seized contraband.
>
> Ms. Sanders plead guilty to violating Health & Safety Code 21350 and received 16 months in state prison, while Mr. McDaniel plead guilty to violating Health & Safety Code 21351.5, had a prior conviction struck, and received a five-year prison term.

> The Court of Appeal reversed the conviction, holding that the protective sweep was unlawful and that since the police did not know in advance of Mr. McDaniel's parole condition, the search could not be justified on those grounds. Neither defendant challenged the lawfulness of the initial entry into the apartment. The California Supreme Court upheld the trial court's ruling, but expressed no opinion on the protective sweep of the apartment.

In his dissenting opinion, Justice Baxter said, "a parole search term significantly diminishes a defendant's reasonable expectation of privacy, whether or not the search officers know the defendant is on parole." **Sanders**, **supra**, at 341. Justice Baxter stated that the Fourth Amendment protects people not premises and that Mr. McDaniel's had a diminished expectation of privacy given his parole status. Justice Baxter also expressed his belief that the majority should have applied a "totality of the circumstances" standard to uphold the lawfulness of the search and that the Court's majority erred because it only focused on the officer's lack of knowledge of Mr. McDaniel's parole search condition.

In **People v. Pleasant** (2004) 123 Cal.App.4th 194, the Court of Appeal upheld the search of a locked bedroom in a probationer's house and the subsequent seizure of firearms used against her adult son in a criminal prosecution. The son resided in that bedroom, but the probationer possessed keys to that locked bedroom.

The majority observed, "[p]ersons who live with probationers cannot reasonably expect privacy in areas of a residence that they share with probationers. (**People v. Woods** (1999) 21 Cal.4th 668, 675-676.)" (**Id**. at 197.) Because of her search condition, "law enforcement authorities could, without a warrant or probable cause, search areas used exclusively by Ms. Pleasant, areas within 'common authority' . . . of the probationer and fellow occupants and areas which she 'normally had access.' [*Citations.*] Since Ms. Pleasant had access to the keys to the room in which the gun was found, [*Mr.*] Pleasant could not reasonably expect privacy in the room and the officers reasonably entered the room under the authority of Ms. Pleasant's probation waiver." (**Id**. at 197-198.)

In this 2 to 1 decision, the dissenting justice noted that the officers were told the room belonged to the probationer's son and that he kept the door locked. Based on this information, the dissenting Justice believed the officers could not reasonably believe she had access to this clearly "differentiated private living space."

FACTS (People v. Pleasant (2004) 123 Cal.App.4th 194)

> On November 22, 2002, San Diego Police and Sheriff's Deputies went to Ella Pleasant's home to conduct a probation search on her. While doing a safety sweep, an officer came upon a locked door and asked Ms. Pleasant if she had a key to the door. Ms. Pleasant told the officer the room belonged to her son, who was not home, and her keys were on the dresser in her bedroom.

The officer retrieved the keys and opened the locked bedroom. Under the bed, he found a rifle.

Monet Pleasant was charged with being a felon in possession of a firearm, possession of an assault weapon and with one strike prior. Following the denial of his motion to suppress, a jury convicted him of the felony charges. At a court trial, the court found the strike prior true, but struck it. The court imposed a suspended two-year prison sentence and sentenced the defendant to one year in county jail.

2.5.4.4 – Own Recognizance (O.R.) Releases

The California Supreme Court ruled in **In re York** (1995) 9 Cal.4th 1133, that a trial court could condition an O.R. release on the defendant's consent to submit to drug testing and warrantless searches, provided the person is charged with a felony and the trial court makes a record, based on a defendant's particular history, that such conditions are reasonable.

2.5.4.5 – Probation Searches and Electronic Devices

Given our technological society and the proliferation of computers, including electronic storage devices such as cell phones, personal digital assistants (PDAs), and thumb drives, the issue often arises as to whether an officer can conduct a warrantless search of a probationer's computer and other electronic items as part of a probation search. The answer to this question is a qualified maybe.

If a probationer is on probation for a crime involving the use of a computer, the trial court may have ordered restrictions on the probationer's use and possession of computer equipment. For example, California Penal Code 2203.047 mandates that a person convicted of a violation of certain subsections of Penal Code 202 or 502.7 be placed on not less than three years probation unless the ends of justice would be served by a shorter term. The section also mandates that "[d]uring the period of probation, that person shall not accept employment where that person would use a computer connected by any means to any other computer, except upon approval of the court and notice to and opportunity to be heard by the prosecuting attorney, probation department, prospective employer, and the convicted person. Court approval shall not be given unless the court finds that the proposed employment would not pose a risk to the public." A probationer's possession of a computer under those circumstances would be a violation of the terms of probation and would justify its search and seizure by law enforcement.

A sentencing court may also impose other restrictions such as specific terms allowing search and seizure of all digital devices in a probationer's possession, including both on-site and off-site analysis by a forensic lab. Such a condition would obviously justify the warrantless seizure, removal and off-site forensic analysis by a lab of the computer and its contents.

However, if the sentencing court did not go so far in issuing probation conditions, but instead issued terms of probation that included stay away orders from online computer chat rooms, a prohibition against the use of pseudonyms in online communications, no credit card use over the Internet and no participation in Internet based auctions or e-commerce, then the situation is more of a close question.

Upon verifying the imposition of some or all of the above probation conditions, it would not violate the Fourth Amendment for an officer to conduct a warrantless search of a probationer's computer files, cell phone information or PDA either at or away from the location of the probation search.

In the absence of those conditions, a very cursory search of electronic items for evidence of dominion and control of the property would be appropriate. For a more detailed search, including removal of the computer for analysis at a forensic lab, the better practice is to freeze the computer and promptly obtain a search warrant allowing its removal from the location. For example, if the court prohibits a probationer from possessing child pornography and a probation officer's cursory search of the computer yields evidence of the presence of picture files containing such items, the officer should seize the computer and suspend any further search pending the issuance of a search warrant authorizing a more detailed off-site forensic analysis of its information.

2.5.5 – Parole Searches

The California Legislature added Penal Code 3067 in 1996. At that time, subsection (a) mandated that "Any inmate who is eligible for release on parole pursuant to this chapter shall agree in writing to be subject to search or seizure by a parole officer or other peace officer at any time of the day or night, with or without a search warrant and with or without cause." Subsection (b) stated that "Any inmate who does not comply with the provision of subdivision (a) . . . shall not be released until he or she either complies with the provision of subdivision (a) or has no remaining worktime credit, whichever occurs earlier."

In passing this legislation, the California Legislature limited its application in subsection (c) "This section shall only apply to an inmate who is eligible for release on parole for an *offense committed on or after January 1, 1997*."

In 2012, the California Legislature amended Penal Code 3067 to eliminate the language in subsection (a) requiring an inmate to agree in writing to be subject to search or seizure by a parole officer or other peace officer at any time of the day or night. The amendment added subsections (b)(1), (b)(2) and (b)(3). The amended statute now reads in part as follows:[19]

[19] All new additions are shown as underlined text. Additionally, only subsection (e), which relates to the power of the Secretary of Department of Corrections and Rehabilitation to prescribe and amend rules and regulations, is omitted above.

(a) Any inmate who is eligible for release on parole pursuant to this chapter or postrelease community supervision pursuant to Title 2.05 (commencing with Section 3450)) of Part 3 shall be given notice that he or she is subject to terms and conditions of his or her release from prison.

(b) The notice shall include all of the following:

(1) The person's release date and the maximum period the person may be subject to supervision under this title.

(2) An advisement that if the person violates any law or violates any condition of his or her release that he or she may be incarcerated in a county jail or, if previously paroled pursuant to Section 3000.1or paragraph (4) of subdivision (b) of Section 3000, returned to state prison, regardless of whether new charges are filed.

(3) An advisement that he or she is subject to search or seizure by a probation or parole officer or other peace officer at any time of the day or night, with or without a search warrant or with or without cause.

(c) This section shall only apply to an inmate who is eligible for release on parole for an offense committed on or after January 1, 1997.

(d) It is not the intent of the Legislature to authorize law enforcement officers to conduct searches for the sole purpose of harassment.

The California Supreme Court initially applied its decision in **In re Tyrell J.**, **supra**, to parole searches in a 4 to 3 decision in **People v. Reyes** (1998) 19 Cal.4th 743. In doing so, the Court disapproved its earlier decisions in **In re Ralph Martinez** (1970) 1 Cal.3d 641, which held that a warrantless search of a residence could not be upheld as a parole search if the officers were unaware of the parole condition at the time they conducted the search, and **People v. Burgener** (1986) 41 Cal.3d. 505, which held that a warrantless search of a parolee must be justified by at least a reasonable suspicion that the parolee had violated a condition of his parole, a law or was planning to do so. However, as stated earlier, the California Supreme Court reversed itself in **People v. Sanders** (2003) 31 Cal.4th 318, just five years later, meaning that **In re Ralph Martinez** and **People v. Burgener** are once again valid California law.

FACTS (People v. Reyes (1998) 19 Cal.4th 743)

An anonymous informant phoned the office of Gordon McClaskey, who was Mr. Reyes' parole officer, and said that Mr. Reyes was using methamphetamine, had lost his job because his employer suspected him of stealing, that Mr. Reyes had made a false police report regarding the theft of his VCR in a burglary, and that Mr. Reyes' wife left him because he had threatened her with a gun. The caller stated that the source of this information was from a drug user named "Shirley." Mr. Reyes was living in Woodlake, California at the time of the report.

Agent McClaskey contacted the Woodlake Police Department in Tulare County and verified that Mr. Reyes had reported a burglary of his home. Agent

McClaskey also requested the police to check Mr. Reyes out for being under the influence of drugs when they saw him.

Later that evening, Woodlake Police Officer Beal drove by Mr. Reyes' house and saw him walk out of a shed in the backyard. Officer Beal called for assistance and contacted Mr. Reyes. Officer Beal determined that Mr. Reyes was not under the influence of any drug and asked Officer Brock, who was a fill officer, to contact Agent McClaskey and obtain permission to search Mr. Reyes' property. After obtaining that authorization, Officer Brock searched the shed and found a piece of tin foil containing 0.9 grams of methamphetamine.

Mr. Reyes was charged with possessing methamphetamine, plead guilty to that, and admitted one prior felony conviction, after the court denied his suppression motion. The Court of Appeal cited **Burgener**, **supra**, and suppressed the seized evidence. The California Supreme Court reversed the appellate court and reinstated the conviction.

In **People v. Middleton** (2005) 131 Cal.App.4th 732, the Court of Appeal ruled that an officer's awareness that a third party was a parolee was sufficient to inform the officer of the existence of a search and seizure clause (see Penal Code 3067(a), **supra**) and provide the officer with authority to conduct a warrantless search of a motel room.

FACTS (People v. Middleton (2005) 131 Cal.App.4th 732)

On November 11, 2002, at 11:30 p.m., Fairfield Police Officers were conducting a security check at the Travel Lodge Motel on Auto Mall Parkway in Fairfield. As they were descending the second floor stairs, they saw a female coming out of a first floor room and detected a strong odor of marijuana. One of the officers stopped the female and questioned her. During the questioning, the female admitted leaving room #126 and that people were smoking marijuana in the room.

A few minutes later, a second female left room #126 and admitted that she had been smoking marijuana in the room. The police arrested her after they determined that she falsely identified herself.

Four officers tried to contact the occupants of room #126, but no one responded. The officers did see a male peek out of a curtain on the side window and then heard movement inside the room. The officers heard room #126 fall silent, but heard movement next door in room #111. An adjoining door connects the rooms.

Officer Trojanowski went to the motel manager's office to determine who resided in room #111 and learned that the room was registered to Maurice Hurth, who was on active parole. Officer Trojanowski decided to conduct a parole search of the room and obtained a passkey and bolt cutters from the motel manager. Officer Trojanowski knocked on room #111 and announced his presence, but no one answered the door. After a second attempt also ended in failure, Officer Trojanowski used the passkey and bolt cutters to enter the room. Seven officers entered the room with their weapons drawn. Five people were located in the room, including the defendant, who was standing in the bathroom with his hands and arms dripping water.

While moving the occupants outside, Officer Moody saw the handle of a handgun protruding from behind an entertainment center, which he later recovered and gave to Officer Clifton. Officer Clifton went back outside and announced that everyone was being detained because of the discovery of the handgun. The defendant spontaneously said, "How can you put that gun on me when you found it back behind there."

The officers still had not located the parolee and began to discuss the possibility that the parolee was in room #126. The defendant then volunteered that the parolee was not in room #126 and said the officers could use his card key to check the room. The defendant also said that all items found in the room belonged to him and he did not want anyone else to get in trouble for what was in the room.

Upon entering the room, the officers saw seven Ziploc baggies of marijuana on the floor and a small scale was on the nightstand. In the bathroom, an officer saw four small bags of marijuana. Three small rocks of cocaine were floating in the toilet. On a shelf above the toilet were two small baggies of marijuana. In a suitcase under the shelf was a scale, 18 cell phones, two semi-automatic pistols and ammunition.

Before leaving the scene, the defendant asked Officer Trojanowski to retrieve his sweat suit from the room. Inside the sweat suit was a large wad of cash, along with credit cards and ID in another person's name.

Upon losing his suppression motion, the defendant plead no contest to possession for sale of crack cocaine with an arming clause, felon in possession of a firearm and receiving stolen property while armed with a firearm. In exchange for the plea, the defendant received a four-year prison term.

In a 6 to 3 opinion in **Samson v. California** (2006) 547 U.S. 843, the U.S. Supreme Court resolved the question it left open in **United States v. Knights** (2001) 534 U.S. 112: "whether a condition of release can so diminish or eliminate a released prisoner's reasonable expectation of privacy that a suspicionless search by a law enforcement officer would not offend the Fourth Amendment." **Samson**, **supra**, at 847. The Court ruled that suspicionless searches of a parolee do not violate the Fourth Amendment prohibition against unreasonable searches and seizures. Based on Proposition 8, California courts are bound to follow this decision. This means that **Samson** supersedes the California Supreme Court's decision in **Burgener**, **supra**, requiring a "reasonable suspicion" standard before an officer can search a parolee."

FACTS (Samson v. California (2006) 547 U.S. 843)

Donald Curtis Samson was convicted in a California court of being a felon in possession of a firearm and was released on parole. On September 6, 2002, San Bruno Police Officer Rohleder saw Mr. Samson walking down the street with a woman and a child. Officer Rohleder had prior contact with Mr. Samson, knew he was on parole, and believed that Mr. Samson had an outstanding warrant for being a parolee at large.

Officer Rohleder stopped Mr. Samson and asked him about the warrant. Mr. Samson correctly told the officer that he "was in good standing with his parole agent" and did not have an outstanding arrest warrant. Officer Rohleder used his radio, confirmed that Mr. Samson was still on parole and did not have an outstanding warrant. Nevertheless, he decided to conduct a parole search of Mr. Samson's person pursuant to California Penal Code 3067(a). During the search, the officer found a cigarette box in Mr. Samson's left breast pocket. Inside the box was a baggie of methamphetamine.

The officer arrested Mr. Samson who was charged with possession of methamphetamine. The trial court denied Mr. Sampson's suppression motion and a jury convicted him of possessing methamphetamine. The trial court sentenced him to seven years in prison. The Court of Appeal affirmed the trial court's decision admitting the seized evidence based on **People v. Reyes**, 19 Cal.4th 743.

In **People v. Sardinas** (2009) 170 Cal.App.4th 488, the Court of Appeal rejected Mr. Saldinas's contention that the two searches occurring within 24 hours of each other, combined with the officer's prior six or seven contacts with him over a five-year period, belied any legitimate purpose for the second search that resulted in the seizure of cocaine from his person, and compelled the conclusion that the search was done for harassment or other arbitrary purpose.

FACTS (**People v. Sardinas (2009) 170 Cal.App.4th 488**)

City of Pomona Police Officer Samuels became a police officer for the city five years before the challenged search. The officer had seen Rolando Sardinas frequently, and usually in an area where he saw Mr. Sardinas associate with cocaine base addicts. After joining the major crimes task force, the officer had more frequent contacts with Mr. Sardinas because the task force dealt with "street level" narcotics and criminal street gangs. Before the December 20, 2007, traffic stop, the officer had contacted Mr. Sardinas on at least six or seven occasions, with the last occasion being about 30 days before the traffic stop. On each occasion, Officer Samuels had confirmed Mr. Sardinas was on parole.

On December 20, 2007, Officer Samuels stopped Mr. Sardinas for driving a van at night without his taillights working properly. Officer Samuels asked Mr. Sardinas to step out of the van and confirmed that he was still on parole. Mr. Sardinas said that he had just purchased the van that day and had not had an opportunity to repair the taillights. Officer Samuels told Mr. Sardinas to repair the taillights but did not issue him a citation. The officer searched Mr. Sardinas, but found nothing of an illegal or suspicious nature on his person. Officer Samuels' partner searched the van, and failed to find any legal violations. Officer Samuels and his partner then drove Mr. Sardinas home in their patrol car and searched his house, but again found nothing of an illegal or suspicious nature.

On December 21, 2007, at approximately 5:30 p.m., Officer Samuels saw Mr. Sardinas walking through the parking lot of a 7-11 convenience store in an area known for narcotics sales. Officer Samuels knew that the apartment complex directly across from the store was a known source of narcotics and had personally made numerous contacts in the area related to the sale, use, and possession of narcotics. As he drove through the parking lot, he recognized Mr. Sardinas based on his prior contacts as well as the traffic stop the night before, but saw nothing that made him suspicious of Mr. Sardinas. However, because Officer Samuels wanted to ensure that Mr. Sardinas was in compliance with his parole conditions, the officer stopped his patrol car, exited and contacted Mr. Sardinas. Before the officer said anything, Mr. Sardinas said, "What's up Samuels?" The officer asked Mr. Sardinas what he was doing in the area and was told, "Just walking through." The officer conducted a parole search of Mr. Sardinas for his own safety and the safety of the public. During that search, he found several pieces of individually packaged rock cocaine in Mr. Sardinas' front waistband.

After a jury trial, Mr. Sardinas was found guilty of violating California Health and Safety Code 11351.5. He waived jury on his strike prior, a prison prior, and three prior 11370(a) and (c) offenses. The trial court found three of the four prior convictions to be true. The trial court sentenced Mr. Sardinas to seven years prison, and he appealed the denial of his pre-trial motion to suppress evidence.

On appeal, Mr. Sardinas argued that the search violated his Fourth Amendment right to be free from unreasonable searches and seizures. He also argued that because of the officer's prior contacts with him, including the search of his person, van and home less than 24 hours prior to the challenged search, those actions compelled the conclusion that the December 21, 2007, search was conducted for purposes of harassment.

RATIONALE

Citing multiple case sources, the Court of Appeal pointed out that a search is arbitrary and capricious when motivation for the search is unrelated to rehabilitative, reformative or legitimate law-enforcement purposes, or when the search is motivated by personal animosity toward the parolee. **Id.** at 494-496.

The court noted that there was substantial evidence in the record to support the conclusion that this challenged search was conducted for legitimate law enforcement purposes and not to harass Mr. Sardinas. The court pointed out that the search was conducted directly across the street from an apartment complex known to Officer Samuels as a location where drug trafficking occurred. The officer knew that Mr. Sardinas was on parole for a drug possession conviction and saw Mr. Sardinas associate with known drug addicts in the past. The trial court found that there was no evidence that Officer Samuels harbored any animus toward Mr. Sardinas and there was evidence that part of the officer's job was to know the identities of parolees in the city and to patrol areas known for drug trafficking. It ruled that

> . . . based on the evidence presented, it was reasonable for the trial court to infer that the two searches within 24 hours were conducted for legitimate law enforcement purposes. The facts found by the trial court concerning Officer Samuels's knowledge and motives and the circumstances surrounding the two searches [were] supported by substantial evidence. That being so, the December 21 first search was not arbitrary or capricious, but rather was conducted for a legitimate law enforcement purpose." **Id**. at 497.

2.5.5.1 – Parolees and Parole Arrest Warrants

In **People v. Lewis** (1999) 74 Cal.App.4th 662, the Court of Appeal ruled that a police officer does not have to obtain an arrest warrant before entering a parolee's house to arrest the parolee. The court reasoned that a parolee has a diminished expectation of privacy by virtue of his parole status and a parolee's protection against warrantless arrests should not be any greater than the protection afforded a parolee against warrantless searches.

FACTS (People v. Lewis (1999) 74 Cal.App.4th 662)

On Sept. 30, 1991, Oakland police officers were looking for the defendant because there had been a rash of robberies near the address where the defendant told his parole officer he lived. A number of robbery victims had already identified the defendant as the robber.

Late in the afternoon on the 30th, another robbery occurred. Oakland Police Officer Grubensky, who had earlier that day told his superior, Sergeant Delgadillo, that he was looking for the defendant was the first officer to speak to the victim of the robbery. Sergeant Delgadillo did not remember if he had informed Officer Grubensky that the defendant was a parolee but later testified that it would have been his practice to do so.

After obtaining a description of the robber, Officer Grubensky immediately went to the defendant's residence and knocked on the door. The defendant's mother asked who it was and Officer Grubensky said "Oakland Police." The mother then opened the door. The defendant then asked his mother who it was and was told, "The police." Officer Grubensky entered the residence and arrested the defendant.

The officer placed the defendant in the back of his patrol car. After several minutes, the latest robbery victim arrived and identified the defendant as the robber. Earlier in the month, the defendant's parole officer had unsuccessfully tried to arrest the defendant at the house. The trial court denied the defendant's motion to suppress and the Court of Appeal later affirmed that denial.

A jury found the defendant guilty of kidnapping for robbery, five counts of robbery, and five counts of vehicle theft. The jury also found several weapons use enhancements to be true. The defendant admitted two strike priors and the court sentenced him to an indeterminate life term and a consecutive 14-year prison term.

2.5.6 – Vehicle Searches

2.5.6.1 – Probable Cause

In **Carroll v. United States** (1925) 267 U.S. 132, the U.S. Supreme Court held the police did not violate the Fourth Amendment when they conducted a warrantless search of a vehicle based upon probable cause to believe that the vehicle contained evidence of a crime, in light of exigent circumstances arising out of the likely disappearance of the vehicle. This rule is sometimes referred to as the *Carroll Doctrine*.

The Court recognized "[a] necessary difference between a search of a store, dwelling house or other structure in respect of which a proper official warrant readily may be obtained, and a search of a ship, motor boat, wagon or automobile, for contraband goods, where it is not practicable to secure a warrant because the vehicle can be quickly moved out of the locality or jurisdiction in which the warrant must be sought." **Carroll,** at 153.

The U.S. Supreme Court reiterated in **Pennsylvania v. Labron** (1996) 518 U.S. 938, that the Fourth Amendment *does not require* both the existence of probable cause and exigent circumstances before the police can conduct a warrantless, probable cause search of an automobile. The U.S. Supreme Court clearly stated, "Our first cases establishing the automobile exception to the Fourth Amendment's warrant requirement were based on the automobile's 'ready mobility,' an exigency sufficient to excuse failure to obtain a search warrant once probable cause to conduct the search is clear." (**Id**. at 940.) "If a car is readily mobile and probable cause exists to believe it contains contraband, the Fourth Amendment thus permits police to search the vehicle without more." (**Id**. at 940.)

FACTS (Pennsylvania v. Labron (1996) 518 U.S. 938)

Police observed Mr. Labron and others engage in a series of drug transactions on a Philadelphia street. The police arrested all the suspects and then conducted a warrantless search of the trunk of the car from where the suspects obtained the drugs. The search resulted in the seizure of bags of cocaine.

The Pennsylvania Supreme Court held that the Fourth Amendment required "both the existence of probable cause and the presence of exigent circumstances to justify a warrantless search." (**Id**. at 939.) Because the Pennsylvania Supreme Court believed the police had time to get a search warrant, they suppressed the evidence.

The U.S. Supreme Court remanded the case to the Pennsylvania Supreme Court to see if it based its decision on the Pennsylvania Constitution.

It is important to remember that except for California, which is governed by Proposition 8, any other State can grant greater rights to its citizens under its own constitution than are granted under the United States Constitution.

Two years after its decision in **Pennsylvania v. Labron**, **supra**, the U.S. Supreme Court in **Maryland v. Dyson** (1999) 527 U.S. 465, issued a unanimous Per Curium opinion reversing the Maryland Court of Special Appeals' decision suppressing the warrantless seizure of evidence from a car. The Court again stated that the finding of probable cause alone justifies the warrantless search of a car based on its holding in **United States v. Ross** (1982) 456 U.S. 798, **infra**.

FACTS (Maryland v. Dyson (1999) 527 U.S. 465)

At 11 a.m. on July 2, 1996, a St. Mary's County Deputy Sheriff received a tip from a CRI that Kevin Darnell Dyson had gone to New York to buy drugs, and would be returning to Maryland later that day with a large quantity of cocaine. He would be in a rented red Toyota, bearing license plate number DDY 787. The deputy investigated the tip and found that the license plate number belonged to a red Toyota Corolla that the defendant rented and that the defendant was a known drug dealer in St. Mary's County.

When the defendant returned to St. Mary's County at 1 a.m. on July 3, 1996, the deputies stopped his car and searched it. During the search, police found 23 grams of crack cocaine in a duffel bag in the trunk. The defendant was convicted of conspiracy to possess cocaine with the intent to distribute it.

The trial court denied the defendant's motion to suppress evidence. The defendant predicated his argument on the idea that the police had sufficient time after the CRI's tip to get a search warrant, but failed to do so.

The Maryland Court of Special Appeals reversed the conviction and incorrectly held that the automobile exception consisted of the following components:

1. Probable cause to believe that evidence of a crime is contained in the automobile
2. A separate finding of exigency, which precluded the police from obtaining a search warrant.

RATIONALE

The second prong of the test set forth by the Maryland Court of Special Appeals is wrong and is squarely contrary to the Court's previous rulings in **United States v. Ross**, and **Pennsylvania v. Labron**.

In **Chambers v. Maroney** (1970) 399 U.S. 42, the Supreme Court refined the exigency requirement related to car searches when it held that the existence of exigent circumstances was to be determined at the time the automobile is seized. In this case, the search took place at the police station where the car had been immobilized and some time after the driver had been arrested. Given the probable cause and exigent circumstances existed at the time the vehicle was first stopped, the Court held that the later warrantless search of the vehicle at the station did not violate the Fourth Amendment.

The rationale derived from the **Carroll** ruling is that an immediate search at the moment of seizure would have been permissible. The Court reasoned in **Chambers**, **supra**, that the police could search later whenever they could have searched earlier, had they so chosen. Following **Chambers,** if the police have probable cause to justify a warrantless seizure of an automobile on a public roadway, they may conduct either an immediate or a delayed search of the vehicle.

An example of the application of the **Chambers** rule is found in **United States v. Johns** (1984) 469 U.S. 478, where the U.S. Supreme Court ruled that a three-day delay in searching containers in a truck was permissible when probable cause existed initially to search the containers seized from that truck.

Another example of the application of the **Chambers** rule is found in **Florida v. Meyers** (1984) 466 U.S. 380. In that case, the police arrested Mr. Meyers for sexual battery and searched his car at the time of his arrest. The police seized several items of evidence. The police had the car towed to Sunny's Wrecker, and impounded it in a locked and secure area. About eight hours after the car's impound, a second officer, without a warrant, searched the car and obtained additional evidence. Relying on its holding in **Michigan v. Thomas** (1982) 458 U.S. 259, **infra**, the U.S. Supreme Court reversed the Florida state court's suppression of the evidence seized in the second search.

The U.S. Supreme Court resolved a long standing conflict over whether a warrantless search of a car included containers in the vehicle when it decided **United States v. Ross** (1982) 456 U.S. 798. The Court held that a warrantless search of an automobile under the **Carroll** doctrine could include a search of a container or package found in the car when such a search was supported by probable cause. The Court reasoned that if probable cause justifies the search of a lawfully stopped vehicle, it justifies the search of every part of the vehicle and its contents that may conceal the object of the search. With probable cause, a vehicle may be searched as broadly as if the officer had a warrant.

In **Wyoming v. Houghton** (1999) 526 U.S. 295, the U.S. Supreme Court ruled by a 7 to 2 majority, that police do not violate the Fourth Amendment when they search a car passenger's personal belongings inside an automobile, as long as they have probable cause to believe the automobile contains contraband and the belongings are capable of concealing the object of the search.

Justice Scalia, writing for the Court's majority implies that the court decision is just a natural extension of **United States v. Ross**, **supra**, and cites Justice Steven's majority opinion from that case in support of the Court's position:

> "It is noteworthy that the early legislation on which the Court relied in *Carroll* concerned the enforcement of laws imposing duties on imported merchandise. . . . Presumably such merchandise was shipped then in containers of various kinds, just as it is today. Since Congress had authorized warrantless searches of vessels and beasts for imported merchandise, it is inconceivable that it intended a customs officer to obtain a warrant for every package discovered during the search; certainly Congress intended customs officers to open shipping containers when necessary and not merely to examine the exterior of cartons or boxes in which smuggled goods might be concealed. During virtually the entire history of our country – whether contraband was transported in a horse-drawn carriage, a 1921 roadster, or a modern automobile – it has been assumed that a lawful search of a vehicle would include a search of any container that might conceal the object of the search." **United States v. Ross**, at 820, n. 26.

FACTS (Wyoming v. Houghton (1999) 526 U.S. 295)

In the early morning hours of July 23, 1995, a Wyoming Highway Patrol Officer stopped a car for speeding and a bad brake light. David Young drove the car while his girlfriend and Sandra Houghton (the defendant) were passengers in the car.

While questioning Mr. Young, the officer saw a hypodermic syringe in Mr. Young's shirt pocket. The officer went back to his patrol car to retrieve gloves and had the occupants watched by two other officers who arrived as back up.

Upon his return, the officer had Mr. Young step out of the car and place the syringe on the hood of the car. The officer asked Mr. Young why he had a syringe and was told that it was used to take drugs.

The back-up officers ordered the two female passengers out of the car and asked them for ID. Ms. Houghton falsely identified herself as "Sandra James" and said she had no ID.

Based on Mr. Young's admission, the officer searched the passenger compartment of the car and found a purse on the backseat, which Ms. Houghton claimed as her property. The officer opened the purse and removed a wallet. Inside the wallet was Ms. Houghton's driver's license with her true name. When asked why she lied, the defendant said, "In case things went bad."

As the officer continued the purse search, he found a brown pouch and a black wallet-type container. The defendant denied ownership of these items and claimed not to know how they ended up in her purse. Inside the containers were drug paraphernalia and a syringe with 60cc of methamphetamine. Ms. Houghton then admitted ownership of the black container, which also contained drug paraphernalia, and a syringe with 10cc of methamphetamine. That amount was insufficient to support the felony conviction for possession of drugs. Ms. Houghton also had fresh needle marks on her arms and was arrested.

The trial court denied Ms. Houghton's motion to suppress the evidence and she was convicted. A divided Wyoming Supreme Court reversed the trial court and announced the following rule:

> " 'Generally, once probable cause is established to search a vehicle, an officer is entitled to search all containers therein which may contain the object of the search. *However, if the officer knows or should know that a container is the personal effect of a passenger who is not suspected of criminal activity, then the container is outside the scope of the search unless someone had the opportunity to conceal the contraband within the personal effect to avoid detection.'* " (**Houghton, supra, Id**. at 299. [Italics added].)

2.5.6.1.1 – Vehicle Search Case Examples

In **People v. Dey** (2000) 84 Cal.App.4th 1318, the Court of Appeal ruled that an officer's discovery of a marijuana bud in a day planner in the passenger compartment of the car provided probable cause justifying the search of the trunk for additional contraband. That search resulted in the discovery and seizure of more marijuana.

The discovery of the additional marijuana resulted in searching the car's engine compartment, which led to the discovery of a flannel shirt hidden between the headlight and battery. Inside the shirt, the officer found a scale and methamphetamine. That search was conducted pursuant to the CHP's inventory policy for seized vehicles with long expired registration. Incident to the defendant's arrest, the police lawfully seized additional methamphetamine and some money that the defendant had tucked in his underwear.

As a side note, the Court of Appeal expressed its opinion that in light of the U.S. Supreme Court's opinion in **United States v. Ross**, and the passage of Proposition 8, **Wimberly v. Superior Court** (1976) 16 Cal.3d 557 and **People v. Gregg** (1974) 43 Cal.App.3d 137 are no longer viable.

FACTS (People v. Dey (2000) 84 Cal.App.4th 1318)

An officer lawfully stopped Eugene Dey for investigation of a possible registration violation in the early morning hours of September 20, 1998. The CHP officers who stopped him determined that his passenger was a wanted parolee. The officers determined that the parolee was under the influence of a stimulant and illegally in possession of a knife with a blade longer than two inches.

While searching the passenger compartment of the car, the officer found the defendant's day planner, which contained a marijuana bud. Following that discovery, the officer searched the trunk and found an additional quantity of marijuana.

At the motion to suppress, the DDA argued that the search was lawful based on probable cause and the CHP's inventory policy. The trial court agreed and refused to suppress the evidence.

At trial, the defendant was convicted of transportation and possession of marijuana and methamphetamine, and strike priors. The court sentenced him to 26 years to life. The Court of Appeal affirmed the trial court's decision.

In **People v. Allen** (2000) 78 Cal.App.4th 445, which is a case involving a bicyclist, the court of Appeal ruled that based on the **Carroll** doctrine, an officer did not need to obtain a search warrant before conducting a search of a bicycle's handlebar tube for contraband. The Court observed that given the mobile nature of a bicycle, it presents the same practical problems in obtaining a search warrant, as does an automobile.

FACTS (People v. Allen (2000) 78 Cal.App.4th 445)

At about 6:45 p.m., on March 27, 1998, Sacramento Police Officers Jennings and Forbeck saw the defendant in an area of town known for the sale of narcotics at all times of the day and night. Officer Forbeck was familiar with the defendant and knew that he had an arrest history for narcotic related offenses.

Although the defendant lived 58 blocks away, the officers had previously seen the defendant in the area. Each time the defendant was riding his bicycle. The officers had stopped the defendant about two weeks earlier and confiscated food stamps the belonged to someone else from him.

Apparently, food stamps were sometimes illegally traded in that neighborhood for narcotics, alcohol and a multitude of other things. The police did not arrest the defendant on that occasion, but his companion was arrested for being in possession of heroin.

On this particular day, the defendant rode his bicycle through a stop sign, which is a violation of the California Vehicle Code. The officers pulled along side of him and told him to stop. Instead of stopping right away, the defendant looked at the officers, continued to ride his bike and moved his right hand to the right handlebar. The defendant appeared to be using his thumb to push something inside. About 25 feet later, and approximately 100 feet after first being told to stop, the defendant stopped his bicycle.

Officer Forbeck seized a knife from the defendant and patted him down for weapons. As Officer Jennings began to look at the bicycle, the defendant became nervous. Officer Jennings turned the bicycle upside down and tapped on the handlebar. Three small rocks of cocaine fell out and he arrested the defendant.

Following the denial of his motion to suppress evidence, the defendant plead guilty to possession of crack cocaine, admitted a strike prior, and received a 32-month state prison sentence.

RATIONALE

Bicycles, like automobiles are subject to similar pervasive regulatory schemes, which results in a similar reduced expectation of privacy. Examples of such regulatory schemes include the following:

- When ridden on a highway, bicyclists are subject to similar duties as drivers of cars
- There are minimum safety standards for bicycles
- Bicycles are sometimes regulated by local ordinances that subject them to registration and licensing requirements.

The officers had ample probable cause to believe the bicycle contained contraband. This included the following factors:

- The officers' prior knowledge of the defendant's drug history
- The defendant's failure to yield to the officers' command to stop after riding through a stop sign
- The defendant's apparent attempt to conceal something inside the bicycle's handlebars
- The change in the defendant's demeanor when the officer began to look at the bicycle
- The defendant had recently been found in possession of food stamps in the same neighborhood and, on that occasion, was also in the company of someone who was found to possess heroin.

In **People v. Molina** (1994) 25 Cal.App.4th 1038, the Court of Appeal upheld the probable cause search and subsequent seizure of drugs and weapons from a lawfully stopped car based on the officer's initial observation of the odor of fresh beer coming from the car.

FACTS (People v. Molina (1994) 25 Cal.App.4th 1038)

Officer Petersen stopped Arturo Molina for driving 65 mph in a 45 mph zone. As Officer Petersen approached the truck, he noticed the smell of fresh beer. He also noticed that Mr. Molina's eyes were red and glassy and that his breath had an odor of alcohol. However, Mr. Molina passed all the field sobriety tests. Officer Petersen believed that there were open containers in the truck and called for a backup officer. Officer Brown arrived.

After asking Mr. Molina's two passengers to exit the truck, Officer Brown searched the truck for open containers. While looking in the passenger compartment of the truck, Officer Brown found a spilled, open bottle of beer on the passenger floorboard. Next, Officer Brown noticed a large, fixed-blade knife strapped to the driver's side of the truck's roll bar.

Officer Brown walked around to the driver's side of the truck and inspected the knife. He then noticed a second, smaller, fixed-blade knife strapped to the roll bar and inspected it.

Officer Brown also noticed a billy club sticking out from underneath the backseat on the driver's side. He pulled the seat forward and found a large machete secured to the backrest.

Officer Brown next searched a number of pockets sewn into the front seat's cover. He found a small nylon bag, capable of concealing a knife. Instead, it contained a gun magazine. Officer Brown searched the area behind the backseat, which he believed was accessible from the driver's seat, and found a duffle bag. Inside the duffle bag was a loaded .380 Beretta. He located a small toiletry-type bag in one of the seat pockets. Inside he found several baggies containing both cocaine and methamphetamine.

The magistrate upheld the search, but the Superior Court judge overruled the magistrate, suppressed the evidence, and granted Mr. Molina's Penal Code 995 motion to dismiss the Information. The Court of Appeal reversed the Superior Court's order suppressing the evidence.

RATIONALE

The officer's observation of the odor of fresh beer gave him probable cause to search the car for evidence of open containers. During that search, he lawfully discovered a billy club in plain view, which gave him probable cause to arrest Mr. Molina. Incident to that lawful arrest, the officer searched the truck and found cocaine.

In **People v. Carrillo** (1995) 37 Cal.App.4th 1662, the Court of Appeal ruled that probable cause to search a car existed even though the defendant was arrested at a gas station and the car that was searched was located back at an apartment complex.

FACTS (People v. Carrillo (1995) 37 Cal.App.4th 1662)

A CI told Deputy Maples that the defendant was a drug dealer. The CI provided Deputy Maples with a description of the defendant and told him that the defendant drove a "Toyota type" vehicle that looked like it had been in an accident.

A few weeks later, a second CI advised Deputy Maples that the defendant was staying in a particular apartment and would soon be delivering a large quantity of cocaine to a nearby gas station. The police staked out the gas station and saw the defendant and two other persons arrive. The defendant was carrying a large black bag over his shoulder.

The police confronted the three men and asked if they had weapons. The defendant admitted he possessed a gun. A loaded .380 handgun was found in his bag. The police arrested the defendant for possession of the concealed, loaded firearm and found him to be in possession of a single vehicle key. However, the defendant denied owning or driving a car.

Deputy Maples took the key back to the apartment complex and matched it to a locked Mitsubishi vehicle. Inside the car, he located a large stash of drugs.

The Court of Appeal found probable cause to be present to search the car and added that a key factor was the false statement of defendant, which was a "consciousness of guilt" that the officer could use in assessing probable cause.

People v. Temple (1995) 36 Cal.App.4th 1219 is an example of officers taking the probable cause search of automobiles too far. The Court of Appeal ruled that while the officers had probable cause to search the vehicle, per **United States v. Ross**, **supra**, the pockets of the vehicle occupants clothing are not containers that could be searched, absent probable cause to arrest the occupants.

FACTS (People v. Temple (1995) 36 Cal.App.4th 1219)

Officers made a car stop on a van for a broken tail light and weaving. The driver met the officer at the rear of the van, while four passengers remained in the van, including Mr. Temple. The officer noted an odor of marijuana on the driver's person and told the driver to return to the van while the officer waited for his back-up officers to arrive.

Once back up arrived, the officer again approached the van and saw that all five occupants were now smoking cigarettes. The officer still smelled fresh marijuana and asked for consent to search the van, which the driver gave.

The officer ordered all of the occupants, including Mr. Temple, out of the van and then searched it. The officer also searched Mr. Temple's person and found him to be in possession of methamphetamine. Following his arrest, more drugs were located in a piece of luggage that Mr. Temple admitted owning.

RATIONALE

Since there was no evidence that Mr. Temple was under the influence of drugs, or made furtive movements, the search of his person violated his Fourth Amendment rights.

2.5.6.1.2 – Canine Alerts

The Court of Appeal ruled in **People v. Bell** (1996) 43 Cal.App.4th 754 that a trained police canine's sniff alert to a car created probable cause justifying a search of the car.

FACTS (People v. Bell (1996) 43 Cal.App.4th 754)

A CHP officer stopped a vehicle on I-40 for speeding. I-40 is a major pipeline for drug traffickers. The officer had a drug-sniffing dog with him. The officer started writing a ticket and, out of the presence of the passenger, engaged in small talk with the driver.

The officer learned that both the driver and passenger were from out of state and learned why they were in California. The officer noted that the driver appeared nervous. The officer then spoke with Mr. Bell, the passenger in the car, and received different information that conflicted with the driver's story. Mr. Bell also appeared nervous.

The officer noted scars on Mr. Bell's legs, which appeared to him to have been caused by bullet wounds. The officer then saw a cellular phone in the car. The officer returned to the driver and asked if there was cocaine in the vehicle, to which the driver replied, "No." The driver verbally gave consent to search the car but would not sign a written consent form.

The officer then asked Mr. Bell for consent to search the car and obtained consent limited only to "Bell's stuff," which Mr. Bell said was in the trunk. The officer asked Mr. Bell to open the trunk. The dog alerted to the area under Mr. Bell's seat when he exited the car. The officer searched under the seat and found cocaine.

In **United States v. Bloomfield** (8th Cir. 1994) 40 F.3d 910, 919, the 8th Circuit Court of Appeals ruled that a trained police canine's alert to luggage or a car provides probable cause that drugs are present.

The 10th Circuit Court of Appeals in **United States v. Klinginsmith** (10th Cir. 1994) 25 F.3d 1507, 1510 ruled that a trained police canine's alert to a car gave officers probable cause to arrest the occupants and to search the vehicle without a warrant under the automobile exception to the warrant requirement, even in the absence of consent.

The 9th Circuit Court of Appeal ruled in **United States v. Lingenfelter** (9th Cir. 1993) 997 F.2d 632, 639 that a reliable police canine's reaction to the exterior of a warehouse provided probable cause for a search warrant of the warehouse. The Lingenfelter Court specifically ruled that "[a] canine sniff alone can supply probable cause necessary to issuing a search warrant if the application for the warrant establishes the dog's reliability." (**Id**. at 639)

In **United States v. Hernandez** (5th Cir. 1992) 976 F.2d 929, 930, the 5th Circuit Court of Appeals ruled that a police canine alert at a secondary border checkpoint provided probable cause to search the car for contraband.

In **United States v. Spetz** (9th Cir. 1983) 721 F.2d 1457, 1464, two trained narcotic detection dogs belonging to the United States Custom's Service, who alerted to a container, provided probable cause for the issuance of a search warrant, resulting in the seizure of 1,440 pounds of marijuana.

In **People v. Salih** (1985) 173 Cal.App.3d 1009, 1015, a trained police canine's alert to an international mail parcel provided United States Custom officials with reasonable cause to believe contraband was inside the parcel and justified its opening.

In **Florida v. Harris** (2013) ___ U.S. ___; 133 S.Ct. 1050; 185 L.Ed.2d 61, the United States Supreme Court addressed the issue of how a court should determine if a drug detection dog's alert during a traffic stop provided probable cause to search the vehicle. The USSC unanimously overruled the Florida Supreme Court's ruling that the State must in every case present an exhaustive set of records, including a log of the dog's field performance, to establish the dog's reliability.

FACTS (Florida v. Harris (2013) ___ U.S. ___; 133 S.Ct. 1050; 185 L.Ed.2d 61)

Liberty County Florida Deputy Sheriff William Wheetley was employed as a K–9 officer on June 24, 2006. He was on patrol with his narcotic detection trained German shepherd, Aldo. Aldo was trained to detect methamphetamine, marijuana, cocaine, heroin, and ecstasy. Deputy Wheetley stopped Clayton Harris's truck due to an expired license plate. As the deputy approached the stopped truck, he saw that Mr. Harris was visibly nervous as evidenced by his inability to sit still, shaking and rapid breathing. Deputy Wheetley also noticed an open can of beer in the trucks cup holder. Deputy Wheetley asked Mr. Harris for consent to search the truck, but he refused to provide consent. Deputy Wheetley then retreat Aldo from his patrol car and walked around the exterior of Mr. Harris's truck.

Aldo learned at the driver's side door handle consistent with his training, indicating that he smelled drugs. Based on that alert, deputy Wheetley believed he had probable cause to search the truck. While the truck search did not reveal any drugs, the deputy did locate 200 loose pseudoephedrine pills, 8000 matches, a bottle of hydrochloric acid, 2 containers of anti-freeze, and a coffee filter for of iodine crystals. All of those items are ingredients used for making methamphetamine. Deputy Wheetley then arrested Mr. Harris. After waiving his **Miranda** [**Miranda v. Arizona**, (1966) 384 US. 436] rights, Mr. Harris admitted that he routinely cooked methamphetamine at his house and couldn't go more than a few days without using it.

While out on bail on that initial charge, deputy Wheetley again encountered Mr. Harris and stopped him on this occasion for having a broken brake light. Aldo again sniffed the truck's exterior, and again alerted on the drivers side door handle. This time a search of the truck failed to reveal any contraband.

In the trial court, Mr. Harris moved to suppress the evidence seized in the initial stop on the ground's that all those alert did not provide probable cause for the search. At the hearing, deputy Wheetley said that in 2004, he any different narcotics detection dog completed a 160-hour course narcotics detection offered by the Dothan, Alabama Police Department. Aldo any different canine handler completed a similar, 120-hour course provided by the Apopka, Florida Police Department. That same year, Aldo received a one-year certification from Drug Beat, which is a private company that specializes in testing and certifying dogs. Deputy Wheetley and Aldo teamed up in 2005 and went through another 40-hour refresher course in Dothan, Alabama. Additionally, they did 4 hours of training exercises each week to maintain their skills. Deputy Wheetley explained that he would hide drugs in certain vehicles or buildings while leaving other blank to determine whether Aldo alerted at the right places. The state also introduced "Monthly Canine Detection Training Logs" that was consistent with that testimony. The log showed bit Aldo always found hidden drugs in that he performed "satisfactorily" (that is the higher of 2 possible assessments) on each training day.

During cross-examination, Mr. Harris's attorney did not challenge the quality of the deputies or all those training. Instead, she focused on Aldo's certification and his performance in the field, particularly the 2 stops of Mr. Harris's truck. Deputy Wheetley acknowledged that the certification, which Florida law did not require, had expired the year before he pulled Mr. Harris over. He also ignored study did not keep complete records of Aldo's performance in traffic stops or other fieldwork; instead, he maintain records only of alerts resulting arrests. Deputy Wheetley opined that Mr. Harris probably transferred the odor of methamphetamine to the door handle, and Aldo was alerting to that residual odor. The trial court concluded that Deputy Wheetley had probable cause to search the truck and denied the motion to suppress.

The Florida Supreme Court reversed that finding and ruled that the fact a dog has been trained and certified is not enough to establish probable cause. Instead, it ruled that "[T]he State must present . . . the dog's training and certification records, an explanation of the meaning of the particular training and certification, field performance records (including any unverified alerts), and evidence concerning the experience and training of the officer handling the dog, as well as any other objective evidence known to the officer about the dog's reliability." **Id.** at 1055. The Florida Supreme Court particularly stressed the need for evidence of a dog's performance history, including how often the dog alerted in the field but no contraband was found. The Florida Supreme Court ruled that an officer who did not keep those records could never have the requisite cause to think that the dog was reliable indicator of the presence of drugs.

RATIONALE

The USSC observed that "[N]o matter how much other proof the State offers of the dog's reliability, the absent field performance records will preclude a finding of probable cause. That is the antithesis of a totality-of-the-circumstances analysis. It is, indeed, the very thing we criticized in **Gates**, [**Illinois v. Gates**, (____) 462 U.S. 213] when we overhauled our method for assessing the trustworthiness of an informant's tip. ... a finding of a drug-detection dog's reliability cannot depend on the State's satisfaction of multiple, independent evidentiary requirements. No more for dogs than for human informants is such an inflexible checklist the way to prove reliability, and thus establish probable cause. ¶ Making matters worse, the decision below treats records of a dog's field performance as the gold standard in evidence, when in most cases they have relatively limited import. Errors may abound in such records. If a dog on patrol fails to alert to a car containing drugs, the mistake usually will go undetected because the officer will not initiate a search. Field data thus may not capture a dog's false negatives. Conversely (and more relevant here), if the dog alerts to a car in which the officer finds no narcotics, the dog may not have made a mistake at all. The dog may have detected substances that were too well hidden or present in quantities too small for the officer to locate. Or the dog may have smelled the residual odor of drugs previously in the vehicle or on the driver's person. Field data thus may markedly overstate a dog's real false positives. By contrast, those inaccuracies—in either direction—do not taint records of a dog's performance in standard training and certification settings. There, the designers of an assessment know where drugs are hidden and where they are not—and so where a dog should alert and where he should not. The better measure of a dog's reliability thus comes away from the field, in controlled testing environments." **Id.** at 1056-1057.

"In short, a probable-cause hearing focusing on a dog's alert should proceed much like any other. The court should allow the parties to make their best case, consistent with the usual rules of criminal procedure. And the court should then evaluate the proffered evidence to decide what all the circumstances demonstrate. If the State has produced proof from controlled settings that a dog performs reliably in detecting drugs, and the defendant has not contested that showing, then the court should find probable cause. If, in contrast, the defendant has challenged the State's case (by disputing the reliability of the dog overall or of a particular alert), then the court should weigh the competing evidence. In all events, the court should not prescribe, as the Florida Supreme Court did, an inflexible set of evidentiary requirements. The question—similar to every inquiry into probable cause—is whether all the facts surrounding a dog's alert, viewed through the lens of common sense, would make a reasonably prudent person think that a search would reveal contraband or evidence of a crime. A sniff is up to snuff when it meets that test." **Id.** at 1058.

However, in a 5 to 4 decision in **Florida v. Jardines** (2013) ___ U.S. ___; 133 S.Ct. 1409; 185 L.Ed.2d 495, the U.S. Supreme Court ruled that "the government's use of trained police dogs to investigate the home and its immediate surroundings is a 'search' within the meaning of the Fourth Amendment." **Id**. at 1417.

FACTS (Florida v. Jardines (2013) ___ U.S. ___; 133 S.Ct. 1409; 185 L.Ed.2d 495

In 2006, Miami–Dade police Detective William Pedraja received an unverified tip that marijuana was being grown in Mr. Jardines' home. One month later, DEA sent a joint surveillance team to Mr. Jardines' home to follow up on the tip. Detective Pedraja was part of that team and watched the home for approximately 15 minutes. He saw no vehicles in the driveway or activity around the home, and could not see inside the house because the window blinds were drawn. Detective Pedraja approached the house in the company of Detective Bartelt, who is a trained K-9 handler and had just arrived at the scene with his drug-sniffing dog "Franky". The detectives approached the front door by the driveway and a paved path, which is the same route any visitor would normally use.

Franky is trained to detect a variety of controlled substances including marijuana, cocaine, and heroin. Detective Bartelt had Franky on a six-foot leash. As Franky approached the front porch, he apparently sensed one of the odors he is trained to detect, and began exploring the area for the strongest point of the source of that odor. After wandering around on the front porch for no more than about two minutes, Franky sniffed the front door and then sat down, which is the way he is trained to react upon discovering the odor's strongest point. After Franky alerted to the front door, Detective Bartelt advised Detective Pedraja of Franky's positive alert and then left the scene.

Based on the information acquired by using Franky, Detective Pedraja obtained a search warrant for the residence. When the officers served a search warrant later that day, Mr. Jardines attempted to flee and was arrested. The search yielded marijuana plants and Mr. Jardines was charged with trafficking in cannabis.

The trial court suppressed the marijuana plants on the grounds that the use of the canine was an unreasonable search. The Florida Third District Court of Appeal reversed, but it's decision was quashed by the Florida Supreme Court, which ruled that the use of a trained narcotics dog to investigate the home was a search unsupported by probable cause and therefore violated the Fourth Amendment. The U.S. Supreme Court granted certiorari to decide whether "the officer's behavior was a search within the meaning of the Fourth Amendment." **Id**. at 1414.

RATIONALE

Justice Scalia wrote the majority opinion for the Court. He stated that "The officers were gathering information in an area belonging to Jardines and immediately surrounding his house—in the curtilage of the house, which we have held enjoys protection as part of the home itself. And they gathered that information by physically entering and occupying the area to engage in conduct not explicitly or implicitly permitted by the homeowner." **Id**.

Justice Scalia said

> ...when it comes to the Fourth Amendment, the home is first among equals. At the Amendment's "very core" stands "the right of a man to retreat into his own home and there be free from unreasonable governmental intrusion." **Silverman v. United States**, 365 US. 505, 511, 81 S.Ct. 679, 5 L.Ed.2d 734 (1961). This right would be of little practical value if the State's agents could stand in a home's porch or side garden and trawl for evidence with impunity; the right to retreat

> would be significantly diminished if the police could enter a man's property to observe his repose from just outside the front window.
>
> **Id**.

Justice Scalia also observed that "a police officer not armed with a warrant may approach a home and knock, precisely because that is 'no more than any private citizen might do.' **Kentucky v. King**, (2011) ___ U.S. ___; 131 S.Ct. 1849; 179 L.Ed.2d 865." **Jardines** at 1416.

However, Justice Scalia also stated that

> ...introducing a trained police dog to explore the area around the home in hopes of discovering incriminating evidence is something else. There is no customary invitation to do *that*. An invitation to engage in canine forensic investigation assuredly does not inhere in the very act of hanging a knocker. To find a visitor knocking on the door is routine (even if sometimes unwelcome); to spot that same visitor exploring the front path with a metal detector, or marching his bloodhound into the garden before saying hello and asking permission, would inspire most of us to—well, call the police. The scope of a license—express or implied—is limited not only to a particular area but also to a specific purpose. Consent at a traffic stop to an officer's checking out an anonymous tip that there is a body in the trunk does not permit the officer to rummage through the trunk for narcotics. Here, the background social norms that invite a visitor to the front door do not invite him there to conduct a search.
>
> **Id**.

Justice Kagan wrote a concurring opinion, which was joined by Justices Ginsburg and Sotomayor. In her opinion, Justice Kagan observed

> Here, police officers came to Joelis Jardines' door with a super-sensitive instrument, which they deployed to detect things inside that they could not perceive unassisted. The equipment they used was animal, not mineral.... They are to the poodle down the street as high-powered binoculars are to a piece of plain glass. Like the binoculars, a drug-detection dog is a specialized device for discovering objects not in plain view (or plain smell). And as in the hypothetical above, that device was aimed here at a home—the most private and inviolate (or so we expect) of all the places and things the Fourth Amendment protects. Was this activity a trespass? Yes, as the Court holds today. Was it also an invasion of privacy? Yes, that as well.
>
> **Id**. at 1418.

Justice Kagan's view, as well as the Court's majority ruling was simply stated in her concurrence by her observation that the Court's rule in **Kyllo** [**Kyllo v. United States** (2001) 533 U.S. 27][20], **infra**, governed the outcome of this case.

> The police officers here conducted a search because they used a "device ... not in general public use" (a trained drug-detection dog) to "explore details of the home" (the presence of certain substances) that they would not otherwise have discovered without entering the premises.

Id. at 1419.

2.5.6.1.3 – Pretext Searches

The U.S. Supreme Court ruled in **United States v. Whren** (1996) 517 U.S. 806, that there is no such thing as a pretext stop. If an officer has probable cause to believe a vehicle code violation has occurred, the officer may stop the car. It is irrelevant that the officer had some other prior knowledge, unrelated to enforcement of the traffic laws, concerning the criminal activity (example, the driver is a drug dealer) of the car's occupant(s).

The Court once again affirmed its position that "[s]ubjective intentions play no role in ordinary, probable cause Fourth Amendment analysis." (**Id.** at 813).

In **Arkansas v. Sullivan** (2001) 532 U.S. 769, the U.S. Supreme Court reversed the Arkansas Supreme Court's holding that the officer engaged in a pretext search of the defendant's car. In so doing, the U.S. Supreme Court found that the Arkansas Supreme Court erroneously ignored the U.S. Supreme Court's decision in **Whren**, **supra**, and reiterated that subjective intentions play no role in Fourth Amendment analysis.

The U.S. Supreme Court also rejected the Arkansas Supreme Court's position that it could interpret the United States Constitution more broadly than the U.S. Supreme Court The Court cited its own precedent of **Oregon v. Hass** (1975) 420 U.S. 714, where it ruled that "a State is free *as a matter of its own law* to impose greater restrictions on police activity than those this Court holds to be necessary upon federal constitutional standards," it "may not impose such greater restrictions as a matter of *federal constitutional law* when this Court specifically refrains from imposing them." **Oregon v. Hass**, at 719." **Sullivan**, **supra**, at 772.

FACTS (Arkansas v. Sullivan (2001) 532 U.S. 769)

Officer Taylor of the Conway, Arkansas, Police Department stopped Mr. Sullivan for speeding and having an improperly tinted windshield. When

[20] The **Kyllo** rule states that when "the Government uses a device that is not in general public use, to explore details of the home that would previously have been unknowable without physical intrusion, the surveillance is a 'search' and is presumptively unreasonable without a warrant." **Jardines**, **supra**, at 1419.

Mr. Sullivan presented his driver's license, Officer Taylor recalled intelligence information about Mr. Sullivan regarding narcotics.

Mr. Sullivan opened his car door and was unsuccessful in his attempt to locate his car's registration and insurance papers. When he opened the car door, Officer Taylor saw a rusted roof hatchet on the car's floorboard.

Following Mr. Sullivan's arrest for speeding, driving without his registration and insurance documents, carrying a weapon, and having an illegally tinted windshield, Officer Taylor conducted an inventory search pursuant to the standard policy of his agency. During that search, Officer Taylor found a bag of methamphetamine and drug paraphernalia under an armrest in the car.

Mr. Sullivan moved to suppress the evidence seized from the car and argued that his arrest was a mere pretext to search him and therefore violated the Fourth Amendment.

The trial court granted the suppression motion and the Arkansas Supreme Court upheld that suppression. It held that it did not have to follow **Whren, supra**. The Arkansas Supreme Court also stated, "there is nothing that prevents this court from interpreting the United States Constitution more broadly than the U.S. Supreme Court, which has the effect of providing more rights." **Sullivan**, at 771.

However, in **People v. Valenzuela** (1999) 74 Cal.App.4th 1202, a California Court of Appeal ruled that while pretext searches are not prohibited in the context of probable cause searches, they are *still prohibited in the context of administrative, inventory or inspection searches.* The Court of Appeal therefore suppressed narcotics evidence seized from a taxicab passenger by a San Diego Police Officer, whose real motivation was not to conduct a taxicab inspection but instead to search the passenger for drugs.

FACTS (People v. Valenzuela (1999) 74 Cal.App.4th 1202**)**

The San Diego Police Department has had a seven-year problem with the sale and use of controlled substances at The End Zone Bar. San Diego Police Sergeant Brogdon had made over a dozen drug related arrests at the bar and has extensive experience in the area of narcotics. Sergeant Brogdon's narcotics experience includes the following.

- He has testified as a drug expert on over 200 occasions
- He had made over 200 drug related arrests
- 5 ½ of his 12 years as a police officer have been in narcotics enforcement
- He worked for a year in a walking enforcement campaign against narcotics

- He worked for 19 months as a vice detective where he purchased drugs in bars and other places subject to the Alcohol Beverage Control Board's regulation.

Sergeant Brogdon was a patrol supervisor at the time. At about 2:15 p.m. on February 6, 1998, the Sergeant was outside The End Zone Bar when he saw the defendant come out of the bar and enter the front seat of a taxicab parked in front of the bar. The Sergeant followed the cab for a short distance and then stopped it for the alleged purpose of conducting a taxicab inspection.

Sergeant Brogdon had conducted about 30 such inspections before this incident. Such inspections are made daily by vice officers and occasionally made by patrol officers. Sergeant Brogdon testified on cross-examination that he made the stop "based upon the knowledge of the establishment." Sergeant Brogdon did not recall if the cab had a medallion on its trunk, which is required by all cabs operating in the city and county. He also did not look for the medallion even though he was parked 20 to 25 feet behind the cab.

After the cab stopped, the Sergeant approached the passenger side of the car and asked the driver for his driver's and cab licenses, registration and insurance papers. He also stated that he was conducting a cab inspection. The cab driver later testified that after he handed his papers to the Sergeant, Sergeant Brogdon returned them right away and never said that he was conducting a cab inspection or explained why he wanted to see the papers.

While the cab driver retrieved the requested documents, Sergeant Brogdon began a casual conversation with the defendant. The Sergeant asked the defendant to step out of the cab, which he did, and then if he had any form of ID. The defendant produced his driver's license.

Sergeant Brogdon then asked the defendant for permission to search the defendant's person and the defendant consented to the search. During the search, Sergeant Brogdon located a small bag of cocaine and arrested the defendant. Following his arrest, the defendant became unsteady on his feet and almost passed out. The Sergeant held onto him while he awaited the arrival of paramedics.

Sergeant Brogdon did not go through the papers the taxi driver had retrieved and, because the defendant was handcuffed, the Sergeant helped the defendant pay the cab driver. The cab inspection was never completed.

RATIONALE

Pretext searches are prohibited in the context of administrative searches but not in the context of probable cause searches.

The Court of Appeal found the stop to be pretextual based on the following factors:

- Sergeant Brogdon appeared motivated by a desire to contact the passenger, not the cab driver
- The Sergeant had vast experience in narcotics and minimal in cab inspections
- Sergeant Brogdon failed to carry out any element of a cab inspection, other than to ask for and receive the cab driver's papers
- He immediately focused on the defendant
- He admitted that he stopped the cab "based on his knowledge of the establishment."

2.5.6.1.4 – Forfeitable Vehicles and Warrantless Seizures

In a 7 to 2 decision written by Justice Thomas in **Florida v. White** (1999) 526 U.S. 559, the U.S. Supreme Court ruled that no warrant is required to seize an automobile from a public place when the police have probable cause to believe that the automobile itself is forfeitable contraband. However, in a cautionary statement in footnote four, Justice Thomas stated, "[w]e express no opinion about whether excessive delay prior to a seizure could render probable cause stale, and the seizure therefore unreasonable under the Fourth Amendment." (**Id**. FN 4, at 565.)

FACTS (Florida v. White (1999) 526 U.S. 559)

On three occasions in July and August 1995, officers saw Tyvessel Tyvorus White using his car to deliver cocaine. Those actions made the car forfeitable under Florida's Contraband Forfeiture Act.

Several months later, the police arrested Mr. White at his place of employment on charges unrelated to the July and August 1995 drug offenses. At the same time, and without first obtaining a warrant, the officers seized Mr. White's car pursuant to the Florida Forfeiture Act. During an inventory search of the car, the police found two pieces of crack cocaine in the ashtray.

Mr. White was charged with possession of cocaine. The trial court denied Mr. White's motion to suppress the seized evidence. After a trial, a jury found him guilty of possession of cocaine.

The Florida 1st District Court of Appeal affirmed the conviction. The 1st District Court certified the question of whether, absent exigent circumstances, a warrantless seizure of a vehicle under the Florida Act violated the Fourth Amendment, to the Florida Supreme Court. In a divided opinion, the Florida Supreme Court held that it did. In so doing, it explicitly rejected the holding of the 11th Circuit, and the majority of other Federal Circuits who have ruled on this issue in the context of the Federal civil forfeiture laws.

RATIONALE

Although the police lacked probable cause to believe the car contained contraband when they seized it, they did have probable cause to believe that the car itself was contraband under the Florida statute.

Since the car was seized from a public area – the employer's parking lot – no invasion of Mr. White's privacy occurred. Therefore, and based on long established precedent, no warrant was required.

2.5.6.1.5 – Vehicle Searches for ID

In **In re Arturo D.** (2002) 27 Cal.4th 60, the California Supreme Court ruled that when a driver is lawfully detained for a vehicle code infraction, and fails to produce vehicle registration or personal ID documentation upon the request of the officer, the officer may conduct a limited warrantless search of areas within the vehicle where the documentation could reasonably be expected to be found.

2.5.6.2 – Inventory Searches

2.5.6.2.1 – Cars

The U.S. Supreme Court upheld the constitutionality of the police inventory search of a car's unlocked glove compartment, following the car's impoundment for parking violations in **South Dakota v. Opperman** (1976) 428 U.S. 364. The officer seized marijuana from the glove compartment as a result of that inventory search. The officer performed the search pursuant to a standardized police department policy authorizing the inventory search of all impounded vehicle.

In **Michigan v. Thomas** (1982) 458 U.S. 259, the U.S. Supreme Court reversed the Michigan Court of Appeals decision that held that the warrantless search of an automobile pursuant to the inventory search exception violated the Fourth Amendment. The Michigan Court ruled that the search was unreasonable in scope because it included the car's air vents, which were not a likely place for the storage of personal belongings or valuables.

Relying on **Chambers**, **supra**, the Supreme Court reiterated that the police may conduct a warrantless search of a vehicle even after it has been impounded and is in police custody. The Court said, "[i]t is thus clear that the justification to conduct such a warrantless search does not vanish once the car has been immobilized; nor does it depend upon a reviewing court's assessment of the likelihood in each particular case that the car would been driven away, or that its contents would have been tampered with, during the period required for the police to obtain a warrant." (**Id**. at 3081.)

FACTS (South Dakota v. Opperman (1976) 428 U.S. 364)

Following the stop of a car for failing to signal for a left turn, the officer cited the 14-year-old driver for not having a driver's license. The defendant passenger, who was an adult, was arrested for possession of an open container of malt liquor, which was standing upright on the floorboard between the defendant's feet. The police impounded the car and conducted a roadside inventory search prior to towing the car. They found marijuana in the unlocked glove box and a loaded revolver in the car's passenger side air vent. The defendant was convicted of possession of the concealed weapon and appealed on Fourth Amendment grounds.

A California Court of Appeal in **People v. Needham** (2000) 79 Cal.App.4th 260, upheld the inventory search of saddle bags temporarily attached to the exterior of a motorcycle since they are considered to be in the vehicle just like containers found inside a car. The Court refused to treat motorcycles differently than cars for purposes of inventory searches. The Court also upheld the oral policy of the Tulare County Sheriff's Department regarding inventory searches because a searching officer did not have unfettered discretion regarding container searches under that policy. There was no evidence that the inventory search was used as a ruse to search for incriminating evidence.

FACTS (People v. Needham (2000) 79 Cal.App.4th 260)

In the afternoon of July 24, 1998, a Hispanic male ran from the backyard of Luz Villegas' home to the front yard and asked if he could hide in her house. Ms. Villegas also saw the defendant, who she described as a White male, driving a motorcycle around Ledbetter Park three times. The Hispanic male stopped the defendant, gave him some white bags, got on the motorcycle, and drove off with the defendant.

A woman, who was driving a white van stopped to tell Ms. Villegas that a man on a motorcycle had just robbed her. Ms. Villegas called 9-1-1 to report that the Hispanic male had stolen something and left on the defendant's motorcycle.

Ms. Villegas described the defendant as a White male adult with tattoos on his arm. She said that he had left through Eddy Road, had dropped off the Hispanic male and then returned to the park. She later called back to tell the sheriff's department that the defendant was parked in the park.

Tulare County Sheriff's Lieutenant Salazar responded to the dispatch call and recalled that the dispatcher told him that a White male on a motorcycle with a Hispanic male passenger had been involved in a theft. His information also included the location of the suspected thieves, which was the Cutler area near Ledbetter Park.

Lieutenant Salazar found the defendant sitting on a motorcycle without a passenger and detained him. The Lieutenant handcuffed the defendant. Ms. Villegas arrived and identified the defendant, but the police later unhandcuffed the defendant when it was determined he was not involved in the robbery.

Deputy Fosnaugh, who had arrived to assist, then noticed expired motorcycle registration tags and confirmed this through dispatch. He also learned that the defendant was not the registered owner of the motorcycle.

Deputy Fosnaugh advised the defendant that the deputy was going to have the motorcycle towed because of the expired registration. Deputy Fosnaugh completed a towing form and inventoried the property on the motorcycle in preparation for the impoundment and towing. In a duffel bag that was attached to the rear seat of the motorcycle with bungee cords, Deputy Fosnaugh found glass pipes that appeared to be drug paraphernalia. He found additional glass opium pipes inside a blue pouch attached to the front handlebars, as well as a small plastic baggie of methamphetamine inside a colored container. The deputy then arrested the defendant.

The Tulare County Sheriff's Department has an oral policy regarding inventory searches, which the department teaches to deputies in field training courses and is based on the California Vehicle Code. The policy requires that all valuables and property in a vehicle need to be inventoried and recorded on the tow form with as much detail as possible. The policy's goal is to prevent unverifiable thefts because the department is responsible for the property. The policy also protects officers from possible weapons that might be concealed in a vehicle or its containers.

An officer does have discretion as to whether the inventoried property will be seized or released to an individual. However, no criterion exists as to when an officer may exercise his or her discretion to seize or release the property.

After the trial court denied the defendant's motion to suppress the evidence, he plead guilty to violating Health & Safety Code 21377(a) and 11364, admitted a first degree burglary strike and was sentenced by the court to 32 months in state prison.

RATIONALE

The Court rejected the defendant's argument that since bags temporarily attached to the exterior of a motorcycle, unlike those found inside a car cannot be secured inside the vehicle, they cannot properly be searched during an inventory search. The Court refused to treat motorcycles differently than cars for purposes of inventory searches.

In **People v. Green** (1996) 46 Cal.App.4th 367, an officer stopped the defendant for driving with expired registration and decided to impound his vehicle and conduct an inventory search. During that search, the officer found rock cocaine and arrested the defendant. The Court of Appeal, in a split decision, upheld the inventory search of the vehicle even though the People did not produce any evidence regarding standardized procedures regarding such searches by the police department. The Court ruled that the vehicle code provided the authority for the officer to conduct an inventory search even though the offense is citable. The dissenting justice expressed the belief that without evidence of "standardized policies" the evidence should be suppressed.

2.5.6.2.2 – Personal Belongings in Vehicles

The U.S. Supreme Court upheld the inventory search of a shoulder bag found on the car seat in **Illinois v. Lafayette** (1983) 462 U.S. 640.

In **Colorado v. Bertine** (1987) 479 U.S. 367 the U.S. Supreme Court upheld the inventory search of a backpack inside a car impounded due to the arrest of the driver for a DUI.

The Court reaffirmed the following language from **United States v. Ross** at 821: "When a legitimate search is under way, and when its purpose and its limits have been precisely defined, nice distinctions between closets, drawers, and containers, in the case of a home, or between glove compartments, upholstered seats, trunks and wrapped packages, in the case of a vehicle, must give way to the interest in the prompt and efficient completion of the task at hand" **Bertine**, at 375.

The U.S. Supreme Court rejected the argument that the inventory search was illegal because the departmental policy gave the officer discretion to choose between impounding or parking and locking the car in a public place. The Court ruled that the discretion was exercised in light of standard criteria, related to the feasibility of parking and locking a car, rather than impounding it. (*i.e.*, risk of damage to car, or arrestee does not approve of leaving it at the scene.) The defendant also failed to show that the officer chose the inventory option in order to investigate suspected criminal activity.

FACTS (Colorado v. Bertine (1987) 479 U.S. 367)

On Feb. 10, 1984, a Boulder, Colorado police officer arrested Mr. Bertine for an alcohol related DUI. After Mr. Bertine was taken into custody, and before the tow truck arrived to take the van to an impound lot, a back-up officer conducted an inventory search of the car.

The officer found a closed backpack directly behind the front seat of the van. When the officer opened the closed backpack, he found a nylon bag containing metal canisters. The officer opened the canisters and found cocaine, methaqualone tablets, cocaine paraphernalia and $700 in cash. The backpack's outside zippered pouch contained a sealed envelope with $210 inside it.

RATIONALE

The backpack was inventoried pursuant to local police procedures, which required a detailed inspection and inventory of impounded vehicles. It reiterated that inventory searches serve to protect an owner's property while in the custody of the police, to insure against claims of lost, stolen or vandalized property and guard the police from danger.

In **Florida v. Wells** (1990) 495 U.S. 1, a Florida Highway Patrol Officer arrested Mr. Wells for DUI. During an inventory search of the car, the officer located and opened a locked suitcase found in the trunk. The officer found marijuana inside the locked suitcase. The Supreme Court invalidated the search because the Florida Highway Patrol had "no policy whatever with respect to the opening of closed containers encountered during an inventory search." (**Id**. at 4-5.)

The U.S. Supreme Court reiterated that in "[o]ur view that standardized criteria [citation] or established routine [citation] must regulate the opening of containers found during inventory searches is based on the principle that an inventory search must not be a ruse for a general rummaging in order to discover incriminating evidence. The policy or practice governing inventory searches should be designed to produce an inventory." (**Id**. at 4.)

California Courts have also ruled that inventory searches extend to locked and closed containers. [See **People v. Nicholson** (1989) 207 Cal.App.3d 707 (briefcase), and **People v. Scigliano** (1987) 196 Cal.App.3d 26 (a box with methamphetamine.)]

2.5.6.3 – Containers in Vehicles

In **California v. Acevedo** (1991) 500 U.S. 565, a package that was known to contain marijuana was picked up from Federal Express and taken to an apartment. Before the search warrant arrived, Mr. Acevedo left with a brown paper bag that was consistent in shape and size with a pound of marijuana. A warrantless search of the bag in the car's trunk resulted in the seizure of marijuana.

In upholding that warrantless seizure, the U.S. Supreme Court expressly overruled its prior decisions in **United States v. Chadwick** (1971) 433 U.S. 1, and **Arkansas v. Sanders** (1979) 442 U.S. 753, and the line of cases based on those two now repudiated decisions.

United States v. Chadwick (1971) 433 U.S. 1, involved a 200 pound, double locked footlocker that had been removed from a train and placed in a waiting car. Federal agents had probable cause to believe that it contained marijuana prior to it being placed in the car. The Supreme Court held that a warrant was required to search the luggage, even though it had been transferred to an automobile.

Arkansas v. Sanders (1979) 442 U.S. 753, involved a suitcase that was being transported in the trunk of a taxi. Like **Chadwick**, **supra**, the police also had probable cause to believe the suitcase contained marijuana before it was placed in the taxi. The Court again held that the automobile exception to the warrant requirement did not extend to the suitcase merely because it was located in an automobile.

2.5.6.4 – Consent

Unless otherwise indicated, consent to search a vehicle extends to closed containers within that vehicle.

In a 7 to 2 decision in **Florida v. Jimeno** (1991) 500 U.S. 248, the U.S. Supreme Court upheld an officer's search of a closed paper bag during a vehicle consent search, and subsequent seizure of a kilogram of cocaine from that bag. The Court found it objectively reasonable for the officer to believe that the defendant's consent to search the car extended to that closed container.

In **Ohio v. Robinette** (1996) 519 U.S. 33, the U.S. Supreme Court explicitly rejected an Ohio Supreme Court rule that required officers to first tell lawfully detained motorists that they were "free to go" before asking for permission to search their car *["1st-tell-then-ask"]*. It is important to note that in this case the officer did not ask the motorist for consent to search the car until after verbally admonishing the citizen for the speeding violation and then returning the driver's license to the motorist.

The Court of Appeal in **People v. Avalos** (1996) 47 Cal.App.4th 1569, ruled that an officer validly obtained the defendant's consent to search a car even though the police officer asked for permission to search for stolen property "in addition to some other contraband."

FACTS (People v. Avalos (1996) 47 Cal.App.4th 1569)

A CI told officers that people were dealing drugs from a specific apartment. The CI identified a "tall male Hispanic in his mid to late 20's with a medium build" as being involved. During police surveillance of the scene, the defendant arrived and fit the description given by the CI.

The officers contacted the CI by phone, who identified the defendant and his vehicle as being involved in the dealing. The defendant then left the apartment carrying a box.

The officers made a traffic stop and informed the defendant he was being stopped as part of a burglary investigation. The officers sought and obtained the defendant's permission to search the trunk for stolen property "in addition to some other contraband." During the search, the officers opened a box and found and seized five pounds of methamphetamine.

RATIONALE

The police had a reasonable suspicion to detain the defendant and the defendant's consent was not vitiated by the officers' misrepresentation of the crime under investigation.

Additionally, the defendant's consent to search for stolen property would have included the box in any event.

A California Court of Appeal ruled that an officer may lawfully ask for consent to search a car following the issuance of a traffic ticket in **People v. Galindo** (1991) 229 Cal.App.3d 1529.

In **People v. Crenshaw** (1992) 9 Cal.App.4th 1403, the Court of Appeal upheld the seizure of weapons and drugs from a car because it was reasonable for the officer to believe the consent to search included unscrewing a door vent panel that showed signs of having been used as a container for contraband.

2.5.7 – Plain View Doctrine

The U.S. Supreme Court first enunciated the plain view doctrine in a plurality opinion in **Coolidge v. New Hampshire** (1971) 403 U.S. 443. There are three requirements to meet before the plain view applies:

1. An officer must lawfully be in a place where the object can be viewed
2. The object's incriminating character must be "*immediately apparent*"
3. The officers must have a lawful right of access to the object itself.

In **Texas v. Brown** (1983) 460 U.S. 730, the U.S. Supreme Court upheld the warrantless seizure of a green balloon containing heroin and noted that "[t]he fact that [Officer] Maples could not see through the opaque fabric of the balloon is all but irrelevant: the distinctive character of the balloon itself spoke volumes as to its contents – particularly to the trained eye of the officer." **Texas v. Brown**, **supra**, at p. 743.

The Court also took the opportunity to clarify the "*immediate apparent*" language from **Coolidge**, **supra**, and held that the language did not establish a requirement that a police officer "know" that certain items are contraband or evidence of a crime before it is seized. Instead, what the Court originally meant is that the police "may not 'know in advance the location of certain evidence and intend to seize,' relying on the plain-view doctrine only as a pretense." **Texas v. Brown**, supra, at p. 743 and ". . . a law enforcement officer may rely on his training and experience to draw inferences and make deductions that might well elude an untrained person." **Texas v. Brown, supra,** at 746. [Powell and Blackman concurring].

The Court recognized that "[d]ecisions by this court since **Coolidge** indicate that the use of the phrase 'immediately apparent' was very likely an unhappy choice of words, since it can be taken to imply that an unduly high degree of certainty as to the incriminatory character of evidence is necessary for an application of the 'plain-view doctrine.'" (**Id**. at 741.)

FACTS (Texas v. Brown (1983) 460 U.S. 730)

On a summer evening in June 1979, Fort Worth Police Officer Maples was assisting in a routine driver's license checkpoint on East Allen Street in the city. Shortly before midnight, the officer stopped Mr. Brown's car. He was alone in the car.

While standing alongside the driver's window, Officer Maples asked Mr. Brown for his driver's license. At about the same time, Officer Maples also shone his flashlight into the car and saw Mr. Brown withdraw his right hand from his right pants pocket. Between the two middle fingers on the hand was a green colored, opaque, party balloon that was knotted about ½ inch from the tip. Mr. Brown dropped this balloon to the seat beside his leg and then reached across the passenger seat and opened the glove box.

Based on his previous experience, Officer Maples believed that the balloon contained narcotics. Officer Maples shifted his position outside the car so he could better view the interior of the glove compartment. He noticed several small plastic vials containing quantities of loose white powder, and an open bag of party balloons.

After rummaging through the glove box, Mr. Brown told Officer Maples that he had no driver's license in his possession. Officer Maples then ordered Mr. Brown out of the car and told him to stand at the rear of the car. Before joining Mr. Brown, Officer Maples reached into the car and picked up the green balloon. He believed there was some sort of powdery substance inside the green balloon and arrested Mr. Brown.

Following Mr. Brown's arrest, the police conducted an on-scene inventory of the car and found several plastic bags containing a green leafy substance, and a large bottle of milk sugar.

In **Arizona v. Hicks** (1987) 480 U.S. 321, the U.S. Supreme Court ruled , that moving a turntable to obtain the serial numbers off an expensive looking stereo system was an illegal search and seizure and did not constitute a plain view observation. Officers, who were investigating a shooting at the defendant's apartment house, had lawfully made a warrantless intrusion into his residence based on the exigent circumstances of possible injured victims in the defendant's upstairs apartment.

In **Horton v. California** (1990) 496 U.S. 128, the U.S. Supreme Court upheld the seizure of weapons during the service of a search warrant in a robbery case, despite the fact no weapons were listed in the warrant. The Court ruled that the plain view exception to the warrant requirement does not have an inadvertence requirement as implied in **Coolidge**, **supra**. All that is required is the following:

- An officer must lawfully be in a place where the object can be viewed
- The object's incriminating character must be "*immediately apparent*"
- The officers must have a lawful right of access to the object itself.

In **Bond v. United States** (2000) 529 U.S. 334, the U.S. Supreme Court ruled that a law enforcement officer's physical manipulation of a bus passenger's carry-on luggage violated the Fourth Amendment ban on unreasonable searches and seizures. The Court ruled that this was not a plain view case because of the tactile manipulation of the luggage as opposed to a mere visual inspection of the item. The Court noted that while a bus passenger may expect that his luggage may be handled, he does not expect that other passengers or bus employees will, as a matter of course, conduct an exploratory feel of the luggage.

FACTS (Bond v. United States (2000) 529 U.S. 334)

Steven Dewayne Bond was a passenger on a Greyhound bus that left California for Little Rock, Arkansas. The bus stopped, as it was required to do, at a permanent border patrol checkpoint in Sierra Blanca, Texas. Border Patrol Agent Caesar Cantu boarded the bus to check on the immigration status of the bus passengers.

After having reached the back of the bus, and satisfying himself that there were no immigration problems, Agent Cantu began to walk toward the front of the bus. As he did so, he would squeeze the soft luggage that passenger's had placed in the overhead storage area above the seats. When Agent Cantu squeezed the green canvas bag belonging to Mr. Bond, he noticed that it contained a "brick-like" object.

Mr. Bond acknowledged the bag belonged to him and gave Agent Cantu permission to open the bag. When the bag was opened, Agent Cantu found an oval shaped brick of methamphetamine that had been wrapped in duct tape and then rolled into a pair of pants.

Mr. Bond's motion to suppress the evidence was denied by the District Court, following his indictment for conspiracy to possess methamphetamine with an intent to distribute it. A federal judge sentenced him to 57 months in prison.

The Court of Appeals affirmed the District Court and held that the Agent's manipulation of the luggage did not constitute a search within the meaning of the Fourth Amendment.

The decision in this case implicitly overrules the California case of **People v. Santana** (1998) 63 Cal.App.4th 543, which held that an officer's "poofing" of the defendant's luggage did not violate any Fourth Amendment rights. The "poofing" resulted in the detection of the odor of fabric softener, which the officer recognized as being consistent with something used to mask the odor of drugs. Following a narcotic detection dog's alert to the bag, a search warrant was obtained and 38 pounds of marijuana were seized.

FACTS (People v. Santana (1998) 63 Cal.App.4th 543)

On September 20, 1995, San Diego Airport Narcotics Task Force officers were watching passengers arrive on a flight that had been used in the past by persons transporting narcotics. The defendant checked two bags for the flight.

One group of officers followed Mr. Santana to the departure gate, while another group followed the luggage to the baggage room. In the baggage room, an officer squeezed Mr. Santana's luggage (also referred to as "poofed").

The officer smelled the expelled air and detected the aroma of fabric softener, which the officer knew is commonly used to mask the smell of narcotics. The police obtained a trained narcotic detection dog who alerted to the luggage. The officers then obtained a search warrant for the luggage and seized 38 pounds of marijuana.

In reaching its conclusion that the officer's poofing of the defendant's luggage did not violate the defendant's Fourth Amendment rights, the Court of Appeal did a great analysis of federal case law and adopted the reasoning by the Arizona Supreme Court in **State v. Peters** (1997) 189 Ariz. 216. The Court of Appeal held that "[w]hile it might be reasonable to expect that packed articles will not be exposed to public view, it is not reasonable to believe that the air contained in checked luggage, and its odors, will remain in the luggage. That in any given case the air is expelled as the result of a bag being dropped to the ground, pushed hard against other bags or squeezed by a police officer is of no constitutional significance." **Santana**, at p. 548.

In **People v. LeBlanc** (1997) 60 Cal.App.4th 157, the Court of Appeal ruled that officers lawfully seized two crack cocaine pipes that were in plain view inside the motel room while arresting Mr. LeBlanc on two misdemeanor warrants at the entrance to the room. However, the search of the rest of the motel room required a search warrant.

FACTS (People v. LeBlanc (1997) 60 Cal.App.4th 157)

Uniformed Long Beach Police Officers Smith and Gibbs drove a marked police car to the Avalon Motel, in order to serve two misdemeanor arrest warrants on Junius LeBlanc. Officer Smith had previously arrested Mr. LeBlanc for a narcotic related offense and had other numerous contacts with him. Officer Smith knew that Mr. LeBlanc was involved in narcotics activity.

The two officers went to room 12 and knocked on the door, which was opened by Mr. Blanc, who was told he had warrants out for his arrest. The officers then handcuffed him while he was still standing in the doorway of the motel room.

From that location, Officer Smith saw a crack cocaine pipe on a dresser on the west wall of the room. The dresser was about five feet away from the entrance to the room. While Officer Smith was handcuffing Mr. LeBlanc, Officer Gibbs saw a rock like object in the back of the closet on a ledge. He then saw a second glass pipe.

During a warrantless search of the motel room, the officers recovered six glass pipes along with a rock of cocaine that was under the carpet. The officers found one of the glass pipes in a shoe belonging to Mr. LeBlanc.

The Magistrate incorrectly found that no warrant was required to search the room after the officers' initial observations of contraband in plain view.

2.5.7.1 – Plain View Doctrine versus the Plain Smell Doctrine

The plain view doctrine is not the same as the plain smell doctrine. Smell by itself does not authorize the warrantless opening of a package by the police when it is left with a common carrier. This point is best illustrated by the case of **Robey v. Superior Court** (2013) 56 Cal.4th 1218. The California Supreme Court addressed two issues: 1) whether a police officer may conduct a warrantless search of a package seized from a common carrier based on the exigent circumstances of a container's mobility and 2) whether a police officer could conduct a warrantless search of the container based on the "plain smell" of contraband inside the container. The Supreme Court ruled that although a container may be seized based on the exigent circumstances of the container's mobility, that fact alone cannot justify a warrantless search of the container following its seizure. With respect to the second issue, the Court ruled that the Riverside District Attorney forfeited the "plain smell" argument by failing to raise it in opposition to Mr. Robey's motion to suppress in the trial court.

FACTS (Robey v. Superior Court (2013) 56 Cal.4th 1218)

On July 23, 2010, Nancy Her was employed by FedEx. She contacted the Santa Maria Police Department to report that a package smelling of marijuana had been dropped off for shipment to an address in Illinois. Officer Totorica responded to the call, entered the business, and walked towards the package. Officer Totorica smelled the odor of marijuana as he approached the package. Ms. Her told the officer that FedEx could not deliver the package and asked for guidance. The officer seized the unopened and sealed box as evidence and took it to the police station.

At the station, Officer Totorica contacted Lieutenant Hailey, who was his supervisor. The Lieutenant also concluded that the box smelled of marijuana. After conferring with the narcotics unit, and without first obtaining a search warrant, the officers opened the box and found 444 grams (approximately 15.66 ounces) of marijuana inside the box.

Three days later, Kewhan Robey went to the same FedEx office to inquire about an undelivered package. Ms. Her recognized Mr. Robey as the man who had delivered the box seized by the police, and telephoned Officer

Totorica. The officer returned to the store and arrested Mr. Robey, who was carrying a packing slip for the seized package.

Mr. Robey was charged with violations of possessing marijuana for sale and transporting marijuana. Mr. Robey moved to suppress the evidence in the trial court. His motion was denied by the court, which found that exigent circumstances justified the seizure and subsequent search that followed under the inevitable discovery doctrine. Probably, under the belief the police had sufficient probable cause to obtain a search warrant had they sought one.

Mr. Robey then sought a writ of mandate in the Court of Appeal, which in turn issued an order to show cause to the superior court. After asking for additional briefing on the issue of whether the plain smell of marijuana by itself, would have allowed the search and seizure of the package, the Court of Appeal granted the peremptory writ of mandate and directed the trial court to grant Mr. Robey's motion to suppress the evidence. The Court of Appeal did not decide the issue of whether the officer was entitled to seize the package but did rule 1) that exigent circumstances did not justify the subsequent search of the package; 2) that the odor of contraband alone cannot justify a warrantless search; 3) that the inevitable discovery doctrine did not apply to the present facts; and 4) that Mr. Robey had not abandoned the package and therefore had "standing" to move to suppress the seized evidence. The Riverside District Attorney then asked the California Supreme Court to review the case on the issues regarding whether the mobility of the package constituted exigent circumstances permitting a warrantless search of the package and whether the plain smell of marijuana constituted an exception to the warrant requirement.

RATIONALE

The California Supreme Court rejected the Riverside District Attorney's argument that Mr. Robey lacked standing to challenge the search of the package because he had abandoned his interest in the package by using a false name and address when he shipped it. However, at the suppression hearing, the District Attorney accepted Mr. Robey's offer of proof to establish a privacy interest in the container. Additionally, the District Attorney did not enter the packing slip into evidence or create any other record of a false name or address to support a claim of abandonment in response to Mr. Robey's claim that he continued to have an interest in the package by checking on its delivery after leaving it for shipment.[21]

[21] In **People v. Pereira** (2007) 150 Cal.App.4th 1106, the Court of Appeal ruled that the defendant in that case did not abandon the package by using a false name and return address because other evidence showed that he really cared about getting it delivered.

After a lengthy discussion of various cases involving the warrantless seizure and subsequent search of containers found in cars, the California Supreme Court concluded the following:

> "In sum, absent unusual circumstances where transporting or storing a container poses practical difficulties for law enforcement, the concerns justifying an immediate warrantless search of a lawfully stopped automobile do not apply to packages consigned for shipment. In this case, there is no dispute as to whether the police lawfully seized the package without a warrant. Because there was no justification for an immediate search of the package once it was seized, the police had no derivative authority to search the package later at the police station without a warrant. {Slip Opn. Page 19}" **Id.** at 1233-1234.

The Court also ruled that the previous case of **People v. McKinnon** (1972) 7 Cal.3d 899, which appeared to stand for the proposition that the mobility of a container was itself sufficient to justify a warrantless search, and had not been followed by a California appellate court for almost four decades, was no longer valid on that point. The Court then ruled that "[A] container consigned for shipment is subject to the same rule as other containers outside of the specific and well-delineated context of an automobile search." **Id.** at 1239.

The California Supreme Court did say that "[I]n the present case, the mobility of the package constituted exigent circumstances justifying Officer Totorica's seizure of the FedEx package without a warrant so long as he had probable cause to believe it contained contraband. But seizure of the package by the police negated its mobility. Absent some other exception to the warrant requirement, the Fourth Amendment required the police to obtain a search warrant before opening the package after it had been seized."

Finally, the Court observed "...neither the United States Supreme Court nor this court has ever upheld a warrantless search of a closed container solely on the ground that its smell, appearance, or other outward characteristic clearly announced its contents. Thus, it is fair to say that the legal theory urged by the District Attorney is unsettled in the extant case law and novel in this court's jurisprudence." **Id.** at 1242.

2.5.7.2 – Computer Files

The general rule is that when an officer is conducting a search of a computer for evidence of one type of crime, and stumbles upon evidence related to a second type of crime, the officer needs to stop the search and seek a search warrant which broadens the authorization to cover a search for evidence related to the second crime. This situation commonly arises when an officer is searching a computer hard drive for files related to some type of financial crime pursuant to a lawfully issued search warrant and stumbles across a file containing child pornography. In order to expand the search to cover the child pornography crime, an officer must obtain a second search warrant.

The two key cases illustrating this point are **United States v. Carey** (10th Cir. 1999) 172 F.3d 1268 and **United States v. Gray** (1999) 78 F. Supp.2d 524, which are discussed in greater detail below.

In **United States v. Carey**, the 10th Circuit Court of Appeals ruled that officers engaged in a general, warrantless, exploratory search of the defendant's hard drive for child pornography despite having first obtained a search warrant authorizing the search of the computer's hard drive for narcotic evidence.

The Court of Appeals ruled that the search of the child pornography files did not fall within the plain view exception to the warrant requirement because each time the officer opened a JPG file he was expecting to find child pornography and not drug related evidence as authorized by the search warrant. Since the contents (child pornography) were in closed files, they were not in plain view. In the Court's view, after the officer found the first image of child pornography he switched from the authorized search for drug related evidence to the warrantless search for child pornography, and thereby violated the Fourth Amendment's prohibitions against general rummaging searches.

FACTS (United States v. Carey (10th Cir. 1999) 172 F.3d 1268)

Patrick Carey was under investigation for some time for the possession for sale and sale of cocaine. Six weeks after the last controlled buy of cocaine from his residence, police obtained an arrest warrant for him. While arresting him, officers saw a marijuana bong and a small amount of marijuana in plain view in his apartment. Officers obtained Mr. Carey's permission to search his apartment after a lengthy discussion and after explaining that they would obtain a search warrant if Mr. Carey refused to consent to the search. Fearing that the officers would trash his apartment during the search, he told them where they would find additional drugs, cash, a scale, and a firearm. He also told an officer where they would find a pornographic tape but was told that the officer didn't care about pornographic videotapes.

The written consent form allowed the police to conduct "a complete search of the premises and property located at 3225 Canterbury #10, Manhattan, KS 66503." (**Id**. at 1270.) The signed form also stated, "I do freely and voluntarily consent and agree that any property under my control . . . may be removed by the officers . . . if said property shall be essential in the proof of the commission of any crime in violation of the Laws of the United States. . . ." (**Id**. at 1270.)

While searching the apartment pursuant to Mr. Carey's consent, officers found cocaine, marijuana, and psilocybin. They also found and seized two computers in the belief that they would either be subject to forfeiture or contain evidence of drug dealing. The police took the computers to the police station and obtained a search warrant authorizing the search of the computers' files for "names, telephone numbers, ledger receipts, addresses, and other documentary evidence pertaining to the sale and distribution of controlled substances." (**Id**. at 1270.)

Detective Lewis and a computer technician searched the contents of the computer by first viewing the directories of the two computer's hard drives and then downloading them to floppy disks and printing out the listed directories. In the directories were several files with sexually suggestive titles or obscene names, including the words "teen" or "young," followed by the file extension "JPG." Detective Lewis began searching the files copied from the computer using a text search with key words such as money, accounts or people, but no drug related files were located. The detective continued to explore the directories and came across JPG files that he could not read on the computer he was using, so switched to another system. He later testified at the suppression hearing that he didn't know what a JPG file was and had never experienced a situation where a drug dealer used that extension to disguise a text file.

Upon opening the JPG file, he found an image containing child pornography. Without the benefit of a follow-up search warrant, he then downloaded 244 JPG files and transferred them to 19 disks. He looked at about five to seven files on each disk, which took about five hours, and then resumed his warranted search for evidence of drug dealing on the computer.

Mr. Carey was charged with one count of possessing a computer hard drive containing three or more images of child pornography that were produced with materials shipped in interstate commerce, which is a violation of 18 U.S.C. 2252A(a)(5)(B). Following the denial of his motion to suppress the seized evidence he pled guilty and appealed the denial of his suppression motion.

In **United States v. Gray** (1999) 78 F. Supp.2d 524, the District Court found that an officer who was conducting a methodical search of a hard drive for theft related files, inadvertently stumbled upon child pornography files contained in sub-directories labeled "Teen" and "Tiny Teen." The initial observation of the child pornography files fell within the plain view exception to the warrant requirement. As the District Court explained, "[i]n searching for the items listed in the warrant, Agent Ehuan was entitled to examine all of defendant's files to determine whether they contained items that fell within the scope of the warrant. In the course of doing so, he inadvertently discovered evidence of child pornography, which was clearly incriminating on its face." (**Id**. at 529.) Upon lawfully making those initial observations, the officer properly ceased his initial search and obtained a second search warrant allowing a further search of the computer hard drive for additional evidence of child pornography.

In rendering its decision, the District Court specifically rejected the defendant's argument that Agent Ehuan knew the two subdirectories did not contain NLM documents or hacked materials because many of the files had ".jpg" suffixes and none of the materials covered by the warrant were believed to be picture files. The Court observed that "Agent Ehuan would have been remiss not to search files with a '.jpg' suffix simply because such files are generally pictures files, and he believed the NLM documents and hacker materials were more likely to be text files. He knew from his experience that computer hackers often intentionally mislabel files, or attempt to bury incriminating files within innocuously named directories. Indeed, in the course of his search of defendant's computer files, Agent Ehuan found some text files mixed in with picture files. This serves to underscore the soundness of the conclusion that Agent Ehuan was not required to accept as accurate any file name or suffix and limit his search accordingly." (**Id**. at 529.)

FACTS (United States v. Gray (1999) 78 F. Supp.2d 524)

On February 5, 1999, FBI agents served a search warrant at the Arlington, Virginia home of Montgomery Johns Gray. The warrant related to a criminal investigation of unauthorized computer intrusions at the National Institute of Health's National Library of Medicine (NLM). The agents seized four computers belonging to the defendant. At the FBI office, Special Agent Ehuan of the Computer Analysis Response Team (CART) made copies of the computers' hard drives. These copies were made on magneto-optical disks and were in digital form. In order to translate the digital information into readable format, Agent Ehuan planned to make a number of CD-ROMs so Agent Sorum, who was the case agent, could read and access the material.

Before making the CD-ROMs, Agent Ehuan made a separate CD-ROM containing a list of the directory structure for each of the four computers' hard drives. Agent Sorum used these CD-ROMs to perform a text string search of the file structures and identified the computers that appeared to contain the text strings most closely related to the NLM search warrant items. Agent Sorum then asked Agent Ehuan to concentrate on the computer containing that information.

Before making CD-ROMs, Agent Ehusan opened a number of the directories and subdirectories on the targeted hard drive to check their size and determine how many directories would fit on a single CD-ROM. Each CD-ROM had a capacity of 650 megabytes, which is substantially less than the capacity of the magneto-optical disks. During the 45 minute copying process, and pursuant to CART routine practice, Agent Ehuan opened and briefly looked at each of the files in the directories and subdirectories being copied. Agent Euhan was able to open approximately 80% of the files from the targeted hard drive. In order to open these files, Agent Euhan used a program called "CompuPic," which provided thumbnail-sized images of all the items contained in a given file, regardless of whether the file was a picture or text file.

As Agent Ehuan was preparing to copy material onto the eighth CD-ROM, he opened a directory entitled "BBS" in order to see the list of files and subdirectories contained in that directory. While transferring files from that directory to the CD-ROM, and pursuant to his normal practice, he opened most of the files contained in the BBS directory. Some of the file contained adult pornography and others were text files. Agent Ehuan opened a sub-directory entitled "Teen" containing several files with a ".jpg" extension, which is usually indicative of a picture file. While viewing those files, Agent Ehuan thought he possibly saw images of child pornography. However, he wasn't certain and continued his search for items in the BBS directory related to the NLM search warrant.

Agent Ehuan saw a subdirectory entitled "Tiny Teen," which caused him to wonder if it contained child pornography. However, he opened the subdirectory because it was the next subdirectory listed and was opening all subdirectories as part of his routine search for items listed in the search warrant. When he opened it he believed some of the photographs contained child pornography and asked another CART agent to look at the photos displayed on the screen. The second agent also agreed that the photos appeared to contain minors. Agent Ehuan notified Agent Sorum, who also viewed the photographs and agreed they contained child pornography. Agent Sorum then sought a second search warrant authorizing a search of the computer hard drive for child pornography.

Mr. Gray was charged with violating 28 U.S.C. 1030(a)(2)(b) and (a)(2)(C) (Unlawful access of a government computer), 28 U.S.C 1030(a)((2)(c) (Unlawful access to a government computer causing damage) and 28 U.S.C. 2252A(a)(5)(B) (Possession of child pornography). He brought a motion seeking suppression of the photographs contained in the "Teen" and "Tiny Teen" subdirectories and argued that the initial search of the those subdirectories exceeded the scope of the NLM search warrant.

In rejecting the motion, the Court observed that few criminals keep documents of their criminal transactions in a folder labeled "crime records" and that "agents authorized by a warrant to search a home or office for documents containing certain specific information are entitled to examine all files located at the site to look for the specified information." (**Id**. at 528.)

In the more recent case of **United States v. Walser** (10th Cir. 2001) 275 F.3d 981, the Court of Appeals found that following Mr. Walser's arrest on narcotics charges and the issuance of a search warrant for his hotel room, officers lawfully seized his computer from the hotel room. Although not listed as an item to seize in the search warrant, this was a lawful computer seizure because the search warrant authorized a search for "records, and\or receipts, written or electronically stored," the computer was in plain view and it obviously could contain electronically stored evidence of narcotics sales. The Court of Appeals also ruled that while still searching for documents related to drug activity, the officer did not exceed the scope of the initial search warrant's authority when he opened a computer file entitled "bstfit.avi" and discovered the first image of child pornography. The Court ruled that the officer acted lawfully after the initial observation of child pornography when the officer sought and obtained a second search warrant, authorizing the expanded search of the computer hard drive for additional evidence of child pornography.

An officer should always exercise caution before engaging in a warrantless search or seizure of a computer. While **Walser** may provide some cover when faced with a challenge to the warrantless search and seizure of a computer, the better practice is to avoid the lack of specificity presented in **Walser** and list computers in the items list portion of a search warrant and affidavit when there is probable cause to believe one is present and may contain evidence. In **Walser**, the officer knew a computer would be located in the hotel room, but did not specifically list it as an item to search or seize in the search warrant. Instead the nebulous phrase of "records, and\or receipts, written or electronically stored" was the only mention of electronic evidence. Faced with similar facts, the 9th Circuit Court of Appeals or a California state court might reach a different conclusion than the **Walser** court and suppress the computer search and seizure.

FACTS (United States v. Walser (10th Cir. 2001) 275 F.3d 981)

On June 1, 2000, the hotel manager for the Radisson Hotel in Casper, Wyoming, went to room 617 to check on an activated smoke alarm. No one was in the room, but while shutting off the alarm, the manager saw two small plastic bags containing what he believed to be cocaine and marijuana. The manager contacted the local police, who secured the room, but did not enter it. The police learned that Mr. Walser and Debbie Wilcox rented the room earlier in the day. The officers found them sitting in Mr. Walser's car in the parking lot and learned that Mr. Walser had brought a computer with him and set it up in the room.

The police obtained a search warrant for room 617 and Mr. Walser's car. The warrant authorized the search for "[c]ontrolled substances, evidence of the possession of controlled substances, which may include, but not be limited to, cash or proceeds from the sales of controlled substances, items, substances, and other paraphernalia designed or used in the weighing, cutting, and packaging of controlled substances, firearms, records, and\or receipts, written or electronically stored, income tax records, checking and savings records, records that show or tend to show ownership or control of the premises and other property used to facilitate the distribution and delivery [of] controlled substances." (**Id**. at 984.)

Special Agent McFarland of the Wyoming Division of Criminal Investigation (DCI) and local police entered the room and searched. They found plastic baggies containing marijuana, drug paraphernalia for smoking and injecting drugs, and a computer with an attached digital camera. The computer was already on when the officers entered the room and had a wallpaper background of an image of Ms. Wilcox that appeared to have been taken inside room 617. Agent McFarland, who had taken a 40-hour "Cybercop" class, thought there might be drug transaction ledgers or images of drug use on the computer's hard drive. Agent McFarland did a cursory search of the "My Documents" folder on the computer hard drive and opened about 10 JPG files. Each of those photograph files contained images of adult pornography. Agent McFarland then shut down the computer and seized it in anticipation of doing a more thorough search at the DCI office.

Five days later and on June 6, 2000, Agent McFarland resumed his search of the seized computer. Agent McFarland followed a specific methodology in conducting the search. He first checked the "Recycle Bin" and found it to contain no relevant information. Next, he used "Windows Explorer" and opened the "Program Files" folder. He located a sub-folder containing a Microsoft Works spreadsheet program. The folder contained 90 files and four sub-folders. Upon opening the second file from the top named "bstfit.avi" (typically an audiovisual or video file) a "Compupic" program started and a "thumbnail" image of the file appeared on the left side of the Explorer window. The thumbnail image showed possibly underage girls engaged in sex acts with men. Agent McFarland enlarged the image and confirmed his belief. He immediately stopped the search and contacted another DCI agent who was more experienced in computer forensics and child pornography. The second agent instructed Agent McFarland to shut down the computer and seek a second search warrant authorizing a search of the computer for child pornography.

The second search warrant led to the discovery and seizure of child pornography. Following the denial of his motion to suppress the seized evidence, Mr. Walser pled guilty to one count of child pornography. The court sentenced him to 27 months in prison and three years of supervised release.

2.5.7.3 – Thermal Imaging Devices

In a 5 to 4 decision in **Kyllo v. United States** (2001) 533 U.S. 27, the U.S. Supreme Court invalidated a search warrant that was based in part on information of a residential marijuana growing operation obtained with the assistance of a thermal imaging device. The Court said, "[o]btaining by sense-enhancing technology any information regarding the interior of the home that could not otherwise have been obtained without physical 'intrusion into a constitutionally protected area' [**Silverman v. United States** (1961), 365 U.S. 505 at 512] constitutes a search – at least where (as here) the technology in question is not in general public use. This assures preservation of that degree of privacy against government that existed when the Fourth Amendment was adopted." (**Kyllo** at 34.)

"Where, as here, the government uses a device that is not in general public use, to explore details of the home that would previously have been unknowable without physical intrusion, the surveillance is a 'search' and is presumptively unreasonable without a warrant." (**Id**. at 40.)

In reaching this split decision, the Supreme Court rejected the following government arguments:

- The device only detected heat radiating from the exterior of the house
- The device did not "detect private activities occurring in private areas."

With respect to the first government argument, the Court said that the **Katz** case [**Katz v. United States** (1967) 389 U.S. 347] rejected that argument when it held that a device capable of eavesdropping on a conversation from inside a telephone booth violated the Fourth Amendment. To apply such a rule here would mean that the search in **Katz** should have been upheld because it was only picking up sound waves leaving a telephone booth. Such an approach would leave a homeowner at the mercy of advancing technology.

With respect to the government's second argument, the Court said that the Fourth Amendment's protections of the home have never been tied to the measurement of the quality or quantity of information obtained. "In the home, our cases show, all details are intimate details, because the entire area is held safe from prying government eyes." **Kyllo**, **supra**, at 37. "Limiting the prohibition against thermal imaging to 'intimate details' would not only be wrong in principle; it would be impractical in application, failing to provide 'a workable accommodation between the needs of law enforcement and the interests protected by the Fourth Amendment." (**Id**. at 38.) The Court did not feel it could develop adequate rules regarding which home activities were "intimate" and which were not intimate details that could be observed by devices capable of peering through walls.

In his dissenting opinion, Justice Steven's observed that "[w]hile the Court 'take[s] the long view' and decides this case based largely on the potential of yet-to-be-developed technology that might allow 'through-the-wall surveillance,' [citation omitted] this case involves nothing more than off-the-wall surveillance by law enforcement officers to gather information exposed to the general public from the outside of petitioner's home." (**Id**. at 42.) "Unlike an x-ray scan, or another possible 'through-the-wall' techniques, the detection of infrared radiation emanating from the home did not accomplish 'an unauthorized physical penetration into the premises,' **Silverman v. United States**, (1961) 365 U.S. 505, nor did it 'obtain information that it could not have obtained by observation from outside the curtilage of the house,' **United States v. Karo**, (1984) 468 U.S. 705." **Kyllo**, **supra**, at 43. "Heat waves, like aromas that are generated in a kitchen, or in a laboratory or opium den, enter the public-domain if and when they leave a building. A subjective expectation that they would remain private is not only implausible but also surely not 'one that society is prepared to recognize as 'reasonable.' **Katz**, 389 U.S. at 361 (Harlan, J., concurring)." **Kyllo**, **supra**, at 43-44.

FACTS (Kyllo v. United States (2001) 533 U.S. 27)

In 1991, United States Department of the Interior Agent Elliot had reason to believe that marijuana was being grown inside Danny Kyllo's home, which was one unit in a triplex located on Rhododendron Drive in Florence, Oregon.

On January 16, 1992, at approximately 3:20 a.m., Agent Elliot and Dan Haas used an Agema Thermovision 210 thermal imaging device to scan the triplex exterior. The device detects infrared radiation, which all objects emit, but it is not visible to the naked eye. The imager converts radiation into images based on relative warmth, with black being cool and white being hot. Shades of gray reflect the spectrum in between those two extremes. The device operates like a video camera showing heat images.

The thermal scan of Mr. Kyllo's home took a few minutes and was performed from the passenger seat of Agent Elliot's car, which was parked across the street from the front of the house and also from the street behind the house.

The scan revealed that the roof over the garage and a side wall of Mr. Kyllo's home were relatively hot in comparison to the rest of the house and substantially warmer than neighboring homes in the triplex. Based on these observations, Agent Elliot concluded that Mr. Kyllo was using halide lights to grow marijuana in his house.

Based on informant tips, utility bills, and the thermal imaging device information, a Federal Magistrate issued a search warrant for Mr. Kyllo's home. During the service of the search warrant, the agents found an indoor marijuana grow operation involving over 100 plants.

A federal grand jury indicted Mr. Kyllo for manufacturing marijuana. Following the denial of his motion to suppress the seized evidence, he plead guilty.

The 9th Circuit Court of Appeal remanded the case for an evidentiary hearing regarding the intrusiveness of the thermal scan. The District Court made the following findings on that remand:

- The device is non-intrusive and emits no rays or beams
- It "shows a crude visual image" of the heat radiating from the exterior of the residence
- The scan did not reveal "any people or activity within the walls of the structure"
- The scan "cannot penetrate walls or windows to reveal conversations or human activities" and "no intimate details of the home were observed."

Based on the above findings, the District Court upheld the warrant and reaffirmed its denial of the motion to suppress the evidence. A divided 9th Circuit panel initially reversed, but that opinion was withdrawn and another panel, following a change in composition, affirmed the District Court. The Court of Appeals made the following findings:

- Mr. Kyllo had shown no subjective expectation of privacy because he made no attempt to conceal the heat emanating from his residence and, even if he did, there is no objectively reasonable expectation of privacy because the imager "did not expose any intimate details of Kyllo's life."
- The image exposed "only amorphous hot spots on the roof and exterior wall."

In **People v. Deutsch** (1996) 44 Cal.App.4th 1224, a California Court of Appeal reached a similar conclusion as **Kyllo v. United States**, **supra**, which was not decided until five years after this decision.

The Court of Appeal ruled that the police needed a search warrant before they could use a thermal imaging device because the device is indiscriminate in registering heat sources and it is an intrusive tool that tells much about the activities inside the home that might not relate to illegal activity.

FACTS (People v. Deutsch (1996) 44 Cal.App.4th 1224)

An officer suspected that the defendant was growing marijuana inside a house. Late one night the officer drove by with a thermal imaging device. The device measures radiant energy in the thermal portion of an electromagnetic spectrum (heat). The officer observed high heat levels and ultimately obtained a search warrant for the house.

Despite the Court's holding, the Court still upheld the validity of the search warrant once it stuck the thermal imaging information from the affidavit.

The California 6th District Court of Appeal in **People v. Gotfried** (2003) 107 Cal.App.4th 254, suppressed the seizure of 106 live marijuana plants that were seized pursuant to a search warrant that was based in part on an earlier search warrant that authorized the use of a thermal imaging device. The Court found that the warrant authorizing the use of the thermal imaging device lacked probable cause and that the good faith doctrine did not apply to the deputy's actions in this case.

FACTS (People v. Gotfried (2003) 107 Cal.App.4th 254)

On September 24, 1998, Monterey County Deputy Sheriff Ruben A. Garcia submitted a search warrant to the trial court asking for permission to use a thermal imaging device at night on a single-wide mobile home located at 70450 Chadwick, No. 21, Lockwood. In support of that affidavit, Deputy Garcia put forth a very detailed expertise statement.

Deputy Garcia disclosed that he had worked for the Sheriff's Department since 1982 and been assigned to the County of Monterey's Marijuana Eradication Team since December 1993. He provided a very detailed listing of the classes and training he received as well as information about several investigations he had been involved in that resulted in the seizure of large marijuana grows. He stated that he had received formal training by the United States Drug Enforcement Administration regarding the use of thermal imaging devices and that he had used the device in eight investigations. He also stated that he testified as an expert on the use of the device in the detection of indoor marijuana cultivation operations.

Deputy Garcia told the magistrate that he received information from an anonymous informant on September 23, 1998. The informant said that Frederic Gotfried was growing marijuana at his residence and had been growing marijuana for three to four years in a 12-foot-by-12-foot room located to the rear of his trailer. He was currently growing between 80 to 120 marijuana plants under four high-pressure lights. The informant said that Mr. Gotfried has moved to the remote area of Monterey County to avoid detection by aerial over flights with infrared camera and the he had been diverting electricity for over three years to conceal his high power usage. The informant told him that Mr. Gotfried sold marijuana for $2,800.00 a pound to his clients in Santa Cruz and that Mr. Gotfried was being evicted from the trailer park and would be moving the marijuana grow operation to a new location. The informant also told him that Mr. Gotfried drove a Volvo as well as a Ford Bronco and provided the license plate numbers for both of those cars.

Deputy Garcia told the magistrate in his affidavit that on September 23, 1998, at around 10:00 p.m., he and Investigator Doug Dahmen drove to the trailer park and were followed by a Ford Bronco that matched the description and license plate number of Mr. Gotfried's into the trailer park. The Bronco parked at space #21 and the driver confronted the deputies in front of space #21. He questioned them about their business at the trailer park and when told they were looking for a particular person, was advised that the person no longer lived at the park and that they should leave because they were bothering the neighbors. Before leaving, they noticed the Volvo described by the informant parked next to the trailer at space #21.

Deputy Garcia disclosed to the magistrate that he had checked the criminal history records for Mr. Gotfried, but found that he had no prior criminal convictions and that a driver's license check showed an address of 2636 17th Avenue, #159, Santa Cruz. Both vehicles were also registered to that address.

Based on the above factual showing, as well as Deputy Garcia's opinion that the use of a thermal imaging device would be able to detect temperature differences indicative of an indoor marijuana grow operation, the magistrate issued the warrant and allowed the use of the device at night.

On September 25, 1998, which was one day after obtaining the search warrant for the use of the thermal imaging device on the trailer, Deputy Garcia sought a second search warrant, but this time for the residence itself. He disclosed in his affidavit that the thermal imaging device detected a large amount of heat coming from the rear and side of the mobile home, but neighboring trailers did not have that same heat signature. The magistrate issued the search warrant on September 28, 1998, and the officers served it the same day.

During the service of the search warrant, the officers located 106 live, growing marijuana plants, 15 drying plants and about eight pounds of dry "shake" marijuana. The marijuana was being grown under high-pressure lights with circulating fans and a climate control device.

Mr. Gotfried was arrested and later charged with the felony offenses of cultivation and possession for sale of marijuana. On January 20, 1999, he filed a motion to suppress the seized evidence and argued that the information contained in the first search warrant affidavit failed to establish probable cause for the issuance of the search warrants. The trial court denied the motion on May 5, 1999, and found that Deputy Garcia's actions sufficiently corroborated the informant's information and that probable cause existed for the issuance of the first search warrant. Mr. Gotfried waived further preliminary hearing and he was held to answer.

On October 12, 1999, Mr. Gotfried renewed his suppression motion, but the court denied it on November 10, 1999. The Court found that while the warrant lacked probable cause, Deputy Garcia acted in good faith when he relied on the magistrate's approval of the use of the thermal imaging device. The defendant then plead guilty to cultivating marijuana, was placed on three years formal probation and appealed the denial of his suppression motion.

RATIONALE

"In this case, Garcia failed to directly establish the veracity or basis of knowledge of the anonymous informant, the informant's information as to the alleged criminal activity was not self-verifying, and the record does not suggest that such corroboration could not be obtained. Garcia simply corroborated defendant's residence and vehicles." (**Id**. at 264.)

"Garcia failed to confirm that defendant had previously sold marijuana in Santa Cruz or even that he was diverting electricity prior to the meter. In short, all Garcia had was an uncorroborated tip from an anonymous informant. The search warrant authorizing the use of the thermal imaging device was issued without probable cause." (**Id**. at 264.)

"Garcia, who was a well-trained officer, knew or should have known that the limited corroboration he undertook was insufficient and that the affidavit requesting the search warrant was 'so lacking in indicia of probable cause as to render official belief in its existence entirely unreasonable.'" (**United States v. Leon**, **supra**, 468 U.S. at p. 923 [104 S.Ct. at p.3421]; see also **People v. Johnson**, **supra**, 220 Cal.App.3d at pp.750-751.)" (**Id**. at 265.)

2.5.8 – Entries to Arrest with an Arrest Warrant

In **Payton v. New York** (1980) 445 U.S. 573, 576, the U.S. Supreme Court ruled that the Fourth Amendment to the United States Constitution "prohibits the police from making a warrantless and nonconsensual entry into a suspect's home in order to make a routine felony arrest." (**Id**. at 576.)

FACTS (Payton v. New York (1980) 445 U.S. 573)

A New York statute allowed the police to enter private residences without any warrant and, if necessary, with force, to make routine felony arrests. On Jan. 14, 1970, after two days of intensive investigation, NYPD detectives had established sufficient probable cause to believe that Theodore Payton had murdered the manager of a gas station on January 12, 1970.

On January 15, 1970, six police officers went to Mr. Payton's Bronx apartment to arrest him. The officers did not have an arrest or search warrant. They could see light and hear music coming from the apartment. However, no one responded to their knock-notice at the metal front door. About 30 minutes later, the officers forced entry into the apartment with crowbars, but no one was found inside the apartment. In plain view was a .30 caliber shell casing that the police seized and was used as evidence against Mr. Payton at trial.

The California Supreme Court reached a similar result in **People v. Ramey** (1976) 16 Cal.3d 263, which it decided four years before the U.S. Supreme Court's decision in **Payton v. New York**, **supra**.

FACTS (People v. Ramey (1976) 16 Cal.3d 263)

On June 30, 1973, James Turner's Sacramento residence was burglarized. Among the items taken were several guns including a .38 caliber Smith and Wesson Airweight. Mr. Turner was a licensed private investigator and former security agent so he investigated his own case.

Mr. Turner's efforts led him to Mr. Reed and Mr. Weaver. Mr. Reed told Mr. Turner that Mr. Ramey purchased the stolen gun from Mr. Weaver. Mr. Turner was slightly acquainted with Mr. Ramey and so, on the afternoon of August 17, 1973, he went to Mr. Ramey's house. Mr. Ramey initially said that he had been offered the stolen gun but did not buy it, but Mr. Turner insisted that he had heard Mr. Ramey bought the Airweight. Mr. Ramey then said, "Oh, that one." and claimed he did not know it belonged to Mr. Turner.

Mr. Ramey then said he owned it briefly but then sold it to "some white guy." However, Mr. Ramey could not provide any other info about the purchaser and Mr. Turner felt Mr. Ramey was being evasive because he still had the gun.

Mr. Turner then told Sacramento Police Detective Garcia about his investigation and contact with Mr. Ramey. Detective Garcia felt he had probable cause to arrest Mr. Ramey for possession of a stolen firearm.

Three hours later, Detective Garcia and three other officers went to Mr. Ramey's house without an arrest or search warrant. The officers knocked on the door, after drawing their guns. Mr. Ramey opened the door and the police identified themselves. Mr. Ramey backed into the residence and moved toward a portable bar in the living room, but one of the officer's grabbed Mr. Ramey as he reached behind the bar.

Detective Garcia looked behind the bar and found a .45 caliber pistol and three lids of marijuana in cellophane baggies, as well as a baggie of benzedrine. The police then conducted a warrantless search of the rest of the residence and seized more contraband. The police never found any evidence linking Mr. Ramey to the Turner burglary.

In **Kirk v. Louisiana** (2002) 536 U.S. 635, the U.S. Supreme Court reversed the defendant's cocaine conviction and reiterated its holding in **Payton**, **supra**. The Court stated, "[a]s **Payton** makes plain, police officers need either a warrant or probable cause plus exigent circumstances in order to make a lawful entry into a home." **Kirk**, at 638.

The Supreme Court did remand the case to the Louisiana courts to determine if exigent circumstances were present or if any Fourth Amendment violation was cured because the police had an "independent source" for the seized evidence.

FACTS (Kirk v. Louisiana (2002) 536 U.S. 635)

In March 1998, officers received information from an anonymous citizen informant that drug sales were occurring at Mr. Kirk's apartment. Officers set up surveillance and witnessed what appeared to be several drug purchases. The officers stopped one of the buyers within one block of Mr. Kirk's residence. The officers believed that because the arrest occurred so close to the defendant's apartment, Mr. Kirk might destroy evidence.

The officers immediately knocked on the apartment door and arrested Mr. Kirk. Incident to the arrest, the officers searched Mr. Kirk's person and found a vial of cocaine in his underwear and money on his person. The police obtained a search warrant only after they entered Mr. Kirk's apartment, arrested him and found the cocaine on his person. Mr. Kirk was later convicted of that offense and received a sentence of 15 years at hard labor.

The Louisiana Court of Appeal, ignoring the clear ruling of **Payton**, **supra**, concluded that because "the officers had probable cause to arrest and properly searched the defendant incident thereto," the trial court correctly denied Mr. Kirk's suppression motion. **Kirk**, **supra**, at 637.

In **United States v. Gooch** (9th Cir. 2007) 506 F.3d 1156, the 9th Circuit Court of Appeals held for the first time that a misdemeanor bench warrant for failure to appear – as opposed to a felony arrest warrant – was sufficient to justify an entry into a residence pursuant to the U.S. Supreme Court's decision in **Payton v. New York, supra, (1980) 445 U.S. 573.** The Court found that a bench warrant validly issued by a neutral magistrate included the limited authority to enter a residence to make the arrest authorized by the warrant.

In a 7 to 2 decision in **Steagald v. United States** (1981) 451 U.S. 204, the U.S. Supreme Court ruled that absent a third party's consent, police need a search warrant to enter a third party's residence to serve an arrest warrant on a guest at that location.

In order to protect a presumably innocent person in their home from an unjustified, forcible entry by the government, the court held that, absent exigent circumstances or consent, a search warrant was required before entry could be made into a third party's private dwelling to conduct a search or effect an arrest.

While the arrest warrant served to protect Mr. Lyon's privacy interests in being free from an unreasonable seizure and a warrantless invasion and search of his home, it did not protect the rights of the third party homeowner against an unreasonable invasion of his home. "[A]bsent exigent circumstances the magistrate, rather than the police officer, must make the decision that probable cause exists to believe that the person or object to be seized is within a particular place." (**Id**. at 214.)

In the course of its opinion, the Supreme Court explained the difference between arrest warrants and search warrants.

- "An *arrest warrant* is issued by a magistrate upon a showing that probable cause exists to believe that the subject of the warrant has committed an offense and thus the warrant primarily serves to protect an individual from an unreasonable seizure." (**Id**. at 213. [*Italics* added].)
- "A *search warrant*, in contrast, is issued upon a showing of probable cause to believe that the legitimate object of a search is located in a particular place, and therefore safeguards an individual's interest in the privacy of his home and possessions against the unjustified intrusion of the police." (**Id**. at 213. [*Italics* added].)

FACTS (Steagald v. United States (1981) 451 U.S. 204)

"Ricky Lyons" was a federal fugitive wanted on drug charges. DEA agents received information from an informant that Mr. Lyons would be in Atlanta, Georgia on January 16, 1978. The informant provided the DEA with a phone number. DEA obtained the address for that phone number and discovered that Mr. Lyons had a six-month-old arrest warrant.

Armed with only the arrest warrant, 12 DEA agents went to the Atlanta address to arrest Mr. Lyons. Upon arrival, the officers saw two men standing outside, one of which was Gary Steagald. The other was Hoyt Gaultney, who resided at the residence.

Officers entered the house, detained Mrs. Gaultney and searched for Mr. Lyons. While the officers did not find Mr. Lyons, they did observe cocaine in plain view and obtained a search warrant for the residence. During the search of the residence, 43 pounds of cocaine were located and seized in a suitcase in the closet.

2.5.8.1 – Protective Sweeps

Under **Maryland v. Buie** (1990) 494 U.S. 325, the U.S. Supreme Court ruled that during the service of an arrest warrant, police may make a "protective sweep" of the entire structure for officer safety if they have reason to believe that someone else, who may pose a danger to them, may be present in the residence.

In **People v. Celis** (2004) 33 Cal.4th 667, the Court of Appeal suppressed the seizure of cocaine because the officers had no knowledge of anyone in the house prior to the protective sweep. The Court observed that while a protective sweep can be justified on the basis of a reasonable suspicion that the area to be swept contains a dangerous person, it cannot be based on a mere hunch.

FACTS (People v. Celis (2004) 33 Cal.4th 667)

The police suspected Mr. Celis of trafficking in kilogram quantities of cocaine via concealment in large truck tires. The officers stopped Mr. Celis behind his house at gunpoint, handcuffed him and had him sit on the ground. They then made a warrantless entry into his residence to see if anyone was inside who might pose a danger to their safety.

While inside the residence, the officers observed 16 wrapped kilograms of cocaine. Inside a large truck tire outside the residence, which Mr. Celis had been rolling toward a waiting truck in the alleyway, the officers seized an additional 25 kilograms of cocaine.

After the denial of his suppression motion, Mr. Celis entered a guilty plea to the charges. The Court imposed a 12-year prison sentence.

2.5.8.2 – Threshold Exception

In a 7 to 2 decision in **United States v. Santana** (1976) 427 U.S. 38, the U.S. Supreme Court ruled that the police lawfully arrested the defendant without an arrest warrant when, following a narcotics transaction, she was standing in the threshold of her home when the police arrived and was therefore in a public place. The fact that the defendant retreated inside the residence upon seeing the police could not thwart the otherwise proper arrest.

FACTS (United States v. Santana (1976) 427 U.S. 38)

On August 16, 1974, Philadelphia undercover narcotics Officer Gilletti arranged to buy heroin from Patricia McCafferty. He had previously purchased narcotics from her. Ms. McCafferty told the officer that it would cost him $115 "and we will go down to Mom Santana's for the dope."

The officer notified his superiors of the upcoming purchase, recorded the serial numbers of the money and then met Ms. McCafferty at a prearranged location. Ms. McCafferty entered the officer's car and directed him to 231 North 5th Street, which is where the defendant lived. Ms. McCafferty took the money and went inside the house. She stopped briefly to talk to William Alejandro, who was seated on the front steps.

A short time later, Ms. McCafferty came out of the residence returned to the officer's location and gave him several glassine envelopes containing heroin. The officer then stopped the car, identified himself as a police officer and arrested Ms. McCafferty. The officer told Ms. McCafferty that the police were going to go back to the residence and wanted to know where the money was. She said, "Mom has the money." Officer Gilletti relayed that information to other officers and then went to the police station with Ms. McCafferty.

Sergeant Pruitt and other officers then drove about two blocks back to the defendant's residence and saw Dominga Santana standing in the doorway of the house with a brown paper bag in her hand. The officers pulled up to within 15 feet of Santana, got out of the van and shouted, "Police". They also displayed their ID. As the officers approached, Ms. Santana retreated into the vestibule of her house and the officers followed. As she tried to pull away, the brown paper bag tilted and "two bundles of glazed paper packets with a white powder" inside fell to the floor. Mr. Alejandro tried to run off with them but was forcibly restrained.

In response to the officer's command, Ms. Santana emptied her pockets and produced $135, $70 of which was marked money.

Ms. Santana and Mr. Alejandro were charged with possession with the intent to distribute heroin. The United States District Court for the Eastern District of Pennsylvania granted their motion to suppress the evidence because the police did not have an arrest warrant and therefore could not follow her into the house when she retreated inside. The Court of Appeals affirmed the decision without issuing an opinion.

RATIONALE

Ms. Santana was not in an area where she had any expectation of privacy because "what a person knowingly exposes to the public, even in his own house or office, is not a subject of Fourth Amendment protection."

[Citations]. (**Id**., at 42.) "Santana was not merely visible to the public but was as exposed to public view, speech, hearing, and touch as if she had been standing completely outside her house." [Citations]. (**Id**., at 42.)

2.5.9 – Administrative Searches

Administrate searches arise in the context of health, fire, building, or commercial and industrial regulatory inspections undertaken for administrative rather than investigatory purposes. In **Camara v. Municipal Court** (1967) 387 U.S. 523, the U.S. Supreme Court ruled that a San Francisco Housing code inspector needed a search warrant to conduct a search of a residence for code violations.

2.5.10 – Computers and Public Employee Office Searches

In **O'Connor v. Ortega** (1987) 480 U.S. 709, the U.S. Supreme Court ruled that no warrant is necessary for a public employer to search an employee's office for non-investigatory, work-related purposes or to investigate work related misconduct.

The Court ruled that the question of whether or not a public employee has a reasonable expectation of privacy in their work place must be addressed on a case-by-case basis. The Court must balance the employee's legitimate expectation of privacy against the government's need for supervision, control, and the efficient operation of the workplace.

Reasonableness under all the circumstances, and not probable cause, is the standard to be used for assessing the employer's intrusions on the constitutionally protected privacy interests of government employees for work-related reasons, including work-related employee misconduct. There are two elements to the reasonableness analysis:

1. Whether the action was justified at its inception
2. Whether the search as actually conducted was reasonably related in scope to the circumstances which justified the interference in the first place and not excessively intrusive in light of the nature of the misconduct.

It is important to note that the Supreme Court did not address the issue of the appropriate standard to use when an employee is being investigated for criminal misconduct or breaches of other non-work-related statutory or regulatory standards. [See **O'Connor v. Ortega**, **supra**, Fn. * p. 729]

FACTS (O'Connor v.Ortega (1987) 480 U.S. 709)

Dr. Magno Ortega was employed as the Chief of Professional Education at Napa State Hospital and was responsible for training doctors in the psychiatric residency program. Hospital officials, including Dr. Dennis O'Connor, the Executive Director of the Hospital, became concerned about some of the doctor's activities such as his acquisition of an Apple II computer by possibly coercing contributions from medical residents, alleged incidents of sexual harassment of female employees, and inappropriate disciplinary action against a medical resident.

The hospital placed the doctor on paid administrative leave while it conducted an investigation of the charges. As part of the investigation, hospital officials searched the doctor's office on several occasions and seized both personal items as well as articles belonging to the State. The stated justification for these searches was to inventory and secure State property. The following items, which a former resident physician had sent to the doctor, were seized:

- A Valentine's Day card
- A photograph
- A book of poetry.

No formal inventory was made of the property in the office, but all the papers seized were placed in storage for the doctor to retrieve. After completion of the investigation, the hospital fired the doctor. The personal items seized from the doctor's office were used to impeach the credibility of the former physician resident who testified on the doctor's behalf before the California State Personnel Board.

The doctor filed a civil rights lawsuit (42 U.S.C.S. 1993) alleging that the search violated the Fourth Amendment. The District Court held that there was no violation because of the need to secure State property contained in the office.

The 9th Circuit reversed, and held that the search was unreasonable, because the doctor had a reasonable expectation of privacy in his office. It granted partial summary judgment for the doctor on the unlawful search claim and remanded the case for a determination of damages.

On certiorari, the U.S. Supreme Court reversed the 9th Circuit and remanded the case for further hearing.

RATIONALE

The doctor had a reasonable expectation of privacy in his desks and file cabinets in this case because

- The doctor did not share his desk or file cabinets with other employees
- The doctor had occupied the office for 17 years and kept personal materials such as personal correspondence, medical files, correspondence from private patients unconnected to the hospital, personal financial records, teaching aids and notes, personal gifts, and mementos
- The doctor kept his work related files outside of his office
- The only items found during a search of the office were personal items
- The hospital had apparently not established any regulation or policy discouraging employees from storing personal papers and effects in their desks or file cabinets.

In **United States v. Simons** (4th Cir. 2000) 206 F.3d 392, the Court of Appeals upheld against Fourth Amendment challenges, the remote, warrantless search of Mr.

Simons' office computer by his public employer, as well as the employer's physical entry into his office to retrieve the computer's hard drive.

The Court of Appeals "... concluded that the remote searches of Simons' computer did not violate his Fourth Amendment rights because, in light of the [employer's] Internet policy, Simons lacked a legitimate expectation of privacy in the files downloaded from the Internet. ... Simons did not have a legitimate expectation of privacy with regard to the record or fruits of his Internet use in light of the FBIS Internet policy. The policy clearly stated that FBIS would 'audit, inspect, and\or monitor' employees' use of the Internet, including all file transfers, all websites visited, and all email messages, 'as deemed appropriate.' ... This policy placed employees on notice that they could not reasonably expect their Internet activity would be private. (**Id**. at 398.)

With respect to the physical entry of his office, the Court of Appeals stated that "[i]n the final analysis, this case involves an employee's supervisor entering the employee's government office and retrieving a piece of government equipment in which the employee had absolutely no expectation of privacy – equipment that the employer knew contained evidence of crimes committed by the employee in the employee's office. This situation may be contrasted with one in which the criminal acts of a government employee were unrelated to his employment. Here, there was a conjunction of the conduct that violated the employer's policy and the conduct that violated the criminal law. We consider that FBIS' intrusion into Simons' office to retrieve the hard drive is one in which a reasonable employer might engage." [*Citations*] (**Id**. at 401.)

FACTS (United States v. Simons (4th Cir. 2000) 206 F.3d 392)

Mark Simons worked as an electronic engineer at the Foreign Bureau of Information Services (FBIS), which is a division of the Central Intelligence Agency (CIA). FBIS provided Mr. Simons with a private office and a computer with Internet access.

In June 1998, FBIS instituted a policy regarding employee Internet use. Employees were authorized to use the Internet only for official government business and accessing unlawful material was specifically prohibited. FBIS also disclosed that it would conduct electronic audits to ensure employee compliance with the policy. The policy explained that the audits would be capable of recording access to the system, including successful and unsuccessful logins. It would also track inbound and outbound file transfers, sent and received email messages and websites visited. The policy explicitly stated that users were to understand that FBIS "will periodically, audit, inspect, and\or monitor the user's Internet access as deemed appropriate." (**Id**. at 396.)

FBIS contracted with Science Applications International Corporation (SAIC) to manage the network and monitor for any inappropriate use. On July 17, 1998, Clifford Mauch, who was a manager at SAIC, began to explore the capabilities of a firewall SAIC recently acquired. Mr. Mauck entered the keyword "sex" into the firewall database and conducted a search for the period between July 14 and 17, 1998. By doing that, he obtained a large number of Internet hits from Mr. Simons' computer. It was clear to Mr. Mauch that the sites visited were not work related and he reported this to Katherine Camer, who was his FBIS contact.

Ms. Camer than worked with Robert Harper, who was another SAIC employee to investigate Mr. Simons' Internet activity. Ms. Camer told Mr. Harper to view one of the visited website. When he did, Mr. Harper discovered that it contained nude pictures of women. From his own remote workstation, and under the direction of Ms. Camer, Mr. Harper examined Mr. Simons' office computer to check for picture downloads. He found over 1,000 similar files. Mr. Harper viewed several of the images from his workstation and confirmed that they were pornographic in nature. Still acting under Ms. Camer's direction, Mr. Harper printed a list of the downloaded picture files and then copies all of the files from Mr. Simons' hard drive.

On July 31, 1998, two representatives from the CIA Office of Inspector General (OIG), including one who was a criminal investigator, viewed the files Mr. Harper copied from Mr. Simons' hard drive. From that review, it was learned that minors were depicted in the pictures. Later that day, Mr. Harper physically entered Mr. Simons' office and removed the original hard drive, which he replaced with a copy. He turned the seized hard drive over to a security officer at FBIS, who turned it over to OIG that same day.

On August 5, 1998, FBI Special Agent Mesisca viewed in excess of 50 of the images on the hard drive removed from Mr. Simons' office and observed that many of the images contained child pornography. Agent Mesisca, Mr. Harper, the two OIG representatives and Assistant United States Attorney Tom Connolly prepared an application for a search warrant to search Mr. Simons' office and computer. The affidavit alleged that Mr. Simons had connected a ZIP drive to his computer and expressed a need to conduct the search in secret.

On August 6, 1998, the court issued a search warrant, which commanded that the executing officers were to leave a copy of the warrant and a receipt for the property taken. The warrant never mentioned or prohibited the secret execution of the warrant. Agent Mesisca and others served the search warrant that night but didn't leave a copy of the warrant or a receipt behind. The search team copied the contents of Mr. Simons' computer, computer diskettes found in his disk drawer, and files stored on the Zip disk[22] or drive, videotapes and documents, including personal correspondence. The executing officers took no original evidence from the office. It was not until 45 days later that Mr. Simons

[22] A "Zip Disk" is defined by the 2008 version of the Internet source Netlingo (www.netlingo.com) as "An advanced version of the floppy disk, created by Iomega. These disks (typically 100MB or 250MB) enable you to store, share, and backup information from your computer using an Iomega Zip Drive."

learned of the search. Agent Mesisca found over 50 pornographic images of minors among the seized materials.

On September 17, 1998, the Government obtained a second warrant, but this one stated that the August 1998 warrant was for a surreptitious search warrant. Officer served the warrant on September 23, 1998, with Mr. Simons being present. This time, the original evidence was seized and a copy of the warrant and inventory were left with Mr. Simons. Mr. Simons was ultimately indicted on one count of violating 18 U.S.C. 2252A(a)(2)(A) (Knowing receipt of child pornography transported in interstate commerce) and one count of violating 18 U.S.C. 2252A(a)(5)(B) (Knowing possession of child pornography transported in interstate commerce). Following the denial of his suppression motion, a court trial was held and the court found Mr. Simon guilty on both counts and sentenced him to 18 months in prison. He promptly appealed the denial of his suppression motion.

Justification for a warrantless search of an employee's workplace computer may be highly fact-dependent. In **United States v. Slanina** (5th Cir. 2002) 283 F.3d 670, the Court of Appeals ruled that while Mr. Slanina had a reasonable expectation of privacy in files stored on his work computer, the warrantless search of his office computer was reasonable based on the U.S. Supreme Court's ruling in **O'Connor v. Ortega** (1987) 480 U.S. 709.

The Court of Appeals found that Mr. "Slanina clearly demonstrated a subjective expectation of privacy with respect to his office and office computer equipment. He had closed and locked the door to his office. To limit access to his computer files, he installed passwords, thereby making it more difficult for another person to get past the screen saver and reboot his computer." **Slanina**, at 676.

The Court of Appeals specifically declined "[t]o hold that a warrant is necessary any time a law enforcement official recognizes the possibility that an investigation into work-related misconduct will yield evidence of criminal acts [because it] would frustrate the government employer's interest in 'the efficient and proper operation of the workplace.' *O'Connor*, 480 U.S. at 723, 107 S.Ct. 1492." **Slanina**, at 679.

"Under *O'Connor*, a search by a government employer must be justified at its inception and reasonably related to the circumstances justifying the interference in the first place." **Slanina**, at 679. The Court of Appeals had little difficulty finding that Director Keller's search passed the test. "At the inception of his search, Smith had already discovered titles of newsgroups suggesting the presence of child pornography on Slanina's computer. Smith had also found an image of adult pornography, which represented a violation of city policy. On this evidence alone, Keller was justified in conducting a full search of the computer and accompanying disks to look for evidence of misconduct. Moreover, the scope of the search was also reasonable. The computer had been provided to Slanina by the city, and any use of it to access pornography was a violation of city policy. Keller was entitled to determine the extent of Slanina's violations." (**Id**. at 679-680.)

In reaching its decision, the Court of Appeal clearly stated that the decision they reached was limited to the unique set of facts presented and that they were not ruling on "the constitutionality of a search of a government employee by a law enforcement officer who is not also the employee's supervisor. . . . or the situation where the criminal acts of a government employee do not also violate workplace employment policy." (Id. at 680.)

FACTS (United States v. Slanina (5th Cir. 2002) 283 F.3d 670)

Wesley Slanina worked as a Fire Marshall for the City of Webster, Texas for nine years. His duties included public safety, fire inspections, enforcement of building codes, responding to arson related calls, and reviewing city plans. He also worked as the Emergency Management Coordinator and focused on hurricanes and explosions.

Mr. Slanina's immediate supervisor was the Fire Chief, Bruce Ure, who answered to Mike Keller, the Public Safety Director. Director Keller was in charge of both the police and fire departments and maintained ultimate control over Mr. Slanina's employment, including any salary increases and reviewing his evaluations.

Before June 1999, Mr. Slanina's desk was located in the City Hall, where he had a city-provided computer with Internet access, but no access to the city's intra-office network. Following the completion of a new fire station, Mr. Slanina office was moved to the new station. While he brought his office computer with him, he had no Internet access or network connection from his new office.

On June 11, 1999, Management Information Systems Coordinator Ryan Smith began installing the city network on the fire station computers. Around 5:00 p.m., he used a grand master key to enter Mr. Slanina's office to continue the installation work. Mr. Slanina's computer was already operating and a password protected screen saver was running. Mr. Smith restarted the computer to bypass the password but found that Mr. Slanina had also installed a BIOS password. Mr. Smith contacted Chief Ure and advised him of the problem. Chief Ure told Mr. Smith to call Mr. Slanina and obtain the password. Since Mr. Smith did not feel comfortable making the call, Chief Ure made the call.

Mr. Slanina did not come to work that day because he was still recovering from recent wisdom teeth removal surgery. Upon receiving the call from Chief Ure, Mr. Slanina was initially reluctant to provide the information but was informed that Mr. Smith was on overtime and the job had to be completed that day. Mr. Slanina agreed to call Mr. Smith and supply him with the necessary information. Mr. Slanina called Mr. Smith and sounded nervous and hesitant and wanted to know exactly what Mr. Smith would be doing to the computer. Mr. Smith assured him that he was just installing the network and configuring the computer to the server. Mr. Slanina then surrendered his password.

Mr. Smith began his work on Mr. Slanina's office computer and left the office to go to the server room. When he returned, he was surprised to see Mr. Slanina at the office, especially since they had just talked on the phone 10 minutes earlier. Mr. Smith noticed swelling around Mr. Slanina's jaw and became suspicious when Mr. Slanina jumped back on the computer when Mr. Smith left the room. Mr. Smith lied to Mr. Slanina and told him that it would take a few more hours to complete the job, so Mr. Slanina left.

After Mr. Slanina left, Mr. Smith noticed that an email application was running, but had been minimized. As he clicked on the email to close it, he noticed the presence of newsgroups. Three months earlier Director Keller told Mr. Smith that no one was allowed to have newsgroups on their computers, but the policy had not been disseminated to the fire station employees, including Mr. Slanina. Mr. Smith maximized the email to look for additional newsgroups and found three titles that suggested the presence of pornography, which is also improper to have on an office computer. Mr. Smith clicked on one newsgroup title, "alt.erotics.xx.preteen" and saw that about 25 of the 60 files had been read. Mr. Smith stopped reading and checked Mr. Slanina's computer for JPG and GIF files. In the recycle bin he found a file containing an image of adult pornography and printed it out for his superiors.

Mr. Smith contacted Chief Ure, advised him of his discovery, and was instructed to secure the office. Mr. Smith changed the office door lock, turned the computer off and left the premises. By the next day, Chief Ure had contacted Director Keller who instructed the Chief to have Mr. Smith remove the computer from the fire station and place it in his office, which was located at the police station. The Chief and Mr. Smith went to Mr. Slanina's office and Mr. Smith showed the Chief the pornography before he removed the computer.

At 3:00 p.m. on Sunday, the Chief and Mr. Smith met with Director Keller and were instructed to get what they needed to view the files and any ZIP disks or drives from Mr. Slanina's office. Upon returning, Mr. Smith showed Director Keller the adult pornography picture he obtained on Friday night from the computer and where he had found it on the computer. Director Keller and Mr. Smith searched the computer and ZIP drive for about two hours and saw images containing explicit child pornography. Director Keller contacted the City Manager and informed him of the discovery. The decision was made to notify the FBI on Monday.

On Monday morning at 7:15 a.m., Chief Ure met Mr. Slanina in the parking lot and told him that they needed to meet in Director Keller's office. At that point, Mr. Slanina became visibly anxious and rocked back and forth. He was told he would be suspended during the investigation of his misuse of city property by obtaining child pornography with a city computer. Director Keller told Mr. Slanina that he was not in custody and could leave at any time. Instead, Mr. Slanina remained and admitted to accessing newsgroups and downloading child pornography on his office computer. Additionally, he confessed that he had more pornography at his house and ultimately consented to a search of his home. Mr. Slanina, Chief Ure, and Captain Smiley of the Internal Affairs Division went to Mr. Slanina's house, where he led the group into his study and invited them to take the computer, ZIP drive, and disks.

Once back at the police station, Director Keller searched the home computer and found more child pornography. Several weeks later it was learned that the home computer actually belonged to the city. The City ultimately fired Mr. Slanina. On February 14, 2000, a grand jury indicted Mr. Slanina on two counts of possessing child pornography in violation of 18 U.S.C. 2252A(a)(5)(b) and 18 U.S.C. 2256. The District Court denied Mr. Slanina's suppression motion. After a court trial, the judge found Mr. Slanina guilty as charged and sentenced him to 33 months in prison followed by three years of supervised release and fined him $2,200.

2.5.11 – Computers and Private Party Searches

As discussed earlier in 2.0 of this document, the Fourth Amendment only protects a citizen from governmental action; it does not protect a citizen from private party actions that law enforcement officers do not instigate or direct, even if those actions are illegal. (See **Burdeau v. McDowell** (1921) 256 U.S. 465.)

In **United States v. Hall** (7th Cir. 1998) 142 F.3d 988, the Court of Appeals found that the viewing of files on Mr. Hall's computer by a repair technician constituted a private search and therefore upheld the later issuance of a search warrant based on those observations. "The Government had no knowledge that Goodwin was going to repair Hall's computer and thus, did not instruct Goodwin to inspect the files. Goodwin did not contact the Government until after the evidence was discovered. The search was initiated by Goodwin, and was completed in the normal course of CDS's business, with the sole purpose of testing Hall's CPU. Therefore, the Fourth Amendment is inapplicable." (**Id**. at 993.)

FACTS (United States v. Hall (7th Cir. 1998) 142 F.3d 988)

Mr. Hall took his computer to CDS Office Technologies in Springfield, Illinois, for repair on November 7, 1995. The next day, Richard Goodwin, who was a CDS employee, began working on the computer. In order to diagnose the problem, he accessed several of the computer's directories. While doing so, he noted a number of files that had unusual names which implied sexual content, such as a file entitled "Boys 612." Mr. Goodwin viewed the file and found it to contain an image of two young boys, between the ages of 10 and 12, engaged in either actual or simulated anal sex. Mr. Goodwin then checked three to five other files and found that they also contained pornographic images of young males. Mr. Goodwin estimated that there were approximately 1,000 video files on the computer that had names implying that they contained child pornography. He believed that many of the files had been downloaded from America Online (AOL) because he found them in the AOL directory.

After Mr. Goodwin saw the files, he received a phone call from Mr. Hall, inquiring about the status of the computer. Mr. Goodwin explained that the computer probably needed a video upgrade and that a CDS salesperson would call him back concerning the price. However, he made no mention of what he had seen on the computer.

Mr. Goodwin called Illinois State Trooper Johnson, who was a friend of his, and told him about his discovery. Mr. Goodwin described two or three of the images to Trooper Johnson, who instructed Mr. Goodwin to make a copy of several of the files onto a 3.5-inch diskette in order to preserve the evidence. While this was improper, the Court found no Fourth Amendment violation because law enforcement never viewed the contents of the disk.

Trooper Johnson contacted Lieutenant Terry of the Illinois State Police, who in turn contacted the FBI. Mr. Goodwin was interviewed by the FBI and he and CDS agreed to cooperate in the investigation. Mr. Goodwin provided the agents with Mr. Hall's home address and phone number and his work address.

After the meeting, a CDS sales representative called Mr. Hall and discussed the video upgrade, which Mr. Hall authorized. The CDS employee explained that the repair would take another week because the video card needed to be ordered. CDS placed Mr. Hall's computer in another CDS employee's locked office while the FBI continued its investigation. The FBI subpoenaed AOL's records and confirmed that Mr. Hall was a subscriber from February 22, 1995, through November 7, 1995. AOL's records also matched up with the address the FBI obtained from Mr. Goodwin.

On November 15, 1995, the video upgrade was completed and FBI Agent Walker obtained a search warrant for Mr. Hall's residence and one for his computer. CDS agreed to keep Mr. Hall's computer for an additional day to allow an FBI expert from headquarters to view the pornographic files that Mr. Goodwin had initially seen on the computer.

At around 8:00 a.m., on November 16, 1995, FBI Special Agent Randolph served the search warrant on Mr. Hall's computer at CDS and confirmed the presence of files containing child pornography. At 9:00 a.m., Mr. Hall arrived and picked up his computer. As he left the store, FBI agents confronted him and seized the computer. The agents told Mr. Hall he wasn't under arrest and was free to leave. They also told him that they were investigating the illegal transmission and receipt of child pornography by Mr. Hall. Mr. Hall cooperated and admitted that he obtained the child pornography via his AOL account and signed a written consent to search his residence and computer.

At his residence, agents seized 42 disks, three of which were found to contain child pornography. Following an inventory review and inspection of Mr. Hall's computer and disks, agents found 403 files containing visual images of prepubescent children engaged in explicit sexual conduct.

On October 10, 1996, the government indicted Mr. Hall for violating 18 U.S.C. 2252(a)(4)(B). Mr. Hall brought a motion to suppress the evidence on December 3, 1996, which the District Court denied on December 23, 1996. Following the denial of his motion, Mr. Hall pled guilty. The court sentenced him to 15 months in prison, followed by three years of supervised release and imposed a $50 special assessment fee.

In **United States v. Runyan** (5th Cir. 2001) 275 F.3d 449, the Court of Appeals addressed two narrow questions in its opinion: "(1) whether a police search exceeds the scope of a private search when private searchers examine selected items from a collection of similar closed containers and police searchers subsequently examine the entire collection; (2) whether a police search exceeds the scope of the private search when the police examine more items within a particular container than did the private searchers; . . ." (**Id**. at 461-462.)

In resolving those issues, the Court of Appeals ruled that the police exceeded the scope of the private search when they examined disks, such as the ZIP disks, which the private searchers [Mr. Runyan's wife and friends] did not examine themselves. However, the Court ruled that the police did not exceed the scope of the prior private search by examining the files on the private-party searched disks in more deal than did the private parties.

FACTS (United States v. Runyan (5th Cir. 2001) 275 F.3d 449)

Robert Runyan lived on a ranch outside of Santa Anna, Texas. He owned and operated Gammon Technologies from the ranch between 1990 and 1998. The business was a computer repair and service company and employed junior high and high school students to perform administrative tasks for the company and odd jobs at the ranch. Mr. Runyan was married to Judith Runyan, who had a daughter named "Rickie" from a previous marriage. In January 1999, Mrs. Runyan left and moved in with a boyfriend in Brownwood, before filing for divorce.

In June 1999, Mrs. Runyan made several trips back to the ranch to retrieve her personal property. On different occasions Rickie and other friends accompanied her. Mrs. Runyan knew that Mr. Runyan would not be present on the ranch at these times and knew that after they separated, Mr. Runyan placed a chain and lock on the gated entrance to the ranch and changed the locks on the house and barn. He also installed surveillance cameras on the property.

On June 17, Mrs. Runyan and Rickie jumped the fence around the ranch and looked through a ranch house window. Mrs. Runyan saw some of her belongings in the house. On June 18, Mrs. Runyan, Rickie and a friend returned to the ranch. This time Mrs. Runyan entered the house through a breakfast room window. After searching the house, they went to the barn next to the house.

Once inside the barn, Mr. Giles opened a black duffel bag and found that it contained pornography, CDs and computers disks, a Polaroid camera with film, a vibrator, and pictures of two individuals, one of whom appeared under age. Under the duffel bag were two ammo boxes that contained more pornography. Mrs. Runyan took the duffle bag back to her residence in Brownwood.

Later that day, Mrs. Runyan and six of her friends returned to Mr. Runyan's ranch and used bolt cutters to cut the chain on the gate. Over the next two days, the group removed items from the ranch house that Mrs. Runyan claimed belonged to her, including a desktop computer. Surrounding the computer were 3.5 inch floppy disks, CDs, and ZIP disks. Mrs. Runyan had Brandie Epp, one of her friends, dismantle the computer and transport it to her residence, where Ms. Epp reassembled the computer. Ms. Epp also took the disks surrounding the computer.

After reassembling the computer, Ms. Epp viewed about 20 of the CDs and floppy disks and found that they contained images of child pornography. Because of a lack of hardware, Ms. Epp could not review any of the ZIP disks. Ms. Epp later called the sheriff's department and informed them of what she saw on the floppy disks and turned over 22 CDs, 10 ZIP disks and 11 floppy disks to a sheriff's deputy.

Over the next few weeks, Mrs. Runyan gave various items she found on the ranch to different law enforcement agencies. She gave the sheriff's department additional CDs of child pornography and gave the Santa Anna Chief of Police a 3.5 inch diskette containing child pornography. She also contacted Texas Ranger Grubbs and gave him the black duffel bag along with the pornographic materials found in the ammo boxes, two additional disks and the Polaroid photographs she took from the ranch. At some point, she also gave him the desktop computer.

Ranger Grubbs reviewed some of the disks given to him by Mrs. Runyan and saw images consistent with child pornography. On June 24, 1999, the Coleman County District Attorney went to the Sheriff's office and viewed several of the images. A number of the images were printed out on a color printer and viewed by other members of the DA's office. DA Investigator Darla Tibbetts tentatively identified one of the subjects in one of the printed photographs. A DA Intern named Melissa Payne then went to the Sheriff's office to assist in the identification and positively identified one of the girls as a former high school classmate named "Misty."

On June 28, 1999, and after learning he was a potential suspect, Mr. Runyan met with Ranger Grubbs and waived his *Miranda* rights. He claimed that he found the bag containing the pornography at a rest stop and it contained the CDs and other items. He admitted that he viewed the materials out of curiosity and used his computer to view child pornography over the Internet. However, he claimed that he never uploaded or downloaded any pornography from the Internet during those sessions.

On July 7, 1999, U.S. Customs Service Special Agent Nuckles happened to be at the DA's office on an unrelated matter, and expressed a willingness to work on the case. He was given copies of all of the reports and statements as well as the physical evidence taken by Mrs. Runyan, including the computer.

Agent Nuckles examined every piece of evidence he received, including the ZIP disks. He scanned two images of Misty into a computer. DA Investigator Tibbets and Ranger Grubbs then interviewed a number of people including Misty. Misty told them that she worked at the ranch doing odd jobs and ironing clothes for Mr. Runyan. When she was 15 years old, Mr. Runyan approached her about posing nude and took sexually explicit photographs of her on many occasions when she was between 15 and 17 years old. Sometimes she was paid $5 per session, but Mr. Runyan promised her more money once he sold the pictures over the Internet to Japanese customers.

Agent Nuckles then obtained two search warrants. The first authorized a search of the desktop computer and all the disks for images of child pornography. The second warrant authorized a search of Mr. Runyan's ranch house for "any and all computers, computer hardware, software and services." A search of the Runyan ranch house yielded a computer back-up tape that contained one picture of child pornography.

A grand jury indicted Mr. Runyan on October 13, 1999, for six counts of child pornography, two of which the government dismissed before trial. He brought three separate motions to suppress the evidence against him, alleging primarily that the police violated his Fourth Amendment rights by searching the disks without first obtaining a search warrant. The trial court denied the motions on April 20, 2000, and ruled that the pre-warrant searches by the police did not exceed the scope of the private search by Mrs. Runyan and her associates.

On April 21, 2000, a jury convicted him of four counts related various federal violations of child pornography laws. The trial court sentenced him to 300 months in prison, followed by three years of supervised release and $400 in mandatory fines. Mr. Runyan appealed his conviction and, among other arguments, renewed his Fourth Amendment claim.

In **United States v. Heckenkamp** (9th Cir. 2007) 482 F.3d 1142, the Court of Appeals affirmed the District Court's decision upholding the warrantless remote search of Mr. Heckenkamp's personal computer, which was connected to the University of Wisconsin network, under the "special needs" exception enunciated in **Griffin v. Wisconsin** (1987) 483 U.S. 868. In that case, the U.S. Supreme Court held that no warrant is required when "special needs, beyond the normal need for law enforcement, make the warrant and probable cause requirement impractical." **Griffin**, at 873. The "special needs" doctrine is discussed in more detail in 2.5.4.1 of this document, dealing with general principles governing probation searches.

In so ruling, the Court of Appeals affirmed the District Court's holding that Mr. Heckenkamp had standing to object to the search of his computer because "the act of attaching his computer to the network did not extinguish his legitimate, objectively reasonable privacy expectations." **Heckenkamp**, at 1146. Mr. Heckenkamp's expectation of privacy was also shown by the fact his personal computer's screen saver was protected by a password, the computer was located in his dormitory room and there was no university policy allowing the university to actively monitor or audit his computer usage.

With respect to the remote computer search, the Court of Appeals ruled that despite Mr. Heckenkamp's subjective and objective expectations of privacy in his computer, "the university's interest in maintaining the security of its network provided a compelling government interest in determining the source of the unauthorized intrusion into sensitive files. The remote search of the computer was remarkably limited given the circumstances. Savoy did not view, delete, or modify any of the actual files on the computer; he was only logged into the computer for 15 minutes; and he sought only to verify that the same computer that had been connected at the 117 IP address was now connected at the 120 IP address." (**Id**. at 1148.) Given the government interest served and the relative unobtrusiveness of the search, the Court of Appeals found that the search did not violate the Fourth Amendment.

Additionally, the Court specifically found that University of Wisconsin Computer System Investigator Mr. Savoy "was acting to secure the Mail2 server, and that his actions were not motivated by a need to collect evidence for law enforcement purposes or at the request of law enforcement agents. This undisputed evidence supports . . . [the] conclusion that the special needs exception applied. The integrity and security of the campus email system was in jeopardy. Although Savoy was aware that the FBI was also investigating the use of a computer on the university network to hack into the Qualcomm system, his actions were not taken for law enforcement purposes. Not only is there no evidence that Savoy was acting at the behest of law enforcement, but also the record indicates that Savoy was acting contrary to law enforcement requests that he delay action." (**Id**. at 1147.)

FACTS (United States v. Heckenkamp (9th Cir. 2007) 482 F.3d 1142)

In December 1999, Scott Kennedy, who worked as a computer system administrator for Qualcomm Corporation in San Diego, California, discovered that someone had hacked into the company's computer network. Mr. Kennedy contacted FBI Special Agent Rankhorn upon making the discovery. Mr. Kennedy managed to trace the hacker back to a computer network at the University of Wisconsin in Madison, Wisconsin. Mr. Kennedy ultimately contacted Jeffrey Savoy, who was a computer network investigator for the university.

Mr. Savoy confirmed that someone using a computer on the university's network did in fact hack into the Qualcomm system and that the user had also gained unauthorized access to the university's system. Mr. Savoy was especially concerned because the hacker had gained access to the "Mail2" server on the university, which housed the accounts for 60,000 persons on campus and processed approximately 250,000 emails a day. Mr. Savoy knew that students were preparing for final examines and a tremendous disruption on campus would occur if the emails were destroyed.

Mr. Savoy traced the intrusion back to a computer located in university housing and that the hacker had an Internet Protocol (IP) address that ended in 117. Mr. Savoy discovered that Jerome Heckenkamp was a computer graduate student and checked his email from that IP address 20 minutes before and 40 minutes after the unauthorized connection between the Mail2 server and the Qualcomm server. Mr. Savoy also discovered that the IP address was regularly used to check Mr. Heckenkam's email address, but no others.

Mr. Savoy knew that Mr. Heckenkamp was terminated from his job at the university computer help desk two years earlier for similar hacking activity and knew that Mr. Heckenkamp possessed the technical expertise to damage the university's system.

Mr. Savoy attempted to verify that the computer used was assigned to Mr. Heckenkamp's dorm room, but the housing department stated the IP address belonged to a room down the hall from Mr. Heckenkamp. However, the housing department also said that the record could be inaccurate and could not verify the information until the next morning. Mr. Savoy then electronically blocked the connection between IP address 117 and the Mail2 server.

Mr. Savoy next contacted Agent Rackhorn and told him about what he discovered during his investigation. Agent Rackhorn told Mr. Savoy that he intended to get a search warrant for the computer, but did not instruct Mr. Savoy to do anything. Later that night, Mr. Savoy checked the status of the computer at IP address 117 from his home because he was still concerned about the integrity of the university's network. Mr. Savoy saw that the computer at IP address 117 was not logged into the network, but checked to see if the computer was now logged in at a different IP address. He discovered that the computer was logged on at IP address 120. By using a series of commands he was able to determine that the computer at the 120 IP address was the same as the computer at the 117 IP address. He did not delete, modify, or destroy any files during that search.

Mr. Savoy re-contacted Agent Rackhorn and University of Wisconsin Detective Scheller and informed them of his discovery. Agent Rackhorn asked Mr. Savoy to wait until a search warrant could be obtained, but Mr. Savoy believed he need to take the computer offline immediately in order to protect the university's system.

Mr. Savoy, and Detective Scheller went to Mr. Savoy's room with other university police officers and found the door ajar and the room empty. Mr.

Savoy disconnected the computer from the network and noted the computer had a password protected screen saver, which prevented him from accessing the computer. Detective Scheller found Mr. Heckenkamp nearby and explained the situation to him. Mr. Heckenkamp voluntarily provided his password, which Mr. Savoy used to verify that he had found the computer used in the hacking. Mr. Heckenkamp also authorized Mr. Savoy to make a copy of the hard drive for later analysis.

Agent Rackhorn did obtain a search warrant and served it the next day. Agents seized the computer and searched the room. Mr. Heckenkamp was ultimately indicted in both the Northern and Southern Districts for California for multiple offenses related to his illegal actions. The cases were ultimately consolidated and Mr. Heckenkamp entered a guilty plea to two counts of violating 18 U.S.C. 1030(a)(5)(b) (Reckless Damage By Intentionally Accessing A Computer Without Authorization), conditioned on his ability to appeal the District Court's denial of his suppression motion.

2.5.12 – Border Searches or their Functional Equivalent

No search warrant is required to conduct a search at the United States border or its points of entry.

2.5.13 – School Searches

In **New Jersey v. T.L.O**. (1985) 469 U.S. 325, the U.S. Supreme Court ruled , that while the Fourth Amendment applies to school searches, there is no probable cause requirement, only a "*reasonable grounds*" standard. School searches are okay if there is a reasonable suspicion of a violation of the law or school rules.

The California Supreme Court in **In re Randy G.** (2001) 26 Cal.4th 556, held that school officials, including uniformed security guards, could detain a minor student *on school grounds* even in the absence of reasonable suspicion of criminal activity or violation of school rules.

The California Supreme Court held "that the broad authority of school administrators over student behavior, school safety, and the learning environment requires that school officials have the power to stop a minor student in order to ask questions or conduct an investigation even in the absence of reasonable suspicion, so long as such authority is not exercised in an arbitrary, capricious, or harassing manner." (**Id**., at 559.)

The Court specifically limited its ruling to school grounds given that school discipline and order are essential for school officials to fulfill their obligations to educate. "If the school can require the minor's presence on campus during school hours, attendance at assigned classes during their scheduled meeting times, appearance at assemblies in the auditorium, and participation in physical education classes out of doors, liberty is scarcely infringed if a school security guard leads the student into the hall to ask questions about a potential rule violation." (**Id**., at 567.)

FACTS (<u>In re Randy G.</u> (2001) 26 Cal.4th 556)

Campus security officer Cathy Worthy, saw the minor and another student between building "C" and the auditorium during a period break between classes at about 9 a.m., on March 16, 1999. They were in an area where students are not allowed to gather.

As Officer Worthy became visible to the minor, he nervously fixed his pocket, although some of the lining of the left pocket was still visible. Officer Worthy asked the students if they needed anything and then instructed them to go to class. Officer Worthy followed the students to their destination because the minor acted "very paranoid and nervous."

After conversing with her supervisor, she summoned assistance and went to the minor's classroom. Officer Worthy asked the minor if she could see him outside, and he complied. In the course of the 10-minute contact outside the classroom, Officer Worthy conducted a consensual patdown on the minor, which revealed a knife with a locking blade in his pocket.

The minor was found guilty of violating California Penal Code 626.10 and placed on probation.

The Court of Appeal ruled in **<u>In re Alexander B.</u>** (1990) 220 Cal.App.3d 1572 that the uncorroborated statement of an unidentified student that another student had a gun was sufficient to justify a search of the other student.

The Court of Appeal upheld the search of the minor's backpack and the recovery of a gun on school grounds in **<u>In re Joseph G.</u>** (1995) 32 Cal.App.4th 1735.

FACTS (<u>In re Joseph G.</u> (1995) 32 Cal.App.4th 1735)

On Wednesday afternoon, the Vice Principal received a call from the mother of a student at the school. The parent identified herself but asked that her identity remain confidential. The mother said that her son had seen Joseph with a gun at a high school football game the previous Friday.

The next morning, the Vice Principal searched Joseph's locker and found only books. However, about five minutes later he saw Joseph place a backpack in the locker. When Joseph left the area, the Vice Principal again searched the locker and found a loaded gun in the backpack.

RATIONALE

The caller was a citizen informant, who is presumed reliable.

The fact that the information was five days old is irrelevant because when the Vice Principal saw Joseph put the backpack in his locker, the Vice Principal had a reasonable suspicion (the backpack would be a likely place to carry a gun) to justify the minimal intrusion of searching the locker and backpack.

In **In re William V.** (2003) 111 Cal.App.4th 1464, the Court of Appeal refused to apply a different standard to school searches simply because Officer Johannes was a police officer, who was assigned to the school as a resource officer, as opposed to a non-law enforcement security officer. The Court ruled that Officer Johannes was a school official for purposes of Fourth Amendment analysis and therefore the search of the minor was justified by the reasonable suspicion that William V. was committing a violation of the school rules.

FACTS (In re William V. (2003) 111 Cal.App.4th 1464)

> Hayward Police Officer Johannes was assigned to Hayward High School as a "school resource officer" for a two-year term. His assignment required that he maintain an office at the school and be on the campus about eight hours a day.
>
> On September 6, 2001, at about 9:15 a.m., Officer Johannes walked toward the administration building. As he did so, he saw William V. standing alone in the hallway. William V. had a neatly folded red bandanna hanging out of the back pocket of his pants. Possession of a bandanna on campus is a violation of school rules because of gang concerns. When Officer Johannes made eye contact with William V., the minor became nervous and started to pace.
>
> Officer Johannes approached William V. and asked him to remove the bandanna. William V. claimed he did not know he had the "red rag." Officer Johannes pointed out the bandanna to William V. and then removed it. The officer decided to take William V. to the principal's office for discipline.
>
> Officer Johannes first conducted a pat search of William V. for weapons because of the recent increase in gang violence on the campus, the way in which William V. was wearing the bandanna which was indicative of something about to happen and the minor's demeanor. During the pat search of William V., Officer Johannes discovered a steak knife with a five-inch blade protruding from the minor's front pocket. William V. admitted he had the knife for protection.
>
> William V. was initially charged with a felony for having a knife on school grounds, but this was later reduced to a misdemeanor. The Juvenile Court sent William V. home on probation.

The Court of Appeal in **In re Lisa G.** (2005) 125 Cal.App.4th 801 found the search of a student's purse to be illegal because the teacher lacked a reasonable suspicion related to the commission of a crime or a violation of school rules regarding the purse. "The only misbehavior Lisa engaged in was being disruptive in class. Mere disruptive behavior does not authorize a school official to rummage through his or her students' personal belongings." (**Id**., at 807.)

FACTS (In re Lisa G. (2005) 125 Cal.App.4th 801)

> On September 22, 2003, Lisa G. began school at San Diego High School. Andrea Craig was her fourth period teacher. During the class, some students, including Lisa G., were disruptive. After being told to sit down and complete their work,

the students complied. Due to a medical condition, Lisa G had permission to use the bathroom at any time. Ms. Craig was unaware of this fact, which was on file with the school nurse. Lisa G. repeatedly asked for permission to use the bathroom, but was denied by Ms. Craig. Ultimately, Lisa G. left the classroom and left her purse behind on her desk. Ms. Craig had taken Lisa G's purse and placed it on her desk to protect it from being taken by someone.

When Lisa G. returned to the classroom, she found the door locked and Ms. Craig would not let her back in the classroom. After Ms. Craig dismissed the class, she decided to write a disciplinary referral on Lisa G. Ms. Craig knew that Lisa G. was outside the classroom, but decided to check Lisa G's purse for her name and student ID number. Ms. Craig never asked Lisa G. to produce any ID, even though Lisa G. was outside the classroom. When Ms. Craig opened the purse, she found a knife inside and summoned school security.

At her juvenile proceeding, the Juvenile Court denied Lisa G's motion to suppress the search of her purse. A plea bargain was struck and Lisa G. agreed to plead guilty to a violation of Penal Code 626.10(a) and the Court placed her on probation for one year.

RATIONALE

Determining the reasonableness of a school search requires a two-fold inquiry:

- Whether the search was justified at its inception and
- Whether the scope of the search was reasonably related to the circumstances that justified the initial search.

In this case, the Court held the search of the purse was not justified at its inception because there was no correlation between Lisa G's wrongful behavior and the intended findings of the search. Ms. Craig had no facts suggesting Lisa G. had engaged in any prohibited activity that justified the search of the purse.

2.5.14 – Drug Testing

The U.S. Supreme Court ruled in **Samuel Skinner v. Railway Labor Executive Association** (1989) 489 U.S. 602, that a Federal Railroad Administration safety regulation mandating or authorizing alcohol and drug tests of employees without warrants or individualized suspicion does not violate the Fourth Amendment.

The Supreme Court did find that the Federal Government's compelling of testing and its encouragement, endorsement, and participation in the testing made the test attributable to the Federal Government and is therefore covered by the Fourth Amendment. The collection and analysis of the biological samples also infringed on the employees' reasonable expectations of privacy, and therefore constituted a search of the person.

FACTS (<u>Samuel Skinner v. Railway Labor Executive Association</u> (1989) 489 U.S. 602)

The Federal Railroad Administration issued regulations mandating blood and urine tests of employees following major train accidents or incidents. The testing requirements extended to those engaged in handling orders concerning train movements, operating crews, and those engaged in the maintenance and repair of signal systems. The testing requirement was mandatory if one of the following train accidents occurred:

- a train accident involving a fatality
- a train accident involving the release of hazardous material accompanied by an evacuation or a reportable injury
- a train accident involving $500,000.00 or more in damage to railroad property.

The railroad also had an additional mandated duty of collecting blood and urine samples for testing after an "impact accident," which is defined as a collision that results in a reportable injury, or in $50,000.00 or more of damage to railroad property.

RATIONALE

The tests mandated or authorized by the Federal regulations were reasonable, and therefore did not violate the Fourth Amendment even though they did not require a warrant or individualized suspicion that any particular employee to be tested was impaired by the use of alcohol or drugs. The concern for public safety justified regulating the conduct of railroad employees who were engaged in safety-sensitive tasks.

Imposing a warrant requirement would cause a delay, possibly resulting in the elimination of a portion of the alcohol or drugs that might be in an employee's bloodstream at the time, and thereby hindering the governmental purpose of determining whether or not alcohol or drugs were in the employee's bloodstream at the time in question.

The Federal Government's compelling interests in deterring on-duty railroad employees' alcohol and drug use and obtaining information about the cause of major train accidents outweighed the railroad employees' privacy expectations, which were diminished by the their participation in an industry that was pervasively regulated to ensure safety.

The U.S. Supreme Court reached a similar result in **<u>National Treasury Employees Union v. Von Raob</u>** (1989) 489 U.S. 656, where it upheld the warrantless drug tests on those persons directly involved in the interdiction of illegal drugs or positions that required the carrying of a firearm.

The Supreme Court remanded the case to the lower court on the issue of testing those persons handling "classified" materials because of a concern that the United

States Customs Service (USCS) had defined the category more broadly than necessary to meet the testing program's purposes.

FACTS (National Treasury Employees Union v. Von Raob (1989) 489 U.S. 656)

The United States Customs Service implemented a drug screening program requiring urinalysis tests of USCS employees who occupied or sought a transfer to positions having a direct involvement in drug interdiction, firearms usage, or handling "classified" materials. Under the rules, test results could not be turned over to any other agency, including criminal prosecutors, without the employee's written consent.

RATIONALE

The Supreme Court found the following governmental factors justified the testing:

- A national crisis in law enforcement caused by the smuggling of illicit narcotics
- Ensuring that front-line interdiction personnel are physically fit and have unimpeachable integrity and judgment
- Preventing the risk to the life of the citizenry posed by the potential use of deadly force by persons suffering from impaired perception and judgment.

The U.S. Supreme Court, found no violation of the Fourth Amendment in **Acton v. Vernonia School District** (1995) 515 U.S. 646 and therefore upheld an Oregon public high school's policy requiring random urine testing of all student athletes.

In **Chandler v. Miller** (1997) 520 U.S. 305, the U.S. Supreme Court invalidated a Georgia statute that required drug tests for all candidates for state offices because it violated the Fourth Amendment.

The California Supreme Court ruled that the City of Glendale's across the board urinalysis drug testing for current employees seeking promotion, regardless of the type of job sought, was unconstitutional in **Loder v. City of Glendale** (1997) 14 Cal.4th 846. Implicit in the holding is that the testing would be constitutional if it was rationally related in some way to the job being sought.

The California Supreme Court did uphold the City of Glendale's policy to have across the board urinalysis drug testing for all new employees.

In **Ferguson et al. v. City of Charleston et al**. (2001) 532 U.S. 67, the U.S. Supreme Court invalidated a non-consensual urine testing program for pregnant women suspected of cocaine use, where the results were turned over to law enforcement for use in the prosecution or substance abuse treatment of the pregnant woman.

Table of Cases

Cases

Table of Statutes

United States Constitutional Provisions

United States Statutory Provisions

California Constitutional Provisions

California Education Code

California Evidence Code

California Penal Code

California Vehicle Code

www.ingramcontent.com/pod-product-compliance
Lightning Source LLC
LaVergne TN
LVHW060026210926
848481LV00013B/3800